THE TARIM MUMMIES

J. P. MALLORY · VICTOR H. MAIR

THE
TARIM
MUMMIES

Ancient China and the Mystery of the Earliest Peoples from the West

With 190 illustrations, 13 in color

 Thames & Hudson

© 2000 Thames & Hudson Ltd, London

First published in hardcover in the United States of America in 2000
by Thames & Hudson Inc., 500 Fifth Avenue, New York, New York 10110

Library of Congress Catalog Card Number 99-66166
ISBN 0-500-05101-1

Printed in Hong Kong

CONTENTS

Rediscovery

The mummies stalked into the world's pressrooms in 1994. London's *Mail on Sunday* could trumpet how the discovery of mummies in western China had stood 'history on its head'. Preserved in a state that surpassed anything to come out of ancient Egypt and decked in clothes that were gaudy even by 'New Age' standards, the mummies of Xinjiang, the westernmost and largest of the provinces of modern China, had clearly caught the public imagination. But it was also obvious from the popular accounts that journalists were going to have a hard go of it. After all, these mummies were housed in a museum in Ürümchi. Where? They were more ancient than the current population of the region, the Uyghur. Who? And what angle should one play? Although the mummies were certainly spectacular enough to fill a page or two of a colour supplement, they came from an area so far removed from the average reader's ken that it was difficult to find common ground, much less talk of revolutionary discoveries. In short, the mummies *looked* very exciting; it just wasn't all that clear why they should *be* so exciting.

What lingered from the journalists' accounts was that the remains of tall, blond Europeans, possibly from northern Europe, had been found in the desert wastes of western China. Their earliest remains dated to about 2000 BC and they were found to have survived in this region down to about 1,700 years ago. And somehow the Chinese historians had got it all wrong: China had not developed its civilization in splendid isolation from the West but had been heavily influenced by prehistoric Europeans, so much so that it may have been Europeans who introduced both the wheel and bronze metallurgy, two of the primary technologies of civilization, to the Chinese. All of this was politically very sensitive and there were hints that the Chinese authorities were trying to keep these important discoveries under wraps. As to what ethnic or linguistic label might be assigned to the mummies, it was suggested that they might have been the ancestors of the Tocharians. Tocharians? The journalists tried their best: the Tocharians seemed to have been closely related to the Celts of western Europe. What did this mean? That prehistoric Irishmen had become lost in western China? But they also appeared to be tall blonds and looked more like Germans or Scandinavians. In short, remains of people closely related to those who read Western newspapers and magazines had somehow trekked their way across Eurasia to settle in the arid wastes between Qäshqär and Lopnur. Where? Before we move ahead we had better travel back a decade and recapture the excitement of the recent rediscovery of the mummies by Victor Mair.

New Friends in Ürümchi

Victor has made regular trips to China since 1981. Usually they have involved visits to archaeological sites in Xinjiang and Gansu, the far western portions of the country, since his research speciality for the past two decades and more has focused on early manuscripts found in that region. He had been to the Ürümchi Museum many times in the past, but the summer of 1988 was different. As he walked through the old, familiar exhibition halls, he was totally unprepared for what he would encounter in a new gallery that had been opened at the end of the archaeological section. Parting the hanging curtains of the doorway, he entered another world.

The room was full of mummies! Lifelike mummies! These were not the wizened and eviscerated pharaohs wrapped in yards of dusty gauze that one normally pictures when mummies are mentioned. Instead, they were everyday people dressed in their everyday clothes. Each one of the half-dozen bodies in the room, whether man, woman or child, looked as though it had merely gone to sleep for a while and might sit up at any moment and begin to talk to whomever happened to be standing next to its glass case.

Although he was supposed to be guiding an instructional tour for the Smithsonian Institution, for the next three hours Victor totally forgot about all else in the world except the mummies in that dark, sequestered room of the Ürümchi Museum. For the remainder of that day, he became a member of the community of ancient souls in the room that, years later, he would return to visit again and again.

Although he swiftly became familiar with all of them, the mummy Victor remembers best from that initial encounter was the one (commonly known as 'Chärchän Man') whom he came to call fondly 'Ur-David'. 'Ur' means 'primal' or 'earliest' and 'David' refers to his second-eldest brother; the resemblance between the two gentlemen is startling. 'Ur-David' was sleeping peacefully in the far-right corner of the room (pls. I, II). He was lying on his back, his head propped up on a white pillow, his knees raised slightly, and his expressive hands – held together by a friendship bracelet twisted from red and blue yarn – placed gently upon his abdomen. 'Ur-David' was wearing a brilliant reddish-purple woollen shirt trimmed with fine red piping and trousers of the same material. His knee-high socks of matted wool fibres (not quite felt) were as brightly coloured as a rainbow – with horizontal

Xinjiang

The common political designation of the far western territory of China is Xinjiang or, as it is to be found in books earlier than the Chinese spelling reform of 1956 which introduced the *pinyin* system of transcription, Sinkiang. The name means 'New Territories', as they only became a province of the Chinese state in 1884. The main ethnic minority of the region are the Uyghurs, a Turkish people who began settling there in the 8th century AD, and the territory is more properly known as the Uyghur Autonomous Region of Xinjiang (altogether there are 47 different ethnic groups in the province). The names 'Eastern Turkestan' or 'Chinese Turkestan' have also been applied to this region, as has the politically more neutral 'East Central Asia' which we will often employ in this work. Xinjiang comprises a territory of over 600,000 sq. miles, one sixth of the entire country of China. Its area is on the order of the British Isles, Belgium, the Netherlands, France, Germany and Italy put together with room to spare or, from an American point of view, well over twice the size of Texas but a bit smaller than Alaska.

1. *Xinjiang, the 'New Territories', is one of the most land-locked regions of the world.*

stripes of flame red and golden yellow, but occasionally alternating with the most deliciously faint blue imaginable. Over the socks were boots of white leather, probably from a deer, that reached to his thighs. There was also a mystifying leather thong wrapped around the middle finger of his left hand; it was secured by passing one end through a slot in the other end. Perhaps it was a crop, signifying that he was a horserider, or merely a means of keeping the deceased from falling on his side.

But it was the face that arrested Victor most. He circled the glass case at least a dozen times, taking in each tiny detail of this human being with whom he felt such an affinity. He wanted to absorb everything about this person from the past, yet it was the face that kept drawing his attention. What was the meaning of the spirals painted in ochre on his temples? Were they solar symbols? The horns of a sheep? Finally, he could do nothing but stare fixedly into those ancient eyes. They were blissfully closed, yet they spoke eloquently and powerfully. Then as his vision shifted to the top of the head he became conscious that the hair of 'Ur-David' was blond. His mind began to race wildly, filled with a thousand insistent and unanswered questions: What is this tall, blond man doing here in the middle of Central Asia where almost every person one sees today is much shorter and has black hair? How did he get here? Where did he come from? When did he arrive? What language did he speak?

Victor looked at the label on the case. It said that the individual lying inside was from Chärchän (Qiemo in Modern Standard Mandarin (MSM)) and that his remains dated to 1000 BC. He paced around the room, avidly reading every single label – 1200 BC, 1800 BC, more individuals from 1000 BC. The shock of seeing these living fossils of Xinjiang first led him to question their authenticity. To be sure, at the turn of the century European explorers such as Sven Hedin of Sweden, Albert von Le Coq of Germany and Sir Aurel Stein on behalf of Britain had all recounted their discoveries of desiccated bodies in their search for the artistic and literary relics of the Buddhist shrines of Central Asia. In their magnificently illustrated accounts,

2. A mummy of an elderly man removed from his coffin, discovered by one of the Swedish expeditions earlier this century.

they had even published drawings and photographs of these remains. In a different world and time, these excited little interest and never prepared Victor for coming eye to eye with the prehistoric people of Xinjiang. With many questions still racing through his mind, he dashed off to recover his Smithsonian charges.

Then the Iceman Came

On the morning of 26 September 1991, Victor was sitting in the newspaper nook of the National Humanities Center in Research Triangle Park, North Carolina. When he picked up the *New York Times*, he was stunned to see the headline announcing the discovery of the frozen body of a Copper Age hunter-herder high in the Ötztaler Alps on the border between Austria and Italy. Except where it had been damaged by a pneumatic chisel in the area of the left buttock and thigh during recovery, the body of this 'Iceman' was almost perfectly preserved.

As Victor read more reports about this remarkable event, he learned that Ötzi (as the Iceman had come to be called) was 5,300 years old, that he was equipped with a bow, arrows, axe, and other implements, that he wore carefully sewn fur and leather garments, and that he bore presumably therapeutic tattoos at strategic spots on his body. For Victor, however, what was most striking was that Ötzi's icy grave was amazingly near to the Austrian village, Pfaffenhofen, in which his father was born and grew up.

While he was devouring the news about Ötzi, almost instantaneously there formed in his mind an ineluctable connection between the Copper Age Iceman of the Austro-Italian Alps and the Bronze Age denizens of the Täklimakan Desert whom he had first seen in 1988. Somehow or other, he sensed a distinct relationship between these ancient human beings. He became possessed by the desire to determine whether this were indeed true and, if so, in what way the Iceman and the desert people were linked.

Within half an hour of learning of the discovery of Ötzi, he resolved to organize a research project on the mummies of the Tarim Basin (throughout this book we will frequently use 'Tarim' as shorthand for both the Tarim Basin proper and the neighbouring regions to its north and east). He was aware that DNA tests would be carried out on Ötzi. Consequently, he thought that it would be both simple and precise to do the same for the Täklimakanians. Once the DNA of the Iceman and the desert people were compared, it should be easy to decide if they were of the same stock. That very afternoon, he began to write letters in preparation for a scientific expedition to the Uyghur region of China.

The Quest Begins

There were three main aspects to the flurry of activity into which Victor immersed himself during the coming months: locating reliable scientific expertise, raising the necessary funds, and obtaining the permission of the Chinese government to engage in cooperative research. He viewed all three tasks as equally challenging. Much to his surprise, he met with swift success in all three areas of endeavour.

The first step was to solicit the guidance and help of a qualified geneticist. He had long known of the outstanding work on population genetics of the distinguished Stanford scholar, Professor Luigi Luca Cavalli-Sforza. He was unprepared for the approachability of this world-class scientist and man-of-ideas. Not only did Cavalli-Sforza enthusiastically declare that he would be happy to participate personally in the research project, he also suggested several possible funding agencies. With one telephone call to Cavalli-Sforza, he had already come close to killing two of the three birds required to set the enterprise in motion.

The Alfred P. Sloan Foundation made a substantial grant to undertake research on the mitochondrial DNA of the Tarim Basin mummies during the 1993 season and they generously doubled the size of their grant in the following two years. Funds were also obtained from Victor's own University of Pennsylvania, the Henry Luce Foundation, and numerous individual citizens who are interested in world history and wish to do their part to clarify the mysteries surrounding the mummies of the Tarim Basin.

The signals he was receiving from various sources in China were sufficiently encouraging to assume that there was at least a chance that he would be able to proceed. In particular, Wang Binghua, Director of the Institute of Archaeology in Ürümchi, exerted himself on behalf of the project. And although there were bureaucratic hiccups enough along the way, permission to go ahead was obtained from the Chinese authorities at the eleventh hour. By this time Cavalli-Sforza had had to abandon the idea of travelling to Central Asia himself because of a heart condition, so he provided a superb substitute in the person of Paolo Francalacci of the University of Sassari in Sardinia. After meeting up in Beijing, Paolo and Victor flew to Ürümchi on 22 June. Lengthy negotiations were required to allay the main concerns of the Chinese. It was agreed that their geneticists and archaeologists would be directly involved in all phases of the work, that they would be listed as joint authors of any significant publications emanating from the project, and that technology transfer would occur in the form of training in the new, advanced analytical techniques the American side would be using. It cannot be stressed too heavily that taking tissue samples was a highly sensitive matter. The Chinese side was also eager for some of their scholars to go abroad for brief visits or for extended periods of study, to raise money from American foundations to support their work, and to seek assistance in building a special museum for the preservation of the scores of corpses that had been excavated and will continue to be excavated in the Uyghur region. Victor readily acceded to the mission of helping the Chinese build what might affectionately be called the 'Mummy Museum'.

Bronze Age People in Poplar Gully

On 25 June, Wang Binghua, Paolo and Victor travelled by car 490 km (304 miles) eastwards across the searing desert to Qumul. Known as Khamil in Mongolian, the name of this important Silk Road town is transcribed in Modern Standard Mandarin as Hami. It is famous for its succulent melons suffused with fragrance and sweetness. Large amounts of cotton are also grown in irrigated fields surrounding the town. Nearby was one of the most important sites for the project.

Approximately 1 km (0.6 miles) to the northwest of the oasis village of Qaradöwä (MSM Wupu) is a terrace of pebble-strewn desert that lies across a little valley called 'Poplar Gully' which separates it from the town. From the terrace one can see at the town's edge a distinctive mound of reddish earth which gives its name to the area. In Uyghur, it is known as Qizilchoqa, which means 'Red Hillock'. A tract of about 5,000 sq. m (53,820 sq. ft) has been fenced in for protection and is under the jurisdiction of the Xinjiang Institute of Archaeology which is responsible for its ongoing excavation.

The Qizilchoqa cemetery was discovered by Wang Binghua in 1978 by following the stream in Poplar Gully from its glacial source high in the Tängri Tagh ('Celestial Mountains', Tian Shan in MSM) to the north. It was his hunch, based on the many years he had spent as a practising archaeologist in the region, that ancient peoples would have located their settlements along the stream because it provided a relatively reliable source of water. As he followed the stream bed, Wang queried the local inhabitants as to whether they had come across any old broken pots, wooden artifacts and so forth. An old man named Imit came forward with some ancient

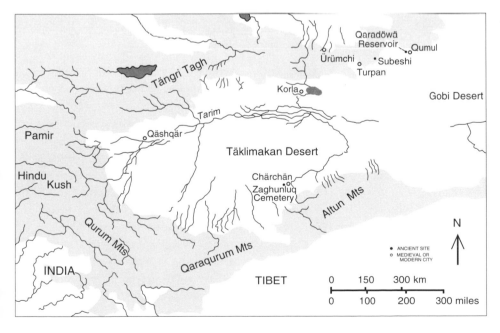

3. Sites mentioned in the introduction.

objects that were exactly what Wang was looking for. When Victor initially visited Qizilchoqa in 1993, Imit was the guard at the cemetery.

During the first year, 29 graves were excavated. In 1986, 82 more graves were dug and, in 1991, two additional graves were excavated in cooperation with a fairly large team of Japanese archaeologists. Judging from the size of the tract and the number of obvious depressions in the surface of the earth (which indicate the existence of a grave beneath), there were probably at least another hundred graves remaining to be dug at Qizilchoqa. But by June 1997, when Victor returned to Qizilchoqa to make a film about the mummies for Nova (WGBH-Boston) and Channel 4 (London), the entire cemetery had been hurriedly rummaged. Few graves remained untouched and litter from obviously hasty 'excavations' was strewn across the pebbly desert surface. In June 1998, Victor returned to Qizilchoqa once again, this time to make a film for the Discovery Channel. The debris from the previous year's shallow scavenging had been cleared up and it appeared that it might still be possible someday to excavate the remaining graves properly.

The Qizilchoqa graves have been dated to approximately 1200 BC by Chinese archaeologists because of the presence of bronze objects, the style of painted pottery, and five radiocarbon dates. This puts the site at a key point in the development of Chinese civilization, the height of the Shang dynasty. It is dated to essentially the same moment as the introduction of the chariot and the rise of writing.

Aside from numerous well-preserved corpses, a wealth of artifacts was recovered from the graves. These were not luxury goods but simple items for use in daily life (combs, mirrors, needles, bowls, pots, hooks, bridles, bells, spindles, bread, etc.). Among those that struck Victor most forcefully was a part of a wheel that he spotted protruding from an unexcavated grave. It was similar to another partial wheel that had been unearthed earlier from one of the other graves, which was kept in the Qumul Museum. These wheels, termed 'tripartite disc wheels', are of a peculiar construction which joins three thick planks (rounded at the edges) with tightly fitting dowels. The same type of disc wheel is found in West Asia and throughout Europe a thousand years earlier. The spoked chariot wheel has not yet been found at such an early date in Xinjiang, but it has been found at a slightly earlier site, Nomhong, in Qinghai (Kokonor) province just to the east.

The Qizilchoqa graves are relatively simple in their construction. About 2 m (6 ft 7 in) deep, they are lined with large, unbaked bricks around the lower part of their sides. The pits were just big enough for the occupant(s) of the grave who were placed in them on mats, lying on their sides or backs with their knees bent upwards. Above the buried individuals, about halfway down in the pit, was a ledge around all four sides. A layer of mats and reeds was placed here to prevent the sandy soil from falling down into the brick-lined burial chamber. The opening of the grave was covered by a row of large, rough-hewn logs strewn with mats and reeds over which was a layer of sand.

4. Mummified corpse on the floor of a brick-lined tomb at Qizilchoqa.

5. Victor Mair with a recently exhumed corpse at Qizilchoqa before it was returned to its grave.

The most impressive aspect of the Qizilchoqa graves is, of course, the ancient corpses themselves. Due to the unique combination of climatic conditions in the area, many of the bodies have been preserved intact through a process of natural desiccation. The corpses are fully clothed in marvellously coloured and patterned woollen fabrics, felt and leather boots, and sometimes leather coats. They are clearly of Caucasoid/Europoid extraction (long noses, deep-set eyes, blondish, light-brown or red hair, and so forth). The men are fully bearded and the women have long, braided hair.

In company with about a dozen local archaeologists and diggers, Victor and his crew spent the entire day at Qizilchoqa exhuming corpses from graves that had previously been excavated but, after preliminary examination and recovery of important artifacts, had been reinterred because of a lack of adequate storage facilities in Qumul or in Ürümchi. As one grave after another was opened, Victor was awed by the sight of bodies that had been lying there for over three millennia.

Paolo, wearing a face mask and rubber gloves to avoid contamination of the corpses with his own modern (and much more potent) DNA, used surgical scalpels to remove small samples of tissue from unexposed areas of the bodies (usually the inner thighs or underarms). He also took fragments of a few bones (parts of ribs that were relatively easy to break off) and teeth which preserve the DNA perhaps even better than do the muscle tissue and skin.

The samples were placed in collection jars, sealed and labelled. While Paolo was doing his work, Victor made a photographic and written record of the tissue collection. Altogether, they took double or triple samples from six corpses at Qumul.

That evening the team feasted on an elaborate banquet held for them in the guest house where they were staying. Paolo was wearing his 'Ancient DNA' t-shirt and beaming broadly.

The Trio From Chärchän

Although the 1993 expedition did not travel to the town of Chärchän (Qiemo in Mandarin), which lies towards the eastern end of the southern branch of the Silk Road, they were able to see half-a-dozen mummies from the very important site of Zaghunluq that lay in the desert nearby. Three of these were the by-now world-famous 'Sunday supplement' family comprising 'Ur-David', the woman who is thought to have been his wife, and the little child with blue bonnet and blue stones over his eyes that was buried in a separate grave close by theirs. The other three mummies from Zaghunluq were kept in the district museum at Korla which the 1993 team did visit. While there, they took tissue samples from two of the corpses that were best preserved, a young woman of about 20 years old and a little boy of approximately 2½ years.

l. The temples of 'Ur-David' were ornamented with designs in ochre.

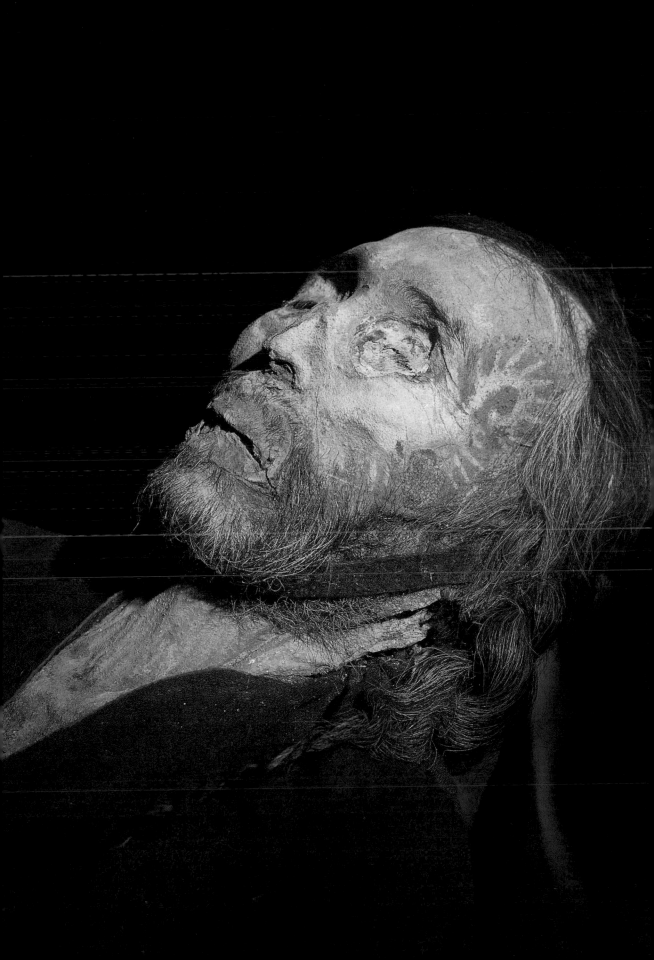

*II. 'Chärchän Man',
Victor Mair's 'Ur-David',
reclines in the
Ürümchi Museum.*

*III. The woman from
Zaghunluq who
accompanied
'Ur-David'.*

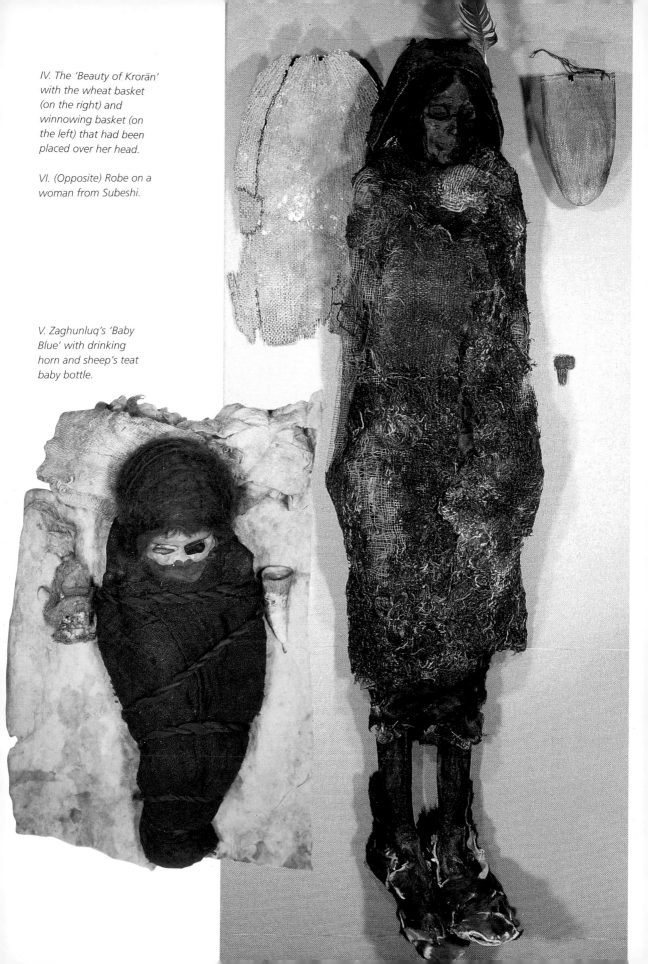

IV. The 'Beauty of Kroran' with the wheat basket (on the right) and winnowing basket (on the left) that had been placed over her head.

VI. (Opposite) Robe on a woman from Subeshi.

V. Zaghunluq's 'Baby Blue' with drinking horn and sheep's teat baby bottle.

VII. Close up of the face and tattoos of a female mummy from Zaghunluq. Note that her nostrils have been stuffed with wool and she wears a false braid.

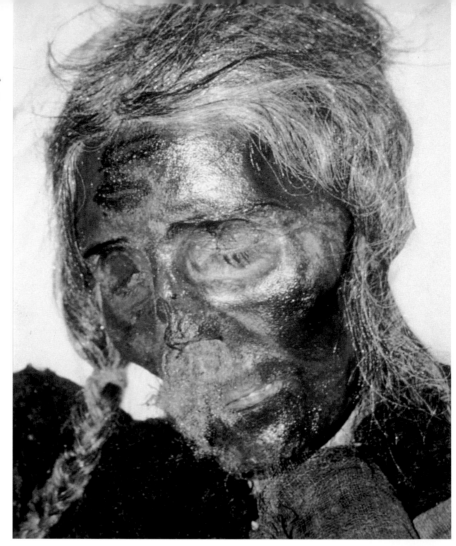

VIII. Tattoos on the woman's hand.

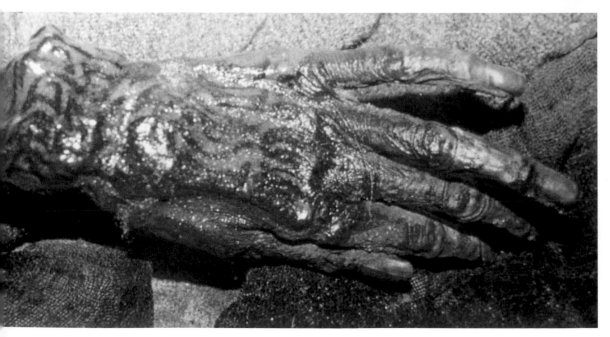

IX. Burial of an aristocratic Europoid couple exhumed from Niyä in 1995. They wore fine silk clothing and matching face covers. Their burial dates to the Han or Jin period (probably 2nd–3rd century AD).

X, XI. (Below left) Fragment of twill from Qizilchoqa. (Below) Qizilchoqa tartan.

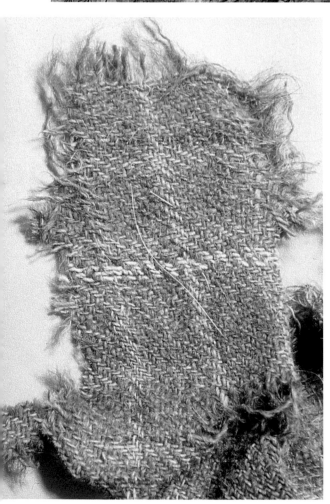

XII. The 'knights with long swords' with their light hair and, where discernible, light eye colour. From the Cave of the Sixteen Sword Bearers in Qizil; early 6th century AD.

XIII. A Tocharian monk and an East Asian monk from Bezäklik; 9th–10th century AD.

The tiny Korla Museum also houses the spectacularly well-preserved and magnificently clad body of a woman in her fifties. At first glance, Victor thought it was a man because the person seemed to have a moustache (pl. VII, ill. 6). It was only when he returned home and examined his photographs with a magnifying glass that he realized that what had seemed like a moustache were actually tufts of wool stuffed in the nostrils. This is particularly interesting in the light of the ancient Egyptian practice of packing the nostrils (and other orifices) of the deceased with linen and/or resin to prevent the escape of bodily fluids which would damage the appearance of the corpse. Another misapprehension about the corpse of the woman had to do with what Victor took to be her extraordinarily long fingernails. He initially assumed that they had continued to grow after death, a common folk belief. Upon further investigation, he learned that the nails of dead people only seem to look longer because more of them is exposed as the flesh on the fingers shrinks. In the case of the older Korla woman, her fingers themselves are preternaturally long and the nails that extend from them seem to be at least an inch in length: they could not possibly have grown so much after she died. Instead, like the Empress Dowager at the end of the Manchu dynasty, she must have worn them this way while she was alive – a symbol of her status as a person who did not have to work with her hands. This was one of the few examples of overt social differentiation that Victor encountered in his investigations of the Bronze Age inhabitants of the Tarim Basin and surrounding areas.

Grave-robbers at Subeshi

As the 1993 expedition was driving to and from Qumul, it stopped near the site of Subeshi ('Water Source') which lies in the gorge of Tuyuq, not far to the east of Turpan (Turfan). Here, during March–April 1992, a team led by Lü Enguo of the Xinjiang Institute of Archaeology had excavated a series of graveyards from the Warring States period (mainly 5th–4th centuries BC but also some a couple of centuries later). The partial excavation, like so many others in China, was undertaken on a rescue basis because of the construction of a small country road in the vicinity and repeated grave robbery at the cemetery. Over a dozen corpses were recovered, as well as an enormous number of artifacts which reveal fascinating details about the customs and material culture of that period (a woman's hat with long horn-like projections, which prompted some Chinese archaeologists to speculate that the number of projections reflected the number of the woman's husbands; medicine pouches to be hung at the waist; operations with horse-hair sutures; a saddle; composite bows of complicated structure with cases and quivers, etc.). It is surprising that, at this rather late date and so far to the east, all of the individuals from Subeshi that Paolo and Victor examined were still clearly Caucasoid; there was not a single Mongoloid among them. The corpses and most of the artifacts were kept

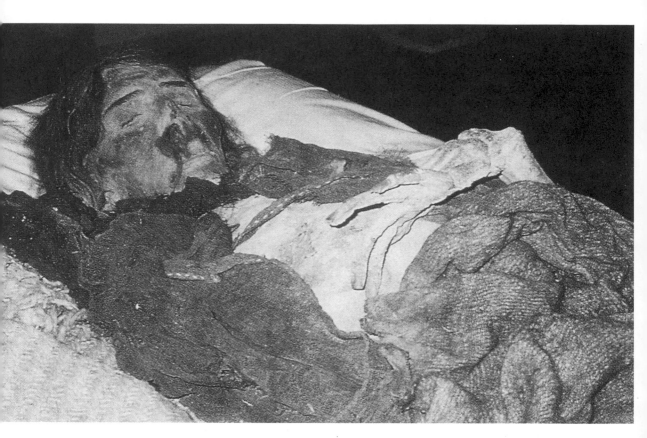

6. Mummified remains of a woman from the Korla Museum whose nostrils have been stuffed with wool.

7. A basement full of mummies from Subeshi at the Institute of Archaeology in Ürümchi (photograph taken in June 1993).

in a damp and cramped basement storage room at the Institute of Archaeology in Ürümchi. After their condition was revealed in the worldwide press, they were moved to a dusty upstairs room. Yet they are still completely exposed to the atmosphere (the windows of the room are kept open all year round); with the exception of several that have been moved to the museum, no measures have been taken to conserve the Subeshi mummies. The situation is particularly frustrating since Victor made a large donation to the Institute of Archaeology in 1994 that was specifically earmarked for the construction of glass cases for the Subeshi mummies. It was promised that the cases would be built in Shanghai and installed within a year, yet by 1999 nothing had been done. There is a desperate need to provide these precious specimens with surroundings that are better designed to ensure their preservation.

Victor visited the Subeshi graveyards again in May 1995 with Lü Enguo (the excavator of the site), Dolkun Kamberi (his Uyghur research associate), Elizabeth Barber (a world-renowned authority on prehistoric textiles), Paul Barber (an expert on mortuary practice) and Irene Good (a textiles specialist from the University of Pennsylvania). What they witnessed at Subeshi was enough to make any sensitive human being cry. Grave robbers had passed through the gorge only months before and systematically ransacked scores of tombs spread over vast acres of the stark landscape. The cemeteries are laid out on sandy, wind-swept terraces high above the deep gorge. The 1995 team saw body parts strewn about callously by the robbers in their mad quest for anything of value. It is sad that such destruction is being unleashed when there is so little prospect of finding anything of great worth. Then, as now, this was a harsh environment, one where subsistence was the rule of the day and the accumulation of luxury was a virtual impossibility. Although the team was devastated by what had happened to most of the cemeteries at Subeshi, they were relieved to see that the main one which had been excavated by Lü Enguo was in much better shape. They were especially excited to come upon the remains of an ancient house. Scattered about its walls were a large quantity of sherds and other artifacts, including fragments of broken wooden plates. It is astonishing that, to date, no systematic archaeological study has been made of this or any other residential area associated with the prehistoric mummies of East Central Asia.

Collaboration

Victor returns to Eastern Central Asia at least once every year and probably will continue to do so for another decade. The Chinese and Uyghur archaeologists of the region are busy with their work from year to year but it is necessary to bring the results of their excavations to the attention of the rest of the world. For this reason, Victor welcomed an invitation in 1995 from the *Journal of Indo-European Studies* to guest-edit a collection of 11 papers from archaeologists, physical anthropologists and linguists who were all eager to comment upon the possible ethnic and linguistic identity of these ancient Europeans who had apparently wandered so far to the east. He followed this up the next year with a major international conference on the mummies at the University of Pennsylvania where 50 scholars from 15 countries scrutinized the evidence for the ethnic identity of these mummies. The four keynote speakers included Victor, Luigi Luca Cavalli-Sforza who had done so much to encourage DNA studies of the mummies, and two of the major protagonists concerned with the origins and dispersals of the Indo-European peoples and their languages: Colin Renfrew of Cambridge University and Jim Mallory of Queen's University, Belfast. A month after the conference Mallory suggested off-handedly that in addition to all the specialist and journalistic accounts that had been or were being produced, Victor might consider writing a thorough, illustrated account of the mummies for the general public that presented them in as full a context as possible. As he had published his own study of Indo-European origins with Thames and Hudson and occasionally pre-reviewed manuscripts for them, he suggested that he would be happy to provide Victor with an introduction to their archaeology editor. Victor had been thinking along similar lines for some time and Mallory's letter prompted him to reflect on the benefits of some form of collaborative effort. Victor's own area of specialization is Sinitic studies in general and the transmission of Indian literature and religion to western China in particular. This expertise could be augmented by an archaeologist who regularly dealt with the larger issues of the Indo-European languages and European prehistory, especially that of the Eurasian steppe region. Also, Mallory's more recent research had been in the area of Indo-European dispersals specifically in Asia. But Victor's return letter, suggesting a collaborative effort, had apparently been the farthest thing from Mallory's mind when it arrived, and Mallory promptly wrote back, solicitous of Victor's sanity and introducing him to the term 'head staggers'. By the time Victor replied that he was very serious about a collaborative effort, however, Mallory had chanced to read the excavator's description of Victor's 'Ur-David' that indicated that like himself he was in his fifties and stood 2 m (6 ft 7 in) tall: the lure of Victor's ancient friend from Xinjiang who, when living, could have looked Mallory straight in the eyes, was too much for him to resist.

Beyond the Sound Bite

The mummies from Xinjiang, one of the most spectacular archaeological finds of the 20th century, deserve far more than a sound bite; they need a context that places them in the broader picture of the cultural history of Eurasia. And the understandable hype, the journalistic compulsion to make everything bigger, older (almost always 'older than the pyramids' if one wishes to attract tabloid notice), first or revolutionary, needs to be tempered with some accuracy. For example, the mummies have become a news item because of *recent* archaeological discoveries but, as we have already seen, the well-preserved remains of Europeans had already been discovered in precisely the same region at the turn of the century and had been published in the dramatic accounts of explorers such as Aurel Stein and Folke Bergman. The mummies have also been presented as if they were the unique evidence of Europeans in western China when there is far more abundant evidence, although not nearly so dramatic, in the hundreds of unmummified skeletons recovered from the same region and in the well-known references in Chinese annals to people who looked like monkeys, unflattering descriptions which European scholars have long seized upon to indicate themselves. One also needs to emphasize the fact that the mummies from East Central Asia are not the products of deliberate embalming techniques such as found in Egypt or closer afield in the Iron Age tombs of the Altai Mountains; rather, they are the results of burial in an arid climate whose preserving qualities have often been enhanced by the salt content of the soil and bitterly cold winters. Nor do the mummies constitute a single culture or physical type but derive from a range of cultures, periods and peoples who inhabited the region. If we are to understand the significance of the mummies and the problems their existence poses, we need to step back first and consider the mummies and the territory in which they are found in as many contexts as possible.

Questions and Contexts

You are at a party and the person standing next to you begins: 'An Englishman, a Scotsman and an Irishman walk into a pub....' We have heard this type of joke countless times before; our background knowledge or, better, the ethnic stereotypes we have endured over the years, prepare us to understand (or brace ourselves for) the punchline when it comes; whether we find it funny or insulting is another thing altogether. But consider for a moment that you are trapped in a corner of the same party and someone pins you against the wall and begins: 'A Kuchean, an Agnean and a Kroränian walk into a pub....' While such a joke might leave a Sogdian camel-driver rolling on the floor, the odds of the average listener getting the joke, much less laughing at the punchline, recede to the minuscule. The point is, whether we are into Irish jokes or Kroränian ones, we cannot understand what is going on unless we understand their cultural context. The same applies to understanding the Tarim mummies. We have no intention of dragging the reader straight into the mummy galleries of the Xinjiang museums and then, only after we have displayed our 'punchlines', informing our audience what the story was really all about. We are going to take it slowly, not just because that is the easiest way to introduce our subject, but also because the discovery, prehistory and history of East Central Asia is such a fascinating and little-known story. The mummies are centre stage but they are not the whole play. We will try to answer the following questions:

Where were the mummies found?

First of all, we need a map (Chapter One), but a map of the lands in which the mummies were buried is hard won. So remote from both the Greek and Chinese worlds was East Central Asia that both traditions ringed it with the monstrosities and demons that imagination supplies when geographical knowledge falters. It was only in the first centuries BC and AD that eastward-probing Greeks and westward-advancing Chinese penetrated the geographical mists that surrounded their own worlds to discover one another. We must, therefore, follow the earlier tracks of Herodotus, Alexander the Great and lesser-known figures such as the 'timetraveller' Aristeas or the more mundane caravan agents of Maës the Macedonian, who pushed Greek knowledge of the world eastwards, so that by the first centuries AD a Greek geographer could draw up a map of the world that acknowledged the existence of the land of the mummies. Discovery was not just one way, however, and we will have good cause to review the incredible wanderings of the indefatigable explorer and ambassador of the Han dynasty, Zhang Qian, and the military adventures of General Li Guangli, the brother of the emperor's favourite concubine, who opened up the way west. The main arena for this process of mutual discovery was the Tarim Basin, the territory that would prove to be both the central and most difficult section of what came to be known as the Silk Road. We will see how the mummies occupied the midpoint of the most important overland trade route in Eurasian history.

Who occupied the land of the mummies?

The discovery of the Tarim Basin by literate civilizations permits us to draw on the evidence of written sources to construct an historical picture of the land of the Tarim mummies and its peoples (Chapter Two). Our sources will be primarily Chinese, often snippets of information that were 'wired' back to the central chancellery of the Han and later dynasties. From these reports we can construct something of the history and ethnography of the major players of East Central Asia. These include those populations who inhabited the oasis towns of the Tarim such as Qäshqär, the westernmost emporium of East Central Asia; Kucha, the largest of the oasis towns of the north; the ancient kingdom of Khotan, the capital of the southern Tarim; and Krorän or Loulan, the statelet that emerged near the barren wastelands around the great salt lake of Lopnur in the east, a territory that has yielded the most impressively preserved of our mummies. Our survey will also include the great nomadic tribes who occupied or swept through the region, in particular the Xiongnu, the masters of the Tarim and the eastern steppe who are often linked to the best known of Eurasian barbarians, the Huns; the Wusun, the major tribal confederation to form in the pasturelands to the northwest of the Tarim; and the Yuezhi, the people who in historical times were forced to make the long trek west from the corridors of frontier China into the eastern realms of the former Persian empire where they founded the Kushan empire, one of the major states of the ancient world. And our final historical context will introduce the Uyghurs, the Turkic-speaking population who currently dominate the Tarim Basin and the people most likely to preserve the genetic heritage of the Tarim mummies.

What languages might the mummies have spoken?

As we will be searching for the ethnic and linguistic identity of those mummies who preceded the evidence of historical records, we can have no hope of even conjecturing possible identities unless we are able to establish what languages were known to have been spoken in the Tarim Basin (Chapter Three). It is here that we are reminded that the mummies do not constitute the sole treasure of Täklimakan: the arid climate preserved not only the remains of its peoples (and trees, houses, shrines, artwork, cupboards, tables, chairs, mousetraps, brooms, etc.) but an enormous quantity of written documents that attest to a myriad different languages. In fact, the most linguistically diverse library in the ancient world has survived in the drying sands of the Tarim Basin. All the languages attested in the Tarim Basin belong to well-known language families and we will attempt to place these in the broader context of Eurasian language geography. For the earliest historical period, with the obvious exception of Chinese, all texts are in languages of the Indo-European family that unites the peoples of Eurasia from Ireland in the west to the Tarim Basin and northern India in the east. The linguistic review will introduce the evidence which many believe indicates that the ancestors of at least some of the Tarim mummies originally derived from Europe.

How do the mummies fit into the archaeological picture?

The final context is, naturally, the archaeological background to the mummies (Chapter Four). We must consider the cultural evolution of the region from archaeological sources which appear so far to suggest that East Central Asia was originally settled from the west or north and that it lay essentially outside the orbit of the Chinese world until the first centuries BC. We will also examine the specific archaeological cultures in which the various groups of mummies are found and consider how they relate to the world beyond the Tarim Basin.

How many mummies? What do they look like?

Once we have established the geographical, historical, linguistic and archaeological background, we can begin our examination into the lives, deaths and identities of the mummies. We will start with the physical evidence of the bodies (Chapter Five) and consider how they managed to be preserved and the archaeologically tragic situation which threatens their survival.

Now some might object to our use of 'mummies' to describe what they might dismiss as mere 'desiccated corpses', arguing that unless you have had your bowels and brain removed, been saturated with natron, embalmed, wrapped in linen sheets, stuffed in a wooden case, sealed in a sarcophagus (and preferably were a native Egyptian-speaker), you weren't a 'real' mummy. To this we can only refer the reader to a good dictionary or, perhaps better, a book on mummies such as Christine El Mahdy's *Mummies, Myth and Magic in Ancient Egypt* ('A mummy is the preserved body of a human being or an animal, by any means, either deliberate or accidental') or Aidan Cockburn in the opening of his classic *Mummies, Disease and Ancient Cultures* ('Today, the term mummy has been extended to cover all well-preserved dead bodies. The majority of these are found in dry places such as the sands of deserts or dry caves, where desiccation has taken place rapidly, doing naturally what Egyptians did by artifice'). This book is about mummies.

What does the clothing of the mummies tell us of their origins?
The Tarim mummies may have entered the world naked but they often exited it well dressed and it might be argued that the preservation of their clothing is every bit as exciting as that of their bodies. It is not just the level of preservation but the detail of the fabrics and weaves as well as the sheer ostentation of their dress that provides clues to the identity of the mummies (Chapter Six). Aside from witches' hats, plain and simple, perhaps most intriguing is the presence of plaid twills which places them in the same category of tartan splendour as the Celts of western Europe. For some, this dovetails nicely with the theory that derives the Tocharians, one of the possible candidates to be equated with the mummies, from western Europe, and we will have to examine how credible this theory actually is.

What do their skeletal remains and DNA tell us of their origins?
The final physical clue as to the identity of the mummies rests with their own bodies and the skeletal remains of the less well-preserved members of their communities (Chapter Seven). We will attempt to sort out the details of the anthropological analyses of the various groups of mummies and the attempts that have sought to link them to other populations in Eurasia. This will also force us to consider to what extent the blood of the mummies still runs through the veins of the current population of the Tarim Basin. We will, in addition, examine the results of the recent application of DNA testing to trace the closest genetic relations of the mummies.

Are the mummies Indo-Iranians?
By now we will have accumulated enough evidence to round up the most likely suspects and run them through an identity parade to determine how well they fit the bill as the ethno-linguistic groups behind the mummies. The first of these is the Indo-Iranians (Chapter Eight), the largest of the

subgroups of the Indo-European world, whose speakers, in a variety of local guises, we know to have both surrounded and penetrated the Tarim Basin. What is the evidence that these people were in the Tarim Basin far earlier than our historical records would have us believe?

Are the mummies Tocharians? Who were the Tocharians anyway?
We must then turn to our final suspect, the Tocharians, the most elusive of the ancient Indo-European peoples (Chapter Nine), and attempt to establish what precisely we know of their language, culture and origins, and how they may lie behind the identity of the earliest mummies.

What happened in East Central Asia?
By now we have assembled all the evidence presently available to us to attempt a reconstruction of the ethnic history of the land of the Tarim mummies (Chapter Ten).

What role did the mummies play in the rise of Chinese civilization?
This book is not just about the identity of the mummies but also their contribution and that of their closest relations to Eurasian culture. The world's oldest surviving civilization still flourishes in China long after those of Mesopotamia, the Indus Valley, Central America (the Maya and Aztecs), and South America (the Incas) have all disappeared. The contribution of China to world culture is so massive (we could begin our examples with the very paper this book is printed on and the cash or cheque that was employed to purchase it) that one could well become predisposed to accepting that China did evolve in isolation from the backward world of European barbarians. The mummies of East Central Asia, however, challenge this assumption and in our attempt to place the mummies in the cultural history of the peoples of Eurasia (Chapter Eleven), we will also seek to discover the contributions of the prehistoric West to the ancient East.

A Note on Transliteration and Reconstruction

Throughout this book we have transliterated letters belonging to non-Roman alphabets (Chinese, Indo-European etc.) to give them approximate values in Roman letters. In addition, an * indicates where words are not actually attested in the given language but have been reconstructed through comparative philology; subscript figures or letters accompanying an h (as in $h_2óu̯is$ 'sheep') indicate laryngeals which have been reconstructed for Proto-Indo-European.

CHAPTER ONE

Beyond the Centres: Tarim Between East and West

The Tarim mummies were discovered in a region remote from the world's early civilizations. Indeed, it may be unfamiliar to many readers. In order to provide a geographical context for the mummies, let us position the various peoples of the ancient and early medieval world as figures on a board game such as chess or draughts (checkers) (ill. 9). In this way we can approach the centre from the two sides of the board, the ends of the literate ancient world. This will permit us to see how geographical knowledge of the world of the mummies, effectively that of the Silk Road, came into being; moreover, it allows us to introduce some of the peoples neighbouring East Central Asia who, as we will see in subsequent chapters, most influenced the culture of the Tarim region. In the next chapter we will shift our game to the type popular in the Middle Ages where we will set the Tarim Basin at the centre of the board and arrange its neighbours on the periphery.

8. The word Zhongguo (China) consists of two hanzi *(characters): the first is* zhong *'middle' (with a line through the middle) while* guo *'country', 'state' depicted a dagger-axe defending a walled town with palisades above and below, around which was later added a box symbolizing a boundary.*

Two Centres

Europeans tend to find their mother culture in that of the ancient Greeks who believed themselves to sit at the centre of the world. According to Greek tradition, Zeus had set loose two eagles, one in the east and one in the west; they were instructed to fly to the centre and it was at Delphi that they met. The Greeks recognized a stone at Delphi, seat of the famous oracle, as the 'navel of the world'. It is little wonder then that when the Greeks drew their maps, Greece was at the centre of a world surrounded by barbarians (*barbaroi*), people who did not speak Greek but could only stammer out something that sounded (at least to a Greek) like 'bar-bar'. Such a misguided perspective was not the way to impress a north Chinese contemporary: the name of the 'best place in the world under heaven' was Zhongguo, which

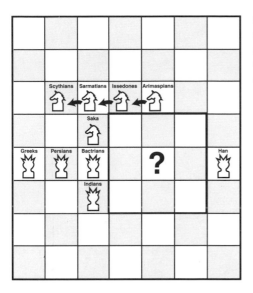

9. Board game 1: The main players before the discovery of the Tarim and Turpan basins by the West. Kings represent settled states; knights indicate essentially nomadic populations.

combines *zhong* 'middle' and *guo* 'country' (hence 'the Middle Country'), as the Chinese knew quite well that theirs was the only civilization and it was they who sat at the centre of a world surrounded by barbarians (*hu*). But explorations during the last millennium BC cured both countries' geographical and cultural myopia as they eventually came to discover one another. In so doing, they also became acquainted with the places and peoples of East Central Asia, the land of the Tarim mummies.

EAST OF GREECE

Herodotus

In the 5th century BC, Herodotus (*c.* 484–420 BC) provides us with one of the earliest Greek attempts to peer eastwards across Asia. Before his time, maps of the known world, such as that attributed to Hecataeus (ill. 10), would have been extremely schematic. An Ionian Greek who sought to prevent his people from rebelling against the Persians, Hecataeus appears to have travelled widely over both Egypt and Persia and we are left with a fragmentary account of his late 6th- or early 5th-century BC travels. On the basis of what little evidence can be gleaned from these fragments and references to a slightly earlier map drawn up by Anaximander (*c.* 610–545 BC), one can fashion something of a world map *c.* 500 BC. It is generally portrayed as a disc with Greece naturally at the centre of three continents: Europe occupies the upper half of the circle with a smaller Libya (Africa) and Asia sharing the lower hemisphere, all surrounded by an ocean that ran around the world. Herodotus was unimpressed with such maps since he believed that the known world was hardly so symmetrical and that the greater part of the

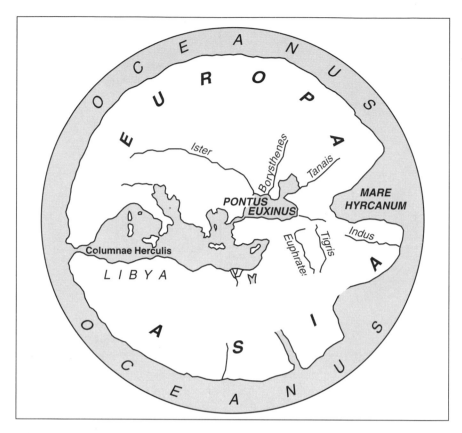

land ran west to east extending an unknown distance in the direction of the rising sun.

The path of knowledge to what lay east of the Greek world could follow two routes. The first was a northern route that would carry one eastwards across the great Eurasian steppe, the rolling grasslands that extended from Hungary on the west to northern China on the east. The second route coursed its way across the south through the lands of the Persian empire, over the Hindu Kush or Pamirs and into the Tarim Basin and eastwards across China. Both of these served as the main routes of trade between China and the West. They also comprised the two corridors of population movements that would have carried Caucasoids east into the Tarim Basin.

The Northern Route

In the mid-5th century BC an intrepid Greek traveller could depart from Athens and sail northeastwards to one of the Greek colonies founded along the northern shores of the Black Sea to provide food, fur, wax, grain, slaves and other commodities to the Greek towns on both sides of the Aegean. These colonies offered a world little different from that of his homeland. He (or she) could worship in his or her temples, attend Greek schools, enjoy the gymnasium and theatre, and find a proper Greek burial in the Greek towns such as Olbia on the mouth of the River Bug or Tanais on the River Don, which was then reckoned to be the dividing line between Europe and Asia (we now consider the border to lie much farther east along the Ural River). Greeks traded with the peoples of the interior, namely farmers who supplied them with grain and the pastoral nomads of the steppelands, the Scythians, who supplied them with whatever they could exploit or extort from the more settled populations of the Black Sea region, together with the products of their own herds.

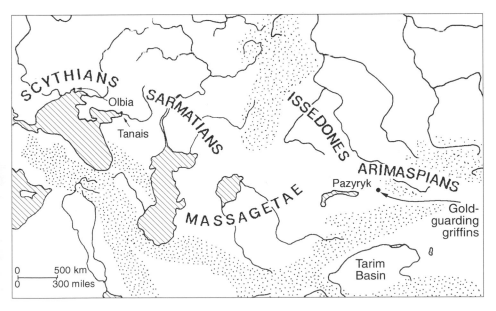

Herodotus provides us with a detailed account of the peoples north of the Black Sea, both the settled farmers who occupied the black earths that formed the breadbasket of the former Soviet Union, and also the Scythians. He portrays the latter as a nomadic people who traversed the steppe in wagons with their herds and flocks. They were armed with the sword and especially the bow. As they did not occupy towns, they did not need to defend territories other than their royal burial grounds. The elaborate burial of the Scythian kings is described by Herodotus and is almost entirely confirmed by archaeology. Large pits capped with tent-like timber structures were built to house the remains of the

11. A Scythian with a peaked hat strings his bow.

king, his retainers and his horses (over 300 in one tomb), as well as a fabulous assortment of golden objects.

12. A map constructed from the descriptions of Herodotus reveals a chain of peoples leading eastwards but no certain evidence that they extended as far as the Tarim region.

13. Reconstruction of a heavily armoured Sarmatian.

Beyond the Scythians, across the River Don, lay the Sauromatae, whom Herodotus explained as the issue of Scythian men and the Amazons, the legendary tribe of women warriors. Herodotus and subsequent writers maintained that the Sauromatae (and as they are known later in Roman sources, the Sarmatians) retained practices of their Amazonian past which was evident in the behaviour of their women who continued to ride horses and hunt and who were not permitted to marry until they had made their first kill in combat. That this story may have some form of rational explanation is suggested by the fact that Sarmatian burials of women include a substantial number which show, in addition to articles that might be regarded as clearly indicating a feminine role in society (cooking and spinning equipment, feminine ornaments), armour and weapons. What is certain is that the Sarmatians came eventually to dominate the European steppelands where they defeated the Scythians who had preceded them. They employed heavily armoured cavalry in battle, which initially proved more than a match for their steppe neighbours but which would later prove too clumsy to withstand the Romans.

Beyond the Sarmatians Herodotus provides us with a catalogue of peoples whose ethnic identity, if not existence, has vexed scholars for generations. We then come to the Tanais, the modern River Don, where the Geloni and Budini shared the enormous wooden settlement of Gelonus which archaeologists have now identified with the modern site of Belsk, one of the largest earth and timber-defended enclosures of Eurasia (although it actually lies west of the Don). Beyond these peoples one would have encountered the Thyssagetae and Iyrkae who lived by hunting and who have been located by some modern scholars somewhere between the middle Volga and the southeast Urals where forest meets the forest steppe. Beyond them lay other Scythians who, Herodotus informs us, had revolted against the Royal Scythians of the Black Sea region (or, as some scholars propose, were Scythians who had remained behind when the rest moved westwards).

Still farther east, according to Herodotus, we encounter the Argippaei who are described as bald from birth onwards (both men and women) and snub-nosed (which is taken by some to suggest a Mongoloid and hence beardless physical type); they dress like Scythians but carry no weapons as they are regarded as sacred and are employed to settle disputes. They make a thick black drink that they call *aschy* which can be consumed straight, mixed with milk, or the lees can be made into cakes. The beverage has been identified as *atschi*, a drink made from the fruit of the bird-cherry (*Prunus Padus*), the national drink of the Kazan Tatars. Herodotus remarks that the Argippaei are linguistically diverse and different from their neighbours, requiring some seven interpreters to deal with their seven languages. Beyond these tribes we enter realms where the geographical location, still more so the ethnic identity, of the peoples cited becomes wildly speculative. But we must maintain our march eastwards if we are to understand how Europeans may have found themselves in what is now western China. Herodotus can only get us so far; to go farther we need another guide.

Aristeas

To carry us beyond Herodotus' own knowledge, we, like Herodotus, must rely on the observations of Aristeas of Proconnesus who is reputed to have lived in about the late 7th or early 6th century BC. One of the most amazing figures of early Greek tradition, Aristeas is reputed to have walked into a fuller's shop in his home town on the island of Marmora, where he collapsed and died. The fuller closed up shop and ran to fetch Aristeas' kinsfolk to retrieve the body, but when they arrived they discovered that Aristeas had disappeared. Six years later, however, Aristeas reappeared in town and revealed that he had spent the intervening time wandering across the steppelands (a reputed time-traveller, Aristeas also re-emerged several *centuries* later in Italy!). He fashioned an account of his initial journey in his *Arimaspeia*, a poem recounting his travels. Only fragments of this poem survive and our knowledge of its contents is largely confined to Herodotus and to snippets from other early writers (in the 2nd century AD the Roman author Aulus Gellius managed to pick up a second-hand copy in Brindisi for an 'astonishingly low' price).

The veracity of Aristeas' account has been the subject of considerable discussion. His 'seizure' in the fuller's shop has been interpreted as a form of religiously inspired catalepsy brought on by his excessive devotion to the god Apollo – he was, as the Greeks had it, *phoibolamptos,* 'possessed by Phoebus Apollo'. Early Greek tradition related that the Hyperboreans, who lived on the outer reaches of the world disc, were those dearest to Apollo;

it was they that started Aristeas off on his remarkable journey in search of his god. Such is the stuff of modern fantasy literature: we have before us an eccentric Greek, either wandering or being passed from one tribe of steppe nomads to another, who tolerantly grant him safe passage as they regard him holy, mad or both. Others reject the whole notion of such a journey and suggest that Aristeas never left the floor of the fuller's shop, but that we are dealing with the archetypal 'vision flight' of a shaman who merely imagined that he made the journey. The problem with Aristeas' account is that no matter how fantastic the individual details, there are enough rational explanations to string us along in the hope that we are onto something that is at least partially real.

By the time we have arrived among the next people, the Issedones, even Herodotus' credulity is frayed. His bald-headed Argippaei have told him that beyond them live mountain people with goat's feet and then we come to people who sleep six months of every year – neither of these impressed Herodotus but he did affirm, following Aristeas, that the Issedones really did exist and he relates some of their customs. We learn that on the death of a man among the Issedones, his closest relatives mixed the diced remains of the deceased with the joints of animals and engaged in ritual cannibalism. The skulls were gilded and taken out for yearly veneration. In his fascinating account of Aristeas, J. D. P. Bolton suggests that before we dismiss this account of ritual cannibalism out of hand, there is some evidence for such practices elsewhere. The missionary William of Rubruck maintained that the population of Kokonor (between northeast Tibet and northwest China) engaged in the same practice in the 13th century; however, as William himself admits, he did not actually see this happen and we might be dealing with a warmed-up reminiscence taken from Herodotus. 'Endocannibalism', i.e. the consumption of one's own people rather than one's enemies, is always possible (and is attributed to a number of other peoples in Herodotus), but we can offer a different 'rational' explanation for dicing up one's deceased relatives. Recently, Eileen Murphy, an osteoarchaeologist from Queen's University, Belfast, has been studying the remains of some thousand Scythian-Sarmatian period burials in Siberia. She has uncovered evidence for widespread deliberate defleshing of many of the deceased, seen in the tell-tale marks of the knife applied to the bone. Her solution to the problem is not that the community were devouring their dead but rather that they were solving a very practical problem that pastoral nomads must invariably face if their cemetery is centrally located and their relatives have inconveniently died in distant pastures. Assistance with a knife in reducing the deceased to clean bones that might be carried back home in a bag resolves the problem of carrying a decaying corpse for weeks or months before returning to the proper burial ground. The evidence of defleshing is primarily confined to those burials in which the skeleton is not in its correct anatomical position. One can easily imagine how this apparent butchery of corpses might be misinterpreted by a stranger unaccustomed to such a practice.

We also learn that the women here shared equal power with the men. Any elevated position of women was always a topic of marvel to the male-dominated 'democracies' of ancient Greece. Despite the graphic portrayals of ruthlessly patriarchal societies that the cinema studios of Hollywood or Rome have been wont to serve up when depicting steppe nomads, there are a number of instances, in addition to the case of the Sarmatians, where we find women occupying some of the more traditionally male social roles. Accounts from the last century of the Mongol Hazaras of northern Afghanistan, for example, describe women riding to both the hunt and war with their husbands, and the motif of the woman warrior is also well known in Celtic and Germanic traditions. Furthermore, we will encounter in the Tarim Basin horseriding women who, like their menfolk, wore trousers. It might be noted that the Chinese shared the same jaundiced view of women as the Greeks. One of the earliest (12th-century BC) Chinese texts we have is inscribed on an oracle bone of the Shang dynasty: the seers predicted that 'The Lady Hao will give birth and it will be good', but the marvellously empirical Chinese also provided the results of their prediction: '... she gave birth. It was not good. It was a girl.' Again like the Greeks, the ancient Chinese also imagined the existence of Nürenguo, 'women's countries', situated far to their west.

Where did these Issedones live? We can fix this position notionally because the Issedones were to be found to the north of the Massagetae whose position is well enough known from other sources. The Massagetae occupied both the agricultural territory between the Amu Darya (Oxus) and Syr Darya (Jaxartes) to the south of the Aral Sea and the semi-desert and steppelands to their north. They practised both irrigation agriculture and pastoralism with their cattle, horses and camels. Those who lived to the north, beyond the range of agriculture, hunted and fished as well, and we are told (rather ingenuously) that their name derives from the Iranian word for 'fish'. We will later see that all these skills were employed by the earliest Caucasoids who occupied the Tarim Basin.

The name of the Issedones has long been linguistically associated with the name of the Iset River which flows from the southern Urals eastward into the Tobol. In the 17th century this region was still known as the province of Isetia. The Issedones have been regarded by some as middlemen, guarding the Ekaterinburg Pass through the Urals, in the vast trade network that extended the length of the Eurasian steppe as far east as the Yenisei River (alternatively, they may have controlled the two ends of the route, on the steppe and on the frontiers of China). Both the name of the river and that of the people have been identified as Iranian, the same language group that also prevailed in ancient Persia and Afghanistan.

On the other hand, the geographer Ptolemy, writing in the 2nd century AD, locates an Issedon Scythica (presumably our Issedones) and an Issedon Serica (Issedones of the Silk-lands or China) in the Tarim Basin. That this was their position (actual or mythic) at the time of Herodotus is quite uncertain and here, on the eastern extremity of Ptolemy's world, it is always possible that the residue of unlocated places may have been conveniently dumped on the outer rim 'so that none of the things inserted to fill up the whole world may have an undefined place'. We will have good cause to return to Ptolemy later on.

We learn one more thing of interest from Aristeas' sojourn among the Issedones. He tells us that their neighbours, the Arimaspians, had driven them from their country and they in turn had pushed westward the Scythians who then dispossessed the Cimmerians of their lands north of the Black Sea. This 'domino' model of one steppe people pressing upon another, from east to west, is essentially confirmed by historical sources that portray a good part of the 1st millennium BC and the subsequent millennium in terms of demographic convulsions arising from somewhere deep in Asia and pushing one tribe after another westwards (we may recall that the Huns, Avars, Turks and Mongols were waiting in the wings). For our purpose, the important thing to note is that by the middle of the 1st millennium BC, the human gradient running across the steppe, at least between eastern Europe and the Urals, seems to have flowed from east to west rather than in the opposite direction. From the perspective of Europeans pouring into the Tarim Basin, the human current at that time seems to have been flowing the wrong way.

Arimaspians

Next, we come to the Arimaspians of Aristeas' poem, and here we have no first-hand account since even Aristeas gained his knowledge of these remote people from the Issedones. In his study of Aristeas, J. D. P. Bolton uses this admission to counter the revisionist interpretation that Aristeas did not visit these lands but rather was engaged in a shamanistic spirit-flight; if this were indeed so, how should we explain Aristeas 'crash landing' among the Issedones from whom he had to pick up the rest of his geography second-hand? He learned from the Issedones that the Arimaspians raised livestock (horses, cattle and sheep), were brave warriors, had shaggy hair and, less credibly, that the men had only one eye in the centre of their forehead (although they had a 'handsome visage'). Herodotus tells us that the Scythians derived their name from *arima*, 'one', and *spou*, 'eye'; a more recent etymology would see them as *arim*, 'friends of' or 'owners of', *aspou*, 'horses'. One of the favourite motifs cited by Herodotus and later writers was that the Arimaspians were

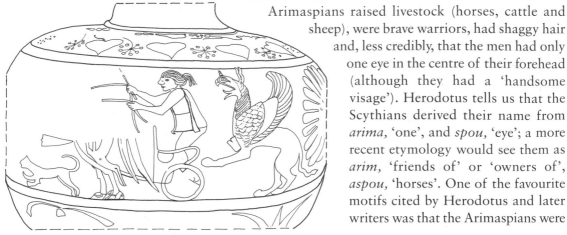

14. A griffin chases an Arimaspian on a Caretian vase.

15. Griffins depicted on a textile fragment from Pazyryk in the Altai Mountains have been associated with the gold-guarding griffins of Herodotus.

able to steal golden treasures from griffins who guarded the gold in a neighbouring land. Milton reprises these motifs in *Paradise Lost* when Satan makes his long downward fall towards earth:

> As when a Gryfon through the Wilderness
> With winged course o'er Hill or moory Dale,
> Pursues the Arimaspian, who by stealth
> Had from his wakeful custody purloin'd
> The guarded Gold.... (*II 943–947*)

By now our traveller would have journeyed to the limits of early Greek knowledge of the Eurasian steppelands.

The precise location of these Arimaspians has taxed the imagination of numerous scholars who have sought not only the possible sources of the gold but also the griffins, or at least the artistic motif which was widespread across the steppe, particularly in the eastern steppe (it has been suggested that the griffin motif itself may have been stimulated by the ancient discovery of fossils of beaked dinosaurs; similarly, the famous Cyclops who dwelt in Sicily may have been prompted by the discovery of the remains of pygmy elephants on the island whose skulls would suggest a monstrous creature with tusks and a single orbit). Modern geographers have dragged the Arimaspians all over the Asian landscape. One of the more popular suggestions has been that if one accepts that the Issedones occupied the southern Urals, then we might locate the Arimaspians in the Altai Moun- tains. Conveniently enough, we not only find sources of gold in this region but the famous royal burials at Pazyryk. These tombs, dated to about 300–250 BC, were plundered in antiquity – tombs in this general region were plundered so often that they were popularly known as 'gold hills' – causing them to fill with water which then turned to ice and marvellously preserved all the organic remains. In the felt and wooden ornaments we find the recurrent motif of the griffin. We will have cause to return to the Pazyryk burials in a later chapter, but for now we should mentally note that the majority of human remains there belonged to Caucasoids and that the Altai Mountains themselves constitute the northernmost natural border of the modern province of Xinjiang, the home of the Tarim mummies.

It may well be argued that any attempt at locating such a remote people is itself an idle one. The motif of a distant people battling monsters is common in Herodotus, who also has the Indians fighting giant ants (identified recently as gold-digging marmots of the Pamirs!), and Arabs pitted against enormous birds and flying serpents. The motif of dragon-guarded gold at the ends of the world is so widespread that seeking a geographical explanation here may be futile. Bolton, however, was impressed since there were even some clues about the ultimate inhabitants of the world, the Hyperboreans.

Hyperboreans

The most distant inhabitants of the world disc, the goal of Aristeas' journey, would have been the Hyperboreans, those who were 'dear to Apollo' and dwelt beyond the source of the wind Boreas. For the sceptical who would wonder why one might search for the source of the most violent of winds in Central Asia, Bolton assembled an impressive series of travellers' accounts of the tremendous winds that pour out through the Dzungarian Gate and blow over Lake Ala Kul threatening the lives of any traveller and decamping any tent. Here, he suggests, is certainly a meteorological phenomenon that could well earn a mythic reputation as being the mother of winds. In short, a remarkable geographical situation could have given rise to a myth that spread widely over Central Asia and was passed from the Issedones on to Aristeas.

And, as for the Hyperboreans themselves, the people who lived beyond the land of the Boreas wind, we know little other than that they lived in harmony, were apparently vegetarians, and dwelt by the sea. Bolton suggests that the most obvious well-ordered society which both dined primarily on grains and dwelt by the sea might be the Chinese.

With so much still and perhaps perpetually in doubt, it is difficult to draw conclusions about the precise position and identity of the easternmost of Herodotus' peoples. It is certainly probable that his geographical knowledge extended as far east as Kazakhstan, which the reader might do well to recall is the ninth largest country (in territory) in the world and would have been a major staging area for any European push into Central Asia. The ancient historian, limited by fragmentary records assembled by dubious witnesses and reported by gullible or uncomprehending writers, can get us only so far in understanding the steppelands that lay beyond first-hand testimony.

On the other hand, from an archaeological perspective we do know that the Eurasian steppelands were a vast area of transit and exchange during the last millennium BC. A recurring package of high-status cultural traits found across the entire steppe – weapons, horse harnesses, 'animal style' art, cauldrons, mirrors, stone stelae, burial under kurgans (mounds) – attests to this intercommunication; regardless of whether ancient or modern historians can assign names to the various peoples or not, the steppe corridor was surely not empty or a *terra incognita* to its many inhabitants who traded, mingled and fought with one another. Peoples, material culture and ideas moved along this corridor through the Iron Age and even earlier during the Bronze Age of the 2nd millennium BC when, as we will later see, we find our earliest evidence for Caucasoids in East Central Asia. Bolton would argue that Greek geographical knowledge might carry one as far as the Dzungarian Gate and the base of the Altai Mountains. Now Dzungaria or, better, the Jungghar or Yarish Basin, is the northern sister to the Tarim Basin. It lies west of the Altai but still north of the Tängri Tagh (or Tian Shan; both meaning 'Heavenly' or 'Celestial Mountains') that form the northern border of the Tarim Basin. We are at the main entry point for any movement southwards into the world of the mummies. But what is still missing is certain evidence that the ancient Greek world knew of the existence of the desert oases of the Tarim Basin itself.

The Southern Route

> As far as India, Asia is an inhabited land; but thereafter all to the east is desert, nor can any man say what kind of land is there. (*Herodotus IV 40*)

If a Greek or any other European wished to trek eastwards and avoid lands teeming with the snub-nosed, bald-headed, one-eyed cannibals and griffins, then there was another route through the great Persian empire. According to Herodotus, the Persian king Darius I (550–486 BC) had divided his empire into 20 provincial governments or satrapies. A Greek could make his way eastwards through the western provinces such as Anatolia (Turkey) and Mesopotamia and then cross into the lands of the Persians and the Medes, whose own territory extended as far as the southeast Caspian and the Araxes River. To push any farther east would carry one into the easternmost provinces (which comprised the easternmost ends of the world so far as an ancient Greek knew). Our immediate perspective of these provinces derives from the time of Herodotus, but we would do well to keep in mind that the territory that we are about to survey briefly would form an alternative staging area for European penetration into East Central Asia, as the populations which inhabited most of the area are, broadly speaking, Caucasoids. The eastern frontier consisted of India, the most populous of the provinces, which was required to supply to Persia a great tribute in gold. To its north

16. *Greek accounts of the empire of Darius could carry one as far east as the peoples of India and Bactria but no farther.*

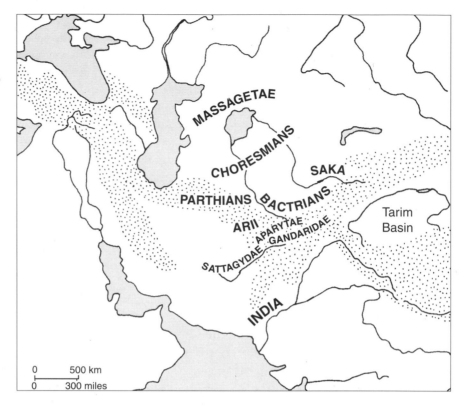

was the 7th province, the lands of the Sattagydae, Gandaridae, Dadicae and Aparytae which carried one into northwest India-Pakistan and the territory known today as Swat. Still farther north, in what is modern Afghanistan, was the 12th province, Bactria. Today the name is of little import unless one is caught in a quiz and has to remember which type of camel has two humps. Newspapers and television confront us with little else from this region than the distressing political turmoil of Afghanistan. Surely this was nothing but a backwater to civilization? How wrong could one be! Bactria was then the major crossroads of movement from west to east, a pivotal territory in the emergence of the historical cultures of the Tarim Basin; in short, Bactria was where the action was and this is something we must consider as we pursue our story. To its north lay the 16th province of the Parthians, Choresmians, Sogdians and Arii, all of whom will also have a part to play later in our story. These peoples held the lands of modern West Central Asia. To their east lay the limits of known peoples in the 15th province, assigned to the Saka, who, we will soon see, spilled over into the Tarim Basin itself and offer us one of the main candidates to be associated with our Asian mummies. North of them lay the Massagetae whom we have already encountered occupying the territory east of the Caspian and on either side of the Aral Sea; according to Herodotus, the Massagetae (under the leadership of their Queen Tomyris) managed to kill the emperor Cyrus (*c.* 590–*c.* 529 BC) when he strayed north of the Oxus. What lay farther east?

Herodotus did not know and, uncharacteristically, he even declined to speculate much other than to mention, as we have seen, that beyond India was desert. This, at least, suggested the possibility of other lands beyond those recognized by his immediate predecessor Hecataeus. In the early 5th century Scylax of Caryanda, who left us with a memorable account of India, its wildlife (unicorns) and peoples (for example, long-lived mountain-dwelling dog-headed people who could understand the speech of the Indians but only bark back in response, one-legged people – we have been here before) posed the question: whence flowed the waters of the Indus? He set their source at Paropamisus or what we would today call the Hindu Kush. There was now a mountain range between the world known to the Greeks and whatever lay beyond.

Geographical knowledge of the east increased but slowly over the next centuries. Alexander the Great might take his armies into Bactria, defeat the nomads of the north or cross into northern India but there seems to have been no great pressure to expand geographical horizons eastwards. The peoples of the east had all fought and surrendered to Alexander, the nomads of the steppe being the hardest to subdue, but geographical knowledge beyond the great mountain ranges was apparently not increased. Geographers still conceived of a world ocean and beyond the mountain ranges lay the Caspian Gulf; to the ancient Greeks the Tarim mummies would have floated in a sea that lay just beyond the borders of the known world. Even Aristotle was of the opinion that one could climb the Hindu Kush and see the great Ocean at the limit of the world. The wind from the east blew from Bactria; there was nothing known beyond it.

Eratosthenes

He was nicknamed 'Beta' by his contemporaries because he was never an 'Alpha', never regarded the best, but always second. But what a second! His colleagues may have regarded him as of low potential but he was definitely a high-achiever. He was Eratosthenes (276–194 BC), one of the librarians of Alexandria, the intellectual storehouse of the ancient world and the product of one of the greatest legacies of Alexander's conquests. Eratosthenes was the polymath who computed the circumference of the earth and arrived at a figure remarkably close to its actual diameter of c. 40,000 km (c. 25,000 miles). (Depending on how one calculates his unit of measurement, the stadion, he may have come within 320 km or 200 miles of the actual figure.) His geographical work was not simply a matter of scale: he also plotted the distances between the known places on the face of the earth derived from marching itineraries, where a day's journey had to be computed into Greek stadia or some other unit of measurement. Here his reckoning was not nearly so good and his estimation of the distance between Cape Verde off Africa and the mouth of the Ganges may have been out by some 3,200 km or 2,000 miles. His eastern limits were the Ganges and the Himalayas (Imaus). He was

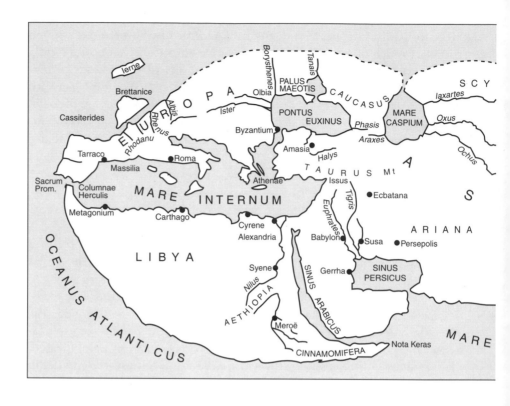

confronted with a major problem: how to account for the distance between
the Ganges eastwards around to the shores of the Atlantic in order to join
up the ends of his maps (the Greeks had no great difficulty with the concept
that they may have lived on a large ball). The world known to Eratosthenes
only occupied a third of the total circumference of the earth that he had
calculated; the remaining two-thirds were variously accounted for by the
ancients as either an enormous sea (wherein one could sail westwards from
Europe to India which would later entice a gullible but very lucky Columbus
to try the same) or populated with the lost continents of ancient and modern
mythologies. This picture of the eastern limits of the world, which ended at
the Tamarus promontory that overlooked the world ocean, was largely
retained up until the beginning of the Christian era. The geographer Strabo
(c. 64 BC–AD 23) leaned heavily on Eratosthenes in drawing up his map of
Asia. That it could not go beyond the Tamarus was curious, for a new
product from the distant east had already begun to attract the attention of
the West.

By the 1st century BC we read of the use of silk for the first time in the
West adorning Cleopatra's dresses, the awnings at the Roman Colosseum
or Parthian flags. A century before this we encounter the name Seres to
designate a people of the far east, while the derivative 'Sericus' might mean
either 'of the Seres' or 'silk', the two having become synonymous. Pliny the
Elder, writing about AD 77, relates an earlier tradition that as one travels
beyond the Caspian one must pass through an uninhabitable region full of

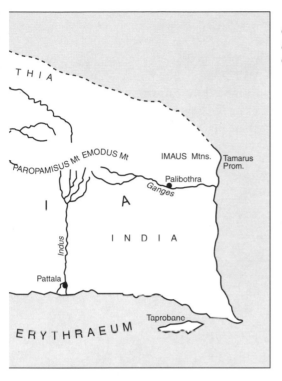

17. Even in the time of Strabo, the world extended only as far as the Hindu Kush, beyond which the West still imagined an enormous sea.

snow, and then a territory in waste where the Anthropophagi Scythae (man-eating Scythians) dwell, then more waste, more Scythians, then desert wastes before one reaches the Tabis, the mountain range that fronts the eastern sea. Along its coast dwell the Seres who supply the west with a 'woollen material from their forests', taken by many to refer to cotton. The Seres are regarded as 'mild in character' (elsewhere 'just' and they were also reputed to have been extraordinarily long-lived, up to 200 years according to Strabo), but they resemble wild animals in that they avoid the rest of humankind and 'wait for trade to come to them'.

But before we presume that the Seres are Chinese, we should look at one of the more fascinating descriptions of this east–west trade recounted by a Singhalese ambassador to the Emperor Claudius (recorded in Pliny VI 88). He tells us how his father made the trip eastwards to trade with the 'Serai' who always ran out to meet them. Goods would be left out on the river bank by both sides and taken away if they were deemed satisfactory. So are these Serai Chinese? Probably not, for Pliny's informant tells us that they are 'more than normal height, and have flaxen hair and blue eyes, and they speak in harsh tones and use no language in dealing with travellers'. Speculation as to who is meant here by 'Serai' is rampant and covers peoples ranging from southern Siberia westwards to the Jaxartes, including the Wusun (of whom we will have much more to tell) and various peoples of the Tarim Basin. As we are for the moment attempting to see things through European eyes, how did western goods come to these people who dealt in silk?

Maës the Macedonian

The major atlas of the ancient world was prepared in Alexandria, Egypt, by Claudius Ptolemy (who was active *c.* AD 127–145). He prepared an impressive gazetteer of the known world which for him ran from Ireland in the west to the frontiers of China in the east. We can behave like a persistent child and ask: how did he know where these places were or what their names

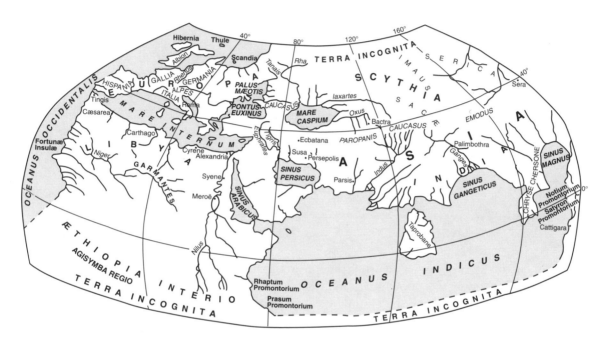

18. By the time of Ptolemy (2nd century AD) geographers could map a world that carried one as far east as the western frontiers of China.

19. The Silk Road, actually several routes that carried one from China across the northern and southern rims of the Tarim Basin and on to the West, was the major overland trade route of the ancient world.

were? He tells us himself that he was forced to rely for many of his locations on his near contemporary, Marinus of Tyre, who flourished in the early 2nd century AD. But how did Marinus know? Here we learn that Marinus himself depended on a caravan itinerary, the closest thing to a road map in the ancient world, which he had purchased from a Macedonian trader named Maës Titianus. The account gave directions for a caravan departing from Syria eastwards to the Bactrian capital, Bactra, and then over the Pamirs to Kasia (probably Qäshqär (Kashgar)) and along the southern route to Throana (Dunhuang), the outpost of Chinese civilization. And how did Maës know? Maës drew his account together from information supplied by his own agents. Marinus was sceptical of information obtained from traders who had a habit of exaggerating distances to enhance their reputation. He might have added also their price, as the longer the journey the greater the overheads, although these were unlikely to be too great. As the historian William McNeill has pointed out, the efficiency of the camel caravan was truly remarkable. Although its speed was only about 3 or 4 miles per hour, it was an all-terrain transport and did not require the building and maintenance of roads; thus camels were more cost effective than wheeled vehicles. Generally, one herdsman controlled 6 camels and it was usual for two men to work a team of 12 camels tied in tandem. The overheads of these earliest caravans is uncertain, but records from a 16th-century caravan from Iran to Turkey indicate that the cost of transport was no more than 3 per cent of the sale price of the silk which was being conveyed. Since we find a change in the unit of distance at Bactra from the Greek *stadion* (*c*. 156–200 m or 512–656 ft) to the Egyptian *schoinos* (*c*. 4.5 km or 2.8 miles), we may presume that the leader of the expedition also changed here.

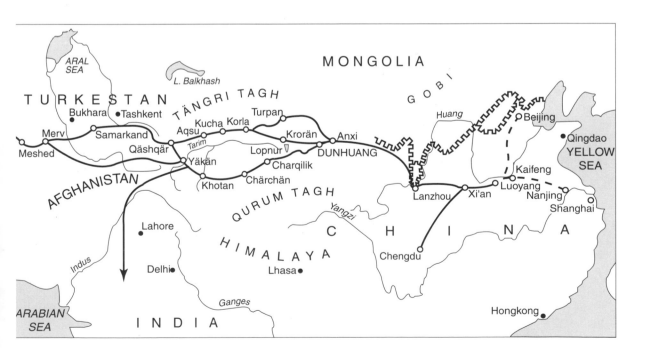

Freiherr (Baron) Friedrich von Richthofen

The name 'Silk Road' (*die Seidenstrasse*), the transcontinental caravan routes that went from China through Central Asia to the Black Sea and Mediterranean Sea, was coined by the uncle of the celebrated World War I flying ace, the 'Red Baron' Freiherr Manfred von Richthofen. Friedrich von Richthofen (1833–1905) was one of the leading geographers and geologists of the 19th century. He taught at the universities of Bonn, Leipzig and Berlin, and was a founder of the science of geomorphology. Himself a formidable traveller, from 1860 to 1862 Richthofen visited Ceylon, Japan, Formosa, the Celebes, Java, the Philippines, Siam and Burma, as they were then called. After that he went to California where he stayed from 1863 to 1868 and carried out geological investigations which, among other things, resulted in the discovery of goldfields. From 1868 to 1872, he undertook a series of expeditions to China, during the course of which he visited almost every part of the country and gathered materials for his magnum opus, *China: Ergebnisse eigener Reisen und darauf gegründete Studien (China: The Results of My Travels and the Studies Based Thereon)*, 5 vols. and atlas (1877–1912). Among other achievements, he located the dried-up lake bed of Lopnur long before anyone else. To honour his tremendous contributions to the knowledge of Chinese geography acquired during his seven expeditions to that country, the range of mountains along the southern edge of the Gansu Corridor – now called the Qilian Mountains – were named the Richthofen Range.

According to Ptolemy, the account purchased by Marinus allotted seven months' journey time from the Pamirs to China. The caravan followed a relatively well-known route as far as the Pamirs but then aimed for a 'stone tower' as the major way station. Many have tried to locate this tower precisely. The words 'stone tower' could be rendered in Turkish as Tashkurgan, the major fortified site on the western rim of the Tarim and a natural outpost (the name Tashkent also renders 'stone tower' in Turkish and was once suggested as the original gathering place of merchants along what Baron Friedrich von Richthofen called the 'Silk Road'). Whatever its precise location, it was within its vicinity that major transactions were made between those trading in silk from the east and their western counterparts who exchanged glass, fragrances, gold and other precious goods. The caravan route continued eastwards to Qäshqär and followed one of the two great forks (ill. 19). The southern route through Khotan, Niyä, Miran (i.e. roughly along the route between modern Chärchän and Charkhlik), Lopnur and then Dunhuang, the main Chinese outpost in the west, was probably the earlier. The other route carried one across Kucha, Korla, Lopnur and then to Dunhuang; this northern route required one to pass through lands teeming with bandits. Either route took one through the lands of the Tarim mummies.

WEST OF THE MIDDLE COUNTRY

Dog-heads and Winged Tigers

Beyond the great ocean or desert of the ancient Greeks lay another empire that simultaneously began straining its vision westwards. Like Greece, it began at the 'centre' or Middle Country. We can reconstruct a map from the Warring States period (403–221 BC) of the enfeebled Eastern Zhou dynasty that purports to depict schematically the political world of the Chinese as a series of concentric boxes (to the ancient Chinese the land was conceptually a square and aligned with the cardinal directions while the heavens were 'in the round'). In the centre lay the *dian fu*, the royal domain of the Zhou king. Five hundred *li* beyond (a *li* measured *c.* 400 m or 1,313 ft) we find the territory of the *hou fu*, the domain of the princes. The map expands again at successive units of 500 *li* through the pacification zone and the zone of compacts to the *huang fu*, the wild zone. And wild it was, for the early Chinese were content to populate the lands beyond their own borders with creatures every bit as weird and wonderful as the one-eyed griffin fighters of the Greeks.

Accounts of the marvels of the western lands are found in the *Shanhai jing* (*Classic of Mountains and Seas*). Legend had it that the founder of the Xia dynasty (*c.* 2205 BC), Yu, and a minister of the former regime travelled across China and neighbouring territories, recording whatever they saw. In actual fact we are dealing with a bestiary which was compiled in the 1st centuries BC and AD, although it contained material some centuries older. In addition to peoples lacking shanks and bellies, or who walk around on tiptoe, are more familiar friends such as red ants as large as elephants, which remind us of the gold-guarding ants recorded in Greek sources about India. Still more striking are the descriptions of two peoples who were at war with the Chinese, the Gui and the Dog Rong. The former had but a single eye (like

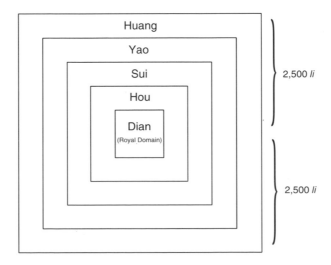

20. A schematic map of the lands surrounding the royal court of China's Zhou dynasty.

21. *The ancient Chinese were a match for Herodotus in their ability to people remote lands with strange beings such as these fantastic creatures from the* Shanhai jing.

the Arimaspians of our Greek sources) and in their region we also find the *qiongqi*, winged tigers, which, if we engage in a bit of feline species re-alignment, provides us with a fair version of a griffin, a winged lion. And beyond the northern sea we find a giant some 1,000 *li* long (approximately 480 km or 300 miles) whose breath makes the wind. We seem to be discovering here a mythic fauna not far removed from that provided in the descriptions of Aristeas. As Bolton suggests, the striking similarity between Chinese and Greek tales may reflect a common Central Asian folkloric tradition that worked its way into the geographical mythologies of both East and West. Nowhere is this seen better perhaps than in the accounts of the land of feathers which exist in both traditions.

Herodotus remarked that in the northern parts of Scythia one could neither travel nor even see because of the incredible quantity of falling feathers (he rationalized this away, explaining that the feathers were merely a metaphor for snow). Pliny the Elder, on the other hand, located this feather-filled country just beyond the land of the Arimaspians which, as we have seen, Bolton and others would locate in the vicinity of the Altai Mountains.

Now, the *Shanhai jing* is not our only Chinese source about the wonders that lay beyond the western borders of China. In the 3rd century AD the Chinese exhumed the remains of a king who had been buried during the Warring States period some 600 years earlier. In his tomb they recovered the text of the *Mu tianzi zhuan*, an account of the travels of the Zhou King Mu (reigned 956–918 BC) who reputedly wandered west from his capital at Luoyang. When he came to the vicinity of what was then called the Kunlun Mountains (but was more likely to be identified then with our Altai or Tängri Tagh), he arrived at a lake of sparkling water in the land of the 'Queen Mother of the West'. Here he found at the water's edge so many large waterbirds shedding their feathers that he was able to carry off as many as a hundred cartloads of feathers. Again we see East Central Asia nurturing the mythologies of both East and West.

Of all the fantastic beings of the west, one of the most pervasive is the dog-headed people, the Dog Rong, who were localized to the northwest of the Han and are recorded as a motif of Chinese lore as far back as the Shang dynasty *c.* 1200 BC. Various 'barbarians' in Han China were provided with a canine origin and here we find a trail of beliefs and even some linguistic evidence that, as we will later see, carries us from the world of the steppe nomads to the very heart of Chinese tradition.

But what about the lands in which we find the mummies themselves? Here we are given descriptions both useful and fantastic. That its mountains possessed jade and copper can be corroborated by geological and archaeological evidence, and East Central Asia was indeed historically noted for its production of jade. But it was also a land full of genetic monstrosities, the type of composite beasts in which the *Shanhai jing* delighted. Along the northern Tarim, for example, dwelt a quadruped that looked like a rat but had the head of a rabbit, the body of an elk, the cry of a howling dog, and flew about through the use of its tail. Or, to the north of this wonderful creature, you might encounter a *zhujian*, an animal resembling a leopard with a long tail, a human head, the ears of a cow and a single eye. Now, not all of these descriptions are purely the product of an overactive imagination, for some of the strange creatures described in the *Shanhai jing* may also be found depicted on Chinese bronzes or may have origins that lie in the mythologies of shamanistic neighbours of the Chinese. And, as we have seen, when the text refers to griffin-like creatures, we may well be dealing with the artistic legacy of the steppe nomads. Of even greater interest is reference to one of the peoples of the west, for we find recorded north of the territory of the 'fish-dragons' the land of the Whites (*Bai*), whose bodies are white and whose long hair falls to their shoulders. Such a description could accord well with a Caucasoid population beyond the frontiers of ancient China and some scholars have identified these Whites as the Yuezhi, whose very existence prompted the first Chinese mission to the west.

Zhang Qian's Expedition to the West

Our first concrete historical information about the west comes from the Han dynasty (206 BC–AD 220). The Han world was ringed by uninviting deserts and barbarians, in particular the Proto-Turkic and Proto-Mongol tribes of the north. Chinese accounts provide us with parahistorical records of some of these people. Parahistorical, unlike prehistorical, means an account of a people who, although themselves illiterate and thus unable to record their own past, did have literate neighbours, in this case the Chinese, who related something of their existence. The Chinese sources mention that during the period 176–165 BC one of the peoples at the western end of their empire, the Yuezhi, had been defeated by the Xiongnu, and their leader's skull had been fashioned into a goblet. The descendants of the Xiongnu or close relations would soon be terrorizing the European world as the Huns. Xiongnu captives in the royal court reported that the Yuezhi had fled westwards over the Tängri Tagh, to the land of the Wusun in the Ili Valley and, still pursued by the Xiongnu, had then fled southwards to seize the kingdom of Bactria. In so doing, they moved out of the historical records of the Chinese into those of the Greek world, and it has long been argued that these Yuezhi refugees are the same Tocharii and Asii mentioned in Greek sources, an issue that we will examine more closely later.

From their confrontations with nomads such as the Xiongnu, the Chinese rulers realized that they too would have to match the equestrian skills of these nomadic raiders and in order to do so, they required strong horses, capable of carrying an armoured warrior into battle. In the tactics of the mounted nomads of the steppe, the number of mounts required of a rider has been variously put at between 3 and 18. The Han court learned from Chinese traders that in the far west, in the region known as Dayuan

(Ferghana), such horses existed. Emperor Wudi (149–86 BC) therefore sent Zhang Qian on an expedition through Xiongnu territory to the west in 138 BC. His mission was also to ascertain what had happened to the Yuezhi, who at least had shared a common enemy with the Chinese and who were reported to be seeking allies for a joint assault against their common foe.

Zhang Qian, whose account of Ferghana is preserved for us in the *The Grand Scribe's Records* (*c.* 90 BC) by Sima Qian, set out with a hundred men from Longxi (in what is now eastern Gansu province), the westernmost limit of Han power. His expedition moved from one oasis to the next and he himself was captured twice by the Xiongnu among whom he is reputed to have spent ten years in captivity. The Xiongnu were rightly suspicious of a Chinese emissary to a people hostile to themselves. Here among them he was given a local wife who bore him children, but after ten years' captivity he managed to escape with his servant and spouse. He finally succeeded in crossing the Tängri Tagh and arrived in Ferghana, where the king had apparently been interested in communicating with the Han empire.

The king of Ferghana had Zhang Qian escorted to the Great Yuezhi where he found the ruler, either the widow or the son of the former decapitated king, uninterested in a rematch with the Xiongnu. Zhang spent a year among the Yuezhi before returning, but was once again captured by the Xiongnu. He, his wife and his old servant, Ganfu, managed to escape again during the turmoil following the death of the Xiongnu king (126 BC). His report to Wudi provides us with our first thorough Chinese description of the west.

He reported that Ferghana lay southwest of the Xiongnu and some 10,000 *li* (roughly 5,300 km or 3,300 miles) due west of China. It was occupied by a settled people who cultivated grain and rice, produced wine from grapes and raised horses that sweated blood, interpreted rationally here as liable to parasitic attacks (*Parafilaria multipapillosa*) that cause minor bleeding of the skin and make sweat appear pink. These horses were descended from heavenly horses. The people lived in about 70 walled towns

22. Zhang Qian's travels and the world he brought to the notice of the Han court.

Zhang Qian

Although traffic had been moving through Central Asia for millennia, whether across the steppe or from oasis to oasis along the edges of its deserts, it was Zhang Qian (d. 114 BC) who brought the Western Regions, including their economic and strategic potential, to the attention of the Han government. As a result of Zhang Qian's missions to the Western Regions, the tempo of east–west communication increased markedly and the Chinese empire began to play a more active role in the politics of Central Asia. Zhang Qian's report, as preserved in the *Shiji* and *Hanshu*, offers the earliest detailed historical information about the area in which the mummies were found. Aside from his verbal and written reports, Zhang Qian introduced new plant specimens, such as grapes and alfalfa, and helped provide access to a superior breed of horses from Central Asia.

In the light of his great historical importance, it is somewhat odd that no cycles of stories or legends grew up around the famed explorer of the Western Regions. Zhang Qian's departure for the Far West was depicted on a small portion of one of the Dunhuang wall paintings, so evidently people (at least some of them in this frontier town) were still talking about his exploits centuries after they occurred . Yet he figures in but a single popular tale relating how he sought the source of the Yellow River which was thought to flow from heaven as a continuation of the Milky Way (known in Chinese as the 'River of Heaven'). Zhang Qian travelled upstream for many days until he arrived at a town where he saw a maiden weaving and a young lad leading an ox to the water to drink. He asked the maiden where he was and she gave him her shuttle, directing him to show it to the astrologer-diviner Yan Junping upon his return, who would know from it where he had been. Zhang Qian did as the maiden told him and Yan Junping immediately recognized the shuttle as that of the Weaver Girl (α Lyræ in the constellation Lyra), declaring further that on the very day and at the very hour when Zhang supposedly received the shuttle he had noticed a wandering star come between the Weaver Girl and the Herd Boy (βγ Aquilæ in the constellation Aquila). Thus Zhang Qian was considered to have sailed upon the bosom of the Milky Way. For his contributions towards the expansion of Han dynasty influence in the Western Regions, Zhang Qian was ennobled as 'Marquis of Extensive Vision'.

23. Tang period wall painting in cave 323 at Dunhuang showing the great explorer Zhang Qian's departure for the Western Regions.

and numbered some 100,000 who fought with the bow and lance and could shoot from horseback.

The lands around Ferghana included Kangju (the Jaxartes region) to the northwest, the Wusun to the northeast, Wushen (Uzun Tati) and Yutian (Khotan) in the east, Daxia (Bactria) to the southwest and the Great Yuezhi in the west. Zhang Qian reported that west of Yutian the rivers flowed into the western sea (like the Greeks, the Chinese imagined a land-based world surrounded entirely by water) while the rivers to the east flowed into the Salt Swamp.

The account of the Salt Swamp is important, because Zhang Qian is offering our first description of the Tarim Basin whence our mummies derive. The Salt Swamp is identified as Lopnur, the dried-up lake at the eastern end of the Tarim Basin which lay some 5,000 *li* from the Han capital of Chang'an. The ever troublesome Xiongnu occupied the area between Lopnur eastwards to where the Great Wall reached Longxi, thus effectively barring China from the west. Zhang Qian also tells us that two peoples lived in fortified cities along the Salt Swamp. These were the Kroränn (Loulan) and Gushi peoples and, as we will see, their territories are identical with those in which we find some of our most spectacularly preserved mummies. Zhang Qian also mentions that this was a land of many precious stones, attesting to the fact that it was from this region that the Chinese obtained their jade.

The Wusun were a pastoral people 2,000 *li* to the northeast of Ferghana who lived a nomadic life like the Huns. They numbered some tens of thousands of bowmen and had been defeated by the Xiongnu but had become powerful enough to avoid attending the annual gatherings of the Xiongnu court, although the Wusun's dependent status remained.

Two thousand *li* northwest of Ferghana was the territory of Kangju (Samarkand), which was occupied by a nomadic people similar to the Yuezhi and who numbered some 80,000–90,000 bowmen. A farther 2,000 *li* northwest of Kangju were the Yancai nomads who were similar to those of Kangju. Here were a people with more than 100,000 archers living alongside a great lake, possibly identified as the Caspian Sea. Some have identified these with the Aorsi or Alanorsi of Ptolemy.

The land of the Yuezhi themselves lay 2,000–3,000 *li* west of Ferghana and north of the Gui River (Oxus or Amu Darya); it was held by some 400,000 people of whom a quarter were described as 'trained bowmen'. Zhang Qian relates something of their history. They originally lived between the Qilian (the 'Heavenly Mountains', commonly presumed to be the Tängri Tagh – not the present Qilian Mountains or Richthofen Range which are just to the south of Dunhuang) and Dunhuang but were attacked by the Xiongnu who slew their king. They fled westwards beyond Ferghana to their present location from which they had expanded south to conquer Daxia (Bactria). Those who could not make the great trek westwards remained behind among the Qiang barbarians, generally considered to be Proto-Tibetans, in the

'Southern Mountains' (another ambiguous location but probably corresponding to today's Qilian and Altun ranges, southwest of Dunhuang) where they constituted the Lesser Yuezhi.

West of the Great Yuezhi by several thousand *li* lay the Parthians, who were described as a settled people who occupied an enormous territory of several hundred towns. They engaged in commerce, merchants setting off in carts and wagons for several thousand *li*. These people employed silver coins with the images of their kings and kept records, written horizontally (the Chinese wrote in columns) on strips of leather. West of them lay Tiaozhi (Mesopotamia), a hot and moist land where one might find birds' eggs as large as a pot (Xenophon tells us that ostriches lived in Persia and Syria) – so much for the 'cradle of Western civilization'! This territory was under the rule of the Parthians.

Daxia (Bactria) is described as lying more than 2,000 *li* southwest of Ferghana, south of the Gui (Amu Darya). Like the people of Ferghana, its occupants were a settled people living in walled towns. They lacked powerful chiefs and rather were divided into small individual towns with their own leaders. Their armies are described as insignificant and cowardly, a clear come-down from their reputation when they faced Alexander, but they excelled in commerce with enormous markets, especially in their capital Lanshicheng (Bactra). They numbered about a million people. While in Bactria, Zhang saw trade goods from Sichuan and asked how they had come there. Here he learned that they were obtained from a land called Shendu (i.e. Sind, the Punjab), which lay in the region of a great river (the Indus) and was occupied by a people who employed elephants in warfare.

From the Chinese perspective the lands could be divided into those that were settled, prized Han goods and were militarily weak and those, such as the Yuezhi and Kangju, who were strong in warfare but could be bought off with Han bribes. And, with designs no less ambitious than those of Alexander in the west, Emperor Wudi planned the expansion of his Chinese domain a farther 10,000 *li* to the west.

The March West

After several false starts, the Chinese armies defeated the Xiongnu and drove them out of the western region between the 'Southern Mountains' and the Salt Swamp. Later, they forced the Xiongnu north of the desert although the latter continued to raid farther south. Zhang Qian was consulted as to the next course of action and he related how the Wusun, having formed a semi-independent nation (from the Xiongnu), might be invited (and bribed) to journey east to occupy the lands formerly held by the Xiongnu. This would provide the Chinese with a buffer zone against the Xiongnu and also help to bring the other westerners into the Chinese orbit. The other obvious reason for expansion was the desire to secure the trade routes to the west which, in effect, required the pacification of the Tarim Basin. Given that this region contributed in a large way to the wealth and armaments of the Xiongnu, a push west might also be regarded as an additional means of defence. Zhang Qian was sent with a mission and suitable gifts. He and his ambassadors ultimately convinced the various western peoples to send envoys to the Han court to see its wealth. The Chinese were particularly anxious to obtain horses which were required if they were to counter the continued threat of mounted northern barbarians. Both the Wusun and the people of Ferghana sent horses, the former possessing 'heavenly horses' but the emperor preferring the hardier 'blood-sweating horses' found in Ferghana.

Intense diplomatic activity spread Chinese influence to the west as major caravans set out; those going to the far west were enterprises that lasted on the order of a decade. The commercial objective of the expansion was trade with Daxia (Bactria), which was hampered by bandits who had to be cleared. In addition, the position of envoy was thrown open to the unscrupulous and thus many who were interested in a quick profit and a bit of embezzlement applied. They discovered in the emperor a man who perfectly understood the character of the people with whom he was dealing and, on return, they would frequently find themselves accused of crimes that required some form of expiation, invariably yet another long journey.

The account of this period of the Han goes on to lay the foundation for the military conquest of the west. The states of Kroränn and Kucha were singled out for attacking the Chinese envoys and the Xiongnu occasionally raided in this area as well. When the envoys complained to the emperor, he dispatched an army to deal with these brigands. An army of several tens of thousands, spearheaded by 700 light horsemen under Zhao Ponu, launched an attack on the Tarim towns. They captured the king of Kroränn and defeated Gushi, after which a defensive line was established from Jiuquan ('Wine Springs') in the Gansu Corridor west to the Jade Gate Pass at its end. Nevertheless, all these barbarians knew full well that China was far away and the Xiongnu were too close at hand to offend openly: the envoys of the Han had to bribe and pay their way across the west whereas the envoys of the Xiongnu were never likely to be given an occasion to take offence. The exchange did see the introduction of the vine for wine and alfalfa for horses in the Chinese capital as well as the establishment of herds of foreign breeds of horses. It was allegedly the question of horses that ultimately moved the expansion from a diplomatic to a military one, although at the heart of the matter was the defence of China's borders against the incursions of the Xiongnu.

A Laughing Stock Among the Outer States

The Han emperor had heard of especially fine horses in Ferghana and he dispatched envoys to purchase them. By now, the people of Ferghana had grown so accustomed to Han goods that they had lost their novelty value.

They were also well aware that the caravans were small, normally consisting of about 100 people, half of whom generally perished along the way. With the vast desert to their south and the Xiongnu to their north, they regarded it as highly unlikely that the Chinese could ever mount a military expedition against them and they dared refuse the request for the horses.

We are told that the emperor was enraged. To give General Li Guangli, the brother of his favourite concubine, some employment, he sent him off with 6,000 men from the dependent states and some 20,000–30,000 young undisciplined troops. This army marched west in 104 BC through the desert towns beyond Lopnur and found that the people had not unpredictably walled themselves in their towns and refused to supply the army with food. By the time General Li had reached Yucheng, he was left with no more than a few thousand soldiers and he was defeated and forced to return to China after a fruitless campaign of two years. Only one- to two-tenths of his army survived the expedition. The prestige and reputation of the Han empire were at stake. The affront from Ferghana had to be punished and the way west placed firmly in the hands of the Chinese or the emperor 'would become a laughing stock among the outer states'.

The emperor gathered together an enormous army of some 60,000 men (many of whom appear to have been 'provincial rabble' from the border states) which was this time well provisioned. General Li led them over the 2,400 km (1,500 mile) journey and besieged the capital at Yuan. Although the Han successfully breached the outer wall, there was still plenty of armed resistance and not a little cunning on the part of the defenders, who made the Chinese an offer they couldn't refuse: they supplied them with the head of their king (who had offended the Han emperor) and told them they would yield up the horses as well if the Chinese would withdraw, but if they continued the assault, the local inhabitants would fight to the death and also kill the horses. General Li and his commanders accepted the offer and returned with several thousand of the finest horses, driving the Xiongnu out of northwest China and spreading Chinese rule into the Tarim Basin. The emperor was delighted and composed his 'Song on the Horses of Heaven':

> *Horses of Heaven came over*
> *From the Western Extreme,*
> *Crossing the Flowing Sand,*
> *Nine border tribes surrender.*

Not everyone was so delighted, however, as revealed in these acerbic remarks by the noted Han period scholar Liu Xiang (79–8 BC): 'Li Guangli … abandoned 50,000 troops, wasted hundreds of millions in expenses, underwent four years of toil, and as a result obtained only 30 fine horses. Although he beheaded Wugua, the king of Dayuan, this still was not enough to compensate for the expense.'

The Judgment of history runs otherwise: with control of East Central Asia in Chinese hands, the Silk Road was effectively begun with the West. In the period 114–108 BC it is recorded that ten caravans a year were making the journey from China to Ferghana. The two centres had finally met and the crossroads of their meeting was the land of the Tarim mummies.

The Later Explorers

With the opening of the Silk Road Buddhism rapidly spread across East Central Asia, where it flourished until the expansion of Islam into the region. The consequent establishment of an eastern Islamic empire which rendered the overland route to the East too perilous, coupled with the growth of sea transport, saw the virtual closure of the Silk Road by the beginning of the Ming dynasty in 1368. Accounts of the region, at least in the West, did not begin again until there were Western scholars capable of reading the necessary Chinese and Tibetan texts. The first was Joseph de Guignes (1721–1800), who prepared an historical study of East Central Asia as part of his general history of the Huns, Tatars and Mongols. Far more important, however, was the work of Abel Rémusat (1788–1832), who gathered together all the available sources to write a history of the kingdom of Khotan, and Julius Klaproth (1783–1835), who wrote an account of the various peoples of the region. Greater knowledge of the region became available in the middle of the 19th century with vastly increased direct experience of the area.

Western travellers into the Tarim region were few until the 19th century, when a new form of explorer began traversing the ancient wastes, this time not in search of trade routes but rather antiquities. The Russian empire provided the earliest such visitor in the person of Chokan Chingisovich Valikhanov (1835–1865), who recovered gold coins from Jungghar and in his mission to Qäshqär in 1858–1859 was the first to discover Buddhist art from the Tang dynasty in the hills near Kucha. He was followed by the great Russian explorer, Nikolay Mikhaylovich Przhevalsky (1839–1888), who gives his name to the major species of Eurasian wild horse. Przhevalsky undertook four expeditions into East Central Asia along both the northern and southern branches of the Silk Road. Among his discoveries were well-preserved burials of people of large stature with long hair. In 1889 a Captain Bower (later Major-General Sir Hamilton Bower), on a hunt for the murderer of a British traveller, discovered one of the earliest books in the Sanskrit language (dating to about the 5th century AD) in his explorations near Kucha. In the period from about 1890 to 1920 there was hardly a major European nation that did not have explorers seeking out ancient ruins, Buddhist art, manuscripts and whatever else might provide ample rewards for the various museums who helped fund the expeditions. And photographs! The mission of S. F. Oldenburg to Dunhuang in 1914, for example, returned with some 2,000 photographs of murals.

Throughout the period of these early discoveries, the Russians maintained a major presence, both through their consuls who busied themselves in collecting antiquities and through their major expeditions. Of the west Europeans, the earliest to make a major impact were the Swedes. The Swedish explorer Sven Hedin led repeated expeditions to the region. In his explorations of 1899–1902 he uncovered the lost town of Loulan, the capital of the ancient kingdom of Krorän. The Swedish explorations received an additional boost with the assistance of the archaeologist Folke Bergman (1928, 1934) who undertook excavations of prehistoric cemeteries in the vicinity of Lopnur and, as we will see, discovered ample evidence of Caucasoid mummies. The Swedes joined forces with the Chinese archaeologist Huang Wenbi (1893–1966), who continued exploration and excavation in East Central Asia after most of the foreigners had left.

The next to lead the way after Hedin was the remarkable Aurel Stein (1862–1943) who mounted four expeditions from northern India, the first in 1900–1901. He devoted most of his work to the southern route and Dunhuang, leaving a legacy of superbly illustrated accounts of his researches which, like those of the Swedes, uncovered evidence of the Tarim mummies as well as an incredible quantity of manuscripts. His second expedition (1906–1908) alone recovered some 8,000 manuscripts. And, as was the case with the Russians, Stein was ably backed by the British consul to Qäshqär, George McCartney.

Within a year of Stein's first expedition came the Germans and their four expeditions (1902–1914) under A. Grünwedel and A. von Le Coq who concentrated their activities largely in the north, again uncovering and meticulously recording a vast quantity of Buddhist art and the manuscript treasures of the Tarim and Turpan basins. The French under Paul Pelliot (1878–1945) explored Kucha, Turfan and Dunhuang in 1906–1908 and, with the scholarly collaboration of the Sinologist Édouard Chavannes, made extraordinary contributions to our knowledge of the region. Finally, expeditions under Otani Kōzui, which began in 1902, established the Japanese as one of the major academic players in the study of East Central Asia.

The achievements of many of these earlier explorers are so remarkable, particularly in the light of the enormous difficulties they faced, that we have no intention of leaving them to this brief account but will return to their exploits over the course of this book. But now it is time for us to clear the peripheral players off the board and go straight to the geographical centre of our story.

CHAPTER TWO

East Central Asia: Players at the Centre of the Board

We have seen how Europeans and Chinese came to discover both each other and the peoples of East Central Asia in the first centuries BC. It is now time for us to shift our focus to the centre of the board, to the lands of the mummies, to see how far the written record can assist us in placing them, or at least their descendants, into some form of historical context. For a region so desolate, the ethnic situation was amazingly complex as a succession of settlers, conquerors, refugees, and passers-by from every direction poured or were pushed into the Tarim and Turpan basins.

We can divide our players into two different groups: settled, semi-urbanized peoples at the core; and pastoral nomads at the periphery. The first group comprise those who occupied the oasis towns and entered the written records of both the West and China during the 1st centuries BC and AD. There must be a strong presumption that some of the Tarim mummies were either ancestral to or members of these various, historically attested peoples. Among the variety of Tarim statelets, we will consider four in some detail. The first will be Qäshqär (Kashgar), the westernmost outpost of the Tarim Basin along the Silk Road where Chinese goods were assembled to be exchanged for Western commodities, especially gold. We will then consider the state of Kucha, the largest of the oasis towns on the northern route. As we will later see, many suspect that the language of the Kucheans is the key to explaining the origin and ethnic identity of the Tarim mummies. The main alternative to linking the mummies to the Kucheans is to be found among the peoples who established the kingdom of Khotan, the premier oasis state along the southern route of the Silk Road, where we will find evidence for an entirely different language. The northern and southern

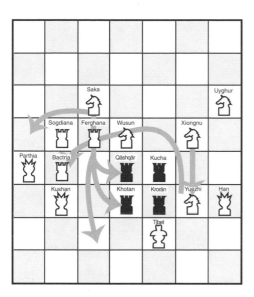

24. Board game 2: The dynamic world of the Tarim statelets (rooks) surrounded by nomads (knights), a theocracy (bishop) and neighbouring empires (kings). The Xiongnu and later the Wusun pushed the Yuezhi from east of the oasis states as far west as Bactria, where they founded the Kushan empire.

routes came together again on the eastern rim of the Tarim near the great salt marsh of Lopnur in the kingdom of Krorän (Kroraina, Loulan) before continuing into the world of the ethnic Chinese. We have very good reason to consider briefly the history of this region as it has yielded some of the earliest and most spectacular of the Tarim mummies.

The history of the Tarim and its peoples, however, did not lie entirely with its farmers and walled towns but also with the pastoral nomads who controlled or frequented East Central Asia. The environment of the region invites two very different economies. The oases of the Tarim and Turpan basins favour those who can live by hunting, fishing or irrigation agriculture with some herding. However, agricultural pursuits would be impossible in the upland reaches of the Tängri Tagh and here, as well as in other highland grasslands, the environment attracted pastoral nomads who could move with their herds and flocks between lowland and highland pastures along the northern rim of the Tarim and Turpan basins. Such an economy, requiring vast expanses of grassland, would have been entirely precluded by the desolate wastes of the Täklimakan Desert. These nomads were regarded by the Chinese as 'barbarians' who continually threatened the northern and western frontiers of their civilization and for this chapter, where we must deal with almost exclusively Chinese sources, we will blithely maintain this fiction. But, as we will later argue, these 'barbarians' were also the people who introduced the new technologies and ideas that periodically galvanized those who occupied the Huanghe (Yellow River) Valley. There can be little doubt that their influence on Chinese civilization was considerable.

The historical pastoralists that we will examine first of all are the Xiongnu, the nomadic warriors who came from the north to exploit the settled peoples of this territory, and fought and ultimately lost their struggle to maintain control of the oasis towns in the face of Chinese expansion. At

25. The three worlds of the Tarim: the central desert, the agricultural oases that rim the desert and the distant mountains with their high valleys, the haunts of the nomadic peoples.

various times subservient to the Xiongnu were two other important nomadic peoples, the Wusun and Yuezhi. The former operated primarily in the highlands to the north of the Tarim Basin, although they were earlier located farther to the southeast; the latter were originally presented as masters of the eastern borderlands of the Tarim Basin and then, when they were driven farther and farther west by the Xiongnu, they created one of the most dynamic empires of the ancient world, that of the Kushans. We conclude our historical survey by introducing the Uyghurs, the Turkish nomads who by the 9th century AD came to establish their own rule over the Tarim and Turpan regions and now represent its major ethnic group. As we will eventually see, today's Uyghurs may well be the final genetic successors of the Tarim mummies.

THE SETTLED

In their account of the western lands, Chinese sources of the Han dynasty record some 36 statelets situated in what we now call East Central Asia. According to Chinese reckoning the Western Regions measured 6,000 *li* east–west by 1,000 *li* north–south (a *li* measures just over half a kilometre or about a third of a mile). These lands lay west of their own Han state, east of the Pamirs, and between the Qurum (Kunlun) Mountains of the south that rise into Tibet and the Tängri Tagh (Tian Shan) Mountains that form the northern barrier to the Tarim Basin. Our historical sources provide us with the names of these oasis statelets and their direction and distance from the Han capital at Chang'an or the seat of the Protector-General of the Western Regions at Wulei. Our primary early historical document, the

Hanshu, also provides us with the number of families in each statelet, the number of people (literally 'mouths'), and the number of soldiers along with an occasional brief description and some historical background.

We should emphasize that the *Hanshu* provides us with figures that do not entirely inspire confidence in their accuracy. For example, at times the distances are clearly rounded off day marches with a 100 *li* equalling roughly a day's march. More importantly, the number of 'mouths' per family can range from a low of 2.5 to a maximum of 12.3, suggesting either rather bizarre variations in fertility between the various statelets or the imprecision of the estimates. And the ascription of precisely 36 statelets is not an accurate reflection of the actual number of towns; it simply reflects a halving of the number 72, seen by the Chinese (as well as by other Eurasian peoples) to be an auspicious magical number. Still, the figures from the *Hanshu* and other documents are the ones available and they, perhaps, provide us with at least a notional idea of the population size inhabiting the Tarim and Turpan basins at the time the Silk Road was opened around the latter part of the 2nd century BC. The total census of the towns comes to just under 300,000 people of whom some 60,000 were capable of bearing arms.

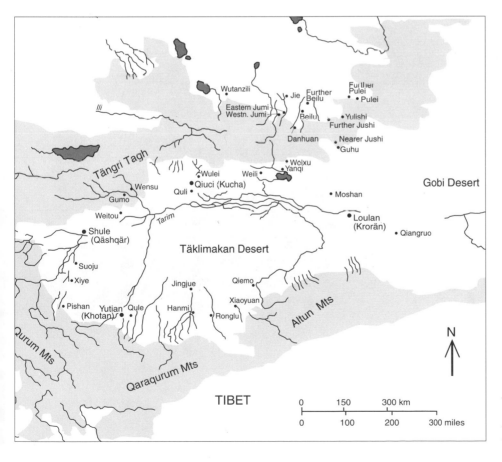

26. The 36 statelets of the Tarim and Turpan basins recorded in the early historical sources.

Populations of the Tarim and Turpan basins (based on the *Hanshu*)

Town	Location	Families	Mouths	Soldiers
Beilu	*c.* 60 km NNE of Ürümchi	227	1,387	422
Further Beilu	beyond Beilu	462	1,137	350
Danhuan	near Ürümchi	27	194	45
Guhu	Lükchün, NE edge of Turpan Basin	55	264	45
Gumo	near Aqsu	3,500	24,500	4,500
Hanmi	Uzun Tati, near Khotan	3,340	20,040	3,540
Jie	*c.* 100 km NW of Ürümchi; N of Sanji	99	500	115
Jingjue	Cadota (near Niyä)	480	3,360	500
Eastern Jumi	S of Manas; Yulduz(?)	191	1,948	572
Western Jumi	S of Manas; Yulduz(?)	332	1,926	738
Nearer Jushi	Yarghul	700	6,050	1,865
Further Jushi	between Fukang and Guchung	595	4,774	1,890
Loulan	Krorän	1,570	14,100	2,912
Moshan	Quruq tagh	450	5,000	1,000
Pishan	W of Khotan; SW of Yäkän	500	3,500	500
Pulei	near Lake Barköl	325	2,032	799
Further Pulei	Ürümchi-Manas area(?)	100	1,070	334
Qiangruo	between Dunhuang and Lopnur	450	1,750	500
Qiemo	Calmadana (Chärchän)	230	1,610	320
Qiuci	Kucha	6,970	81,317	21,076
Qule	?near Khotan	310	2,170	300
Quli	Chärchi, near Kucha	130	1,480	150
Ronglu	near Xiaoyuan	240	1,610	300
Shule	Qäshqär	1,510	18,647	2,000
Suoju	Suoju (Shache), near Qäshqär	2,339	16,373	3,049
Weili	NE of Korla	1,200	9,600	2,000
Weitou	Sapar bay, near Üch	300	2,300	800
Weixu	Chaghan-tungge, NE of Qarashähär	700	4,900	2,000
Wensu	near Üch and Aqsu	2,200	8,400	1,500
Wulei	near Kucha	110	1,200	300
Wutanzili	between Manasa and Ebi-nor	41	231	57
Xiaoyuan	'Little Yuan'	150	1,050	200
Xiye	near Yäkän	350	4,000	1,000
Yanqi	Qarashähär	4,000	32,100	6,000
Yulishi	*c.* 125 km NNE of Turpan; 275 km E of Manas	190	1,445	331
Yutian	Khotan	3,300	19,300	2,400
Totals:		37,673	301,265	64,410

Qäshqär (Shule)

For a traveller from the West who had endured a truly hair-raising journey across the 'Roof of the World', the Pamirs, the first major town encountered on the western edge of the Tarim Basin was Qäshqär where the Silk Road divided to follow either the northern route or the southern route east to Lopnur. The pilgrim Xuanzang tells us that its name in Sanskrit was Śrīkrītāti, which means something like 'Fortunate Hospitality'; the local name was transcribed in Chinese as Shule, at the time pronounced something like ṣi̯o-lək, which provides fairly dramatic evidence for what happens when a Chinese tongue tries to articulate Indo-European clusters of sound. From the perspective of the Chinese traveller, Shule was a main emporium *en route* to Ferghana and Bactria; it is highly likely that General Li Guangli led his forces through it in his quest for the 'heavenly horses' of Ferghana. During the Han period its population was initially recorded as about a quarter of the size of Kucha, i.e. 1,510 households, 18,647 people of whom 2,000 could bear arms (but the town was booming by the 2nd century AD when the

Ban Chao and the *Hanshu*

'If you don't enter the tiger's den, how can you catch the tiger's cub?' This, along with 'Throw away your writing brush and join the army!' are sayings as familiar to any Chinese as 'War is hell' or 'Peace in our time' to Americans and the British. They come from General Ban Chao (AD 32–102), whose family both wrote and made history. His father, Ban Biao (AD 3–54), had begun the compilation of the *Hanshu (History of the Western Han Dynasty)* in AD 36 and it was completed by his son Ban Gu (AD 32–92) and Ban Chao's sister, Ban Zhao. It is thanks to the *Hanshu* that we have such precise data (names and locations, population figures, socio-economic descriptions, cultural and anthropological details) about dozens of countries in Central Asia during the Western Han dynasty (206 BC–AD 9). The fact that Ban Chao was responsible for Chinese colonial administration of the Western Regions means that the Ban family could have received accurate information about conditions in Central Asia directly from him. As for Ban Chao's own accomplishments in bringing the many scattered peoples of East Central Asia under Chinese control – if only for a relatively brief period of time – they were nothing short of phenomenal. Relying on a combination of ruthlessness, cunning and sheer bluff, Ban Chao, who was said to be hopelessly outnumbered, was swiftly able to subdue the various groups living in the Western Regions by playing on the internal dissensions among the tribes. In AD 91, he was made Duhu (Protector General) of the Western Regions with his headquarters at Kucha, and proceeded to expand his conquests across the Pamirs all the way to the shores of the Caspian Sea. Only Parthia separated Ban Chao from the Roman empire and he actually dispatched an envoy in an attempt to make contact with representatives of the government in Rome. For his services to the empire, Ban Chao was granted the title 'Marquis Who Stabilizes Distant Places'.

number of families was about 21,000 and it was fielding ten times the earlier number of soldiers). We are informed that there were markets with stalls in the town. It was an important garrison town in the Western Han dynasty (206 BC–AD 9), but early in the 1st century AD it fell to Khotan only to be retaken by the Chinese under General Ban Chao . Thus, the trade route west was secure at the time that Marinus of Tyre was gathering information about the Silk Road through the agents of Maës the Macedonian in the early 2nd century AD.

During the early 1st century, Qäshqär was under the influence of the Kushans, the empire established in Bactria by Yuezhi refugees from East Central Asia. These Kushans may have introduced Buddhism into the Tarim Basin at this time, if it had not arrived still earlier. Buddhist monks provide us with the few ethnographic accounts of the region in the centuries c. AD 400–700. Among the relics of Qäshqär, for example, was the Buddha's alms bowl which was said to change weight when placed on one's head (like pieces of the true cross, such a relic was also encountered at other towns as well); the Buddha's stone spittoon was also venerated at Qäshqär. The monk Xuanzang visited Qäshqär and tells us that its territory measured 5,000 *li* in circuit, and the town sat in a desert region with little cultivable land. Regarding the people themselves we are informed that the inhabitants flatten the heads of their infants against the cradleboard. The people are tattooed (this will be typical of some of our mummies as well) and have green eyes, the latter a clear indication that we are dealing with (mixed?) Caucasoid populations. As to their character, several accounts give them a bad press: the 'disposition of the men is fierce and impetuous, and they are mostly false and deceitful', a description that Marco Polo was to reprise ('a covetous, sordid race') if not plagiarize in his own account of 'Cascar' (which supports those who argue that he never really reached China). They also 'esteem learning very little'. Reference to the fact that they sacrifice to the sky god indicates that in addition to Buddhists, Zoroastrians (followers of the ancient religion of Iran) dwelt in Qäshqär. Nestorian Christians would likewise occupy Qäshqär although probably at a somewhat later date. The language of the people of Qäshqär was regarded as 'different from other countries' (repeated anachronistically by Marco Polo: 'the language of the people is peculiar to themselves') but would appear to have been written in one of the alphabets of India. Qäshqär produced textiles: wool or felt and carpets.

Qäshqär effectively drifted out of Chinese control until the 7th century when the Tang dynasty began its march westwards and incorporated Qäshqär as one of the 'Four Garrisons'. By the 670s Qäshqär had fallen to the Tibetans, but was subsequently retaken and held by the Chinese until 791 when the Tibetans recaptured the area. The Uyghurs came to dominate it in the 9th century. By the 10th century the population had abandoned Buddhism for Islam and Qäshqär, earlier condemned for its lack of erudition, became the centre of Islamic learning in East Central Asia.

Marco Polo

While Marco Polo (c. 1254–1324) is universally acclaimed as one of the greatest travellers in human history, grave doubt has been raised about the veracity of his claims and the details of his life. Viewed in the best possible light, the most sympathetic reader must admit that there are serious gaps, contradictions, inconsistencies, plagiarisms and inaccuracies in the fabled Venetian's account. For example, for a man who was supposed to have spent 17 years in China and claimed to have ruled one of its most populous and important cities for three of those years (an appointment not recorded in any Chinese source) his entire book mentions but two (or perhaps three) personal names that are vaguely Chinese, and these appear to have been filtered through Persian (and, to a lesser extent, Arabic or Turkish). The large number of place names in China that he does mention bear a strong Persian stamp and many of them are mislocated. In fact, there are enough similarities between Polo's references to places and those of the great Persian geographer and historian, Rashīd ad-Dīn (a Jewish convert to Islam) to suggest that the former was directly or indirectly relying on the latter (or the same types of sources as the latter) for much of his information. Rashīd himself was dependent upon Mongol records and high officials of the Mongol empire for his information about China. The slightly earlier *firsthand* accounts of the Mongol realm by the Franciscan friars Giovanni da Pian del Carpini (John of Plano Carpini, c. 1180–1252) and Willem van Ruysbroeck (William of Rubruck, c. 1215– c. 1295) are far more historically reliable, although they lack the storytelling panache of Polo.

One of the more disturbing features of Polo's book is that the very sorts of things one might well expect to find in it if he had really sojourned in China are conspicuously missing: chopsticks, the Great Wall, bound feet, extraordinarily long fingernails (worn by men who wished to advertise that they did not have to engage in manual labour), woodblock printing, books, tea, any mention of the unusual Chinese script, to name only a few phenomena of the Middle Kingdom that would almost certainly have impressed a European. The failure to notice tea is particularly peculiar because it was so ubiquitous in China by the end of the 13th century and because of Polo's obvious interest in foodstuffs, plus the fact that many of the cities Polo was supposed to have visited were famous for their tea and the drink was vital to their cultural and commercial life.

It is also hard to imagine how Polo could have avoided making note of women with bound feet who were essentially crippled and incapable of walking very far. Their hobbling gait would have been striking to a visitor, especially one like Polo who did take the time to describe courtesans in Kinsai (Hangzhou). Also puzzling is the deafening absence of dates, which leaves the roughly quarter of a century ostensibly covered by the book suspended in an inexplicable timelessness.

Regardless of (or perhaps because of) all the tremendous problems surrounding Marco Polo's captivating book, scholars will continue to argue over its authenticity and reliability. In the process, we will learn more about the true history of Asia, so we can only be grateful to the author of what is popularly known as *Il Milione*, whoever he was, and whether or not he ever reached China.

Kucha (Qiuci)

The towns of the Tarim oases, as we have seen, were brought into the Chinese orbit at the conclusion of General Li Guangli's second (successful) quest for the 'heavenly horses' of Ferghana. Of the towns along the northern route, Kucha was by far the largest and sat about midway between Qäshqär, where the northern and southern routes forked, and Lopnur, where the two routes rejoined to continue their way into China. Not only was it on the major east–west route but the road north over the Tängri Tagh also began at Kucha. The general established a military colony at Bügür and Quli (south of Chadir) and so Kucha began to pass under the influence of the Han dynasty. By 21 BC it appears that the residence of the *Duhu*, the Chinese governor of the 'Protectorate' that comprised the Tarim Basin towns, who formerly lived in Wulei (Chadir), was relocated to Kucha itself. Kucha was pivotal in holding the northern route against the Xiongnu and its history reflects a small state maintaining a precarious balancing act between its two highly aggressive 'protectors', the Xiongnu and the Chinese, but always ready to flex its own independent muscles when it perceived weakness in central authority or nomadic confederation. During the resurgence in Chinese power in the Tang dynasty, Kucha became one of the four garrison towns of the Tarim Basin, along with Qäshqär and Qarashähär in the north and Khotan in the south, before it ultimately fell to Uyghur control in the 9th century.

In describing one of the major populations of the Tarim, the Chinese documents emphasize that the peoples were native so far as the Chinese could determine, unlike nomads such as the Xiongnu who constantly disturbed the northern and eastern frontiers of China. They were also urban and their entire way of life was distinguished from the nomadic Xiongnu and the Wusun. If we glean what we can from the occasional references to the peoples of Kucha over a period between the Early Han and the establishment of Uyghur domination of this region, we can produce a potted ethnography of the Kucheans. This is about as close as the Chinese texts get us in describing what life was like in the Tarim Basin in the 1st millennium AD.

The Chinese name for Kucha is given as Qiuci (in Han and medieval times pronounced *kiwəg-tsiəg* or *kjwi-tsi*). The *Hanshu* gives the population of Kucha for the period *c.* 206 BC–AD 8 as 6,970 households, which comprised 81,317 people and 21,076 soldiers, i.e. soldiers comprised about a fifth of the entire population. Kucha as a regional power embraced not only the town of Kucha itself but also Bügür, Bay, Aqsu, Üch, Toksu and Shayar. Kucha was, it might be noted, not only the largest town of East Central Asia but also markedly larger than the imperial seat of the *Duhu* at Wulei, some 350 *li* distant. Wulei housed only 1,200 people and 300 elite soldiers. Other administrative centres of the Han were of a similarly modest size and when the Chinese determined that Kucha deserved punishing in the 1st century BC, a force of some 50,000 troops gathered from the western lands were required

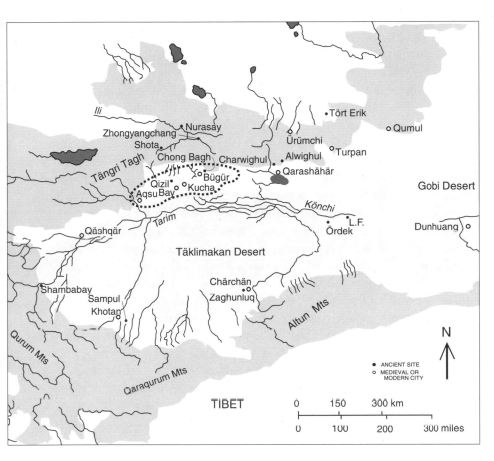

27. *The political territory of Kucha (indicated with a dotted line), the largest of the Tarim oasis states, extended over the neighbouring region.*

to take the town. Some of the other Tarim towns were moderately large, e.g. Wensu (near Üch-Turpan) had 8,400 people and 1,500 elite soldiers while Gumo (near Aqsu), which lay some 670 *li* to the west of Kucha, had 24,500 people and 4,500 soldiers.

Descriptions of the town itself are exceedingly few. The *Jinshu* (*History of the Jin Dynasty*) mentions that during the Jin period (AD 265–419) Kucha consisted of both an inner town and an outer town and that the inner citadel itself was enclosed by three walls. Within this precinct were a thousand stupas (shrines) and Buddhist cloisters. The circumference of the town was likened to that of the Chinese capital of Chang'an and the *Beishi* (*History of the Northern Dynasties*) describes the town as 5 to 6 *li* square. The royal palace was splendid and reputedly contained a large wine cellar.

The population lived by agriculture and sources from the 6th century AD listed the agricultural products of Kucha: red millet, wheat, rice, legumes, hemp, grapevines and pomegranates; livestock included horses, cattle, sheep and camels. When General Lü Guang recaptured Kucha in AD 352, he required 20,000 camels to transport back the foreign valuables; he also returned with 10,000 horses. Kucha was famous for its peacocks and the royal house of Kucha maintained a flock of a thousand on which it could dine. The peacock was introduced to China from the west, probably along the Silk Road through the Tarim Basin.

In addition to a sound agricultural subsistence basis, the wealth of the northern Tarim towns rested on exploiting the mineral resources of the surrounding mountains. The Boshan ('White Mountain') in the Tängri Tagh Range north of Kucha yielded copper, iron, lead, gold, tin, coal, sal ammoniac, copper oxide, orpiment, sulphur and other commodities. Some 200 *li* north of Kucha lay a mountain that reputedly exhibited fire by night and smoke by day. This mountain (identified as the present Hamam or Eshek-bashi Ola), provided sufficient iron to equip the entire Tarim Basin with arrows, swords, lances and armour, weapons that were also important to the Xiongnu nomads, which explains why they attempted to maintain control of the territory. The ammonia, which the *Songshi* notes could only be exploited by those with wooden soles on their shoes as leather ones would burn, was employed in leather-working to make the lassos of the Tarim riders so feared by the Chinese. The population also produced fine felt and rugs, while silk was obtained from China. Exchange was facilitated by two media – cotton goods and coins of copper, silver and gold.

According to the *Hanshu*, the Tarim towns were organized under a prince (*Hou*). Under him was a commanding general (*Duwei*), then a general (*Jiang*), a captain (*Jun*) and a chief translator (*Yizhang*). Kucha apparently diverged from this model by having its *Duwei* as the highest office and inserting another military rank, the *Qianzhang* (leader of a host of a

28. Cave painting of the king and queen of Kucha as Buddhist donors. From Qizil, Cave 205.

thousand) above the chief translator (of which four are listed for the town). The soldiers were armed with bows, swords, armour and long spears. The necessity of employing translators – Zhang Qian required nine on his first mission – will become blindingly apparent in the next chapter.

The Chinese regarded the marriage practices of the population of Kucha as similar to those obtaining in Qäshqär (without telling us what was so special about either). Little is mentioned of legal practices other than that murder carried the death penalty and theft could result in the loss of an arm or a foot.

Both men and women were described as wearing their hair cut so that it hung to the nape of the neck. An account dating to about AD 630 also mentions that the population of Kucha, like that of Qäshqär, employed a hard cradleboard to flatten the backs of their children's skulls, a practice found widely throughout the world, e.g. among the Pueblo Indians of the American Southwest. The people wore caps and their clothes consisted of brocades and rough wool. The king, at least according to an account from the Tang dynasty (AD 618–906), wore a long cloak (*pao*) and a belt (*dai*) with precious stones. A cave painting from Qizil (5th–8th centuries AD) (ill. 28) shows the king with a long cloak reaching to his knees, a style often replicated in depictions of the Kuchean nobility which would place the populations of Kucha in the orbit of Iranian costume rather than the dress styles of China. When Jiangbin, the king of Kucha, returned from a year-long stay in the imperial capital and attempted to introduce Han dress and ceremonies, he was likened by the local 'barbarians' to a mule, a (cultural) bastard born of an ass and a horse.

As to the physical appearance of the populations, the Chinese sources leave us no direct information. One possible line of inference is the name of the first historically recorded dynasty in Kucha and the name of the town itself. It has been suggested that the indigenous name Kucha means 'white' because the Chinese designation of the first dynasty was *Bo* which means 'white'. It is possible that this is an ethnonym meaning 'the white people', although this need not necessarily refer to skin colour but could also denote 'the brilliant ones' or something similar. As to the language of the population, Chinese testimony is minimal. In the 4th century references were made to the many mistakes that might be found in translations of Buddhist texts from the '*Hu*' language; *Hu* was a general term employed to refer to the barbarians and where it occurs in Buddhist contexts it usually refers to Sanskrit (it could also specifically designate Sogdian). That Sanskrit was employed at least as an ecclesiastical language in Kucha there is no doubt, since the town housed such Buddhist luminaries as Kumārajīva (which the Chinese rendered as Jiumoluoshi), whose father came from India, crossed the Pamirs, and arrived in Kucha to marry the sister of the local king. But as we will see in the next chapter, Sanskrit was hardly the language of the people and the Kucheans employed several other languages whose trail will take us much farther abroad than India.

Throughout the period of historical records, Buddhism would appear to have been the primary religion of the Kucheans. Although Buddhism is generally presumed to have entered the Tarim in the first centuries AD, there is some circumstantial evidence that it may have come earlier. It was later recorded that a water-jug (*kuṇḍikā* in Sanskrit) was sent from Kucha as tribute to the Han emperor in 109 BC and as such a vessel was a typical item of tribute among Buddhists, the historian Liu Mau-tsai has suggested that it may attest to the presence of Buddhists in Kucha as early as the 2nd century BC.

The populations of Kucha were particularly noted for their musical talent where they excelled on flutes and stringed instruments. So impressed were the Chinese by Kuchean music that the celebrated Tang emperor Xuanzong (r. AD 712–756) completely reorganized the instrumentation of China to accommodate Kuchean music (among the stringed instruments were some of the earliest precursors of the violin). Apparently, in a reversal of ethnic stereotyping, in the eyes of the medieval Chinese it was the European barbarians who possessed 'a great sense of rhythm' and Kucha was the Harlem of the Tang dynasty. Dancers and musicians participated in New Year festivals during which fights were staged between different animals – cattle, horses, camels and sheep – in order to predict the fertility of the various species in the coming year. Scholars regard the practice of wearing animal masks (both dogs and apes) at festivals as originally an Iranian practice which diffused eastwards, arriving in China by the early 8th century. The Kucheans reckoned dates according to the Chinese system and on the 15th day of the 8th month there were Buddhist celebrations involving the display of statues of the Buddha.

29. An East Central Asian orchestra, several of whose instruments (such as the harp) derive from western Asia. From Khocho; c. mid-9th century.

Finally, burials in Kucha were contrasted with those of China in that the population cremated their dead (as they did in Qarashähär) and mourned them for a period of seven days. Obviously, the rite of cremation, apparently introduced by the Buddhists, distances the Kucheans from their predecessors but, as we shall see in later chapters, the linguistic evidence from Kucha and neighbouring towns will play a critical part in establishing the identity of the prehistoric populations of East Central Asia.

Khotan (Yutian)

The major oasis of the southern Tarim Basin, Khotan, was favourably set amidst the Yurung-kāsh and the Qara-qāsh, the only two rivers to carry the melt waters of the Qurum (Kunlun) Mountains northwards to join the Tarim rather than, like so many others, dissipating into a sea of sand. The fertile loess soils of the Khotan oasis ensured that its agricultural foundation would support a major settlement, and when Aurel Stein and other explorers visited it at the turn of the century, they observed that the region was underpopulated given its agricultural potential (the population at that time was estimated roughly at *c.* 200,000, approximately ten times larger than that given in the *Hanshu*). But despite its fertility, like all other oases its agricultural potential depended entirely on irrigation.

Khotan was also the centre of silk production in the Tarim Basin and Stein suggested that it might have been the actual Serindia of the ancient geographers (rather than China) whence the West learned of the product itself. The legend tells that at the time when the Chinese prohibited the export of silk worms, mulberry trees and the knowledge of the manufacture of silk, a wily king of Khotan requested the hand of a Chinese princess in marriage. Before she departed to her new land, her husband made it clear that if she expected to be kept in silks, she had better procure what was necessary for their production, so she secreted silkworms' eggs and seeds of the mulberry tree in her headdress and carried them to Khotan. The paper mulberry tree (*Broussonetia papyrifera*) is also found primarily in the region of Khotan and its bark was pulped into the earliest paper in the region, another gift of Chinese technology to the West. Both cotton and wool

30. A painting on a wooden plank or panel said to depict the smuggling of silkworms and mulberry seeds to Khotan in the headdress of a Chinese princess. From Dandan-iliq, 6th century AD.

77

production have been major products of Khotan since antiquity, while Khotan was also a major supplier of jade to China (the 'Jade Road' between Khotan and China is considerably older than the Silk Road).

Khotan also occupied a remarkably strategic position. To its south, the forbidding Qurum and Qaraqurum ranges were absolutely desolate and Stein could count but a mere 400 people scattered across a territory of 9,000 sq. miles. To its east one could follow the Silk Road, but beyond Niyä (Minfeng) the oases were so few and far between that it would have been difficult to facilitate any major approach to Khotan other than one that had been highly organized, such as might be found in Chinese military operations. To the north lay the full expanse of the Täklimakan Desert. Only the west provided a relatively easy route through which populations might have entered this region in deep antiquity. Khotan itself, despite its prestige, was surprisingly small. The sole historical source (*Beishi*) to provide a dimension of the town reckons its circuit at 8 or 9 *li* and this is roughly confirmed by Aurel Stein's own excavations at Yōtqan which discovered that the circumference of the town was merely about 2.5 to 3.2 km (1.5 to 2 miles). Stein also both witnessed and recorded how centuries of treasure hunting had been obliterating the archaeological evidence of the region. As early as the 16th century the ruler of Khotan and Qäshqär, Abū Bakr, is reputed to have employed convict labour to undertake vast excavations in the hunt for precious stones and metals from antiquity, the smaller objects being recovered by water sieving, a technique that modern archaeologists would applaud, although hardly Abū Bakr's motives.

In accounting for their own foundation, the Khotanese have left us with traces of the origin legends that have survived both in the account of the Buddhist pilgrim Xuanzang and in Tibetan translations of Khotanese documents. The various accounts suggest that Khotan was originally settled from both northwest India (in the expulsion of the son of King Aśoka to the desert regions beyond the mountains) and from China, where an exiled king established his own colony. After a battle, the two colonies merged under the leadership of the eastern king (in some versions it is the son of Aśoka who founds the kingdom). There are many layers of interpretation in the origin myths but key elements suggest that they were composed to account for the Prākrit-speaking Buddhists (employing the language and script of northwest India) of the region. They may also suggest the establishment of Indian colonies in the region, perhaps induced by the opening of the Silk Road, even before the spread of Buddhism. That the kingdom was founded from east and west, i.e. in the form of two colonies, helps explain why, since Han times, Khotan was divided into a western and an eastern city. The earliest coins would appear to date from the period of the Kushans (*c.* 1st–3rd centuries AD). Coins of Chinese issue are also recovered but even here we find the inscription in Prākrit (in the Kharoṣṭhī script) on the reverse side.

The earliest non-legendary source for Khotan, known to the Chinese as Yutian (anciently pronounced as *giwo-d'ien* or *jiu-d'ien*), is the *Hanshu* which informs us that at the time of Zhang Qian there were 3,300 households with a population of 19,300 of whom 2,400 bore arms. Other than its location and rivers, we are informed that there is 'an abundance of jadestone'.

The kingdom of Khotan apparently began its political expansion about the 1st century AD. After having been first made subject to Suoju (Yäkän/ Yarkand), it revolted in the period AD 25–57 and managed to subdue Yäkän and the territory to the northwest as far as Qäshqär. In so doing, it, along with the kingdom of Krorän (Kroraina, Loulan or Shanshan, centred on Lopnur), controlled the southern Silk Road. When the Chinese 'pacifier' of the region, the redoubtable general Ban Chao, came to Khotan, he found the king in league with the Xiongnu nomads. Insulted by the Khotanese king, Ban Chao personally liberated the head of the king's adviser with his own sword; properly admonished, the king of Khotan obligingly slaughtered the Xiongnu emissaries. The Khotanese remained as useful auxiliaries when Ban Chao was forced to subdue a rebellious Yäkän in AD 88, although they later murdered a Chinese commissioner in 151.

The succeeding centuries saw the growth of Khotanese power which periodically tested the grip of the Chinese but never broke into open rebellion. By about AD 400 the pilgrim Faxian made his famous journey to the west, stopping for three months in Khotan, and leaving us a description of its monasteries (the one called Gomatī, 'abounding in herds of cattle', reputedly housed as many as 3,000 monks) and religious festivals.

The next distinguished visitor to leave us with a detailed account of Khotan was the pilgrim Song Yun (travelling in 518–521) who arrived in Khotan from Krorän in 519. Again we read of how Buddhism was flourishing and gain some interesting ethnographic details. The women of Khotan, for example, are reputed to have worn girdles, vests and trousers and rode on horseback like their menfolk, characteristics that would accord well with the Sarmatians and other steppe peoples. The dead were cremated and buried under the stupas (Buddhist shrines) with the exception of the king who was buried in a coffin. Mourners cut their faces and hair, abandoning mourning when their hair had grown back to 10 to 13 cm (4 or 5 in) in length. At this time, the Khotanese acknowledged the sovereignty of the Hephthalite Huns. Of these, Song Yun makes a curious

31. Ritual hair-cutting and mutilation were part of expressing one's grief over a death both in the steppelands and in the oasis states. From Cave 244 at Qizil, 6th century AD or earlier.

remark that, as we will later see, our mummies may help to explain: in the country of the Hephthalites, the wives of the king wear on their heads 'a kind of horn three feet high' which is variously decorated with jade and pearls.

The 'Master of the Law', Xuanzang, visited Khotan as a pilgrim in 644 (box pp. 82–83) and left us an invaluable account of its people and legends. The kingdom sustained itself on both agriculture (cereals and fruits) and industry (carpets, felts, silks and jade). Few of the people wore wool or fur by this time; most dressed in light silks or white cotton. There were about a hundred monasteries and 5,000 monks. We are told that their writing resembles that of the Indians (from this period we can clearly see the use of Sanskrit as a liturgical language). So detailed were Xuanzang's descriptions of the Buddhist sites that they provided a reliable guide for Aurel Stein's own explorations of the region.

In 648, when the Tang dynasty reasserted Chinese authority in the Tarim, Khotan became one of the 'Four Garrisons'. At this time it is reputed to have housed some 4,000 troops. The *Tangshu* provides us with a superbly eclectic view of the people of Khotan (and the rats as large as hedgehogs that dwelt in the desert nearby!). Jade, which was recovered from the river when its reflection was seen in the moonlight, was an important commodity. The people wrote with sticks of wood rather than with brushes and when they received a letter (other than official 'post'), they held it over their heads before opening it, expressing the same degree of respect as one in China would greet a letter sent from the emperor. (Another feature of letter-reading etiquette is recorded in the travels of Song Yun, who unsuccessfully upbraided the king of Gandhara in north India for not reading letters addressed to him from the Chinese emperor standing up.) Of their religion, we learn that they were still devout Buddhists but also that some worshipped the 'celestial god' which is taken to indicate that Zoroastrianism flourished here as well as at Qāshqär. The people were given to singing and dancing, and, in another notice, we read that like the Kucheans, the people of Khotan ran brothels which were taxed as a source of revenue. Unlike the people of Qāshqär, those of Khotan are described as 'mild by nature and respectful, they love to study literature'.

Occasional actions against the Turks were taken by the Chinese during the 7th century until a much more formidable enemy appeared. In 665 the king of Khotan required Chinese assistance against attacks from the Tibetans. In the following years, Chinese policy found itself continually forced to confront the Tibetans in order to keep the southern route to the west open. By about 790 the Four Garrisons slipped from Chinese control and notice for over a century as the Tibetans succeeded in taking most of the Tarim Basin and the Gansu Corridor. One can imagine the shock then of emissaries from Khotan turning up out of nowhere at the Chinese court in 938, bearing presents for the emperor and requesting his assistance against Tibetan harassment. Although by this time the Uyghurs had taken the northern Tarim Basin, their power did not stretch so far south and a 'silent century and a half' of Khotanese history was apparently spent in a constant struggle against Tibetan power. Gifts were regularly offered to the Chinese court. In 969 the main gift was a block of jade weighing some 237 pounds and in 971 the Khotanese managed to present a dancing elephant that they had captured in their war against Qäshqär. It was this war which would ultimately seal the linguistic fate of Khotan. The Islamic Turks, who then controlled Qäshqär, were apparently the victors and Chinese sources again become silent on the fate of Khotan until 1009 when we read that tribute was once more being offered by the king of Khotan. But this time it came under the licence of an Islamic Turkish king. Arabic sources provide us with enough information from the other perspective to see that the conquest of the 'infidels' of Khotan was a long and hard-won affair. By the time Marco Polo supposedly passed through Central Asia (around 1271–1275), the people were all Muslims and under the rule of the Kublai Khan.

Krorän (Loulan)

The statelet that formed about the great salt marshes of Lopnur was known in Chinese sources originally as Loulan and then later was called Shanshan (*dian-dian* or *źiän-źiän*) when the territory came under Chinese dominion in 77 BC. The name Loulan reflects an attempt to render in Chinese what we find in later Indian (Kharoṣṭhī) documents from the region as Krora'ina or Krorayina (now Krorän). We have already seen the Chinese turn Kumārajīva into Jiumoluoshi but something like Krorayina into Loulan! How? Well, the ancient pronunciation of Loulan was roughly *glu-glân* (in the Han period; the asterisk indicates that the word is not actually attested as such but has been reconstructed through the techniques of comparative philology) or *ləu-lân* (in the early medieval period). We can take care of the r's when we recall that the Chinese (like the Japanese) have difficulty in distinguishing between a foreigner's *r* and *l* (hence *glu-glan* came from something like *gru-ran*) and the Chinese g here comes from the foreigner's *k*, leaving us with a proto-form *kru-ran* which is now close enough to Krorayina. Difficult clusters of sounds (for a Chinese speaker) such as *gl* were ultimately simplified by dropping the initial consonant which leaves us with *Loulan*. (Regarding these difficult clusters, if an English speaker is feeling superior: how do *you* pronounce *pneumonia* or *pterodactyl*? Do you hear the laughter of ancient Greeks?) As for the name 'Shanshan', this has been seen as a precursor to the name 'Chärchän', where some of the most spectacular mummies have been recovered. This is hardly unexpected as the region possesses immense deserts laden with salt that both early Chinese guidebooks and modern explorers have described in detail. A 1st-century BC document informs us that from the Chinese outpost at Dunhuang to Krorän there was a desert that stretched for 500 *li* in which there was neither water nor grass. Naturally, the combination of arid conditions and the preserving

Xuanzang

From the 3rd to the 9th centuries AD, hundreds of Chinese Buddhist pilgrims travelled by sea or land to the holy land of India. They went to visit the sacred sites associated with the Buddha and his disciples, to study in Buddhist monasteries and universities, and to obtain scriptures for translation into Chinese. Among these, the most famous are Faxian (his journey lasted from 399 to 414), Song Yun and his monk-companion Huisheng (travelling 518–521), Xuanzang (travelling from 629 to 645), and Yijing (on the road between 671 and 695). All of them left behind accounts of their travels which are of great historical importance and literary worth. Indeed, it would not be an exaggeration to state that, except for a limited number of inscriptions, most of the solid dates in early medieval Indian history are based on the reports of these Chinese travellers. Xuanzang is by far the most famous of them all.

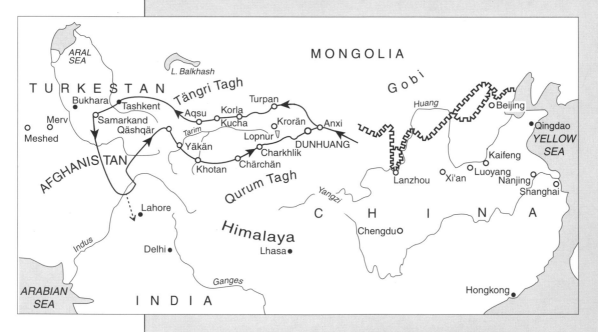

32. The route of Xuanzang's travels in the period AD 629–645 (excluding those in India).

Xuanzang (c. 600–664) is said to have entered a monastery at the age of 13. He went to the Tang capital, Chang'an and was fully ordained as a monk in the year 622. Troubled by philosophical problems that Chinese masters were unable to solve and disturbed that China lacked many of the Buddhist scriptures, he decided to go to India to seek guidance and to procure those texts that were missing in his own country. He set out surreptitiously around the year 629 and arrived in India in 633. There he visited many sites associated with Buddhism and studied intensively in several of the most distinguished Buddhist institutions. In 645, after an absence of 16 years, Xuanzang returned as a hero to the Chinese capital where he presented to the imperial court the 657 texts he had collected, together with 'many images and pictures, and one hundred and fifty relics'. He translated approximately 75 of the works that he had brought back from India and elaborated the abstruse doctrine known as Consciousness Only within the Yogācāra school.

His *Records of the Western Regions during the Great Tang Dynasty* is the longest and most detailed account of the countries of Central Asia and India we possess by a Chinese Buddhist pilgrim. Everywhere he went, Xuanzang made precise observations about religious life, society and cultural customs. He occasionally recorded interesting legends and stories associated with the places he visited. Xuanzang also included information on countries he had heard reports of but was not able to visit himself.

There is an iconographical form of a supposed pilgrim-monk that is almost universally recognized to be that of Xuanzang, yet the image actually evolved from portraits of Central Asian monks of the Tang period: long noses, deepset eyes, no epicanthal fold, long and narrow face usually covered with stubble, etc. Gradually, though, the monk's features changed so that by around the 13th century he started to look Mongoloid, but it wasn't until still later that the form was identified as Xuanzang.

33. *The popular depiction of Xuanzang, with a portable library on his back, is actually modelled on portraits of Caucasoid monks of East Central Asia.*

nature of salt has ensured that this would be an important region for the survival of ancient burials. The weird landscape also provided the impetus for a local version of the Atlantis story where a 'Town of the Dragon' was reputed to have been inundated by a local lake and only the foundations of the town could still be seen; in fact, as Aurel Stein demonstrated, there was no town, but the extensive remains of odd geological formations (e.g. *yardang*, a wind-eroded ridge found in deserts) helped to generate such a myth.

Although the desert region was regarded as barren of all living things save 'demons and strange beings', the geographical position of Krorän with respect to the Silk Road was absolutely strategic. We might recall that Ptolemy's gazetteer places 'the great race of the Issedones' in the Serica region and mentions the names of towns and mountains whose identity has eluded historians for generations, although they are clearly to be set in the

Sven Anders Hedin

' ... [T]he adventure, the conquest of an unknown country, and the struggle against the impossible, have a fascination which draws me with irresistible force.' These words neatly encapsulate the difference between Sven Hedin (1865–1952), the intrepid Swedish explorer, and his contemporary, the more cautious Aurel Stein. By the age of 20 Hedin had already travelled through the Caucasus, Persia and Mesopotamia and he spent most of his life engaged in numerous explorations of remote places. Between 1893 and 1898, Hedin crossed Asia to Peking (Beijing) via the Urals, the Pamirs, and Lopnur. His 1895 explorations in the Täklimakan Desert between Qäshqär and Khotan, which almost cost him his life, were highly influential for bringing to the attention of scholars the existence of Indian, Greek and Persian cultural vestiges in this uninhabited region. From 1899 to 1902, he explored the Gobi Desert and followed the course of the Tarim River through the Täklimakan. Among the important archaeological and geographical findings of his later (1927–1933) expeditions to these areas was the discovery of extensive Stone Age cultures at 327 sites between Manchuria and Xinjiang.

These expeditions, nicknamed 'the Travelling University', were of large scope and great complexity, requiring tremendous organizational skills to coordinate the activities of numerous research stations that stretched from the Great Wall to the Caspian Sea, and were staffed by geologists, meteorologists, philologists, zoologists palaeontologists and other experts. Incidentally, nearly every European who participated in Hedin's Travelling University, no matter how limited his baggage allowance, elected to bring along a copy of Marco Polo's *Description of the World*, and Hedin himself carried no fewer than four different editions! In 1928, Hedin solved the mystery of the shifting location of Lopnur throughout history and prehistory by relating it to changes in the lower course of the Tarim River, along the remnants of which were excavated the oldest mummies in East Central Asia, those associated with the Qäwrighul Culture. Hedin was also the first person to provide detailed maps of the Trans-Himalayan Range of Tibet (1905–1908) and, against enormous odds, he organized the first motorized expedition through the deserts of Central Asia – at the age of 69! Hedin and other members of his expeditions encountered numerous ancient human remains in the sands of the Täklimakan. While they did not

Tarim Basin. And, of these identifications, it has been suggested that Ptolemy's Issedon Serica might well have been Yixun (anciently pronounced *i-dzwiən or *ē(d)-sdūn hence, some would argue, a phonetic stone's throw from Greek *Issēdōn*) in the kingdom of Krorän. When the Xiongnu controlled the region between Krorän and the Great Wall to the east where their territory met that of the Tibetans, China was effectively blocked off from all contact with the west.

During the Han period the population of Krorän is given as 1,570 households, with 14,100 people of whom 2,912 could bear arms. The agricultural potential of the region is described as limited, its soils being too sandy and salty, and food crops had to be brought in from neighbouring states. There was an important nomadic component in the region where asses, horses and many camels are reckoned. Other products were jade, rushes, tamarisk and balsam poplar.

transport any of them back to Europe for in-depth scientific research, their observations in the field are of great importance for corroborating sketchy reports from more recent finds.

Hedin's works often read like 'ripping yarns'. One of his earliest desert journeys was when, with perfect *sang-froid*, he set out to cross a section of the desert never before attempted, even by the local camel-men. His only chance of survival was a rumour, impossible to check in advance, that water could be found on the other side of the crossing. The journey proved to be a nightmare for Hedin, his four hired camel-drivers, and the eight picked camels. They lost their way and ran out of water; in places the sand was so loose and treacherous that a passage had to be dug for their camels; and one by one the animals began to falter and die. Even Yoldash, Hedin's pet dog, lost its senses and ran off into the wastes to perish. Two of the camel-men in desperation tried drinking camel's urine mixed with sugar and vinegar, and in consequence suffered terrible cramps. Finally only Hedin and one of the guides were left on their feet, and they made a desperate sortie to try to fetch water. Hedin realized that they could only hold out for another two or three days at most, and in one last gesture he changed into his sole remaining suit of clean clothes so that if he should die in the desert, he would at least be decently dressed. For two days the pair struggled on, marching by night and resting by day, buried up to the neck in sand to escape the fierce sun. Finally the guide collapsed, pleading that he could continue no longer, and it was left to Hedin to stagger and crawl forward on his own. Semi-delirious, he bumped into some bushes and chewed their sap to give him the strength to make one last spurt, which brought him, stumbling and falling, to the long-awaited river. There he filled his boots with water and carried them back to his companion. One of his camel-men was miraculously picked up alive by nomads, but two had died in the desert, and only one of the eight camels survived the fearful ordeal.

Hedin's many published works, some of which were quite popular worldwide, include *Through Asia* (1898), *Southern Tibet*, 13 vols. (1917–22), *My Life as an Explorer* (1926) and *The Silk Road* (1938).

Krorän was included in the lists of conquests carried out by the Xiongnu leader Modu in 176 BC and, with the westward expansion of the Han, it found itself caught in the middle of the two warring empires. The territory was regarded of dubious loyalty as it harassed Chinese missions to the west and served as 'eyes and ears' for the Xiongnu. About 108 BC it was taken by a Chinese force of 700 cavalry and, after it had sent its gifts to the Chinese emperor, the Xiongnu attacked. The king of Krorän found himself then sending two sons as hostages, one to the Han (who was later indicted under Han law and, as the euphemism goes, 'sent to the silk-worm house', i.e. he was castrated) and another to the Xiongnu. The king saw that it was imposs- ible to navigate between two such masters and tilted his hand towards the Han, who took advantage of the situation, assassinating one king and beheading another until they had installed someone they could trust, and in 77 BC the name of the state was changed to Shanshan. Although ostensibly under Han control, as late as AD 25 it was recorded that Krorän was still in league with the Xiongnu.

Understandably, during the floruit of the Silk Road, Krorän was a place of great strategic importance. About AD 119 Ban Yong, the son of General Ban Chao, recommended that the Chinese governor be sent to Krorän with 500 men to establish a Chinese colony (such colonial programmes are incidentally still part of Chinese policy in this region, much to the annoyance of the local Uyghur population). It was intended that this colony dominate all approaches to Dunhuang, the main Chinese outpost in the west, by way of both the northern and southern routes and it was also intended to check any Xiongnu incursions. In order to provide the colony with a secure agricultural basis, major irrigation works were required and a much later account depicts how attempts to place a barrage across a river in order to dam the water for irrigation were thwarted by an intractable river throwing itself against and over the barrage. First the governor tried prayers and sacrifices to get the water to recede but when these failed he sent his troops in to assault the waters with swords, spears and arrows, and the river, apparently cowed, dropped its water level and supplied the desired irrigation channels.

The administrative capital of Krorän was discovered and investigated by Sven Hedin (box pp. 84–85), Aurel Stein and Hou Can. The 429 documents found in these investigations provide contemporary evidence of the running of the Chinese colony in the 3rd century AD and the approximate date of its abandonment in the 4th century (the most recent document dates to *c*. 330). In addition to the documents written in Chinese there were tablets in Prākrit, a north Indian language, which also contained traces of the language of the native inhabitants, about whom we will have much more to say later. Stein could only speculate that physical changes robbing the region of adequate water supplies led to its current deserted state and Hou Can supports this theory with documentary evidence, indicating pressure on water resources and the need to build a reservoir upstream. The Chinese abandoned the territory and did not attempt to resettle it during their reconquest of the Tarim in the 7th century. Krorän apparently went out with a whimper rather than a bang: in his excavations of the home of one of the leaders of Kroränian society Stein discovered thick layers of sheep dung that preceded its total abandonment – animals had been stalled in rooms where nobility had once dwelt.

THE NOMADS

Xiongnu

The Xiongnu (pronounced 'Shyoongnoo') were a pastoral nomadic people who exploited both their own herds and the peoples subject to them (in pastoral nomadic societies the distinction between cattle ('four-footers') and chattel ('two-footers') was at best a trivial one). They are pivotal to understanding the Chinese expansion into the Tarim Basin or, as the earliest major historical source about this region would put it, the 'Western Regions'. These were identified as the lands that lie west of the Xiongnu and which were at one time 'all subject to the Xiongnu'. The imperial policy of the Han state to rid their western frontier of the Xiongnu threat was what prompted the Chinese to expand into the Tarim Basin.

The first great history of China before the 1st century BC, the *Shiji* (box p. 88), relates that the Xiongnu raised horses, cattle and sheep (children trained to ride on sheep before they advanced to horses) and, to a lesser degree, also herded much rarer animals such as camels, asses, mules and wild horses. One source remarks that the human:animal ratio among the Xiongnu was on the order of 1:19, a figure not far off that of traditional Mongolian society. It also says that they had no walled settlements or fixed dwellings, nor did they practise agriculture. How true this observation is or to which period precisely it pertains is difficult to determine as archaeologists have uncovered both Xiongnu dwellings and even fortified settlements (four

34. This reconstruction of a Xiongnu dwelling suggests a more sedentary way of life than that portrayed in Chinese sources.

ramparts surrounded Ivolga near Lake Baikal where 54 houses were excavated) dating to the first centuries BC. Their clothes were fashioned from hides, felt or fur. Letters to the Xiongnu addressed by the emperor contrast the Xiongnu with the Han (Chinese) who 'wear hats and girdles'. Tattooing is implied by the Xiongnu custom that required envoys from the Han emperor to have their faces tattooed in black before they entered the tent of the Xiongnu king.

Sima Qian and his *Shiji*

The *Shiji (The Grand Scribe's Records*; also frequently rendered as *Records of the Grand Historian)* is a general history of China starting from the founding myths (most of which actually first appear just before, during, or after the Han dynasty) up to about the year 90 BC when the book was completed. The *Shiji* was begun by Sima Tan (fl. 140–110 BC) and completed by his son, Sima Qian (145–c. 85 BC), who is often hailed as China's Herodotus, i.e. the 'Father of History'. There is some controversy over the meaning of *shi* in the title of Sima Qian's book. The earliest forms of the character (c. 1200 BC) used to write *shi* depict a hand holding what has been interpreted as a bow drill and this in turn is explained as referring to a type of divination or part of the divination process. Occurrences of the character in the royal oracle and shell-bone inscriptions of the Shang period make it clear that there was an office of *shi* and that those who held this office were indeed involved in some form of divination. During the Western Zhou and Spring and Autumn periods, there was established at court the office of *taishi* ('Grand *shi*') and the holder of this office was charged with record keeping, the maintenance of annals, preparation of documents, astronomical observations, and calendrical adjustments, so it is fair to render the title as 'Grand Scribe' in these circumstances. Sima Tan held the office of *taishi* and his son Sima Qian succeeded him in it. Regardless of what they were supposed to be doing in that office (history, astronomy or astrology), they took it upon themselves to compile what may legitimately be thought of as historical records.

Before Sima Qian was able to complete the history, however, he infuriated the emperor by coming to the defence of the general Li Ling. The unfortunate general had been entrusted with an expedition against the Xiongnu but, when his 5,000 soldiers were surrounded by 30,000 of the enemy and had exhausted all of their arrows, he was forced to surrender. Simply giving in to the enemy under any circumstances was an unpardonable offence. Naturally, it was foolhardy in the extreme for Sima Qian to attempt to vindicate Li Ling. No sooner had he done so than the emperor ordered his execution. Sima Qian pleaded to have his sentence commuted so that he could finish the *Shiji*, whereupon the emperor had him castrated instead. Feeling profoundly shamed, for the rest of his life Sima Qian poured all of his energies into the writing of his historical masterpiece. The *Shiji* is generally regarded to be less reliable than the *Hanshu* as a source of historical data. On the other hand, it is universally appreciated for its vivid writing and engaging style. Together with the *Hanshu*, the *Shiji* established the format for all the succeeding official dynastic histories of China.

It was said of the Xiongnu that they gave their best food to the young and the scraps to the old as they prized youthful vigour and disdained the feeble; the Xiongnu retorted that it was really no different with the Han whose families were forced to give up their own food to their sons when they were drafted into the army. Children were taught the use of the bow, first targeting birds and rats and later hares and foxes. Warriors fought with bows and arrows for long range and swords and spears for close combat. The defeated were either beheaded or brought back as slaves and their property seized by their captor. The Xiongnu regarded warfare as the business of all men, but when not engaged in warfare, they enjoyed themselves, having little else to do; this they contrasted with the Chinese who in times of war had to build defensive walls (against the Xiongnu!) and in times of peace exhausted themselves trying to make a living. Their burials reputedly involved both an outer and inner coffin and were accompanied with gold, silver, clothing and fur; ministers and concubines would accompany their ruler to the grave. We should remember this later when we uncover fairly grisly evidence for possible human sacrifice in the burial of mummies from Zaghunluq. The Xiongnu did not employ burial mounds or plant a tree over the deceased. On the death of his father, the Chinese related, a son married his stepmother and similarly if a man died, his brother married his widow.

According to Chinese historical tradition, the Xiongnu were equated with the 'Mountain Barbarians' who are mentioned as attacking the Chinese at least as early as the 8th century BC, but under their actual name they are mentioned in Chinese written sources (they left no literature of their own) only from about the 3rd century BC when their raids against the Chinese prompted the erection of the nucleus of that most famous of Chinese monuments – the Great Wall. Initially, three independent states erected walls against the Xiongnu along China's northern frontier and these were subsequently joined together into a single defensive line some 10,000 *li* (over 3,000 miles) long by the first emperor of Qin (the one who was buried with his terracotta army) in the years after 214 BC. The Chinese technique of defending against these superb horseriders and archers not only involved the construction of walls but also emulation, and in 307 BC a king of one of the Chinese states ordered his people to adopt both the dress and the tactics of the Xiongnu. Within a few generations, a force of 100,000 Xiongnu horsemen were crushed by a Chinese army of chariots, cavalry and archers.

Although occasionally defeated, the Xiongnu rose again under Modu who assumed the office of *shanyu* ('chief') in 209 BC. Remarkably cruel, Modu reputedly ordered his men, under penalty of death, to fire at any target at which he shot a whistling arrow. Imposing a fairly ruthless learning curve, he took his men through birds, animals, then his favourite horse (some of his men were executed for failing to shoot at it), then his favourite wife (again a few had still not quite got the idea), then his father's favourite horse (all now knew what to do) until he finally fired his special arrow in his father's direction on a hunting expedition.

35. The two Chinese characters for Xiongnu (pronounced *hyung-no in the Han period), superficially mean 'breast-slave', but are actually used here to transcribe the name that is rendered in the West as 'Hun'.

36. There was a wide variety of whistling arrows employed on the Asiatic steppe over many centuries.

After his father's tragic hunting accident, Modu quickly began stripping back the gains made by the Chinese so that by 198 BC, a peace alliance was made between them in which the Xiongnu were initially bought off from raiding by their leader's marriage to a Han princess and gifts of silk, wine and food from the Chinese. This system was known as *heqin*, i.e. *he* 'peace' and *qin* 'marriage'. But as each successive *shanyu* attempted to exert his authority through further conquest of China, the bribes offered in the peace treaties became increasingly large and, finally, required the establishment of frontier markets where the Xiongnu could acquire various Chinese goods, in particular rice, wine and cloth. Established at the Xiongnu's request, these also came to play an important role in imperial policy when it came to be recognized that dependence on Chinese goods could be turned to the advantage of the Han. But in the face of continuous Xiongnu pressure, the bribes continued to grow in size. A Han eunuch who went over to the side of the Xiongnu warned them of the Chinese agenda of weakening them through dependence on Han goods. ('When you get any of the Han silks, put them on and try riding around on your horses through the brush and brambles! In no time your robes and leggings will be torn to shreds and everyone will see that silks are no match for the utility and excellence of felt or leather garments.')

The Xiongnu enter our story because of their expansion into the Western Regions of the Tarim Basin. We can maintain with relative certainty that at least some of the mummies owed obedience if not allegiance to the Xiongnu *shanyu*. The Xiongnu defeated both the Wusun and the Yuezhi, and the latter were mainly driven west into southern Sogdiana. The Xiongnu controlled the Tarim Basin through what the Chinese called their *Tongpu duwei* whose title 'Commandant [in Charge] of Slaves' neatly expresses the relationship between the Xiongnu and the peoples of the Tarim Basin. The towns were required to pay the Xiongnu in both goods and labour, and such was the wealth of the region that the Tarim Basin was regarded by the Chinese as the 'right arm' of the Xiongnu and an area which imperial policy must detach from these troublesome nomads if they were ever to rid themselves of the Xiongnu threat. From 130 BC onwards, the Han mounted ambushes and military offensives against the Xiongnu. It was in the context of this campaign that the Han emperor applied to the chief of the Greater Yuezhi for aid and sent Zhang Qian on his extraordinary mission to the west. And it was the emperor's putative need for the 'heavenly horses' of Ferghana that drove his military expansion farther west when the Han court wrested control of the Tarim Basin from the Xiongnu, and replaced their 'Commandant of Slaves' with their *Duhu* 'Protector General'. The Chinese then began the establishment of *tuntian* settlements, consisting of 500 soldier-farmers who could supply both the army and envoys with food in the region. The Xiongnu continually attempted to re-establish themselves in the Tarim Basin whenever Han power waned since its resources (foodstuffs, manpower, raw materials, and manufactured goods, including iron swords) were crucial to Xiongnu power. Han policy was hardly constant and with an uncannily modern ring to them the Chinese annals often depict central government pondering whether the taxes and trouble involved in confronting the Xiongnu in the west were really in the strategic interests of China. Ultimately, the Xiongnu began to accept client status under the Han (for which they were well rewarded) and when the Xiongnu leader came to pay homage to the Han emperor in 51 BC, it marked the shifting of allegiances of the peoples of the Western Regions from the Xiongnu to the Han court. But by the middle of the 1st century AD the Xiongnu had once again asserted their authority over the region until the Han effectively drove them from any power base in the Tarim Basin at the end of the century.

Wusun

The *Hanshu* defined the Western Regions, the territory of the Tarim Basin and surrounding areas, in terms of the Xiongnu, who occupied the region to its east, and the Wusun, who dwelt north of the Tarim Basin. The great traveller Zhang Qian included the Wusun in his itinerary of the peoples he encountered in his travels west. He situated the Wusun 2,000 *li* northeast of Dayuan (Ferghana in Western sources), the land of the 'blood-sweating horses'. According to the *Hanshu*, the Wusun numbered 120,000 households with 630,000 people and 188,800 under arms, which, if these figures are to be believed, would render them over twice as numerous as the entire settled population of the oasis states. They occupied a land that was flat, covered with vegetation (particularly pine and elm), and experienced heavy rainfall and cold. This territory is commonly identified as the Ili Valley and the Wusun 'capital' of Chigu ('Red Valley') may be on the upper reaches of the Tekäs River. We are told that the lifestyle of the Wusun was very much like that of the Xiongnu in that they were pastoral nomads. Their character was not highly regarded by the Chinese: they were described as 'hard-hearted, greedy, unreliable ... and much given to robbery', but it also had to be admitted that they formed 'an exceedingly strong state'.

As to their origins, the *Hanshu* emphasizes that they had only recently taken up their positions in the west and that their present territory had been previously occupied by the Sai. This name, in its earlier pronunciation (**sək* or **səg*), is commonly equated with the Iranian word *Saka*, the name applied in Iranian sources to the peoples rendered as Scythians in Western sources (the earliest reference to Scythians is in Near Eastern sources where an Assyrian document of Esarhaddon (680–669 BC) renders their name *iš-ku za-ai*, taken to derive from **škūz-*, hence our Greek *skythos*). The Sai were reputedly pushed out of their territory first by the Yuezhi (*c.* 177 BC) and then the Wusun, who at the time of the Han incorporated elements of both the Sai and the Yuezhi 'races'. It has been suggested that the Wusun may also be identified in Western sources as their name, pronounced then **o-sən* or **uo-suən*, is not far removed from that of a people known as the

Asiani who the writer Pompeius Trogus (1st century BC) informs us were a Scythian tribe. There is another school of thought that has regarded the Wusun as the Issedones of Herodotus (see ill. 37 for yet another).

Where did the Wusun come from? We are told by Zhang Qian that the Wusun occupied the same territory as the Da Yuezhi in Gansu in the region between Dunhuang and the Qilian Mountains (presumably the Tängri Tagh) and most scholars today would more precisely locate them near Lake Barköl, north of Hami, before their transit across Jungghar to the Ili Valley. Such a location is marginal to most of the evidence of our mummies but a record from a Chinese military settlement of the 1st century BC speaks of how one was destroyed by 'Wusun brigands'. Some have suggested that the attacked post was situated near Lopnur, the region which has produced a considerable quantity of Caucasoid mummies dating from the 1st centuries BC and AD.

In 176 BC, the *shanyu* of the Xiongnu indicated that he had conquered the Wusun along with more than 20 other tribes, thus uniting under his power all those who lived by 'drawing the bow'. But by about 128 BC it was apparent that the Wusun had begun throwing off the Xiongnu yoke, and although they still acknowledged themselves part of the Xiongnu confederation, they no longer felt compelled to attend the court of the Xiongnu. This break occurred during the reign of the remarkable Kunmo, the son of a previous Wusun king who had been killed by the Xiongnu. Cast out as an infant, he was reputedly sustained by wolves and ravens, an origin myth that is also to be found among various Turkish tribes as well as the more familiar story of Romulus and Remus. The Xiongnu took these as portents that the boy was a deity and he was put in command of troops. His own contingent grew and when the *shanyu* died, he led his people off. It became Han policy to entice the Wusun eastwards to settle the previous lands of an obscure people called the Hunye in the Gansu corridor, in order to cut off the 'right arm' of the Xiongnu and provide the Chinese with a buffer zone. On his second mission to the west Zhang Qian was sent with massive gifts of cattle, sheep, silk and gold. But Kunmo could not decide such an important move on behalf of all his people since they had split into three factions over the issue of his successor. Zhang Qian then sent out other envoys to the neighbouring states and the Wusun provided them with guides and interpreters. Wusun envoys were also sent to the Han court since the Wusun had no idea how large the Han empire was. Returning to their own lands, they were greatly impressed and when the Xiongnu divined what was happening and prepared to attack, the Wusun sued for a pact of brotherhood with the Han and an imperial princess was married off to their king.

It was the Wusun who first supplied the Han with 'heavenly horses' (so named because their gift of horses arrived at the emperor's court when their coming had been predicted in the *Yijing* (*Book of Changes*, better known in the Wades-Giles romanization as *I Ching*); but when the emperor encountered superior horses from Ferghana, he demoted the Wusun horses to 'horses from the western extremity'. There were 1,000 horses in the

烏孫

37. The two Chinese characters for Wusun (pronounced *ʔaḥ-swə̀ in the Han period) superficially mean 'black grandson', but the name here may actually be cognate with that of the Ossetes, an Iranian people of the Eurasian steppe, who have survived only in the Caucasus.

original betrothal gift sent by Kunmo to the Han (the account of this transaction makes it clear that this was not a great sum as a wealthy man among the Wusun might possess as many as 4,000 or 5,000 horses). Kunmo named his Han bride his 'Bride of the Right' and the Xiongnu promptly played the same gambit and provided him with a 'Bride of the Left' (and, as is likely if the Wusun shared the same social values as the Xiongnu, the one on the left, the Xiongnu bride, was regarded the more important). The poor Chinese princess, saddled with the status of second-place wife to an ageing Lear (Kunmo was described as *lao*, an old man of 70), who met with her only once or twice a year and shared no verbal communication, poured out her sorrow into the following song:

> My family married me off to the other side of heaven:
> They sent me to a distant, alien land, to the king of the Wusun.
> My house is a domed yurt with felt for walls.
> My food is meat and my drink is koumiss (fermented milk).
> Here I live, constantly thinking of my native land, alas, my heart is
>   aching;
> I wish that I were a yellow swan, flying back to my native home.

(trans. V. Mair)

Moved by this plea, her father the emperor sent the princess 'drapes, brocades and embroideries' but when the old king wished to marry her off next to his grandson and she refused, the princess' father reminded her that she was an instrument of state policy and she duly became the grandson's wife. The customary marriage of a Chinese princess to a Wusun king provided the Chinese with a frequent excuse to interfere in decisions of royal succession, a perennial source of political instability among the Wusun, but as some of the Han court argued, no great advantage to the Chinese either, as it regularly dragged them into an alliance that required the expenditure of both money and soldiers.

The physical appearance of the Wusun has been of considerable interest. The Chinese commentator Yan Shigu (AD 579–645), presumably working from earlier sources, wrote: 'Of all the Rong of the Western Regions the Wusun looked the most peculiar. Those of the present Hu [Barbarians] who have cerulean eyes and red beards and look like Mi monkeys are their descendants.' This unflattering description is taken to suggest the appearance of Europeans through the eyes of the Chinese and supports the contention that the Wusun were of the European physical type (when they first encountered the Russians, the Chinese thought them to be descendants of the Wusun as well). Skulls presumed to derive from the Wusun and excavated and studied by Soviet archaeologists and anthropologists have ranged in their descriptions from primarily Caucasoid with some Mongoloid admixture (like Uzbeks or Tadjiks) all the way to pure Europeans on the basis of six skulls dating to the first centuries BC/AD at Semirech'e. In any event, the Wusun are one of the historically named peoples of a European physical type who occupied East Central Asia.

Yuezhi and Hephthalites

The Yuezhi emerge in historical records as the first major victims of Xiongnu expansion. The Xiongnu leader had sent his son (and future assassin) Modu as a hostage to the Yuezhi and when he had been delivered to them, his father attacked the Yuezhi hoping that they would kill his son in retaliation (his father wished the throne for Modu's younger brother). But instead of being killed, Modu managed to steal a horse and escape, eventually gaining revenge on his father with his 'whistling arrow' ploy described above. About 177 BC Modu led the Xiongnu southwards into Gansu and his son continued the campaign which culminated in the death of the Yuezhi king whose head was fashioned into a drinking cup (a popular cultural motif among the steppe nomads). The Yuezhi fled west where they divided into two groups. The Lesser Yuezhi (Xiao Yuezhi) moved south to settle among the presumably Proto-Tibetan Qiang, where some of them were said to be assimilated into Qiang culture. The Great Yuezhi moved west to settle in the Ili Valley where they had to confront the Wusun whom they at first defeated. With the assistance of the Xiongnu, however, the Wusun turned the tables and about 155–125 BC drove the Yuezhi farther west through Ferghana. As the Yuezhi were pushed westwards, they in turn drove the Saka southwards into Bactria where they brought about the end of the Indo-Greek state. The Yuezhi held Sogdiana and established their capital north of the Oxus. From there they too conquered Bactria (which the Chinese emphasized had an urbanized population that amounted to more than a million people) from the Greeks although they did not physically occupy it until about 126 BC.

Although the trail of the Yuezhi ultimately leads to Bactria, it does not take them out of our story. As we have seen, there were essentially two main routes to the Tarim from the west – the Eurasian steppe to the north and Bactria to the immediate west. We have already seen Bactria emerge as one of the satrapies of the Persian empire and its subsequent fall to Alexander the Great. It was first part of the Alexandrine empire but by 246 BC it emerged as an independent state that would endure as a Greek-led power for the next two centuries. It combined a rich agricultural basis with a pivotal position in commercial exchange to provide it with the wealth to foster expansion if the social drive were there. In the latter half of the 2nd century BC, the Greeks of Bactria pushed south to conquer the Punjab region of northwest India and penetrate deep into the Ganges system. From this they are often known as the Indo-Greeks. At its apex this Indo-Greek empire controlled most of present Afghanistan and segments of Central Asia and Pakistan. It should be emphasized that this was a Greek world where Hellenistic traditions fused with the local cultures of Bactria but maintained its own language. Greek was spoken and taught in the schools, was engraved on coins, and was the vehicle of dramatic expression in the theatre. The Greek theatre at Ay Khanum, for example, sat 5,000 spectators and was only a little smaller than the one in Greece itself at Epidauros.

Recently, the linguistic world has been excited by claims that a considerable proportion of the vocabulary of a people known as the Bangami who dwell in the Himalayas may have preserved the language of Alexander's Greeks who had wandered into the region and settled (shades of H. Rider Haggard's *She*), and attempts were made to demonstrate that the foreign elements were actually Macedonian. Unfortunately, this lovely romance has been challenged and it has been argued that many of the supposedly foreign words had been misconstrued and that the Bangami, who were anyway quite remote from Indo-Greek movements, had as good an Indian pedigree as their neighbours.

When the Yuezhi took over Bactria they organized it into five major provinces, each governed by a *yabgu*, thus adopting the existing provinces of the region. One of these, that of Guishuang, expanded to rule over the entire country and Chinese sources inform us that the ruler of this unified kingdom was known as the king of Guishuang although the Han preferred to use their earlier designation of Yuezhi. Guishuang renders in Chinese what is known in the west as Kushan (Kuśāṇa).

The Yuezhi were the goal of Zhang Qian's mission to the west to find a powerful ally against the Xiongnu. The son of the beheaded king, however, comfortably distant from both a very dangerous enemy and the entreaties of the Chinese emperor, had his thoughts on the pleasure of his new realm rather than revenge, and the mission was a failure in this sense. Zhang Qian tells us that the Greater Yuezhi lived several thousand *li* west of Ferghana and north of the Oxus (Gui). In his time they were still described as culturally little different from the Xiongnu in that they were pastoral nomads. They could field an army of 100,000 to 200,000 mounted archers. A description of the Yuezhi country in the *Hanshu*, compiled mainly around AD 80, informs us that the capital of the Great Yuezhi was Jianshi. Its population was reckoned at 100,000 households or 400,000 people with 100,000 soldiers, larger than the settled population of East Central Asia but still smaller than the Wusun. Although originally nomadic, the Yuezhi are then described as similar in their cultural practices to the Parthians (Anxi). In their land they raised two-humped (Bactrian) camels. The *Nanzhouzhi*, a gazetteer of exotic lands, peoples and things, especially in the west, provides us with a mid 3rd-century description of the kingdom of the Yuezhi; it tells us that the people were of a 'reddish-white colour' (Caucasoids), and that they were skilled in archery and on horseback, possessing several hundred thousand horses.

Chinese sources emphasize how the Yuezhi (Kushans) exercised influence on the Tarim towns. Ban Chao, in his attempt to pacify the Tarim Basin, appealed successfully to the Yuezhi in AD 84 to prevent the Sogdians from assisting the king of Qāshqār who was in revolt. They had also assisted the

Han in their attack on Turpan (Turfan). By AD 86 the Yuezhi felt themselves of sufficient status to request a Han princess, but though they sent tribute of precious stones, antelopes and lions, they were rebuked. Humiliated, they launched a force of 70,000 troops against the wily Ban Chao who, though greatly outnumbered, knew that these troops would be exhausted and hungry after such a long march. Eventually, the Yuezhi retreated, their leader happy to escape alive, and the Yuezhi were so impressed by the might of the Han that they sent tribute regularly from then on. In the period AD 114–116, the maternal uncle of the ruler of Qäshqär was sent into exile among the Yuezhi and when the king died without adult male issue, the Yuezhi successfully had the uncle installed as king of Qäshqär; the annalist emphasizes that the people of Qäshqär feared the Yuezhi.

Once established in Bactria, the Yuezhi are far better known in the West as the Kushans. Their history is recorded in Western sources, although dates for their principal rulers, particularly Kaniṣka who led the Kushans to the height of their power, are still the subject of major controversy. In about the 1st century AD Kushan power extended from south of the Aral Sea to the mouth of the Indus and eastwards to the Ganges, Kashmir, and the western frontier of Xinjiang. Ruled by kings who claimed divine status, it brought together under a central government a vast array of different peoples, religions and languages. Its coinage, replete with the images of both its rulers and the gods of its various nationalities (Greeks, Iranians, Indians, etc.) attest to a remarkably cosmopolitan society. An inscription of Kaniṣka II lists his titles as *mahārājasa,* 'of the great king' (Indic), *rājatirājasa,* 'king of kings' (an Iranian epithet), *devaputrasa,* 'son of god/heaven' (an Indic translation of a Chinese epithet) and, to cap it off, *kaisarasa,* 'Caesar'. The great Kushans stimulated monumental irrigation projects (the Kirkkiz canal in Choresmia alone required the shifting of some 222 million cu. m of earth)

38. The Kushan empire when it controlled the central part of the Silk Road and could interfere in the affairs of the oasis states of the Tarim Basin.

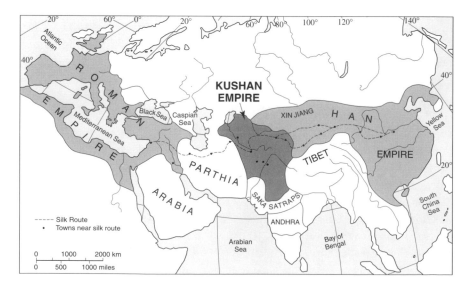

and it brought into cultivation vast areas of Central Asia. Along the lower Amu Darya and Syr Darya rivers, an area larger than the modern state of Belgium was brought under the plough. Besides agriculture, urbanism also flourished, with the expansion of older towns and the founding of new ones. Just as the Chinese had secured control of the eastern approaches to the Tarim Basin, so had the Kushans expanded their power to the east to overlap with that of the Chinese. The Kushans controlled the exchange of goods as they moved east and west. The Roman world shipped gold, silver, woollen and linen textiles, wine and some spices; from India came cotton, spices, Kashmir wool and semi-precious stones; Bactria and the Tarim Basin offered their own rubies, lapis lazuli and silver; and China, of course, sent its silk.

The Kushan empire was the main vector for the diffusion of Buddhism to the east and it was out of this region that Mahayana Buddhism (the Greater Vehicle) emerged and spread to the Tarim Basin and then on to China and Japan. Its artistic achievements, famously eclectic in combining Greek, Indic and Iranian influences, comprised the Gandhara and Mathura schools of art. It is through the various art styles of the Kushan empire that we and the rest of the world inherit our distinctive depictions of the Buddha in his various poses, and the lush, indeed often erotic, figures from the life of Buddha. Initially, the language of the empire indicated in the coinage was both Greek and Indic (coins would be inscribed in Greek on the obverse and Kharoṣṭhī on the reverse) and the civil service comprised people of Greek, Saka and Indic descent, although the Kushan empire became increasingly Indicized. As to the original language of the Yuezhi, we will review this complex problem later but for now note that names such as Kaniṣka are best explained as Iranian Saka or Bactrian and from the viewpoint of Westerners (Romans), the conquest of Bactria was undertaken by Scythians, i.e. Iranian-speaking peoples. The empire also became increasingly Buddhist (Kaniṣka presented himself as a supporter of Buddhism who alternated between ruthless military conquest and remorse throughout his life until his servants smothered him to death), but was essentially eclectic, with many other religions, including Zoroastrianism, Jainism and Hinduism, being practised as well.

The impact of the Kushans on the Tarim Basin was immense. Their missionaries and artisans carried not only Buddhism but also Kushan art, Prākrit (the administrative language of some of the oasis towns), and Sanskrit (the liturgical language of Buddhism) to the east. The arid climate of the Tarim preserved both the artistic and literary legacy of the Kushan empire until it was discovered at the turn of this century by Swedish, French, German and British explorers.

During the 3rd and 4th centuries AD, the struggle between the Eastern Roman empire and the Sassanians, the Persian dynasty that had recovered Persia from the Parthians, diminished but did not erase the Silk Road. The Sassanians expanded eastwards to incorporate into their state the northern part of the disintegrating Kushan empire. This territory, incorporating what

39. *The Hephthalite empire extended into the Tarim Basin.*

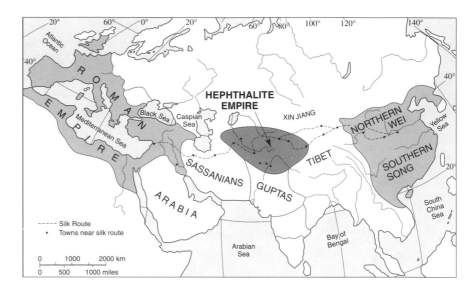

was known in the West as Tokharistan (northern Afghanistan, southern Uzbekistan and Tadjikistan), then fell to the Kidarites, a nomadic people who seized power in the 4th century but had to relinquish it again by 467 when the Sassanians reclaimed the territory of their previous conquest. By the middle of the 5th century a people known as the Hephthalites moved south from the steppe and crossed Central Asia, exacting tribute and establishing their own empire over Bactria. The Hephthalites are of disputed origin (ancient testimony is contradictory: some have claimed that they were of Mongolian stock while Procopius informs us that 'they alone of the Huns are white-skinned and are not ugly', a marked distinction in description to that usually accorded the Huns). Their military force in Tokharistan was set at some 5,000 to 6,000 warriors but, unlike previous usurpers, the Hephthalite Huns (as they were called) pushed their conquests as far south as India. They also pushed east and advanced into the Tarim Basin taking Turpan and holding it during the later part of the 5th century. In this they matched the territorial spread of the Kushans and they also oversaw further development in urbanism, trade and art. Their empire endured from *c.* AD 450 to 563 when a new player, the Turks, began its massive expansion from the steppelands across Central Asia and also into the Tarim Basin.

So far we have skirted the most contentious issues concerning the ethnic and linguistic identity of the Yuezhi as this would have greatly unbalanced the structure of this chapter. The problem is that the Yuezhi of China and the Kushans of Bactria have been credited with being masters of ethnic disguise, lurking behind many of the other names of peoples of Central Asia and even farther afield. Da (Greater) Yuezhi or in the earlier pronunciation *d'âd-ngiwăt-tiĕg* has been seen to equate with the Massagetae who occupied the oases and steppelands of West Central Asia in the time of Herodotus; here *Massa* renders an Iranian word for 'Great', hence the 'Great Getae' (alternatively, Massagetae has been divided as **mah* 'great'

+ *saka-ta* 'Saka', i.e. 'Great Saka'). Others have seen in this word an attempt to capture in Chinese the name of a tribe that is rendered in Greek as the *Iatioi* who are recorded in Ptolemy's geography. The original pronunciation has also been reconstructed as *gwat-ti* or *got-ti* or *gut-si,* which opens up distant lexical similarities with the Goths (the German tribes of northern and eastern Europe), the Getae (the Dacian, i.e. Balkan, tribes northwest of the Black Sea), the Guti (a people on the borderlands of Mesopotamia), the Kusha (our Kushans), the Gushi (a people mentioned in Han texts and regarded as brigands along with the peoples of Krorän), the Kucheans (the people of the largest of the north Tarim oasis states), or a combination of some but not all of the above. To compound confusion, as the Chinese employed the same name, Yuezhi, for both those who lived between Dunhuang and the Tängri Tagh *and* those who ran the Kushan empire which frequently attempted to interfere in the politics of the Tarim Basin, we are not entirely certain whether references to Yuezhi in East Central Asia are to remnant populations of Yuezhi or references to later Kushan power-brokers or, still again, the inheritors of Kushan culture. Does any of this really matter? Very much so, but we will not need to examine these problems in greater detail until a later chapter.

Ruanruan, Sogdians and Turks

The end of the predominance of populations speaking 'western' languages in the Tarim Basin was brought about by a series of incursions by members of the Turkic language family. In what amounted to a dry run for the later Turkic domination of the Asian steppe, the Ruanruan (Avars) emerged as a major power to confront the Northern Wei dynasty from *c.* AD 386 to 534. (The Northern Wei was ruled by the Tuoba (Tabgatch) royal clan of the Proto-Mongol Xianbei (Särbi).) They carved out an empire that stretched from Qarashähär eastwards as far as Korea. They occupied Khotan and defeated the leader of the town of Khocho which would later become the Uyghur capital. The ethnic and linguistic identity of the Ruanruan is unknown and, although often assumed to be Turkic or Mongol, the evidence of Ruanruan names in Chinese transcriptions provides no firm support for either theory and they must be regarded as linguistically anonymous. Within their territory in the Altai were a people whose language was described as *Türk* who worked in metal. The Turks overthrew their masters (3,000 Ruanruan were beheaded in 555) and established over the same territory the first Turkish empire in 553.

The Turks moved to expand their empire, making a successful alliance with the Sassanids, the ruling dynasty of Persia, with whom they encircled and destroyed the Hephthalite empire in *c.* 563. This brought the western Turks control of the Tarim Basin and the Silk Road, but they then had to confront the commercially hostile Sogdians who did not want the Turks to usurp their lucrative role as middlemen between China and Byzantium.

The homeland of the Sogdians was Sogdiana, generally set by the ancients between the Oxus (Amu Darya) and the Jaxartes (Syr Darya). Its principal city was Maracanda (Samarkand). When Alexander the Great attempted to fortify the frontier to exclude the dangerous Scythians from his newly won empire, both they and the Sogdians revolted and provided the greatest military opposition to Alexander in his advance through Asia, slaughtering 2,000 of his men on the banks of the Zeravshan. Alexander ultimately pacified the region when he abandoned his own harsh policy and accepted local rulers, even marrying the daughter of one.

After Alexander's death a variety of small states formed in Sogdiana and, although occasionally united under a foreign power, the story of Sogdiana is essentially one of small states experiencing a dynamic relationship with various nomadic peoples to their north. The Sogdians were the great entrepreneurs of the Silk Road and it was their caravans that carried goods between east and west. The Sogdian language, a variety of Iranian, became the *lingua franca* of the Silk Road in the Middle Ages and was spoken widely over East Central Asia.

The Turks made two unsuccessful diplomatic advances against the Sogdians – during the second mission many of their ambassadors found the Persian climate 'fatal' to their health – and then entered into a series of relations with the Byzantine empire. But by the 7th century the Eastern Turks were being brought under Chinese power through both military force and acculturation and by 659 the empire of the Western Turks also collapsed, the Chinese holding their lands as far west as Samarkand and Bukhara. The Turks in Mongolia, however, initiated a series of revolts which led to the re-establishment of a Turkic confederation under Bilgä kaghan (716–734). But upon his death one of the constituent tribes, the Uyghurs, successfully gained the upper hand and by 745 could present the Chinese emperor with the head of the last Turk king.

Uyghurs

The Uyghurs, united in 742, also spoke a Turkic language, closely related to Turkish. They were known to the Chinese under a variety of names, the earliest recorded being Yuanhe. They reached their maximum expansion under the rule of Mouyu, who claimed the impressive title 'The brave, blessed and wise Uyghur Khan who rules the land and who, through his virtue, obtained fortune from Sovereign Heaven'. Mouyu adopted the Manichean religion, a religion founded in Mesopotamia in the 3rd century AD which spread to China, although it had long been persecuted there. Manicheism became the state religion of the Uyghurs around 762, the only state in which this religion achieved such status. In 840 the centre of Uyghur power in Mongolia collapsed in the face of an invasion by the Kirghiz, another Turkic people. The Uyghurs fled southwards, both east into China (where they fared very badly) and west into Gansu where they established their own mini-state until 1028. More important for our story were those Uyghurs who migrated to the Tarim and Turpan basins and established their capital at Khocho (Gaochang).

In East Central Asia, the Uyghurs settled and adopted agriculture, and shed Manicheism for Buddhism. However, this did not happen until they had left us with Manichean religious texts that, along with those in Sogdian, provide our primary knowledge of this religion that was so heavily persecuted elsewhere. Manicheism was a gnostic religion that combined elements of Buddhism, Christianity and Zoroastrianism to found a universal religion. The Uyghurs established a kingdom in the Tarim and Turpan basins that flourished from 850 to 1250 which combined, apparently harmoniously, a myriad different ethnic groups, religions and languages. The Uyghur king came to be titled *kaghan*, employing an old Turkish word, but his consort was titled *kunchuy* (from the Chinese *gongzhu*, 'princess'), while the king wore a *didim*, a 'diadem', a word borrowed ultimately from Greek via the Sogdians. When the German expeditions explored the area of the Uyghur capital at the turn of the century, they claimed to have retrieved written documents in 17 languages and one might reflect on the origin myth of the Uyghurs who, when they sought to choose their own first king, selected Buku khan who 'knew all the languages and writings of the different peoples'. It is time for us to take our cue from Buku khan and tackle the linguistic landscape of the Tarim Basin.

40. An Uyghur depicted on a wall painting from the Uyghur capital at Khocho.

CHAPTER THREE

The Linguistic Landscape

In order to investigate the ethnic identities of the Tarim mummies or where they came from we will need to establish what languages they may have spoken. While they may not have died with 'letters in their pockets', their probable descendants certainly left enough to provide us with some clues to their identity. As we have just seen, when the Berlin Ethnological Museum expeditions of 1902 to 1914 had finally unpacked all their cases of material excavated from the desert sands of the northern Tarim and Turpan basins, they claimed to have recovered the remains of no fewer than 17 languages recorded in 24 different scripts! Some of the languages were well known outside East Central Asia; others have so far proven to be unique to the region. In order to paint the linguistic landscape of East Central Asia and the surrounding territory, we will have to abandon our analogy of the board game: there are few if any games that can tolerate the number of different players (languages) that we will have to place on the same square. But we will at least be able to follow in roughly the same footsteps as when we set East Central Asia within its geographical and historical context.

THE LINGUISTIC PERIPHERY

Aramaeans and Alphabets

The evangelists Matthew and Mark record the last words of Christ on the cross, *Eloi, Eloi, lamma sabachthani* 'My God, My God, why hast Thou forsaken me', not in Hebrew but in Aramaic, the most widespread language of the ancient Near East at the time of Christ. Written languages obviously require some form of writing system or alphabet. For those in the West it was the Phoenician alphabet that provided the model for alphabetic Greek, Etruscan, and the Roman and Cyrillic alphabets of Europe. Most of the languages of Central Asia also derive their scripts from a common source. The state or official language of the Persian empire at the time of Herodotus

	Es	Pa	MaSo
ʾ			
b			
g			
d			
h			
w			
z			
ḥ			
ṭ			
y			
k			
l			
m			
n			
s			
ʿ			
p			
ṣ			
q			
r			
š			
t			

41. Just as the West owed its alphabets to the Phoenicians, the East derived theirs more immediately from the Aramaic alphabet. The writing changes over time and here are shown examples of Estrangelo (Es), Palmyran (Pa) and the type employed in Manichean Sogdian (MaSo) documents. The column at far left gives the transliteration of these alphabets.

and Alexander was not that of its rulers but rather its civil service. And like the evangelists, they employed Aramaic, a Semitic language closely related to both Hebrew and Phoenician, whose script emerged about 1000–900 BC to play a major role in the subsequent development of writing systems across the Near East and much farther abroad. At the height of its use between 300 BC and AD 650 the language was employed from Armenia south to Egypt, and from the Mediterranean coast east to Iran. Its versatile alphabetic system suited it as a chancellery language or *lingua franca* that helped unite the linguistically and ethnically divided peoples of the Persian empire; in this its role has been likened to that of English in India. The Aramaic script played a similar role in the development of the alphabets of Western and Central Asia. From it were derived the writing systems of Iran, Sogdiana and perhaps India, all of which were subsequently transplanted to the Tarim Basin. When the Uyghurs arrived, they too adopted the Aramaic-derived Sogdian script and this was later adapted to serve the needs of the Mongols and ultimately the Manchus.

Greek

Alexander's conquest of the Persian empire interrupted the predominance of Aramaic as Greek began to compete with it as one of the main chancellery languages of the new Graeco-Persian empire. Greek continued in the Greek kingdom of Bactria and here it was more than just a legacy, since inscriptions have been found, ranging from translations of Buddhist precepts by the proselytizing Indian emperor Aśoka to a copy of the 150 maxims of proper Greek behaviour that was erected on a stela around 275 BC at Ay Khanum on the upper reaches of the Amu Darya. The same Greek town provides circumstantial evidence for the spread of Greek in its gymnasium where its young would be educated in the Greek manner and its 5,000-seat amphitheatre provided Greek drama for the colonists.

Old Persian

The native language of the leaders of the Persian empire was neither Aramaic nor, of course, Greek, but an Iranian language which is today known as Old Persian. The word 'Iran' derives from an earlier Iranian *ērān śahr which meant, quite literally, 'land of the Aryans' as the Iranians comprised the Aryan tribes of ancient Persia. The ancient Aryans, or at least those who employed the term as an ethnic or social designation, were the Iranians and Indians, although the label was later sometimes applied to all members of the Indo-European language family and, more notoriously, adopted as an ethnic designation by racists of the late 19th and earlier 20th centuries.

Old Persian is poorly attested, primarily in a series of about 200 inscriptions (or copies of inscriptions) written in cuneiform, the ancient Near Eastern system of writing that was originally made with a wedge-shaped stylus on clay tablets. Unlike the wildly cumbersome cuneiform of their imperial predecessors of the Sumerian and Akkadian empires, the Persians employed a streamlined version of this writing system. The Old Persian inscriptions, made primarily to commemorate the deeds of Darius I (522–486 BC) and Xerxes I (486–465 BC), are often trilingual and are provided with translations in Akkadian, a Semitic language used by the Assyrian empire which preceded that of the Persians in Mesopotamia, and Elamite, a separate language (neither Semitic nor related to Iranian) that was spoken in southern Iran, and which again preceded that of the Persians in its home region.

We should not be surprised then that official inscriptions of Persian kings required translation for we are not dealing with an empire whose linguistic roots lie buried deep in the local soil. The earliest references to the Persians and their cousins, the Medes who occupied neighbouring Media, occur in Assyrian sources of the 9th century BC. Until this time the lands of the historical Persians were occupied by peoples of other language groups, some of whom were ruled as part of Semitic-led empires. Darius appears to have been the first Persian to have had his words written in his own language; generally, all Persian state communications were translated by Aramaean scribes into Aramaic (or by Elamites into Elamite) and so when Darius employed Old Persian to recount his achievements in a large inscription carved into the face of a cliff at Behistun, he was also flexing his linguistic muscles.

Avestan

In addition to the cuneiform inscriptions of Old Persian, there was also a closely related liturgical language known as Avestan. The *Avesta* is the central religious document of the religion of Zarathustra, or Zoroaster as he was known to the Greeks. The *Avesta* was preserved orally and its original date of composition has been the subject of great argument. Many presume that the earliest parts date to around the year 1000 BC but the leeway here, on either side of this mark, can be up to about 400 years (the usual historical date assigned to Zarathustra, who presumably composed the earliest parts of the *Avesta*, falls between 630 and 540 BC but the language of the texts would appear to be much older). The earliest versions of the *Avesta* that have survived were written in an alphabet that did not appear until the 3rd to 6th century AD and the world of European scholarship only learned of these documents in the middle of the 18th century. Avestan played the same role in the Zoroastrian religion that Latin did in the Catholic Church. And like Latin, it was not originally a liturgical language but was the spoken language of a region (in the case of Latin, obviously this place was Rome and its environs). The home of Avestan is often presumed to have been in the territory known as Choresmia, the region of West Central Asia to the south of the Aral Sea. The Zoroastrian religion eventually spread far beyond the borders of ancient Iran and we find its distinctive fire-temples first in Qāshqär, that crossroads of the East and West along the Silk Road, and then farther east in Khotan; by AD 621 a Zoroastrian fire-temple had been established in the Chinese capital itself at Chang'an.

Comparison of some basic terms in Old Persian and Avestan

Old Persian	Avestan	
adam	*azəm*	I
ardata-	*ərəzata-*	silver
aθaga-	*asənga-*	stone
daraniya-	*zaranya-*	gold
dragah-	*zragah-*	sea
marta-	*mərəta-*	dead
taumā-	*taoxman-*	family
xaudā-	*xaoda-*	hat

Iranians of the European Steppe

When Herodotus considered the forces arrayed against the small Greek city-states, he emphasized that they were a multi-national force under Persian military command. He did not see the conflict in terms of a war between Greeks and Iranians or a Greek and Iranian 'race'; had he been a better linguist, however, he might well have reconsidered the nature of the world that confronted the ancient Greeks.

The peoples of the Ukrainian and Russian steppelands that Herodotus so vividly describes (here as the first opponents of the expansion of the Persians) were themselves also, at least in part, speakers of Iranian languages. Their linguistic legacy is still to be found in the major river valleys of the steppe and forest-steppe. The Iranian word for 'river', seen in the Avestan word *dānu-*, is found to underlie the name of the River Don, which flows into the Sea of Azov north of the Black Sea as well as *Dānu apara* 'the river to the rear', now preserved in Slavic *Dnieper*, and the *Dānu nazdya* 'the river to the front', the modern *Dniester* (*dānu-* by another derivation also underlies the name of the *Danube*). Names of Scythians and Sarmatians and occasional words that caught the interest of classical writers (the weapon wielded so effectively by the Scythians, the bow, was called *taxša* in their language and in the later Persian language was known as a *taxš*) are all Iranian. We also know that the Iranians of the steppe had an important impact on the vocabulary of their Slavic neighbours who absorbed a number of Iranian words into Slavic, e.g. Russian *bog* 'god', is generally derived from Iranian. Hence the Scythians and the Sarmatians to their east were all Iranian-speaking. To this might be added the Alans whose very name may, like the name of Iran, be derived from *aryana*. These nomads of the western or European steppe were eventually absorbed into the surrounding communities or dispersed across Europe (over 5,000 Iranian-speaking horsemen came to settle in Britain in the 2nd century AD; others crossed France and Spain to help establish a kingdom in North Africa) only to disappear after the great migrations impelled by the entry of the Huns into Europe. One remnant, however, still survives: those who retreated into the fastness of the Caucasus persist today as the Ossetes and they number on the order of 400,000 people. The Ossete word for 'water' is *don*.

Old Iranian

Now all these languages (Old Persian, Avestan, Scythian, etc.), dating from the 1st millennium BC, constitute what linguists refer to as 'Old Iranian'. The linguistic picture of that time portrays much of the area on the western approach to Chinese Turkestan as Iranian-speaking. The European steppe to the Urals was occupied by Iranians and northern and eastern Iran also saw early Iranian settlement. It is clear that the Iranian languages in Central and Western Asia had come from either the north or east to the south and west to spread over earlier Elamite-speakers. As for when this happened, where we have some historical control (for example, in Mesopotamia where historical texts date from the 3rd millennium BC onwards), it would appear that the spread of most of the Iranian languages into their historical seats was largely a process of the 1st millennium BC.

Middle Iranian

During the period of Greek rule, the Old Persian language survived and changed through time to emerge once again as a state language in AD 226 with the accession of the Sassanid dynasty. The new language, Middle Persian, reflected a marked simplification, at least in terms of grammatical forms, of the earlier Old Persian language and it has left an enormous legacy of texts in a wide variety of genres. But Middle Persian was not the first of the Iranian languages to retaliate against Greek hegemony. Out of the earlier satrapy of Parthia, the territory of modern Khorāsān (the northeast province of Iran), arose the Parthian empire (247 BC–AD 224) with its own regional language whose alphabet was derived from Aramaic. First attested in the form of inscribed pot sherds indicating wine deliveries, it was also the vehicle for state inscriptions and, after the collapse of its empire, it was one of the media for the literature of the Manichean religion.

The earlier (probable) homeland of Avestan, Choresmia, has also left some traces of its later language, again an Iranian language that survived until it gradually disappeared in the 12th and 13th centuries in the face of Turkish expansion.

The ancient kingdom of Sogdiana has also left us Middle Iranian documents, primarily dating from the 7th to 9th centuries. We have already seen how the Sogdians were among the foremost to exploit the Silk Road (Samarkand was one of their major towns) and, as skilled traders, their language expanded as a *lingua franca* over Central Asia. Eventually Persian began to replace it in the 9th century and later Sogdian disappeared in the face of Islamic expansion. Its sole modern legacy is the Yaghnobi language, spoken by an estimated 2,000 people in the remote fastness along the Yaghnob River about 50 miles north of Dushanbe in Tadjikistan.

Saka

If the western steppe was Iranian-speaking, what was the situation east of the Urals on the immediate approach to the Tarim Basin from the north? Here too we find evidence for Iranian languages. The Massagetae who lay to the north of the Persians (in the south and east Caspian region) are generally believed to have been Iranian speakers (whether native or by acquisition may be disputed). Greek tradition labelled all the peoples occupying the steppelands to the west or east of the Urals as Scythians. The Persians employed the name Saka in the same way – both for their own

42. A cylinder seal from the Persian Achaemenid dynasty (550–331 BC), which portrays Saka archers with their characteristic pointed caps.

43. (Right) From a linguistic perspective, the steppelands and those lands east of the Caspian were occupied largely by Iranian-speaking peoples.

'Scythians' as well as for those who roamed the European steppe. An Old Persian inscription erected during the reign of Darius I lists three Saka confederacies: 1) the *Sakā Tayaiy paradraya* (Overseas Saka), presumably those of Europe (the Scythians of Herodotus), the *Sakā Haumavargā* who we believe occupied Ferghana, and the *Sakā Tigraxaudā* (Sakas who wear pointed caps) who are generally set between the Syr Darya and Semirech'e. When we come to examine the headgear of some of the Tarim mummies, we will have good cause to remember our Saka with their pointed caps. There is also some evidence that the Saka, like the Sarmatians, recognized a role for women in warfare. Dionysius tells us that they were once ruled by a woman named Zarina 'who was devoted to warfare and was in daring and efficiency by far the foremost of the women of the Saka'. In the 6th century BC when the Saka king had been captured by Cyrus the Great, his queen, Sparethre, avenged him by leading an army allegedly numbering 300,000 men and 200,000 women to defeat Cyrus.

Bactrian

If we turn our attention to the pivotal land of Bactria, a major staging area for movement into East Central Asia, our linguistic evidence for the native language (before the incursions of Alexander's army) is meagre indeed and is confined to about 56 words recovered from southern Afghanistan, just beyond the ancient borders of Bactria. All of these are written in the Aramaic script which, although quite useful for composition on parchment or leather like so many other Semitic writing systems, was deficient in vowels which must be restored in order to make sense of the words.

After the Greek conquest of Bactria, the introduction of the Greek alphabet makes our translation of Bactrian somewhat easier and there are various documents known in Bactrian up until the 9th century AD. These provide ready comparisons with other Iranian languages, e.g. Bactrian σαδο (*sado*) and Avestan *satəm* 'hundred', Bactrian ασπο (*aspo*) and Avestan *aspa-* 'horse'. The language would appear to be an independent local representative of East Iranian, comparable to Sogdian, Choresmian and other neighbouring languages. The most important point to consider is that the language of Bactria as well as the language of the Kushan empire was

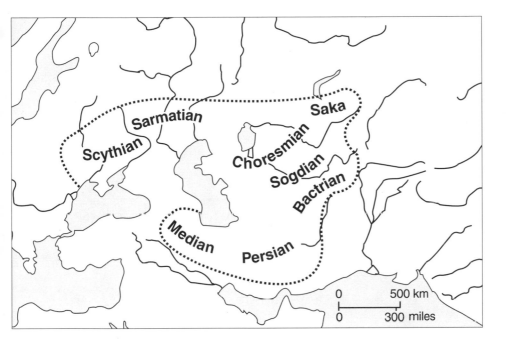

Iranian. Before and after its conquest by the Yuezhi, our linguistic remains are in an Iranian language. This is something we will have to remember later on.

We can see now that most of the European and western Asian approaches to the Tarim Basin, at least during the 1st millennium BC, involved early Iranian-speaking peoples. The *Shiji* informs us that in the lands west of Ferghana 'there are many different languages spoken, but they are in general the same and people understand each other clearly'. And since the Iranian language dominated among those states that were most concerned with the Silk Road, it is hardly surprising when we find Iranian languages farther east in the Tarim Basin.

THE LANGUAGES OF EAST CENTRAL ASIA

As we have mentioned above, at the turn of this century, a series of expeditions headed by Germans, Russians, British (from India), French, Chinese, Japanese and Swedes discovered that the sands of Chinese Turkestan had concealed a treasure trove of antiquities. Whole towns had disappeared under the sands only to be resurrected again by the archaeologist's spade (actually 'hoe') to reveal streets still lined with mulberry trees after over a millennium had passed. The treasures included a vast quantity of written documents. Some of these languages were already known from India and West Central Asia where they were native but the arid conditions of the Tarim Basin provided documents that were either earlier or far more abundant than ever recorded before. In some cases the

Manicheism

The founder of Manicheism, the prophet Mani, was born in southern Babylon in 216 and died at the hands of the Persian state in 274 when, after initial successes in converting the Persian aristocracy, Zoroastrian priests managed to have him tried and imprisoned. At the age of 24, Mani experienced a vision from an angel that prompted him to found a new religion which, he believed, would be superior to all preceding religions which he saw as confined to local areas and languages; Manicheism was an overtly universal religion and his missionaries spread his doctrines, which borrowed from Judaism, Christianity, Zoroastrianism and Buddhism, the founders of these religions being regarded as precursors to the completion of enlightenment by Mani (compare the modern universal religion of Baha'i, founded in Iran by Husayn 'Ali in 1863). Manicheism tended to be more influenced by Christianity in the West and Buddhism in the East. Mani determined that his religion would be well organized and he promulgated his own doctrines in a series of canonical texts including the *Gospel of Life*, the *Book of Secrets* and the *Book of Giants*.

His religion embraced the concepts of a dualistic universe of light and dark, spirit and material, above and below, and preached the fundamental tragedy of human existence which could only be overcome by spiritual knowledge of the self. Strict adherents, the elect, were to avoid meat, wine and all pleasures of the flesh; the saved went to paradise while the fallen were forced to undergo cyclic rebirth. The religion comprised a rich mythology of personified attributes, e.g. Mother of Life, Father of Light, Darkness, and figures lifted from other religions such as Jesus, Eve and Hormizd. It relied heavily on visual representations to convey its doctrines, Mani himself being responsible for the first Manichean picture book. This is in stark contrast to Islam which is staunchly opposed to all artistic depictions of human beings and deities (this helps to explain why the adherents of Islam systematically destroyed the wall paintings and sculptures of Buddhism and other religions in Central Asia). Manicheism spread west across North Africa (St Augustine was a temporary convert) to Gaul but was crushed by the Christian Church and the Roman government during the 5th century and in the eastern empire by the 6th century. Nevertheless, it flourished in East Central Asia where missionaries carried the new religion by the 7th century.

Our knowledge of Manicheism outside East Central Asia is largely limited to attacks by Christians. One of the more exciting finds of the excavations of East Central Asia was a substantial quantity of Manichean texts which dated largely to the 7th and 8th centuries. In the spirit of their founder, the Manichean texts were recorded in Middle Persian, Parthian, Sogdian, Bactrian, Uyghur, Coptic and Chinese; there is also a document in Tocharian. Mani himself presumably spoke Aramaic and his own books were in Middle Persian and Aramaic. After persecution in Persia, the capital of the religion was moved to Samarkand and one of the main vectors for its spread in East Central Asia was, consequently, the Sogdians. Manicheism was embraced by the Uyghurs as a state religion during the 8th century and its centre was that of the Uyghur government in Mongolia.

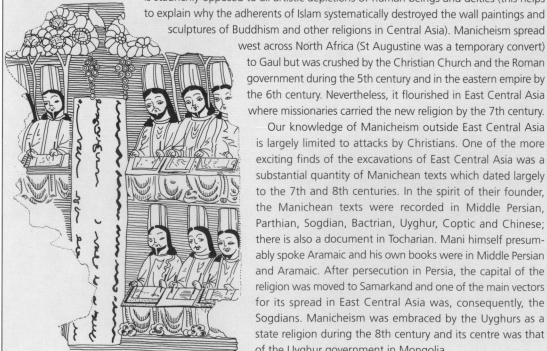

44. The Manichean scribes depicted here were also members of the elect of the Manichean religion.

significance of the documents goes far beyond their purely linguistic importance. Before the Tarim discoveries, our knowledge of the Manichean religion, for example, was almost entirely based on its detractors' attacks; excavations in the northern Tarim revealed the actual beliefs of this widely persecuted faith that was adopted as the state religion by the Uyghurs. Even more exciting was the discovery of documents in languages never before known or imagined. Graphic accounts of these discoveries by such explorer-archaeologists as Aurel Stein, Paul Pelliot and Albert von Le Coq are enough to drive most archaeologists mad with envy. Stein, for example, recounts how he followed a worker to a room where a few wooden tablets had been discovered and within a short time uncovered more than 85 precious documents.

The variety of media employed in writing was great. Chinese records were often found on thin wooden strips of poplar, long enough for a column of 20 to 30 characters, which echoed in their shape the bamboo tablets of the centre of the empire. Iranian documents were sometimes found on wedge-shaped wooden tablets some 18–38 cm (7–15 in) long; such a tablet, primarily a medium for Indic documents, was bound together with a cord and the address stood on the outer surface. Leather, silk and paper, the last of which is said to have been invented in China in AD 105, were also employed. The German and French expeditions also recovered an enormous quantity of documents as well as works of art. Von Le Coq records the discovery of an entire library of Manichean literature, 2 ft deep in manuscripts, utterly destroyed by water, as well as a room stuffed with the

45. Chinese document from Niyä, engraved on a poplar slip, reading '(aged 30 years); medium height, dark complexion; large eyes; he wears a moustache and a beard'.

Paul Pelliot

Paul Pelliot (1878–1945) was the consummate Sinologist. He knew well all the major languages required for the unfettered investigation of Chinese history: Classical Chinese, Arabic, Persian, Turkic, Tibetan, Mongolian, Manchu and Japanese, not to mention all the scholarly languages of Europe. Thus, although Pelliot was the only Sinologist to lead a mission to Central Asia, we may say that he was the perfect person to do so. Pelliot's knowledge of ancient Chinese texts was prodigious and his philological acumen was awesome. He was famous for writing articles that consisted of many more annotations than text. A good specimen of his ability to write critically and voluminously on minute particulars is his two-volume collection of posthumous notes on terms in Marco Polo's book. Pelliot arrived at Dunhuang in February 1908, almost a year after Stein. He stayed there for four months, during which he surveyed all of the 500 or so caves. Most important of all, he somehow managed to convince 'Taoist' Wang to let him inside cave number 17. Whereas Stein had to be content with whatever manuscripts the caretaker of the caves brought out for him, albeit nearly 10,000 in number, Pelliot – with his phenomenal linguistic ability – was able to choose the best of what remained, concentrating on manuscripts in Tibetan, Sanskrit and Sogdian, and Chinese manuscripts that bore informative colophons or were not Buddhist sutras.

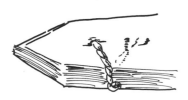

46. Wedge-shaped tablet, typical of those recovered in abundance by Aurel Stein.

slaughtered bodies of some hundred Buddhist monks dispatched by the Chinese in the 9th century. Graffiti are also an important source of the languages of the Tarim Basin. In the north, religious texts were found in Buddhist shrines while in the south at Endere, Aurel Stein discovered on the wall of the fort a Tibetan inscription that read: 'At Pyagpag in the province of Upper Jom lom this army was outwitted and a tiger's meal was obtained (i.e. a great slaughter)' to which a different hand scrawled: 'Now eat until you are fat', apparently the boast of a victorious Tibetan soldier.

Khotanese

Aurel Stein devoted particular attention to the ancient kingdom of Khotan from which we now have a large quantity of documents attesting to no fewer than seven different languages. The native language of the population is known today as Khotanese or, in the native language, *hvatanau*. In this language are found primarily translations of Buddhist texts and an assortment of commercial and legal transactions recording deliveries of cloth: 'Makali gave cloth, 22 feet …. Senili gave cloth, 9 feet, 8 inches.' We also have occasional lateral references to the language of the more dishonest of its scribes. One of the Chinese documents recovered by Stein from Dandān-Uiliq indicts two Barbarian (=Khotanese) scribes who, having purchased an ass from a certain Silüe (Khot Sīḍaka) for 6,000 units of currency, had still not paid him after ten months. Khotanese clearly belongs to the Saka group of Eastern Iranian languages and offers our most abundant evidence for this branch of Iranian. There is some evidence that Saka was also the language of Qäshqär, and Saka documents are known from oasis sites north of the Täklimakan Desert at Tumshuq, near Aqsu and Murtuq, near Turpan. The Saka documents date from the 7th to the 10th centuries.

Although the Saka dialects became extinct both within Turkestan and over much of their former territory, it is alleged that they have survived among a number of small language groups spoken in the more remote areas of the Pamirs. Recently one of the groups, the speakers of Sarikoli, migrated from the Pamirs into Xinjiang where they settled south of modern Tashkurgan.

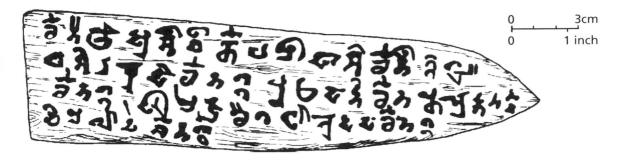

0   3cm
0   1 inch

47. A document in Khotanese Saka.

Sogdian

As we have seen, the Sogdians were quick to exploit the Silk Road and they and their language spread eastwards into the Tarim Basin. The evidence for Sogdian, like that of Saka, is more abundant in the Tarim Basin than in its homeland in Sogdiana. In the Tarim and Turpan basins there are found Sogdian texts that testify to the proselytizing activities of Manicheans, Buddhists and Nestorian Christians (box p. 114), the latter dating somewhere around the 8th to 10th centuries when the Sogdians began the translation of Christian documents. The Manichean documents begin earlier and are composed not only in Sogdian but also in Middle Persian and Parthian. The Sogdian documents are concentrated along the northern route (primarily recovered by the German expeditions in the Turpan region) and are found as far east as Lopnur and in the area of the Great Wall (especially Dunhuang). Some of the texts are ostensibly translations of Indian originals, while others are from Chinese translations (of Sanskrit works). The documents themselves may date from the 4th century to the 10th century and indicate the spread of Sogdian influence throughout the northern Tarim Basin. Finally, in this pot-pourri of texts we may include one of the earliest documents in modern Persian: the site of Dandān-Uiliq yielded up a fragmentary letter dated to about 718 from a Jewish sheep merchant complaining to his superior of bad treatment.

Both the western approaches and the Tarim Basin itself would then appear to have been very much part of the Iranian world at the time of our earliest written records. In some cases, we have reason to suspect that the entry of a particular Iranian language may have been late and accomplished in a particular historical context, e.g. the survival of Parthian liturgical documents or those of Sogdians who attempted to follow the Silk Road trade. But others such as Khotanese Saka would appear to have been spoken by a considerable native population in the southern Tarim. Belonging to a vast chain of steppe-nomadic languages, the Saka will prove to be obvious suspects in our search for the identity of some of the Tarim mummies. Iranian dialects, however, do not exhaust our roster of languages recovered from East Central Asia.

Nestorian Christianity

48. The cross borne by this figure clearly marks him out as a Nestorian.

The spread of Christianity in Asia was very much associated with the doctrines of Nestorius (d. 451), the bishop of Constantinople who had been condemned for his beliefs, e.g. rejection of Mary as 'Mother of God', and emphasis on the human nature of Christ. Although it was suppressed in the Roman empire, the religion survived in Asia where it was known as the Church of the East or the Persian Church, and the seat of its Patriarch was Ctesiphon and then Baghdad. It spread in two directions: towards India and across East Central Asia via the Metropolitan of Samarkand to China. The work of Christian missionaries in East Central Asia is recorded in documents preserved in Syriac, Sogdian, Middle Persian and Turkish. There is also a stela in the Chinese capital of Chang'an bearing a Nestorian inscription in Chinese and Syriac and dating to the 7th century, while translations of Christian documents into Chinese were recovered at Dunhuang. Christianity spread into East Central Asia by the 6th century and reached China by the 7th century. The religion ultimately spread to the northeast and Nestorian Christians were established in the court of the Mongol khan. The primary language vector for the spread of Christianity was Sogdian (Nestorian Christianity had arrived in Sogdiana by the 5th century) and it is presumed that Sogdian colonies carried the religion eastwards with their trading missions. Christian documents were primarily found in the north (near Turpan and Khocho) and hence discovered by the German expeditions under von Le Coq. The content of the Sogdian documents varies widely, including translations of the gospels, hymns, homilies, etc. The religion survives today with *c.* 170,000 adherents in Iran, Iraq and Syria.

Indo-Aryan

The early Iranian languages abutted on the languages of India. The earliest form of Indic was Vedic Sanskrit which, like Avestan, was an ancient liturgical language. Again like Avestan, the earliest texts of Vedic were purely oral; the Vedas were the central religious texts of the ancient Indic religion and were memorized for recitation by the priestly class, the brahmins. The traditional dates for the earliest hymns in Vedic Sanskrit are set to about 1200 BC, although our earliest written manuscripts date no earlier than the 11th century AD; their prior existence was initially maintained in oral religious literature where they were and still are recited by the priests of the Hindu religion, although they were probably written down by the first centuries BC, when a writing system for the language was devised. The earliest written evidence for an Indo-Aryan language is in the inscriptions of the Emperor Aśoka which were erected in the mid-3rd century BC.

49. Brāhmī and Kharoṣṭhī, the two 'Western' scripts most commonly encountered in the Tarim Basin, derived from India. The first and fourth columns give the transliteration.

	Br	Kh		Br	Kh
a			ḍ		
i			ḍh		
u			ṇ		
ā		–	t		
ī		–	th		
ū		–	d		
e			dh		
ai		–	n		
o			p		
k			ph		
kh			b		
g			bh		
gh			m		
ṅ			y		
c			r		
ch			l		
j			v		
jh			ś		
ñ			ṣ		
ṭ			s		
ṭh			h		

These inscriptions include the two different alphabetic systems of ancient India: one was Kharoṣṭhī, which was written from right to left and survived until the mid-5th century AD or perhaps slightly later. It was derived ultimately from Aramaic and some have claimed that it takes its designation after a family name Kharoṣṭha which means 'lip of an ass'. The other writing system, far more widespread, was Brāhmī, written from left to right, which has provided the basis of all subsequent Indian alphabets, including the Nāgarī script which was employed both for Sanskrit and most of the modern Indo-Aryan languages among Hindus. Aramaic is the uncertain ancestor of Brāhmī; some suggest it derives from Phoenician.

Although Sanskrit was the vehicle for the earliest Indo-Aryan literature, it was not the Vedic religion that was carried from India but rather Buddhism. Buddhism, in contrast to the Hindu religion, did not originally employ the ancient liturgical and classical language but, initially at least, used vernacular languages which linguists refer to as Middle Indian or Prākrits (unrefined, natural), whose exact identity (which Prākrit?) is uncertain. The Emperor Aśoka also employed a Prākrit in his inscriptions. But by about the 1st century AD the Buddhists had adopted their own liturgical language by taking the Prākrits and transposing them back into Sanskrit, which gave rise to an artificial language commonly known as Buddhist Hybrid Sanskrit. This language flourished from about the 1st to 7th centuries AD.

The Spread of Indic

The Indic languages and their scripts were in the process of expanding outside India as early as the Graeco-Bactrian kingdom where we find inscriptions on coins given in Greek on one side and in Kharoṣṭhī on the other. The use of Prākrit increased in the subsequent Saka and Kushan administrations but was by then prompted not only by administrative concerns but also the spread of Buddhism. Indic traders followed the Silk Road eastwards across the Pamirs where their inscriptions can be traced back to the 1st century BC and Buddhist missionaries carried both their language and the translations of their sacred documents into the heart of the Tarim Basin to found Buddhist monasteries. The same expeditions that were uncovering the Iranian documents also found some 800 administrative documents on wood, leather and paper in the southern Tarim at Niyä and farther east at Krorän. These Prākrit texts offer the earliest administrative accounts of one of the kingdoms of the Tarim oasis towns and their texts have been dated to the period *c.* AD 230–330. While not riveting from a literary point of view, the texts provide us with a real insight into the world of ancient Krorän. One text, complaining of mismanagement, begins: 'These people Kunge and Ogana are *klasemcis* [some rank] for four divisions of the army, but you are making them keepers of the royal camels. They are performing another state duty which on top of their army work makes five jobs. In this you are certainly not acting rightly, you are acting differently from the command of me, the great king [*maharayasa*, compare Sanskrit *mahārāja*].' We will later see that buried within these mundane texts is one of our most important clues concerning the identity of our Tarim mummies.

In addition to administrative texts, of course, are the numerous liturgical works pertaining to Buddhism which make up the canon of originals that most of the other languages in the Tarim Basin were attempting to translate. We should emphasize that the presence of Indic documents (in Sanskrit, Buddhist Hybrid Sanskrit, Prākrit, etc.) in the Tarim Basin is to be explained in large measure by the spread of Buddhism eastwards towards China. The evidence certainly attests to the establishment of monasteries housing Indo-Aryan-speaking monks but it does not really suggest a large Indo-Aryan population in the Tarim to whom Buddhist missionaries came to minister.

THE WIDER PICTURE

Indo-Iranian

The Indic languages under discussion are also known as Indo-Aryan languages, which emphasizes that although Indo-Aryan reflects a different language group from Iranian, the two are very closely related. For example, the earliest form of Sanskrit was so similar to that of the *Avesta* that with relative ease one can transform one language into the other by applying a few basic rules of sound substitution, e.g. Avestan *z* = Sanskrit *j*. As linguists have often shown, if one takes the Avestan hymn to the god Mithra and translates it into Sanskrit, the resulting text is so close to the Avestan original that the two languages give the appearance of having been mutually intelligible. A comparative linguist can reconstruct forms, ancestral to both of these languages, which we call Proto-Indo-Iranian.

Yašt (Hymn) 10.6

Avestan	*təm amavantəm yazatəm*
Old Indic	*tám ámavantam yajatám*
Proto-Indo-Iranian	**tám ámavantam yaĵatám*
	This powerful deity

Avestan	*sūrəm dāmōhu səvištəm*
Old Indic	*śū́ram dhā́masu śáviṣṭham*
Proto-Indo-Iranian	**ćúram dhā́masu ćáviṣṭham*
	strong, among the living the strongest

Avestan	*miθrəm yazāi zaoθrābyō*
Old Indic	*mitrám yajāi hótrābhyaḥ*
Proto-Indo-Iranian	**mitrám yaĵāi ĵháutrābhyas*
	Mithra, I would honour with libations

It should be noted that the ancient Proto-Indo-Iranian language, the language directly ancestral to both Indo-Aryan and Iranian, is nowhere attested in written form but is a product of reconstruction (and hence its forms are preceded by an asterisk).

Other Languages

If we were going to paint in the linguistic landscape of the western approaches to the Tarim Basin, we would need but two shades of a single colour – to represent Indo-Iranian – and we would extend our brushwork over much of East Central Asia itself. The one non-Indo-Iranian language on the immediate west is Burushaski, a language spoken by some 20,000 people in the region of Hunza and Yasin in Pakistan on the southwestern approaches to Xinjiang. This language is generally treated as an 'isolate', a language with no known relations, although there have been abundant attempts to relate it to one of the known language families of Eurasia. Regardless of its affiliations, it has not been possible (whether through investigations of place names or through other types of analysis) to demonstrate a significant Burushaski presence in the Tarim Basin. The southern Tarim is bordered not only by Indo-Aryan but also Tibeto-Burman languages. We have already seen that the historical expansion of the Tibetans into the Tarim Basin is a late phenomenon recorded in Chinese annals as well as Tibetan documents. From the east naturally comes Chinese and there is abundant documentary evidence for the use of Chinese in the Tarim Basin, but only from the time of its historical expansion into the region during the establishment of the Silk Road and the attempts of the Han dynasty to wrest control of the Tarim towns from the Xiongnu.

This leaves only the northern approaches into Xinjiang unaccounted for. We know from historical testimony that at least one of the major components of the steppelands was the Saka so we should expect a substantial, if not exclusively, Iranian presence to the north. We have also seen that the various Iranian-speaking tribes were under pressure from tribes farther to the east such as the Xiongnu whose own language is so poorly attested – only in Chinese transcription – that conjectures that it is a Turkish or Mongolian language, while plausible enough, remain unsubstantiated.

Indo-Europeans

The exceptionally close relationship between Iranian and Indo-Aryan was not recognized by scholars until the end of the 18th century. And when these similarities were recognized, it was part of a vastly larger process of linguistic discovery. The original key was Sanskrit, a knowledge of which began among Westerners with the expansion of British power in India. To those educated in the classical languages, it was only a matter of time before it was recognized that Sanskrit bore certain striking similarities to both Greek and Latin. A simple 10-word list of fairly basic vocabulary should suffice.

English	Sanskrit	Greek	Latin
mother	mātár	métēr	mater
father	pitṛ	patér	pater
name	nāman-	ónoma	nomen
bad	dus	dus-	dis-
right	dákṣina-	dexiós	dexter
belly	udara	-óderos	uterus
knee	jānu-	gónu	genu
big	mahā-	mégas	magnus
cloud	nabhas	néphos	nubes
house	dama-	dómos	domus

The fact that the European classical languages and the ancient language of India were similar was only the beginning of a chain of revelations as it became increasingly clear that all the languages of Europe (with the exception of Finnish, Lapp, Estonian, Hungarian, Maltese and Basque) exhibited systematic correspondences in their vocabulary and grammars with the three ancient languages. Although there were predecessors, a speech by Sir William Jones to the Royal Asiatic Society in 1786 has been traditionally regarded as the starting point in this process of discovery.

The Sanskrit language, whatever be its antiquity, is of a wonderful structure; more perfect than the Greek, more copious than the Latin, and more exquisitely refined than either, yet bearing to both of them a stronger affinity, both in the roots of the verbs and in the forms of grammar, than could possibly have been produced by accident; so strong indeed, that no philologer could examine them all three, without believing them to have sprung from some common source, which, perhaps, no longer exists: there is a similar reason, though not quite so forcible, for supposing that both the Gothic and the Celtic, though blended with a very different idiom, had the same origin with Sanskrit; and the old Persian might be added to the same family, if this were the place for discussing any question concerning the antiquities of Persia.

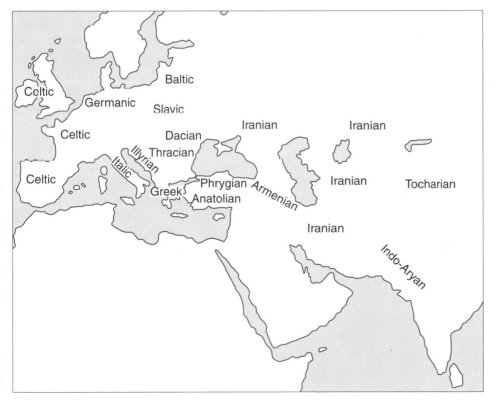

50. Distribution of Indo-European languages.

At the time of Jones, one could also add the Gothic, i.e. what today we would call the Germanic languages (Icelandic, Norwegian, Swedish, Danish, German, Dutch, Frisian, English, etc.) and the Celtic (Irish, Welsh, Breton, etc.) to this list of languages that derived from 'some common source.' As the study of comparative philology developed it was possible to add the Baltic (Old Prussian, Lithuanian, Latvian) and Slavic languages (Russian, Belorussian, Ukrainian, Polish, Czech, Slovakian, Slovenian, Serbo-Croatian, Bulgarian, Macedonian, etc.), Albanian and Armenian. By now the term for all these languages was Indo-European or Indo-Germanic in order to emphasize that they were found from India westwards across Europe. In 1870 inscriptions identified as Hittite were discovered in Turkey, but it was not until about 30 or 40 years later that sufficient material had been excavated for one to assert that the ancient Anatolian languages also belonged to the Indo-European language family.

In classifying the various Indo-European languages, 19th-century philologists observed what they regarded as a crucial difference between the languages of the east (Asia (Sanskrit, Avestan), eastern Europe (Baltic, Slavic)) and those of the west (Europe (Celtic, Italic, Germanic, Greek)). Western languages often showed a 'hard' *g* or *k* where eastern languages revealed in the same place a *j, z* or *s*, e.g. Greek *gérōn*, 'old man', but Sanskrit *járant-,* 'elderly'. In linguistic terms, the velars (*g* and *k*) in the west had been palatalized in the east. Palatalization, the shifting of a sound so that it is made by the blade of the tongue against the hard palate (notice how your tongue moves when you say *keys* and then the palatalized *cheese*), is a frequent enough sound change in many languages. For example, when the ancient Romans referred to the barbarians to the north of them as Celtae, the initial *c* of the word would have been pronounced in ancient Latin as a hard *k* sound (as in the Greek word for the same people, *Keltoi*). But in English we gain the name of this people through French (*Celte*) and the French regularly palatalized Latin *c* when followed by an *e* or *i*. Consequently, we often find that the name is pronounced in the palatalized form, e.g. the American basketball team is always known as the Boston Celtics [/seltiks/]. Palatalization is by no means restricted to Indo-European languages but is a very widespread form of sound change. For example, palatalization has been occurring in Chinese where it appeared first in the north (Mandarin) around the middle of the 17th century and has been steadily spreading south, but not quite to the southern border of China (Cantonese). A customer in a Cantonese restaurant hungry for 'mushroom with chicken slices' orders *moogoo gai pan* (where *gai* means 'chicken'), while the same dish in a Mandarin restaurant is known as *mogu ji pian* where the initial *g* has been palatalized to *j* in Mandarin. Incidentally, palatalization is also to be seen in the name of the Chinese capital which, in Milton's time (1608–74), was spelled *Paquin* (*Paradise Lost*, XI 390, our Peking) while the second syllable is now palatalized in *Beijing*.

When one surveys the correspondences in the Indo-European languages, one finds Latin *centum* 'hundred' but Sanskrit *śatám* and Avestan *satəm* (and Bactrian *sado*) which prompted linguists to term those languages without palatalized forms as *centum* languages and those with palatalization as *satem*. The satem languages comprise Indo-Aryan, Iranian, Slavic, Baltic, Armenian and Albanian. With the exception of Albanian, they all lie to the east of the non-palatalizing centum languages. The discovery of the Anatolian languages which also proved to be centum complicated matters although it did not disturb a broad pattern which portrayed a swathe of languages extending from the Baltic across the steppe and down into India as all having shared a common linguistic change (palatalization). These four (Baltic, Slavic, Indic and Iranian) also share one other significant change involving the special development of the sound *s* after *r*, *u*, *k*, and *i*, the so-called *ruki*-rule. All of this suggested that there must have been some form of common linguistic development in the east, an innovation that distinguished the eastern languages from those of the west. This symmetry, however, dissolved in the desert sands of the Tarim Basin.

Tocharian

The same expeditions that returned with the texts in Iranian, Indic, Chinese, Tibetan and Turkic also came across documents in languages never before encountered. Again the texts were primarily translations, in this case, almost

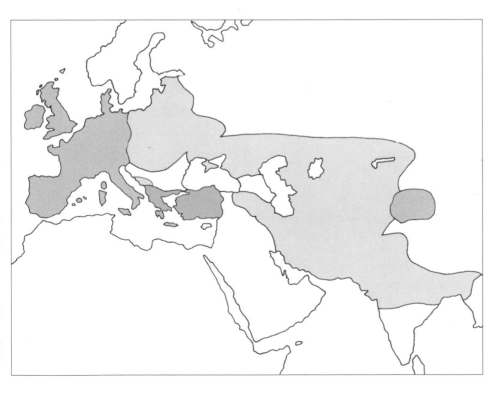

51. A map of centum (dark shading) and satem (lighter shading) languages finds Tocharian isolated in the far east.

exclusively Buddhist with a few Manichean, but there was also a quantity of monastery records, caravan travel passes and other routine documents. To linguists it was obvious that the language of the texts was neither Iranian nor Indo-Aryan. The texts were written in a version of the Brāhmī script of northwest India so that reading the words in the documents was not too difficult; the fact that much of the literature involved translations of Buddhist texts known elsewhere in their original Indic versions, and that there were even bilingual documents, facilitated their rapid translation.

Once translated, it was clear that the explorer-archaeologists had discovered two entirely new Indo-European languages. A number of different names have evolved for the new languages but the consensus today labels them Tocharian. Documents in Tocharian A or East Tocharian are found principally in the area of Turpan and Qarashähär. Tocharian B is found in the west around Kucha but also in the same area as Tocharian A. The documents date from about the 6th to the 8th centuries AD.

The impact of Tocharian on Indo-European studies in general can be readily appreciated when we consider the Tocharian words that correspond to those where we find palatalization in the satem languages. A short table should suffice to show the differences.

English	Sanskrit	Tocharian A	Tocharian B
hundred	*śatám*	*känt*	*kante*
ear	*śrótra*	*klots*	*klautso*
tear	*áśru*	*ākär*	*akrūna* (plural)

Here we see that where we find palatalization in Indic or any other satem language, Tocharian behaves like a 'western' language. How 'western' Tocharian might prove to be we will explore later, but one of the obvious consequences of this discovery was that it predisposed scholars to accept that somehow people speaking a 'European' language had managed to trek their way from Europe to the Tarim Basin.

Domains

The immense linguistic complexity of East Central Asia can be made somewhat less bewildering if we consider the concept of social domain. While native speakers of English in the West have achieved an unenviable reputation of being monolingual, the ability to speak more than one language is far more common throughout the world. In ancient East Central Asia where numerous languages were spoken, many at the same time and in the same general region, bilingualism or multilingualism was probably very much the norm. The governing factor of language choice was the social domain – where one was and what language was expected to be spoken there. To give an extreme case as a hypothetical example, imagine that you are a citizen of Kucha about the 7th century AD. At home and to your parents you might have spoken Tocharian B, but when complaining about the behaviour of ill-mannered camels to a passing caravan leader, you would have to speak Sogdian (shouting louder in Tocharian B might let off steam but probably would not convey much to a Sogdian). If you were a monk, you would be engaged in reading Buddhist scriptures in Sanskrit but would also be expected to be able to read them in Prākrit as well; indeed, the latter may have been the administrative language of your monastery. But if confronted with the imperial authorities, you would have to make recourse to Chinese. You would have had to distinguish then between your native language (spoken at home) and the various other languages suited to the different social domains in which you found yourself in the course of a lifetime. For the inhabitants of East Central Asia, we can prepare a very rough table of the social domains and languages that may have been spoken in the early historical period. With the obvious exception of Chinese and Tibetan and the later Turkic languages, all the languages that we find spoken in East Central Asia belong to the Indo-European language family. Where did all these languages come from?

Tarim languages

North Tarim/Turpan

	Kucha	Turpan
written	Chinese	Chinese
spoken	*TochB*	*TochB*
religious	*Prākrit/Sanskrit*	*Prākrit/Sanskrit*
trade	*Sogdian*/Chinese	*Sogdian*/Chinese

South Tarim/Lopnur

	Khotan	Krorän
written	*Prākrit*	*Prākrit*/Chinese
spoken	*Saka*	*? Kroränian*
religious	*Prākrit/Sanskrit*	*Prākrit/Sanskrit*
trade	*Prākrit*	*Prākrit*

Some of the major languages of the Tarim and Turpan basins and their general social domains.

Prākrit etc. = Indic, *Sogdian* etc. = Iranian, *TochB* etc. = Tocharian

Asian Beginnings

As long ago as Sir William Jones' 18th-century pronouncement on the affinity of the Indo-European languages, scholars sought to locate the original territory from which the earliest speakers of the Indo-European languages had dispersed. The reasons for presuming that the Indo-

Europeans had spread from a more confined homeland were initially far more implicit than explicit: the earliest Indo-Europeans must have constituted a nation, and nations occupied geographically defined territories. The biblical account had assigned the origin of the various languages to the dispersion of the sons of Noah after the Deluge, and discussion of the Indo-European origins adopted a similar model; no one imagined that the earliest Indo-Europeans had always occupied the entire area of their historical distribution. Moreover, 19th-century linguists adopted the biological model of language development, drawing up family trees of the Indo-European languages whose various branches (language stocks such as Indo-Aryan, Germanic and Celtic) all diverged from a Proto-Indo-European trunk and root This model almost invited scholars to translate the trunk into a geographical concept in which the Proto-Indo-European language sprang up from fixed roots and then spread to the territories in which one found the various Indo-European branches.

As comparative linguistics and historical understanding of the past developed, the reasons for seeking a more confined homeland became more solid. Historical testimony indicated that in some regions of Eurasia the Indo-European languages were obviously intrusive. For example, Iranian had spread over Near Eastern languages (both Semitic and Elamite), Latin had spread over Etruscan, and the Celtic and Latin languages had spread over Iberia where there was linguistic evidence for earlier non-Indo-European languages both in early inscriptional form and in a contemporary non-Indo-European language, i.e. Basque. More importantly, it was obvious from the study of languages that the coherence of any language depended on the area

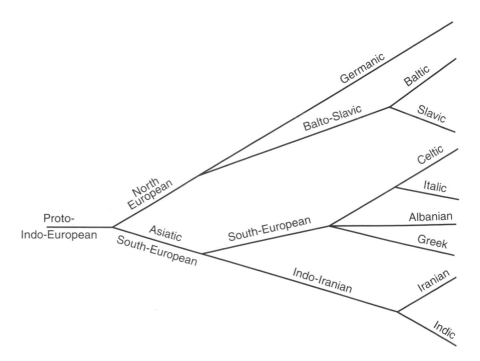

52. The family tree of Indo-European languages as known in the 19th century before the discovery of Anatolian and Tocharian.

that it covered and the length of time that it had existed. The larger the area of a language through time, the greater the linguistic change that might be expected. It was impossible to imagine an unchanging language, here proto-language, stretching over a vast area for millennia. There was no conceivable way to explain why the Irish and the Indians should share the same vocabulary for both the wild and domestic animals of their respective worlds unless their linguistic ancestors had once been drawn from some more confined home. This presented a tremendous problem: where was the home?

The earliest attempts to resolve what has become known as the Indo-European homeland problem found it difficult to detach a solution far from the model of Noah and his sons. That the Near East was the seat of great Semitic empires indicated that this was not the area of the homeland, but one close to it could be devised if the homeland was placed farther east. The area from northern India to West Central Asia became the earliest preferred homeland solution. As Sanskrit was regarded as the 'oldest' Indo-European language and Asia as the traditional 'Mother of Nations', the homeland, one might argue, had to be in the vicinity of greater Iran and northern India. The most popular homeland solution was Bactria which was argued on the basis of linguistics and Indian mythology; to this, in 1826, Julius Klaproth added additional evidence: Chinese texts mentioned an ancient fair-haired and blue-eyed people living on their western borders and these might be our elusive Indo-Europeans.

The Homeland Moves to Europe

By the mid-19th century other theories were being promoted that looked towards Europe rather than Asia as the homeland. The first European solution, argued by Roger Latham, was grounded at least on a principle that was both reasonable and explicit. In the biological sciences, for example, if one sought to locate the geographical origins of a particular genus of plant or animal, it would be presumed to lie where there was the greatest genetic diversity since it is here that the genus should have existed the longest in order to account for so much change. In Latham's time, with only Indo-Aryan and Iranian known in Asia, it seemed far more logical to derive these two closely related stocks (Indo-Iranian) from Europe, where there was far greater linguistic diversity (number of different and not closely related languages), rather than the reverse. The distribution of a relatively uniform language group over a wide area suggested that it had only spread recently or we should have expected far greater differentiation. Hence, it was the Indo-Iranians who had spread east and south into Asia and not the Europeans who had spread west.

Latham's reasons for locating the homeland in Europe did not impress the academic world which, nevertheless, did eventually adopt Europe as the homeland, but initially for the most specious of reasons. By the 1870s the subject of race was in the ascendant and a series of scholars (and those not so scholarly) began to argue that the earliest Indo-Europeans must have been blonds and that tracing the origins of blond populations provided a way of tracing the spread of the Indo-Europeans. The trail led to the Nordic peoples of northern Europe and by the end of the century, a large and vigorous school of thought was supporting a homeland in the Baltic region. Support for a northern homeland was augmented by the linguistic argument that proposed that the homeland should lie where we find the Indo-European language that had changed the least, i.e. was closest to the original form and, consequently, had moved the least and been influenced by non-Indo-European languages the least. It was seen that although attested remarkably late (in the 16th century), Lithuanian was comparatively speaking the most conservative of the Indo-European languages. This, many argued, indicated that it had moved the least which confirmed that the homeland should be located in or near the Baltic.

Indo-European Culture

Throughout the 20th century, archaeology has come to play an increasing role in locating the earliest Indo-Europeans or at least providing various possible solutions to the homeland problem. What was essentially being sought were cultures offering an environmental, material and behavioural context which accorded well with that predicted by the reconstructed Indo-European vocabulary and also showed evidence of dynamic expansion.

The shared vocabulary of the Indo-European languages indicates the nature of their environment and culture at the time prior to their dispersal, or at least before the various languages had begun to diverge so far from one another that words could not pass as readily among them as if they had been inherited from a single parent. This reconstructed Proto-Indo-European indicates that its speakers lived in an area where at least some trees were known (alder, birch, elm, fir, hawthorn, maple, pine, yew and probably others such as oak). The wild mammals would have included hare, squirrel, beaver, mouse, fox, wolf, bear, otter, deer, boar and aurochs (wild cattle). Birds included crane, goose, eagle, duck and thrush, while there was a word for fish and trout. The early Indo-Europeans were clearly farmers and stockkeepers: they had a number of terms for cattle, sheep, goat, pig and dog, and the word for horse is generally taken to indicate the domesticated horse. Both milk and wool were among the products produced by the livestock. Agriculture is attested in the words for cereals, the sickle, quern, pottery and the plough. They dwelt in solidly built houses (we have words for house, door and door-jamb) and even some form of fortified enclosures. Material culture included weapons (bow, arrow, spear and dagger) and they had rudimentary knowledge of metals (copper, perhaps gold and silver), and possessed wheeled vehicles.

Their social vocabulary indicates that, upon marriage, a woman went to live with her husband's family and there is a fairly extensive list of kinship terms which some would argue indicates that the Proto-Indo-Europeans had an Omaha type kinship system (where generations were skewed, e.g. grandfather and mother's brother were designated by the same word). We have some indications of the vocabulary of exchange (including gift-exchange), strife, war and blood-feud to indicate the type of civil violence that played a part in their lives. Their concept of law appears to have placed particular importance on the maintenance of 'order', both cosmic and social. The vocabulary concerning religion attests the existence of a 'Father Sky' and a 'Dawn' goddess. Belief was expressed by the frozen compound 'to place heart', libations were offered to the gods and we have several words for 'pray' or 'venerate'.

Archaeological Solutions

Our capsule description of the Proto-Indo-Europeans derives entirely from what may be solidly attributed to the Proto-Indo-European linguistic period. As the level of culture clearly indicates a population familiar with domestic plants and animals, Indo-European dispersals could not have occurred before the beginning of the Neolithic, the inception of farming in Eurasia. The date for the Neolithic depends very much on geography as it appears earliest (*c.* 8000 BC) in Southwest Asia and most recently on the European periphery (*c.* 4000 BC). The fact that Proto-Indo-European also possesses words for the plough, wool, wheeled vehicles and probable exploitation of the domestic horse, points to a still more recent date, perhaps about 5000–3500 BC.

Matching the cultural picture of the Indo-Europeans gained from the evidence of language against the archaeological record of Eurasia has proved

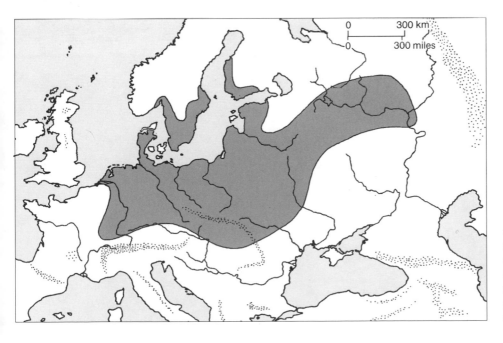

53. *The Corded Ware culture of northern, central and eastern Europe (dark shading) was once held to be associated with the earliest Indo-Europeans.*

a far more difficult enterprise than might be imagined. Most of the environmental items could be found almost anywhere in the temperate parts of Eurasia and the cultural indicators are only diagnostic if one knows precisely *when* Proto-Indo-European existed, since they were all eventually carried over Eurasia in the prehistoric period. Certain European cultures became particular favourites because they at least could accommodate the linguistic picture and they demonstrated dynamic borders. For example, the Corded Ware culture spanned Europe from the Netherlands to beyond Moscow in the period *c.* 3200–2300 BC (ill. 53). It possessed some evidence for horses, certain evidence for wheeled vehicles and the other items assigned to the Indo-European culture, and today it is still widely regarded as 'Indo-European'. But it is not regarded as *the* Proto-Indo-European culture since it does not explain the Indo-Europeans beyond its borders in the Aegean, Anatolia, the Eurasian steppelands, Iran, India or East Central Asia. Throughout the course of the 20th century there have been numerous candidates for Proto-Indo-European but few have presented a case robust enough to be still standing by the end of the century.

Currently, the prevailing theory cast in the traditional archaeological mould is known as the Kurgan theory which employs the *kurgan* (Russian for 'barrow' or 'tumulus', i.e. burial mound) as one of the cultural markers of Indo-European expansions. Championed most vigorously by the late Marija Gimbutas, this has fairly widespread support among both Indo-

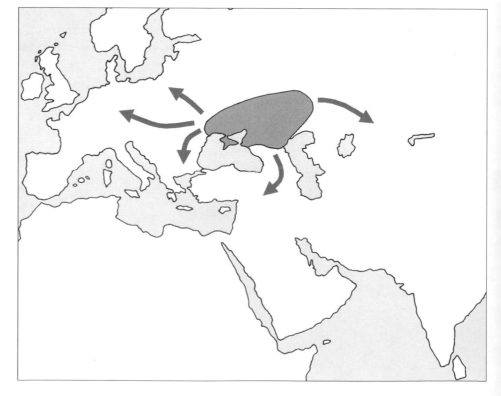

54. According to the Kurgan model, the Indo-European languages spread from a centre north of the Black and Caspian seas during the 5th and 4th millennia BC.

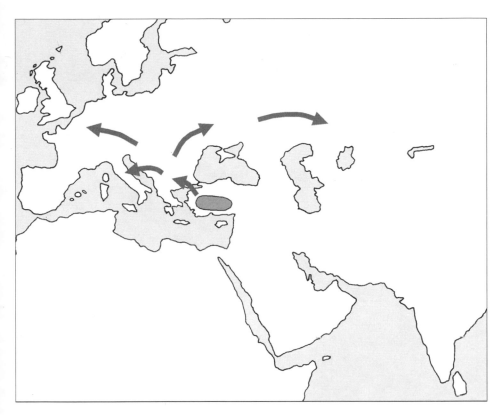

55. The Anatolian model of Indo-European origins suggests that the earliest Indo-Europeans came from the territory of modern Turkey in the 7th millennium BC and then spread through Europe, around the Black Sea and into Asia.

European linguists and many archaeologists. It proposes that the Indo-Europeans emerged from a hunting-gathering life in the region between the Dnieper and the Ural rivers where they adopted both agriculture and, more particularly, a mobile form of stockkeeping, including the domestication of the horse. From there they moved east into Asia to form the Bronze Age cultures that are ancestral to the Indo-Iranian languages. They are also reputed to have moved south, either by way of the Caucasus or around the western coast of the Black Sea, to enter Anatolia and spread the Anatolian languages. Finally, they are envisaged as having pushed into Danubian Europe in three waves from about 4500 BC to about 3000 BC where they either brought about a major transformation of culture to a more mobile lifestyle or they took advantage of a structural collapse in early farming systems to absorb displaced farming communities. Later in Central Europe Bronze Age cultures emerge which are held to be ancestral to most of the Indo-European languages of Europe.

More recently, the theory of an Asian origin has been resurrected which has some vogue, although is not particularly popular among Indo-European linguists who hold it to be incongruent with both the culture and time depth of Proto-Indo-European. It maintains that the spread of the Indo-European languages was coincidental with the spread of farming itself from Anatolia across Europe. This would push the dates for a European expansion back to nearly 7000 BC (Greece). It would see agriculture spreading north through

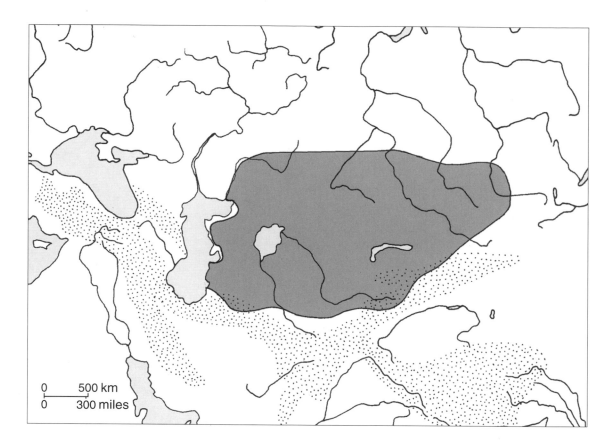

0 500 km
0 300 miles

56. The Andronovo cultural horizon of the 2nd millennium BC (dark tinted area) is often associated with a segment of the Indo-Iranian expansions.

the Balkans and then eastwards and, at least in the model as it is currently expressed, it would derive the steppe populations from earlier farming populations to their west. Once on the steppe, the explanation for the Indo-Europeans of Asia would basically follow the same model as the Kurgan theory, i.e. an expansion of Indo-Iranian languages by way of Bronze Age elites moving south from the steppe.

Indo-Europeans in Asia

Explaining how the Indo-European languages found their historical seats in Asia has proved extraordinarily difficult. All models that attempt to derive the ancestors of the Indo-Iranians from Europe (or via Europe if one adopts the Anatolian Neolithic theory) look to the west Asiatic steppe and forest-steppe as the Bronze Age staging ground for Indo-Iranian migrations southwards. Here one may point to the Andronovo culture (*c.* 2000–900 BC) which makes as fair a fit with the earliest Indo-Iranian society as one might wish. It offers us evidence for the type of pastoral, chariot-riding society that one encounters in the earliest Indo-Iranian descriptions of themselves. It also fills an area known to have been occupied by Iranians during the 1st millennium BC . Immediately south of these mobile steppe tribes lies a band of urban complexes stretching across West Central Asia. These were the Bronze Age descendants of earlier Neolithic farmers who pushed into the oases east of the Caspian and south of the Aral Sea, presumably from the highlands of Iran. We know that the Andronovo tribes were in contact with these Central Asian urban populations because we find Andronovo pottery on their sites and in some regions there is even evidence of steppe tribes settling down and adopting agriculture or at least leaving their burials in the valleys of West Central Asia. But what is missing is a clear trail of Andronovo or any other steppe culture farther south into the historical seats of the Persians, Medes and Indo-Aryans of north India. Here, arguments for immigrants from the north are muted and the best current working hypothesis is that as the steppe tribes passed through the filter of the Central Asian towns of Bactria and Margiana, they adopted the material culture of its Bactria-Margiana Archaeological Complex (BMAC) before passing farther south to spread their language. Some typical BMAC burials are found to the south on the approaches to northern India but a really solid case for such a migration is still far from a reality.

If tracing the arrival of the Indo-Aryans and Iranians in their 'home' countries were not difficult enough, both archaeologists and linguists have been completely incapable of explaining the arrival of the earliest Indo-European groups in East Central Asia. We must resolve these problems before the end of this book and a necessary step in the direction of any solution is to review the evidence for our final context – the archaeological record of Xinjiang.

CHAPTER FOUR

The Testimony of the Hoe

Early explorers such as Aurel Stein recovered mummified bodies near Lopnur where it was possible 'to look down on figures which but for the parched skin seemed like those of men asleep' (and more prosaically, he also discovered mummified mice who had died pilfering a grain-storehouse). Likewise, the German expeditions under von Le Coq uncovered the naturally preserved corpses of Buddhist monks who had been cut down during the 9th-century attempt of the Chinese to secularize society. The sands of the Täklimakan will no doubt yield more desiccated bodies of unfortunate travellers who were set upon by 19th-century bandits. The point of all this is that the mummies cannot be assigned to a single culture or period and we cannot understand them unless we place them within the general cultural context of East Central Asia. In this chapter we briefly survey the cultural evolution of society in the Tarim Basin as it is revealed through archaeological evidence, devoting particular attention to those

Mummies and their cultures

Site	Culture	Location	Date
Qäwrighul	Qäwrighul	Lopnur	2000–1500 BC
Töwän River	Qäwrighul	Lopnur	1800–650 BC
Zaghunluq	Zaghunluq	S. Tarim	1000–600 BC
Qizilchoqa	Yanbulaq (or Sidaogou)	Qumul	*c.* 1000 BC
Subeshi	Ayding	N. Tarim	*c.* 400 BC
Sampul	Sampul	S. Tarim	300 BC–AD 100
Ördek's	Krorän	Lopnur	?*c.* 300 BC–AD 300
Yingpän	Krorän	N. Tarim	300 BC–AD 500
Niyä	Sampul(?)	S. Tarim	0–AD 500
Astana	Khocho	Turpan	AD 300–700

A list of the major sites yielding remains of mummies and their different cultural and chronological associations.

cultures that have yielded mummified remains. In practical terms, unlike the standard trowel, spade or shovel familiar to Western archaeologists, the most frequent digging tool employed in the early excavations was that most Chinese of agricultural implements, the hoe.

Earliest Farmers in Gansu

As we will be going into a region whose archaeology still remains very poorly investigated, it will be easier to get our bearings by starting with the Tarim Basin's better-known neighbour to the east – Gansu, a Chinese province about the size of Germany or California. Along with Southwest Asia, Mesoamerica and South America, China is one of the centres of the Neolithic Revolution, the period in prehistory that marks the transition from a hunting-gathering economy to one based on the domestication of plants and livestock. The precise course of its transition is still obscure, although the heartland of early farming would appear to have been in northern China along the Huanghe (Yellow River) whose middle reaches in Shaanxi province offer some of the earliest evidence for agriculture in East Asia. By the 6th millennium BC, small farming communities had also begun to appear along the upper reaches of the Huanghe in Gansu. These are assigned to the poorly known earliest phase at the site of Dadiwan which was then succeeded by the local variant of the Yangshao culture, the best represented farming culture of the Middle Neolithic of northern China.

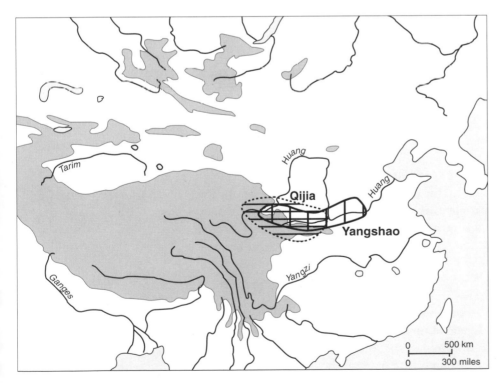

57. Early cultures of Gansu: the Neolithic Yangshao culture extended westwards into Gansu; the Qijia culture (marked with a dotted line) was the earliest Bronze Age culture of Gansu.

The Yangshao in this region extended from about the 5th to the 3rd millennium BC during which settlements increased in size and stability. The Yangshao farmers lived in rectangular structures and as many as 30 houses have been found in a single village. The economy included the raising of pigs and the cultivation of millet. Known to Americans as an animal fodder and confined to budgie cages by the British, millet was a major food source in northern China and was only gradually replaced by rice, which was domesticated earliest in the south of China. There was also weaving and pottery manufacture which included a fine painted ware tradition. Burials were near settlements and in Gansu might include extended inhumation or secondary burial, i.e. the mourners defleshed the bones before burying them a second time. Grave gifts were typically pots, and traces of wooden coffins have been discovered.

First Contacts with the West

The transition to the Bronze Age in Gansu is reflected in the Qijia culture (*c.* 2200–1600 BC). Qijia settlements reveal small houses, measuring about 10 sq. m (108 sq. ft), with their floors slightly below the surface of the ground. The economy included pig, the mainstay of the Chinese farm and menu, and the hunting of deer but now we also find cattle and sheep. The latter shows connections farther west as sheep are not native to China and had to be introduced either across the steppelands or through East Central Asia. Millet was still the primary cereal crop. Cemeteries figure prominently among the 450 sites attributed to this culture. They included pit graves and timber coffins (plank-built or tree-trunks); the deceased might be extended or flexed and were accompanied by a variety of grave goods – pottery, ornaments, tools, etc. – and animal remains, among which the jaws of pigs, followed by those of sheep, were especially popular. At Dahezhuang cemetery the graves yielded 194 pig jaws, 56 sheep, 6 cattle, 3 horse, 2 dog and several from wild animals; although in no way connected, the custom of depositing pig jaws, especially boars, with male burials (the original 'male chauvinist pig') is also found in some European cultures. Some copper tools were recovered from the cemetery at Huangniangniangtai. It should be noted that all burials so far uncovered in Gansu in this period are attributed to people of the Mongoloid physical type. For the purposes of the history of cultural and ethnic development, it is clear then that the 'ethnic' borders of Chinese civilization extended at least as far west as Gansu. But it should also be emphasized that the Qijia culture was in contact with peoples of the steppe to its northwest whence it obtained livestock (sheep, donkey and horse), metal implements typical of the Seima-Turbino horizon of the Eurasian steppe, and possibly even some of its burial traditions (also found elsewhere across Eurasia), for example, the occasional deposition of a man and a woman together in a grave suggestive of the practice of suttee, the execution of the wife on the death of her husband.

The Earliest Occupants of East Central Asia

In the meantime, what was happening in East Central Asia? The western extension of the major farming cultures of northern China can only be traced as far as Gansu and we are largely ignorant of the specific developments farther west. We are even uncertain when humans first settled in East Central Asia. Stone artifacts from near Tashkurgan have suggested to some that Palaeolithic (Ice Age) hunters may have crossed the Pamirs into the western reaches of the Tarim Basin but this is most uncertain. As the earliest evidence for human remains in the north and west Pamirs is assigned to the Mesolithic period, the era of hunter-gatherers following the last Ice Age that extended across much of Eurasia, it is more likely that this indicates when populations first began to settle in the west of the Tarim Basin. A more likely area of settlement would be the Jungghar Basin which, environmentally at least, resembles regions of Kazakhstan where we do have good evidence for Palaeolithic people, and recently Chinese archaeologists have claimed to have recovered some 600 Palaeolithic artifacts in the neighbouring Turpan Basin.

A large assemblage of microliths (small stone tools typical of the Mesolithic period) collected from north of Ürümchi has been tentatively dated on stylistic grounds to *c.* 9000–8000 BC. Other areas in the Tarim Basin have revealed similar tools which show stylistic similarities with Mesolithic sites in north Afghanistan, particularly in the Bishkent Valley. It is possible then that human colonization of the Tarim Basin may have been initiated from the west before the advent of agriculture in the region, but even this is very uncertain.

Setting aside the possibility of earlier settlement, Chinese archaeologists assign most of the evidence of the microliths in East Central Asia to the Neolithic period, contemporary with the farming communities of Gansu and farther east. As with the earlier evidence, most finds derive from surface collections where microliths and, on occasion, pottery have eroded out of the sand dunes. The meagre evidence available suggests that while their eastern neighbours were enjoying village life, those occupying the Tarim Basin were more mobile. Huts tend to be small and round, and communities probably subsisted primarily by hunting, fishing and, possibly, stockkeeping. Farming may have been practised but was unlikely to have been extensive since agriculture without irrigation is nearly impossible in this region. The origin of this Neolithic population, or at least, its economy, is also difficult to determine for certain. While some of the flint tools bear similarities with those of Inner Mongolia, we have already seen that the microliths also share close parallels with cultures from the west in northern Afghanistan. It is possible then that stockkeeping also entered the Tarim from the west, but this is impossible to determine without further evidence. All we can say is that when we do have positive evidence for domestic livestock (sheep) and cereals (wheat and barley) in the Bronze Age, these must have come from the west. The physical type of the population is unknown as there are so far no human remains from the Neolithic period, but again, when we do uncover evidence for human physical types in the Bronze Age, they are largely Caucasoid rather than Mongoloid. Not quite a smoking gun perhaps, but the circumstantial evidence suggests that it was from the west or northwest that East Central Asia was first settled.

The Bronze Age (2nd Millennium BC)

Our earliest mummified remains belong to the Bronze Age and here we need to pay close attention to their archaeological context. There is a series of regional cultures across East Central Asia that date to the period between 2000 and 400 BC. The evidence for the Bronze Age, unlike that of the Neolithic of the same region, is largely confined to burials which always leaves us with a one-sided picture of cultural development (archaeologists are used to this, however, since major areas of Europe are also far better represented by the houses of the dead than those of the living in both the Neolithic and the Bronze Age). If the dead were buried without grave goods, our knowledge of their way of life would be poor indeed but, fortunately, we do have some environmental, economic and technological evidence from the graves as well. Bronze Age communities enjoyed both agriculture and stockkeeping and, in varying degrees, provide evidence of metallurgy. The earliest bronze-working may well have come from the west (or more precisely, the northwest); it began to spread after 2000 BC and dominated industrial production everywhere in East Central Asia by about 1000 BC. Local sources of the constituent elements of bronze, copper and tin may possibly have been mined as early as the 2nd millennium BC, but it is not until *c.* 600–400 BC that we have certain evidence of local copper mining and smelting sites in East Central Asia. At Nurasay (Nulasai) the copper mine shafts extended tens of metres underground and were reinforced with timbers to prevent collapse.

In addition to this establishment of an industrial basis, we also look to the Bronze Age for the rise of regional centres, particularly in the vicinity of the oases, where our historical statelets first appear during the Han dynasty. Although our evidence for settlements is poor, the size of the cemeteries may possibly be seen as an indication of the size of social communities; if so, we can suggest that the later fortified towns of the Silk Road began to emerge in the Bronze Age and it is to this period that we may also ascribe the foundation of some of the major ethno-linguistic groups of East Central Asia.

Qäwrighul: Dawn of the Mummies

Archaeologists regard the Qäwrighul culture, known also in Chinese literature as the Gumugou ('Gully of Ancient Graves') culture, as among the earliest manifestations of Bronze Age settlement in the Tarim Basin.

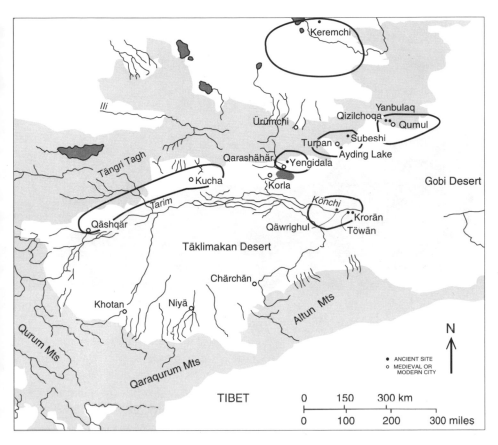

58. Cultures of the 2nd millennium BC in Xinjiang. The Qäwrighul culture centred on the Könchi River region; the Yanbulaq culture occupied the Qumul (Hami) region; the Ayding Lake culture lay to its west; the Yengidala culture centred on the Qarashähär region while the Qaradöng culture extended from Kucha westwards to Qäshqär; and the poorly dated Keremchi culture lay far to the north in the Jungghar Basin.

The culture was situated 70 km (45 miles) west of the great dried salt lake of Lopnur along the Könchi (MSM Kongque, 'Peacock') River, and is best known from its eponymous cemetery which dates to *c.* 2000–1550 BC. The culture occupies the region that coincides with the later kingdom of Krorän during the Han period. It is of major interest to us because it also yields the earliest evidence for Caucasoid mummies in East Central Asia and it shares some similarities with cultures outside the region, thus providing important clues concerning the origin of some of the peoples of the Tarim Basin.

At Qäwrighul excavations recovered some 42 graves which were divided into two groups. The larger group consisted of 36 burials in vertical pits. The Qäwrighul people placed their dead in the extended position on the sandy bottom of these pits; they then encased the bodies in coffins of wood (Euphrates poplar, *Populus diversifolia*) and sealed the top of the burial with animal skins, carpets or a basket-shaped cover. The remaining six tombs all belonged to males and they had a special surface feature: seven concentric rings of wooden stakes radiated out from the centre of the pit to provide what has been interpreted as a solar configuration some 50–60 m (164–197 ft) in diameter. In effect, this produced a forest of upstanding timbers with one of these configurations containing as many as 894 upright posts. Such alignments invite some form of cosmic interpretation, the

59. Circles of concentric posts mark out the later Qäwrighul burials.

arrangement of the posts reflecting in miniature some aspect of the world view of its builders.

The deceased wore ornaments of jade about their necks and wrists. Unlike burials from later periods which were dressed in trousers, coats and skirts, most of the Qäwrighul burials wore no clothing other than leather shoes; the bodies had been wrapped in woollen blankets. Organic objects such as baskets were preserved in outstanding condition. Moreover, in two instances – an adult woman and a child – the remains were sufficiently well preserved to be numbered among the mummies. The deceased were accompanied by a small bag of *Ephedra sinica* which was probably employed for medico-religious use. There are about 40 species of ephedra known across Eurasia and it has been found in association with hemp in Central Asian Bronze Age sites where it is believed to have been one of the primary ingredients of *soma* or *haoma*, the sacred drink of the Indo-Iranians. The effects of ephedrine, which is derived from the stem of the plant, tend to stimulate the metabolism and raise blood pressure. Its medicinal uses could include inducing perspiration, reducing fever and asthma-related coughing and protection against inflammation of the respiratory tract. It grows widely in the Lopnur region. The other grave goods provide what little evidence we have for the economic basis and material culture of its population.

The people of the Qäwrighul culture engaged in both agriculture (small baskets for wheat also accompanied the deceased) and stockbreeding (cattle, sheep, goat, horse and camel). This is a European or West Asiatic 'menu' which contrasts sharply with the typical north Chinese agricultural diet of millet and pork; the domestic pig would always be absent from the dry Tarim Basin. Wheat was domesticated in Southwest Asia as also were sheep and goats which were imported eastwards into China. The horse was domesticated earliest on the steppelands of Eurasia and would have derived ultimately from the north, while the camel came by way of western Asia and then east across Central Asia. The earliest evidence for its domestication derives from a settlement in central Iran dated to the 3rd millennium BC. Although the physical differences between wild and domestic camels are minimal, the presence of camel dung on a settlement site suggests that this was not likely to have been the result of a chance visit by a lost camel. Camels are recorded in north Kazakhstan by *c.* 1700–1200 BC. The Qäwrighul people hunted deer, wild sheep and birds, and fished. Crafts included leather-working, weaving of woollen fabrics, felt-making, and working in jade, wood and bone. Archaeologists recovered some fragments of copper but there is circumstantial evidence that much harder bronze tools were employed. The Chinese archaeologist Wang Binghua examined the markings of axe-blades on hard wooden posts and coffin planks and concluded that they must have been made by a much harder-edged instrument than a stone or copper axe; nothing less than a bronze alloy could have made the marks. Far to the northwest there are also chance findings of bronzes dating to the same period which derived from the great Andronovo steppe culture, for example, a hoard of 13 bronze weapons and tools was recovered from Toquztara in the Ili Valley which dates to *c.* 1500–1000 BC. There were five wooden female figures accompanying the graves (some were still wearing fragments of textiles and they clearly showed the whittle marks of a sharp carving instrument) and one of stone. Although there were containers of

60. The favourable conditions for organic preservation account for the survival of this superb woven basket from Qäwrighul.

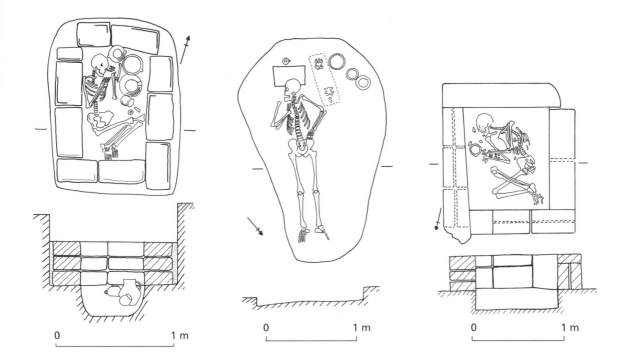

61. The three tomb types from the cemetery at Yanbulaq.

wood and evidence for grass-weaving (including basketry), there was no evidence of ceramics associated with the burials.

Archaeologists have uncovered similar burials from other nearby sites such as one next to the Töwän (Modern Standard Mandarin Tieban) River near the northern tip of Lopnur where a date of *c.* 1800 BC was obtained from the goatskin blanket surrounding the magnificent mummy of a 40-year-old woman, popularly dubbed the 'Beauty of Krorän'. Her people had set her in a shallow pit, only about a metre deep, which was covered with dried branches, reeds and sand. She was accompanied by a comb and a straw basket, while a huge winnowing basket covered her face. We will naturally have much more to say about the 'Beauty of Krorän' in the next chapters. The burial traditions exhibited at Qäwrighul persisted in this region into the 1st millennium AD and, as we will see later, suggest some form of continuity between the earliest settlement of the region and the emergence of the historical kingdom of Krorän.

East Meets West at Yanbulaq

A series of cultural groups mark the earliest Bronze Age settlements that were located in the oases to the east of the Tarim Basin. This was a region from which earlier microliths have been recovered, but evidence for continuity between the local Neolithic (if indeed the stone implements date to that period) and the subsequent Bronze Age cultures is still very uncertain.

Near the modern town of Qumul (Hami) is the Yanbulaq culture whose eponymous site, located near a spring which emerges out of the desert hillside to form a small oasis, yielded both a settlement and a cemetery. The settlement measured some 50–60 m (164–197 ft) on a side and was surrounded by a wall built of stamped earth and mud brick (which until 20 years ago was standing up to 5 m (16 ft) in height and is estimated to have stood up to 7 m (23 ft); local farmers have since quarried it away for top soil so that the only thing left is a single corner). The construction of the surrounding wall seems to have combined elements of two architectural traditions: mud brick is typically found among Bronze Age settlements of the Bactria-Margiana oases culture farther to the west, while stamped earth (*hangtu*) was the characteristic structural technique employed in ancient China. Outside the wall were found the remains of two rectangular houses (no larger than 4.5 m or 14 ft 10 in on a side) constructed of mud brick.

The cemetery of Yanbulaq yielded some 76 graves which its excavator separated into three different types (ill. 61). The graves of type I comprised large vertical shafts divided into two levels, the walls of the lower one built of earth and mud brick and separated from the upper chamber by wooden planks and reed mats. The number of burials in these pits ranged from one to nine. The community buried their deceased in the flexed position, on their sides with heads to the southeast. An abundance of grave goods, especially painted wares, accompanied the burials. The second type of grave revealed vertical shafts that had been simplified into a single chamber and there was less use of mud brick. Usually, only a single individual was placed in each grave, unlike the first type where single burials were rare. The deceased were deposited on their left side and the grave goods were reduced in quantity and included very little painted ware. The third type saw the use of mud brick largely confined to the base of the pit or as a lining; grave goods and the reduction of painted ceramics continued. The full range of artifacts across the three types was large and included knives, arrowheads, ornaments (agate beads, a silver hairpin, cowrie shells) and mirrors; metallic objects were fashioned from both bronze and iron. As was the case at Qäwrighul, wooden human figurines were also found.

Unfortunately, the date range of the site has been disputed: some would divide the cemetery into two main periods, *c.* 1750–1300 BC and 750–550 BC, while others suggest a single period of *c.* 1000–700 BC. And do the different types of grave reflect different periods or something else? This is an important question since Yanbulaq reveals our earliest encounter between East and West in the territory of the mummies. Analysis of the physical type of 29 adult burials reveals that the majority (21) were of Mongoloid stock, similar to the Khams Tibetans (rather than the Han, the primary ethnic group of China), and only eight were Caucasoid (one skull had a blond braid still attached). Anthropological study has revealed that the burials in the type I graves are exclusively Mongoloid while those of type II and III show the presence of Caucasoid populations, specifically related to those found at Qäwrighul. If the distinctions are chronological (and only one type II grave is stratigraphically later than a type I burial) then we may be witnessing the

62. Small wooden figures, both male and female, were recovered from among the Yanbulaq burials.

141

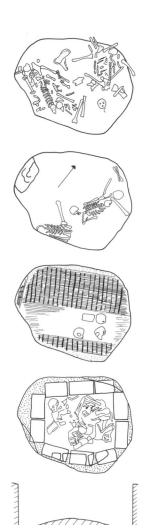

63. The brick-lined pits from Qizilchoqa comprised layers of buried remains and coverings.

movement of Caucasoid populations into a territory in which Mongoloid populations had already established themselves from the east. On the other hand, iron objects have been found in type I tombs and this would suggest that there may not be a great chronological distinction between the various types. In this case the distinctions in burials might be social or ethnic: Mongoloids burying their dead with many grave goods in larger chambers while Caucasoids adopted single-grave burial in less elaborate tombs. The painted ware is similarly mixed: some of the shapes are said to be related to ceramic styles in neighbouring Gansu while painted motifs have been compared with decorations found on ceramics in Ferghana. In short, in the cemetery at Yanbulaq we have clear evidence of two human physical types with Mongoloids predominating. We cannot be certain whether the Mongoloid type arrived earlier or what the precise ethnic or social relations between the Mongoloid and Caucasoid types might have been at this time. Cultural influences also appear to have come into the region from both east (ceramic form, stamped earth) and the west (mud brick, ceramic ornament, irrigation agriculture, western livestock). The presence of iron suggests that the culture should be dated towards the later part of the ranges indicated. One final observation about the Yanbulaq culture concerns the teeth of the deceased. Recent studies have revealed that some 50 per cent of those examined, both males and females, showed evidence of asymmetric wear on their teeth: instead of wearing down evenly, they were worn down at an angle, suggesting that they had experienced hard use, perhaps in pulling fibres or working leather with their jaws.

Some would associate with the Yanbulaq culture the cemetery of Qizilchoqa (Kezierqueqia) near the modern oasis of Qaradöwä (Wupu), some 60 km (37 miles) west of Qumul, where about a hundred tombs had been hurriedly excavated as of 1993. The cemetery was initially dated to *c*. 1400–800 BC but a recent radiocarbon date from a textile places the cemetery as late as 800–550 BC which could argue that the culture was closer to the lower end of the initially proposed span, and perhaps more easily assigned to the Tört Erik (Sidaogou) culture. The earliest graves were single burials in the flexed position that had been inserted into the base of a pit which was then covered with large logs smoothed on one side. The later graves comprised double burials in brick-lined pits; above was a second chamber whose base was sealed by reed mats that protected the burial chamber from falling sand and the top of the chamber was covered with timbers. The two chambers were dug down to a depth of about 2 m (6 ft 7 in). This cemetery also yielded mummies and extraordinarily well-preserved clothes (of which we will have more to say later) and other organic remains, usually Euphrates poplar. The mummified remains here are of a Caucasoid type with light hair and large noses. The hands, arms and upper backs reveal traces of tattoos, a trait again encountered slightly later among the Pazyryk burials in the Altai Mountains. Among the wooden objects found in the tombs there are also traces of wheeled vehicles such as three-piece disc wheels

64. This disc wheel from Qizilchoqa reveals the tripartite construction techniques encountered across Eurasia.

and hubs. There is no evidence to suggest that wheeled vehicles were independently developed in China and the general range of the earliest vehicles in Eurasia runs from Southwest Asia northwards across the Caucasus and then spans Eurasia from the Netherlands to the Yenisei (the Afanasevo culture or, more certainly, its successors, the Okunevo and Andronovo cultures). The large disc wheels mark the initial horizon of wheeled vehicles which persist alongside a later horizon of spoked-wheeled vehicles (c. 2000–1600 BC), particularly the chariot. A number of other features are reminiscent of the later Iron Age burials from Pazyryk, e.g. small wooden tables and trays, and a bronze mirror. Economic evidence comprises faunal remains from cattle, sheep, horse, donkey and camel, while flat cakes of millet and barley have been recovered. Timber remains of what is thought to be a plough some 90 cm (3 ft) long have also been recovered and among the wood, bone and leather remains is harnessing equipment. As we will later see, Qizilchoqa was one of the cemeteries sampled for ancient DNA.

Cultures of the Gushi (Jushi)

Some 300 km (186 miles) to the west of Qumul lie sites in the vicinity of the Turpan oasis that have been assigned to the Ayding Lake (Aidinghu) culture. The lake itself occupies the lowest point in the Turpan region (at 156 m (512 ft) below sea level it is the lowest spot on earth after the Dead Sea). According to accounts of the historical period, this was later the territory of the Gushi, a people who 'lived in tents, followed the grasses and waters, and had considerable knowledge of agriculture. They owned cattle, horses, camels, sheep and goats. They were proficient with bows and arrows.' They were also noted for harassing travellers moving northwards along the Silk Road from Krorän, and the territories of the Gushi and the kingdom of Krorän were linked in the account of Zhang Qian, presumably because both were under the control of the Xiongnu. In the years around 60 BC, Gushi fell to the Chinese and was subsequently known as Jushi (a different transcription of the same name).

There was variation among the different cemeteries of the region with some burials on wooden platforms or under timber beams and reed mats; other cemeteries revealed burials covered by small stone cairns. Burial was in the extended position, head to the west, and might occur singly or as a double grave. Black-on-red painted handmade ware accompanied the burials and there were also some wooden figures similar to those found in the Qäwrighul culture. The Ayding culture itself is dated to c. 1400–700 BC but part of the cemetery at Subeshi, commonly regarded to be related to the Ayding culture, must run later into the Iron Age c. 300 BC. The portion of the Subeshi cemetery excavated in 1992 consisted of some 40 low stone cairns covering burials set on wooden beds. There were special entrances into some of the burial shafts and goods from later burials included iron. Evidence of diet was graphically preserved in such forms as a bowl filled with millet and another containing the coccyx of a goat. Among the burials were seven very well-preserved mummies and the partial remains of some dozen more. One of the men wore leggings and woollen underpants and was accompanied by a bow in a leather case and a set of arrows with wooden, bone, horn and iron tips, apparently fashioned for different intended prey (ill. 66). The archery equipment is reminiscent of that of the Scythians that we have seen earlier. There was also the superbly preserved mummy of a woman clad in a fur-lined cloak and multi-coloured woollen skirt which dated to about the 4th century BC. As the Subeshi cemetery provides us with our 'three witches', we will have more to say about it in the next chapters.

Settlements in Yengidala

About 200 km (124 miles) to the southwest in the vicinity of Lake Baghrash (Mongolian Bostnur) are various sites of the Yengidala (Xintala) culture which dates c. 1700–1400 BC. Here we have evidence of settlement mounds,

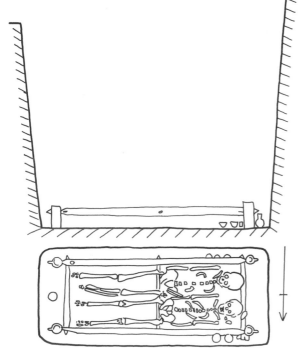

65. Double burial from a pit at Subeshi.

one at Yengidala 5 m (16 ft 5 in) high and about 150 m (492 ft) in diameter. Situated within the district of Qarashähär (Yanqi), the Yengidala group affords us our earliest picture of sedentary communities in the vicinity of this important oasis centre, one of the four garrison towns of the historical period.

There was evidence for wheat, millet and stone sickles and querns; domestic animal bones were also recovered. The finds include painted pottery decorated with geometric and zoomorphic (bird or fish) motifs as well as incised ware which has been likened to that of the Andronovo culture of the steppe. Surface finds of bronze implements such as a socketed axe have been retrieved. Unfortunately burials of this region remain unknown although some disturbed human remains are reported from Chokkur (Quhui).

Kucha

A farther 250 km (155 miles) was the Qaradöng (Haladun) culture which is so far known almost entirely from surface finds except for a small excavation at the settlement of Qaradöng itself. Here, near the major oasis town of Kucha, archaeologists uncovered timber-post-built houses, traces of millet, sickles, grinding stones, a distinctive red-on-white painted pottery and about a hundred bone artifacts (arrowheads, awls, etc.). The site is dated to *c.* 850–750 BC and is succeeded by settlement remains from the period of the Tang dynasty. Surface finds of similar stone tools and pottery have permitted archaeologists to extend the culture's distribution nearly 700 km (435 miles) to the west to the foot of the Pamirs. As with the Yengidala culture, there is evidence that the nuclei of the oasis towns were already forming many centuries before the historical emergence of the Silk Road. But, unfortunately, again we are unable to tie the evidence for the settlements with those from cemeteries, nor do we have any evidence of a continuous development which would take us from Bronze Age beginnings to the appearance of historically attested statelets.

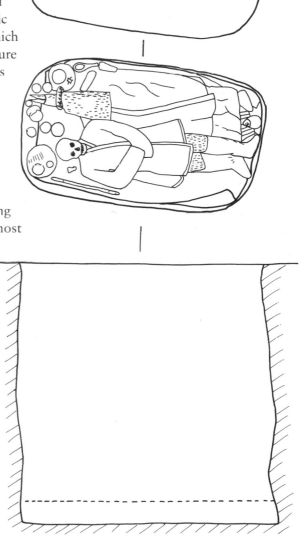

66. This burial from Subeshi included a woman with a tall peaked hat and facial covering, and a man, like her, dressed warmly for winter; both were accompanied by everyday utensils.

The Jungghar Basin

Beyond the Tängri Tagh and immediately north of the Tarim Basin lies the next major region of broad settlement, the Jungghar (Zhunge'er) or Yarish Basin (also known as Zungaria or Dzungaria), the region in which Bolton suggested lay the source of the winds beyond which the Hyperboreans so dear to the god Apollo dwelt. Early Greek geographical speculation aside, this area is critical in that it is one of the directions from which one might presume that 'European' cultural influences, including the people themselves, may have penetrated the Tarim Basin. What is found here is the poorly dated Keremchi (Ke'ermuqi) culture.

At the cemetery of Keremchi in the foothills of the Altai, archaeologists uncovered 32 graves which apparently spanned a very long time. The burials were either grouped or in single tombs, the latter sometimes covered with a stone cairn. Those burials found together might have been covered with stones laid flat on top or set within a rectangular stone or earthen enclosure. Generally, those set within the enclosures did not have a covering although a few did have round cairns over them. The pits consisted of vertical shafts whose base might contain either a stone or wooden structure. Large stone slabs were used to construct cists (box-like stone chambers), some of which were roofed with huge stone slabs. Sometimes, a smaller stone cist was inserted into a larger one. In other instances a rectangular wooden frame was employed. Burials were in the flexed position and decapitation is recorded with one cist containing no fewer than 20 headless individuals, presumed to be sacrifices.

In front of some of the cemetery enclosures and single burials stood a stone statue (*baba*) or simple long stones set upright. The *baba*, some of which revealed traces of human faces, usually faced east and stood in front of the stone burial chambers. The tomb architecture bears close similarities with cultures farther north in southern Siberia such as the Afanasevo culture of the Altai-Yenisei region, the later Okunevo and Karasuk cultures. Here too we find the erection of stone images associated with cemeteries. The ceramics are round-bottomed vessels decorated all over with impressions; these features are characteristic of the Afanasevo culture of the Yenisei-Altai region. Flat-based vessels display similarities with the later Andronovo culture and it has been suggested that the Keremchi graves, which are found widely dispersed over Jungghar, should be set to the 2nd millennium BC.

Whence the Bronze Age?

In this survey we have seen that in the period *c.* 2000–700 BC, the inhabitable areas of the Tarim Basin were occupied by communities practising mixed agriculture (wheat, barley and millet) who, at least in the northern Tarim, were establishing stable settlements in the vicinity of the later historically identified oasis towns. Excepting the Qäwrighul culture, the cultures discussed above are associated with painted wares and coarse wares that place them under the influence of both ceramic traditions in Gansu and those of the steppe regions to their northwest, in particular the Andronovo culture of Kazakhstan. Burials are in shaft graves, frequently prepared with timber or mud-brick chambers, and containing evidence of textiles, ceramics (excepting the Qäwrighul culture), wooden, bone and stone tools, some bronze, and animal remains. Burials tend to be single or double, either in the extended or flexed position. Mummified remains have been recovered from several different cultures, e.g. the Qäwrighul, Yanbulaq (or Sidaogou) and the most recent burials of the Ayding culture. The physical type associated with the earliest Qäwrighul burials tends to be broadly Caucasoid, whose origins should lie farther to the northwest. The Yanbulaq cemetery near Hami also indicates the presence of Mongoloid physical traits in the northeast of Xinjiang. Whether Mongoloids occupied the region prior to the penetration by Caucasian populations is impossible to determine without evidence from Neolithic burials, but the fact that the earliest Mongoloid burials are largely confined to the east and that there are so few recorded from the Bronze and Iron Age sites (only 10 per cent of 274 skulls examined so far) suggests that they may well have entered the Tarim region from the east later than Caucasoid populations coming from the north or west.

If the weight of the admittedly patchy evidence is applied, a good circumstantial case can be made for a major influx of Bronze Age 'Caucasoid' populations whose subsistence basis (wheat, barley, domestic sheep, horse, donkey and camel), material culture (bronze and wheeled vehicles) and mortuary constructions were similar to those found across the steppelands and West Central Asia (e.g. wooden chambers, mud-brick constructions, concentric circles, *baba*, and stone-walled enclosures).

Contacts with the east, i.e. the Shang and Zhou dynasties, would appear to have involved some westward migration of Mongoloid populations and just possibly some impact on ceramic styles. On the other hand, the general trajectory of west-to-east movements, either through or north of East Central Asia, seems to have been far more important. Western livestock, the chariot and possibly bronze metallurgy would appear to have entered China from the west. Exchange relations specifically with the Tarim Basin are seen in the transport of jade from East Central Asia to the heart of the Shang empire. In the royal burial of Fu Hao (*c.* 1200 BC), 756 pieces of jade were deposited, the overwhelming majority of which derived from East Central Asia.

Late Bronze Age–Iron Age (1st Millennium BC)

The introduction of iron objects does not constitute a major break in continuity among the cultures of the Tarim Basin. Iron itself enters the region in the 10th to 7th centuries BC and the earliest iron artifacts show greatest similarities with those to the west in Ferghana; it also predates the

67. Distribution of major sites of the 1st millennium BC.

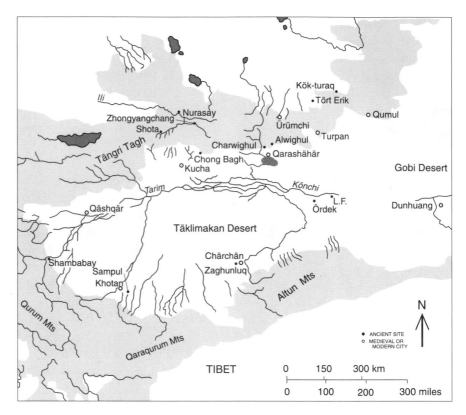

earliest appearance of iron in China. As we have already mentioned, in some regions such as the Ayding and Qäwrighul cultures, there is continuity of burial tradition from the 2nd millennium BC until the early centuries BC and AD; in other cases we define new cultural groupings but these are based more on ceramic styles than on major industrial changes. By the end of the 1st millennium BC we are able to assign some of the archaeological cultures with varying degrees of probability to historically attested ethnic groups.

Ördek's Necropolis

Our knowledge of the southern Tarim during the Iron Age is extremely limited compared with that of the northern rim. The survival of cemeteries similar to those of the Qäwrighul culture has already been mentioned for the southeastern Tarim. Aurel Stein discovered a burial similar to the earliest cemeteries during his excavation in the Lopnur region (Tomb L.F.4) and the Swedish expeditions uncovered a major cemetery which also included the remains of mummies. Ördek, an aged Turkish servant who had assisted Sven Hedin in his explorations at the turn of the century, was recalled into action in 1927–1928 (when he was 72 years old) to assist in locating a number of intriguing monuments that he had claimed to have discovered during his treasure-hunting expeditions. At first he failed to locate a cemetery he had described, even going so far as attributing its disappearance to supernatural

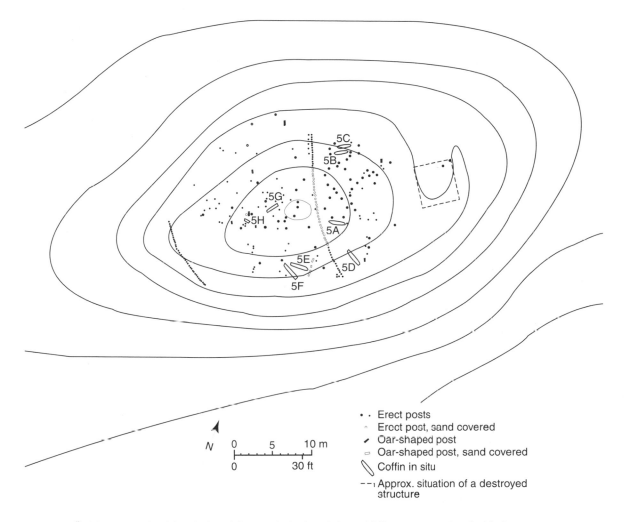

• • Erect posts
◦ Erect post, sand covered
↗ Oar-shaped post
▱ Oar-shaped post, sand covered
⬭ Coffin in situ
--⌐ Approx. situation of a destroyed structure

68, 69. Ördek's necropolis. (Above) Plan of the site. (Below) Upright and fallen posts associated with the cemetery.

70. Ördek's necropolis: the curved boards are from plundered coffins.

powers, but finally Cemetery 5, which the Swedish expedition dubbed Ördek's necropolis, was rediscovered.

Folke Bergman found there an entire sand hill with upright and fallen posts comparable to those marking the graves of the earlier Qäwrighul culture. He estimated over a hundred upright posts, on average 4.5 m (15 ft)

71. Two wooden
figures set upright at
Ördek's necropolis.

high and their bases, protected by the sand, were originally painted red.
Another 75 posts had fallen. In addition there were upright and fallen oar-
like objects. The top of the hill was littered with planks from wooden coffins
of which Bergman estimated there must once have been 120 although only
eight were found in place. The hill was strewn with human remains in

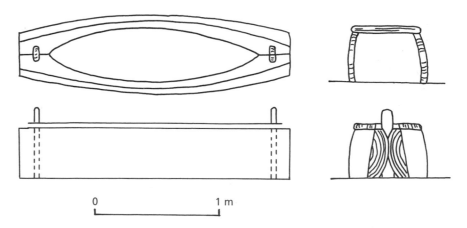

72. Plan of coffin from Grave 5A at Ördek's necropolis: note that it lacks a floor board but was constructed around the body rather than as a container for the deceased.

0   1 m

various stages of decomposition. The level of archaeological vandalism was staggering. Nearby were recovered wooden figures comprising a man 'with strongly marked features of a rather non-Mongolian character' and two female figures. Bergman undertook some excavation. The best-preserved remains were in Grave 5A. The mummified body of a young man, possibly killed by a blow to the head, had been lain in a pit in the sand and a two-piece tree-trunk coffin had been assembled around his sides while wooden planks covered the top which was in turn protected by a couple of ox hides. The coffin had no base. He wore a woollen mantle and a felt headdress tied under his chin; at his head was a small bag of wheat. Although millet and wheat were recovered from the burials, Bergman suggested that the economy was primarily pastoral and that, as the *Hanshu* relates, in this desolate region cereals had to be obtained from neighbouring states. However, the earlier Qäwrighul site which produced very similar interments also yielded remains of wheat, and we may still be dealing with mixed agriculturalists. The only ornament in the grave was an opal bead. A basket filled with the makings of millet porridge was also found. The young man clutched a tamarisk twig in his right hand, and grains of wheat and ephedra were strewn over his front. Four arrowshafts, without heads, were found under his back. Pieces of the ears of calves had been placed near his throat. The other coffins yielded similar contents with one possessing the a vulture's jaw and another yielding a complete horse leg. Scattered across the cemetery were other arrows (but tipped in stone rather than bronze), baskets and combs.

As we have seen, the association of timber uprights with the cemetery, the use of ephedra, grain baskets, and the absence of ceramic goods in the graves are all characteristic of the Qäwrighul culture. These burials continued into the period of the Han dynasty when the Chinese state began its expansion into Xinjiang. The most recent of such cemeteries is from Yingpän, approximately 200 km (124 miles) west of Lopnur, where organic vessels rather than ceramics were still found, and chambers were surrounded by wooden poles. But now the textiles included silk and cotton and there were iron artifacts which would date this cemetery to *c.* 300 BC–AD 500.

The Mummies of Zaghunluq

The remains that first inspired Victor Mair's interest in the Tarim mummies were discovered about 400 km (250 miles) southwest of Lopnur. Here lies the town of Chärchän (Qiemo Xian) where a cemetery of potentially several hundred graves has been discovered at Zaghunluq (Zahongluke). The region, previously well watered by the standards of the Tarim Basin, has since been reduced largely to barren desert. A combination of excavating for rock salt (the salt layer here is a metre thick) and treasure hunting has transformed the cemetery to a plain some 1.1 km by 750 m (0.7 by 0.5 miles) in size, scattered with textiles and other remains ripped from its tombs. In 1985 the Uyghur archaeologist Dolkun Kamberi and his colleagues uncovered five tombs, only two of which had not been looted. One of the tombs, a shallow shaft grave covered with a willow coffin, contained an infant mummy wrapped in wool who was accompanied by a drinking horn and what would appear to be a sewn-up sheep's teat that served as a primitive baby bottle; the head of a sheep had been deposited nearby. The more spectacular tomb (85QZM2) began

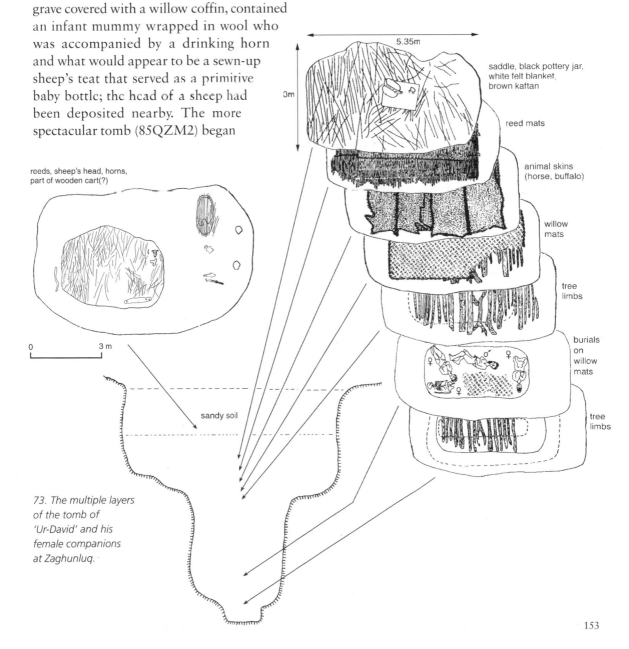

73. The multiple layers of the tomb of 'Ur-David' and his female companions at Zaghunluq.

with a large overpit and then a smaller lower pit. Below a thick layer of reeds and a wooden plank (with remains of a sheep skull, cow horn and pieces of leather) the excavators penetrated through five more layers of covering material. The first consisted of reed mats, a blanket and then a brown robe. Then came another layer of reeds and then a layer of skins of three different animals – a horse, an ass(?) and a buffalo or yak. Bound wooden twigs and then timber beams provided the final covering. Willow mats and branches served for a floor. Within the main burial chamber were the bodies of a man (Victor's 'Ur-David') and three women; the man and one of the women were in a remarkable state of preservation. Grave goods included a round-based clay jar, wooden combs, a milking pail, knitting needles, arrows and a variety of textiles. Less than 2 m (6 ft 7 in) away from the burial pit was another pit with the remains of the skull and foreleg of a horse, the latter of which had had the bone removed and the hide stuffed with reeds.

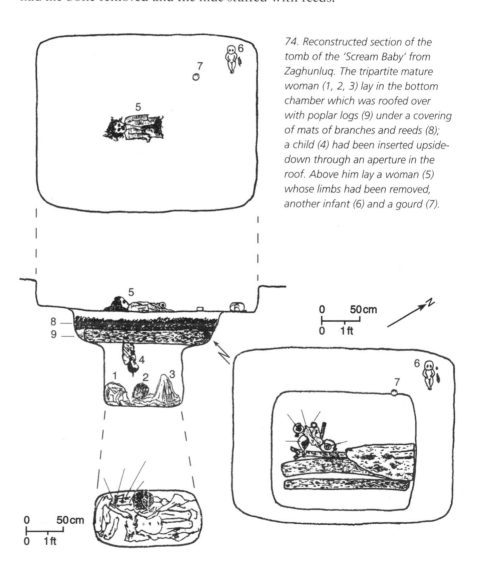

74. Reconstructed section of the tomb of the 'Scream Baby' from Zaghunluq. The tripartite mature woman (1, 2, 3) lay in the bottom chamber which was roofed over with poplar logs (9) under a covering of mats of branches and reeds (8); a child (4) had been inserted upside-down through an aperture in the roof. Above him lay a woman (5) whose limbs had been removed, another infant (6) and a gourd (7).

In 1989 He Dexiu uncovered two more tombs during rescue excavations. One of these included the remains of five skulls and a headless torso; the other tomb was, according to the interpretation of its excavator, even more dramatic (ill. 74). This tomb (89QZM2) was a large wide shaft grave divided into two layers. At the base of the pit was the main burial, the mummified remains of a mature woman whose body had suffered severe disturbance: her upper body had been severed from her lower body, the legs of which were flexed upwards, while the head had been removed and placed in the middle of the chamber near the wall (she has since been reassembled for museum display). In the upper chamber were two individuals who, the excavator argues, certainly did not appear to have gone gently. A young woman, about 20 years old, had her eyes gouged out and her arms and legs hacked off. He Dexiu notes that the woollen gown she was dressed in was bloodstained and there were hard lumps of congealed blood under her body. Through the floor of the same chamber a male infant had been inserted alive (according to the excavator) through a 30-cm (1-ft) wide hole in the roof and had died suspended upside down in the chamber, his eyes tightly closed and mouth wide open. A metre north of the young woman were the remains of a male infant lying naked on a woollen blanket; as with 'Baby Blue', this child had his eyes covered with small stones (green in this instance) and was accompanied by a cow's horn and a gourd with its top removed.

Accompanying a number of the graves are small bundles of sticks or reeds, usually around eight altogether, some of which had different coloured yarn tied around their tops or were kept in special cloth-carrying pouches. Their purpose has so far defied explanation but it might be recalled that both the Chinese classic on divination, the *Yi jing* (*I Ching*), and classical descriptions of divination practices among the Celts, Germans and Scythians, allude to the use of sticks for divination. So far, the remains of Zaghunluq have not been associated specifically with any other culture but its use of the double-chambered pit, timber, mat and hide layers, and animal remains are hardly far removed from the other cultures of East Central Asia.

Sampul

One of the four garrison towns and the major oasis centre of the southern Silk Road was Khotan, yet embarrassingly little is known about the region in which it sits before the opening of the Silk Road. East of Khotan itself, we find a local culture typified by a cemetery at Sampul (Shanpula). It is located near the administrative centre of Lop County (Luopu). Here a cemetery of 52 graves dated to about the 1st century BC has been excavated. The graves are divided into several types. Among the earliest were two large shafts measuring about 5 m by 4 m and 2 m deep (16 ft 5 in by 13 ft and 6 ft 7 in deep) containing collective burials of 133 and 146 people respectively. Accompanying the burials were textiles – felt, wool, silk and cotton – which included a rather amazing pair of trousers. These were fashioned from cut-

up tapestry (which, on the basis of their dyes and weave would appear to have been a western import), decorated with a centaur and a Roman-looking (others have suggested Saka) human face with blue eyes. The figure holds a spear against the right side of his body. Other objects of wood and bronze were recovered. There were also burials in timber-built graves and boat-shaped coffins. Anthropological analysis of 56 individuals from the collective burials indicates a mainly Caucasoid population similar to the Saka burials of the southern Pamirs. Smaller collective burials were also found with the deceased wrapped in reed mats while 41 burials saw individual secondary inhumation. Remains of wheat, peaches and apricots were recovered from the tombs.

The excavated portion is but a minuscule part of an entire series of cemeteries which stretches along a 1-km wide strip for a distance of about 23 km (14 miles). Many of the graves have been robbed and the entire area is littered with bones, textile fragments and other artifacts that have been dug up by local people searching for valuables, firewood or while digging new graves. The human remains contain sufficient evidence to identify the deceased as blond- or brown-haired and the number of burials originally interred is probably to be counted in the many thousands.

75. A pair of trousers from Sampul were fashioned from a cut-up tapestry portraying a Westerner (Roman?). Twenty-four different shades of thread were employed in its production.

New Cemeteries at Charwighul

In the western part of the former territory of the Yengidala culture, there emerges the Charwighul (Chawuhugoukou) culture which has been regarded as the prehistoric predecessor, dating to *c.* 1000–400 BC, to the state of Qarashähär, one of the garrison towns of the northern Tarim region. Whereas previously we had no evidence for burials, we now have them in great number in the five cemeteries recently excavated at Charwighul which were spread over an area some 10 km (6.2 miles) long. The cemetery at Charwighul I held approximately 700 burials while its contemporary, Charwighul IV, held 250. The dead were covered by low mounds encircled with stones. Altogether some 2,000 tombs have been identified in the area as belonging to this culture. The deceased were laid on their backs or sides in the flexed position, oriented to the northwest. The chambers of the pit were lined with stones with a plank floor and plank sides. The Charwighul people laid out their dead on a wooden platform and covered them with reed mats. As elsewhere at this time, collective burials were becoming increasingly more frequent with up to 30 individuals in a single pit in the later period of the cemeteries; analysis of the burials suggests that they may have

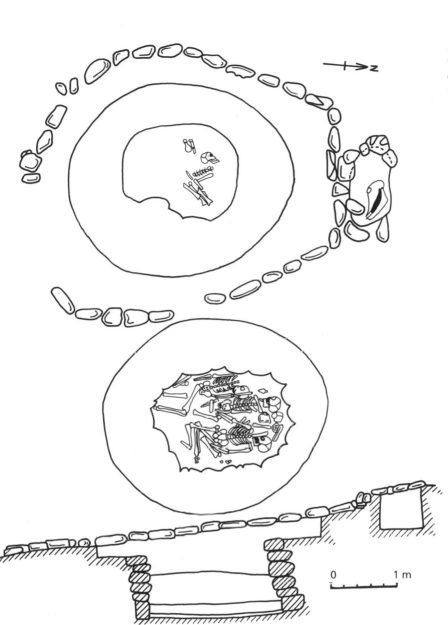

76. A Charwighul grave with a small sub-chamber containing the head of a horse.

been sexually segregated and males clearly predominated. Children were not normally admitted into the main burial rite in the earliest phases but were accommodated only in the later collective tombs. Small circular ancillary pits were sometimes placed about the main pit and here were found the remains of horses (skulls, hooves and sometimes an entire skeleton) or burials of infants. Near Cemetery IV were found ten large circular platforms erected out of stone to a height of 2 m (6 ft 7 in) and a diameter of 10 m (33 ft) that archaeologists presume to have had cultic significance.

Grave goods included pottery, both coarse wares and painted wares, among which spouted vessels, presumed to have served for preparing milk,

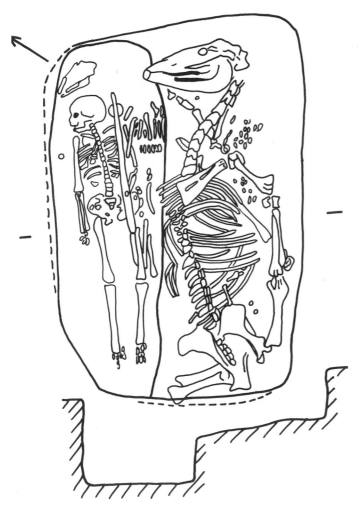

were quite prominent. Wooden objects (containers, arrows, a bow, weaving implements), bronze knives, weapons and ornaments of gold, silver or iron were also present. The finds included some bronze horse-bits and other material associated with horseriding.

The graves yielded remains of sheep, horse and, more rarely, cattle. The human remains, of which about a hundred have been studied, revealed a high incidence of dental caries and many trepanations, the technique of 'healing' an individual by drilling holes into his or her skull. There was also evidence for artificial skull deformation, i.e. lengthening the skull for ethno-cosmetic purposes. Cemetery IV, dated to about 500–1 BC, provided 77 skulls for analysis which were of European type. Cemetery III, with a different mortuary tradition and material culture, dated to about AD 200 and revealed mixed Caucasoid traits consonant with its identification (by some) with the Xiongnu.

The Charwighul culture reputedly shares ceramic parallels with cultures farther east in Gansu as well as to the north and west in Kazakhstan. The burial rite, in particular, with the use of lateral chambers for the remains of horses, is known from the Andronovo culture and among the nomadic cultures of the Altai in the 7th–6th centuries BC. The bronze horse-bits, well known from the northern steppelands, also direct our attention that way. It is, therefore, not coincidental that the Charwighul culture occupies an elevated tableland adjacent to a major pastoral route through the mountains and no agricultural tools have been found in association with the burials.

Closely related to if not included in the Charwighul culture is the cemetery of Chong Bagh (Qunbake), over half way between Qarashähär and Kucha. The cemetery consists of three fields of burial mounds whose dates range from *c.* 800 to 400 BC. The mounds vary in size from 20 cm (8 in) to 2 m (6 ft 7 in) high and from 4 to 40 m (13 to 131 ft) in diameter. Among some of the tombs, a circle of timber posts or stones was discovered inside the chamber which might be compared with the outer rings

77. This burial from Charwighul is accompanied by the complete remains of a horse.

surrounding the burials of the Qäwrighul culture in the eastern Tarim. The grave shafts were covered with logs and reed mats which were then topped with soil. As was the case with the Charwighul cemeteries, the burials were in the flexed position, collective (up to 42 in a single grave), and included subsidiary pits with either the remains of an infant or animals (horse heads, camel heads, sheep/goat and dog).

The economy was mixed with remains of wheat, grinding stones and iron sickles indicating agriculture alongside the remains of domestic animals. Wooden vessels, bronze and iron weapons (knives, daggers and arrowheads) and bronze ornaments were all recovered.

Sites of the Tängri Tagh

Assigned by some to the Charwighul culture but now treated as a culture in its own right is the Alwighul (Alagou) complex of sites situated near Turpan. The complex comprises three types of burials that span the period from *c.* 700 to 100 BC. The graves of the first type are low mounds with pits some 2 m (6 ft 7 in) deep and 2–3 m (6 ft 6 in–9 ft 10 in) in diameter, roofed with timber planks and with walls covered with pebbles. They hold from 10 to 30 burials, here in the extended position, heads to the west. There was excellent preservation of textiles, and occasionally of human hair. Animal remains derived from sheep, horse, cattle and camels while agriculture was attested by flax seeds. Pottery and a wide assortment of wooden containers and tools, including wooden fire drills, were also found alongside bronze and iron implements (knives) and ornaments (bronze plaques). The second type of grave was structurally similar to the first but also included timber frames on which the deceased were laid. Silks and lacquered cups attest to trade relations with China. Physical anthropology of the first two groups reveals primarily a Caucasoid physical type (47 skulls) against only seven Mongoloid skulls. The remains of the few Mongoloid individuals were found within the same tombs as the Caucasoids and if the collective tombs

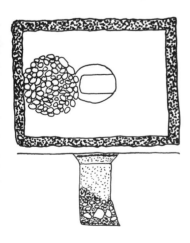
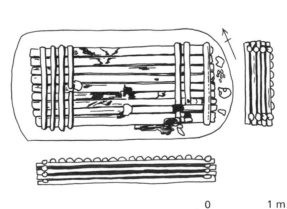

78. Plan and cross-section of an Alwighul grave of the second type of burial (left), with an elaborate wooden platform (detail right) upon which the deceased was placed.

0   1 m

79. This gold figure from Alwighul is in the characteristic 'animal style' of the steppelands.

reflected distinct social groups, then we may have evidence for intermarriage, which would hardly be unexpected.

Very different in structure were the later burials of the third type. Here there were four tombs covered with large stone cairns. The funerary chambers were vast, on the order of 200 cu. m. The base was filled with sand and stones on top of which was a large timber chamber built of pine and covered with a pine roof. The deceased, who numbered only one or two and who were not particularly well preserved, may have been covered with some red pigment. They were accompanied by a rich assortment of ornaments, particularly gold (of which over 200 pieces were recovered despite the fact that the tombs had been plundered) and some silver beads and plaques executed with figures in the 'animal style', the artistic style found widely across the steppe region. Other grave goods included silk and lacquered objects, attesting to trade with China, and the burials, presumed to be aristocratic, date from the 3rd to 2nd centuries BC. The architecture of the tombs bears close parallels with the royal tombs at Pazyryk in the Altai or the tomb from Issyk Kul in Kazakhstan while the ornaments are also clearly connected with the steppe cultures. It has, therefore, been suggested that these tombs should be connected with a pastoral people such as the Saka or Wusun who were pushed west by the Yuezhi and forced to migrate to the Ili Valley.

Across the Tängri Tagh

At the foot of the northern slopes of the Tängri Tagh lies the Tört Erik (Sidaogou) culture which dates to *c.* 1000–100 BC. There are traces of settlements in the vicinity of the oases along with tool-kits (stone querns, mortars, pestles, etc.) that clearly indicate agriculture (wheat) as well as stockbreeding (horse, sheep/goat). At Tört Erik archaeologists found a large circular building with stone foundations, timber posts and fireplaces; other structures were built in mud brick with wooden beams daubed with clay. An even more impressive settlement was found at Kök-turaq (Lanzhouwanzi) where the remains of a structure were found under a rubble mound some 30 m (98 ft 6 in) in diameter and still standing 2 m (6 ft 7 in) high. The building had a floor space of 200 sq. m (2,153 sq. ft) and was divided into several rooms. The walls were 2 m (6 ft 7 in) thick and built of enormous dressed stones (the larger stones were up to 1.5 m (5 ft) long and 0.5 m (1 ft 7 in) wide and high). In addition to the usual finds attesting to a settled agricultural economy, e.g. querns, wheat and painted ware, there was also found a bronze cauldron typical of the steppe cultures of this period. The structure contained the remains of seven skeletons (women and children only), suggesting the possibility that the building for the living (if it had ever really served as such) may have become a house for the dead, in effect, a kurgan.

80. The stone foundations of Kök-turaq.

The tombs consisted of low mounds, some 20–50 m (65 ft 7 in–164 ft) across and 1–4 m (3 ft 4 in–13 ft) high. As in the southern Tarim, we find collective tombs with the burials of a number of individuals. Analysis of the human remains from Tört Erik indicated that the physical type was Mongoloid, but at Kök-turaq it was Caucasoid.

The Saka

Finally, a series of tombs situated in the uplands where nomads may have pastured their herds and flocks have been attributed to the Saka. The southernmost of the sites assigned to the Saka is the cemetery at Shambabay (Xiangbaobao) near Tashkurgan in the Pamirs which archaeologists date to *c.* 900–400 BC. There are 40 tombs known, covered with stone cairns, under which the 17 inhumation burials have been identified as Saka while another 19 cremations have been attributed to the Qiang Tibetans. The putatively Saka tombs have their chambers lined with timber and are accompanied by coarse pottery, some painted ware, and various bronze and iron artifacts. Physical anthropological analysis has suggested that at least some of the population were of a Caucasoid type identical to the Saka of the southern Pamirs.

More numerous are the cemeteries attributed to the Saka situated to the north of the Tängri Tagh. They date from *c.* 555–250 BC, after which Chinese historical sources indicate that the Wusun were pushed westwards into the Ili Valley. There are a number of cemeteries where the details of the mortuary ritual varies considerably. At Zhongyangchang (the Sheep/Goat Stud Farm) there were 30 great mounds, the largest of which was 300 m (985 ft) in diameter and more than 10 m (33 ft) high. The walls of the funerary chambers were often lined with stones, and both timber compartments and traces of coffins have been recovered. The graves are rich in bronze and iron objects, both weapons and ornaments. Animal remains (sheep, dog, horse) are found in numbers. An anthropological study of the cemetery at Shota (Xiatai), here dated to *c.* 250 BC, revealed that 11 of the 13 skulls were Caucasoid while the remaining two skulls, both belonging to females, indicated Mongoloid traits. The remains from the cemetery derive from contexts that historical sources might identify as either Saka or Wusun (there is no apparent difference in the physical types). Also from the Ili Valley (at Künäs) comes the chance find of a collection of bronzes which included a cauldron, a bronze tray and a marvellous sculpture of a bare-chested man (Caucasoid) kneeling on one leg and wearing a wide-brimmed hat topped with a forward-facing crest and a pleated kilt (ill. 82). Perforations through his clenched hands suggest that he held weapons or banners. Items such as the cauldron are typical of the steppe cultures but we should emphasize that ascription of any given culture to the Saka generally rests on the geographical evidence of Chinese historical documents as well as elements suggesting pastoral nomadism and possession of accoutrements common to the Eurasian steppe cultures, e.g. 'animal style' art, horse-gear, arrowheads,

0   1 m
0   3 ft

81. The stone cairn or kurgan covering this tomb at Shambabay is typical of the steppe nomads.

cauldrons and bronze mirrors. Although sites or even cultures may meet the general requirements of the 'Saka', they tend to be so loose that it is always possible that we are dealing with different historical or ethnic groups, albeit inheritors or participants of the great Eurasian continuum of Iron Age steppeland cultures. Even if we cannot be absolutely certain of the ethnic identity of many of these more nomadic cultures, the material culture and behaviour (e.g. supine burial on mats or planks under a tumulus, sacrifice of mobile livestock) indicates that there was a continuum of steppe cultures that stretched from Herodotus' Scythians on the Black Sea east into the northern and western margins of the Tarim Basin.

Wusun

Burials from Mongghul Kürä (Zhaosu) have been specifically identified with the Wusun of the historical period. Here a cemetery of kurgans, arranged in a north–south row, has been excavated. They possess (like the Pazyryk graves) both an outer timber chamber and an inner chamber covered with felt. The deceased were placed in wooden coffins or wrapped in felt. Grave goods usually amount to little more than pottery and some small iron objects; occasionally, more richly furnished graves are known. The tombs have also yielded remains of silk indicating that this region had entered the exchange system of the Silk Road.

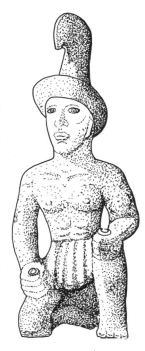

82. A bronze figure from the Ili Valley with a markedly peaked hat.

The 1st Millennium BC

The 1st millennium BC saw a series of cultural developments that help provide a connecting link between prehistoric archaeology and the emergence of historically identified peoples whose existence we have seen is first recorded during the Han dynasty. The evidence for settlements in the oasis regions becomes even more substantial and we clearly see contacts between the Central Asian farmers both with tribes of the steppe to their north and also with the Han whose luxury goods of silk and lacquerware begin to appear in Central Asian sites.

Cemeteries show a greater tendency towards large collective tombs. Many of the cultures discovered have been assigned, within varying degrees of latitude, to pastoral types, e.g. the Charwighul, Yanbulaq, Alwighul, Chong Bagh cultures and sites. This, it must be noted, is problematic since if most of our cemeteries are assigned to nomadic groups, these are the least likely to have produced the textual evidence of the 1st millennium AD; alternatively, those who established the agriculturally based oasis towns, the populations most likely to be reflected in historical sources and through their own written testimony, are those about whose burials and physical type we are most poorly informed. As for the physical types that have been examined from what are presumably pastoral cultures, we now discover not only Caucasoid populations as were typical for the Qäwrighul culture but also

Mediterranean types (Shambabay, Tashkurgan, Sampul and Krorän) whose origins are suspected to lie in the native populations of Central Asia, i.e. the area southeast of the Caspian, and who apparently penetrated the Tarim Basin by the southern route through the Pamirs.

From the cultural point of view, some of the bronze assemblages in the Tarim Basin and surrounding areas such as those recovered from Shambabay and Sampul are presumed to be related; the bronzes from Charwighul seem to have a different source and here also are some painted wares which may have been produced under eastern influence. Otherwise, the ceramic evidence as well as the structure of the tombs looks westwards to Ferghana and the lower reaches of the Vakhsh River. Taken in conjunction with the evidence of physical anthropology, it has been suggested that at about 1000 BC Caucasoid populations from south Tajikistan crossed the Pamirs and pushed along both the northern and southern routes through the Tarim Basin. Those in the north followed the Tarim as far east as Charwighul where they encountered Mongoloid peoples moving westwards while those in the south pushed beyond Khotan as far as Lopnur. In effect, they were establishing the Tarim's western link of the Silk Road.

The Han Period

The period of the Han dynasty (202 BC–AD 220) coincides with the struggle between the Xiongnu and the Han for control of what we have already seen were reckoned as the 36 towns comprising 'The Walled City States of the Western Regions'. An integrated archaeology of this period eludes us, although we do have the results of the exploratory-archaeological expeditions of the turn of the century. The major settlement excavated from this period was the site of Niyä which was explored by Aurel Stein (ills. 84 and 87). Here, over an enormous area (reckoned to be over 20 km (12.4 miles) in circumference) were spread houses of wattle and daub, the timber uprights still preserved after some two millennia (ill. 85). The site was divided into two sections, a smaller southern section with only 10–20 structures and a much larger northern section with several hundred structures. These were dispersed in clusters of three or four houses, stupas, iron-smelting furnaces, etc. Excavation of the houses, generally accomplished by shovelling out several feet of sand, revealed an incredible world of household items ranging from wooden cupboards, tables and chairs down to mouse-traps. Wooden tablets were recovered everywhere, written in both Chinese and Kharoṣṭhī Prākrit. These constituted a major archive of documents, and there was hardly a structure excavated which did not testify to the literacy of its population. Surrounding the houses were remains of their orchards (mulberry trees) and vineyards, while Chinese documents record the importation of *hu* (barbarian) grapes (box p. 169), gourds and peaches as well as alfalfa. The preservation of textiles from this period is abundant and it reflects not only native production of linen and wool but also the massive

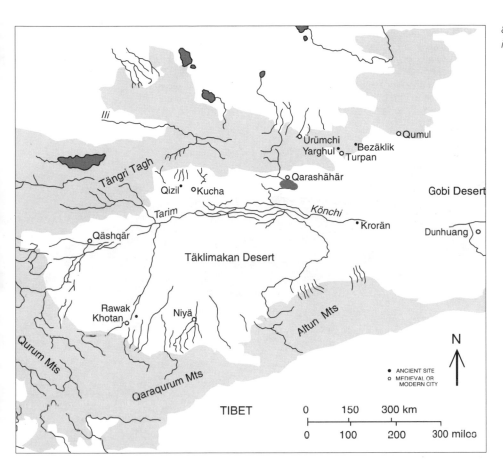

importation of silk. Several pieces of cotton, whose origin is uncertain, have also been recovered from Niyä. The artistry depicts possible Buddhist motifs derived from India but also dragons from the Chinese artistic repertoire. Silk has been recovered from tombs attributed to the Wusun in Mongghul Kürä (Zhaosu) and in the vicinity of Lopnur. Likewise, at Niyä were recovered a wide assortment of silks from the tomb of a mummified man and woman. Another important fibrous product invented in the Han period also appears in our region – paper, which began its inexorable spread westwards towards Europe at this time.

Another prominent site to see some excavation is the town of Kroran which was excavated by Sven Hedin, Aurel Stein and, most recently, by Hou Can. Its stamped-earth walls still stand up to 4 m (13 ft) in height and ran about 330 m (1,083 ft) on each side. It housed clusters of temples, the government central office, residential quarters and what has been dismissed as a 'slum'. Within 5 km (3 miles) of the town Hou Can uncovered seven tombs. Among the burials was a middle-aged woman who had a child placed over her head, reminiscent of the 'Scream Baby' excavated at Zaghunluq.

One other oasis town is currently under excavation. At Yarghul (Jiaohe), 10 km (16 miles) west of Turpan, archaeologists have been excavating

84. General plan of Niyä from the survey of Aurel Stein.

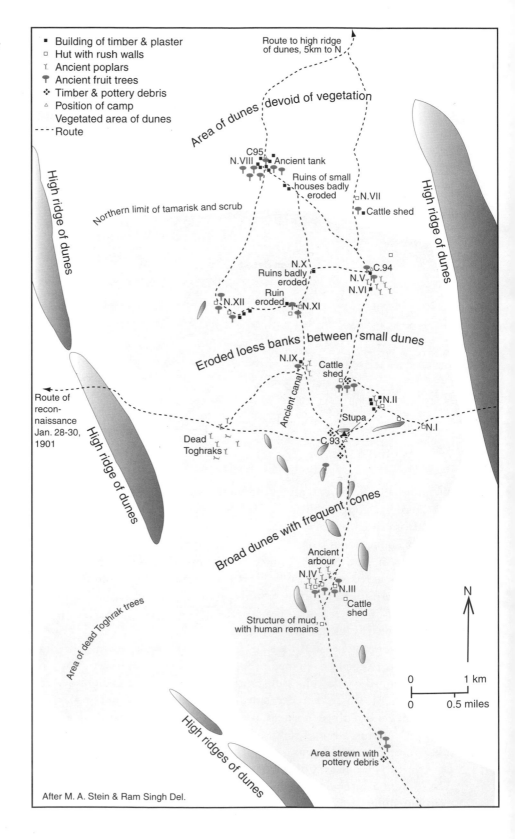

Legend:
- ■ Building of timber & plaster
- □ Hut with rush walls
- ⌇ Ancient poplars
- ⍊ Ancient fruit trees
- ❖ Timber & pottery debris
- △ Position of camp
- Vegetated area of dunes
- - - - Route

Route to high ridge of dunes, 5km to N

Area of dunes devoid of vegetation

High ridge of dunes

High ridge of dunes

C95
N.VIII Ancient tank
Ruins of small houses badly eroded
N.VII
Cattle shed

Northern limit of tamarisk and scrub

N.X
Ruins badly eroded
C.94
N.V
N.VI
Ruin eroded
N.XI
N.XII

Eroded loess banks between small dunes

N.IX
Cattle shed
Ancient canal
N.II
Stupa
N.I
Route of reconnaissance Jan. 28-30, 1901
Dead Toghraks
C.93

High ridge of dunes

Broad dunes with frequent cones

Ancient arbour
N.IV
N.III
Cattle shed
Structure of mud with human remains

N

Area of dead Toghrak trees

0   1 km
0   0.5 miles

High ridges of dunes

Area strewn with pottery debris

After M. A. Stein & Ram Singh Del.

85. The site of Niyä today still reveals upstanding timber walls.

remains of the old Jushi capital, a long (1,700 m (5,580 ft)) but narrow (200 m (656 ft)) town between two rivers. From the Han period they uncovered vast collective shaft tombs (one was nearly 10 m (33 ft) deep). The bodies had apparently already been removed from these tombs but accompanying them were other pits containing from one to four horse sacrifices, with tens of horses for each of the larger burials.

The industrial base, alluded to in Chinese annals, is also supported by archaeological testimony. We can see the strategic production of iron tools and weapons in the mines and foundries dating to the Han period which indicate the local production of iron and steel. With Chinese control there was initiated coinage which almost exclusively comprised the distinctive perforated coins of the Han dynasty. These so-called *wuzhu* coins are found all over the oasis towns which did not mint their own currency; the exception is Khotan where we find unperforated coins with a Chinese seal on the obverse and a horse or camel on the reverse, with an inscription in Prākrit (in the Kharoṣṭhī script) listing the name of the local Khotan king. These show Kushan influence but not necessarily power as the coins make it clear that the local kings regarded themselves the equals of those of Kusha itself.

Further vestiges of Han power are to be found in the archaeological traces of its army. The most obvious features are the tall watchtowers scattered across the Silk Road to provide advance warning of Xiongnu attack. They were built of stamped earth and some still stand to a height of 10 m (33 ft)

86. Han coin, one of the most typical finds of the early historic period.

87. Aurel Stein's plan of one of the house complexes from Niyä with its adjoining orchards.

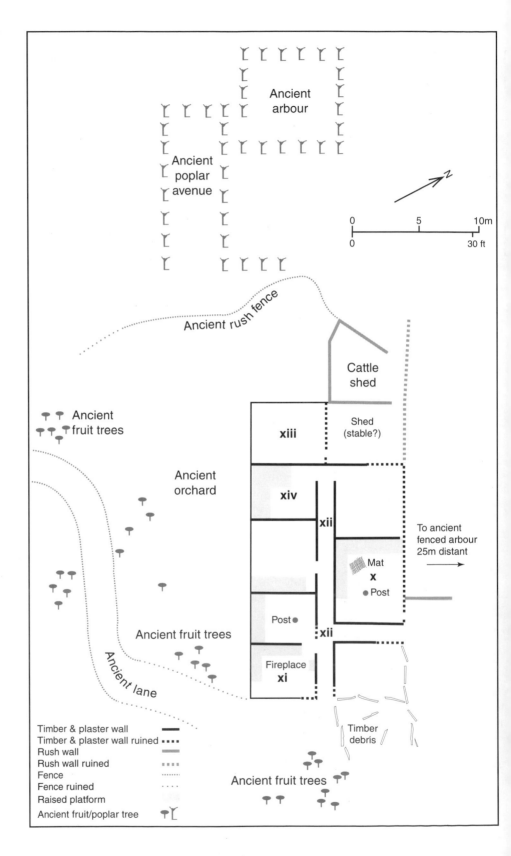

Ancient arbour

Ancient poplar avenue

Ancient rush fence

Cattle shed

Ancient fruit trees

Ancient orchard

xiii

Shed (stable?)

xiv

xii

Mat

x

Post

To ancient fenced arbour 25m distant

Post

xii

Ancient fruit trees

Fireplace

xi

Ancient lane

Timber debris

Timber & plaster wall
Timber & plaster wall ruined
Rush wall
Rush wall ruined
Fence
Fence ruined
Raised platform
Ancient fruit/poplar tree

Ancient fruit trees

or more. Atop was brushwood with which Chinese guards could send messages rapidly, using smoke by day and fire at night. The soldiers themselves were garrisoned in the *tuntian*, the military colonies established by the Han to be self-sufficient in terms of providing foodstuffs and also to augment the military protection of the west. The irrigation canals and field ridges of some of these sites can still be seen today and they provide rich areas for the recovery of Chinese military documents on wooden tablets. The irrigation systems of the walled towns are also traceable; in some areas they are known up to 100 km (63 miles) in length.

88. The Chinese maintained a system of enormous watchtowers to signal to one another and warn and protect against nomad incursions. This is the famous Han watchtower at Qizilqagha ('Red Crow') near Kucha, one of the highest (approximately 15 m (49 ft)) and best preserved in China.

Grapes

Grape vines grow naturally all over the northern Iranian region. The Chinese name for 'grapes' is *putao*, a non-native word which clearly has been borrowed from one of the Iranian languages, cf. Old Persian *batiák* 'wine vessel' and Middle Persian *bātak*. If the historical sources are to be credited, it is likely that the word came, along with the grapes, from Ferghana after the Han made contact with the region for the 'heavenly horses'. Viticulture was one of the important economic activities of the northern Tarim oases (recall the wine cellars of Kucha) and now that seedless Thompson grapes have been introduced to Turpan, they, along with the famous Qumul melons, are the most celebrated fruit of Xinjiang. The fame of the Tarim and Turpan grapes may be preserved in another word. The popular etymology of Täklimakan, the name of the vast desert of East Central Asia, is 'you go in but you don't come out'. But Turcologists have seen in the word either a compound built with Uyghur *tä(r)kli* 'abandoned' and Persian *makan* 'place', i.e. 'abandoned place', or *täkli* 'grape', i.e. 'grape place'.

The Buddhist Tarim (3rd–8th Centuries AD)

Much of the activity of the early explorer-archaeologists was directed at recovering artifacts from Buddhist shrines and temples. The exploration was museum driven, either emanating from a museum itself, as was the case with the German expeditions from the National Ethnological Museum in Berlin, or at least supported by museums, for example, the British Museum which paid some two-fifths of the £5,000 cost of Aurel Stein's second expedition, in expectation of receiving a corresponding percentage of the 'archaeological proceeds'. A large number of these 'archaeological proceeds' cover the period after the Han dynasty when Buddhist art and Chinese administration flourished side by side, expressed architecturally in the form of military colonies, forts and watchtowers on the one hand and Buddhist temples, stupas, cave shrines and secular buildings associated with the silk trade on the other. The material reported fills enormous volumes of accounts describing both the archaeology and also the means by which it was undertaken, frequently spiced with harrowing accounts of the expeditions' passages through glacier-blocked mountain passes or across deserts under conditions which would defeat a modern-day Indiana Jones. The following

89. A Buddhist stupa 23 km (14 miles) northeast of Kucha, the western member of a pair. This was the site of the famous Zhaohuli monastery, originally founded in the 3rd century, though the ruins seen today date from the 7th century.

is only intended to provide some of the archaeological flavour of the period in which many of the written documents were uncovered.

In the Lopnur region at Miran, Aurel Stein uncovered a fort of the Tibetan period, complete with an enormous quantity of Tibetan documents, and earlier monuments belonging to about the 4th century AD. These included a Buddhist shrine with seven massive stucco Buddhas (2 m (6 ft 7 in) across at the knees) as well as a number of stupas. The stupa was one of the most characteristic architectural remains of the Buddhist world; they are not found in Hinduism at all. In function we may view them as a specialized type of tumulus: they were circular in shape with a domed top and they were built to cover the relics of the Buddha, his earlier followers, or some other essential symbol of the Buddhist religion. It might be recalled that the Buddha was *Śākyamuni* ('Sage of the Śākyas' i.e. the Sakas) and, within an Indic context, Buddhism was a kind of 'Iranian heresy'. To the stupas were carried offerings, often letters, while the devoted performed their rituals, walking around the shrine keeping their right shoulders (*pradakṣiṇa*) towards the stupa. In the Tarim Basin the stupas were built of mud brick and then covered over with stucco which might be ornamented in relief, paintings and even gilding. The stupa spread with Buddhism to China and Japan and it inspired the development of the Chinese pagoda, both architecturally and linguistically. Sanskrit *stūpa* gave Prākrit *thūpo* which the Chinese variously treated as **tabo* or **sutab/po*, now simplified to *tā* 'pagoda'. They were a primary target of all the explorer-archaeologists. At Miran, Stein discovered a series of frescoes in an outstanding state of preservation depicting scenes from the life of the Buddha and his followers. These were executed in the Gandhara style, the figures reflecting Indians (complete with an elephant), Graeco-Scythians and even eastern Romans, the latter executed by an artist bearing the name of Tita (Titus) who, Stein argued, came all the way from the eastern extreme of the Roman empire.

In the northern Tarim, the expeditions concentrated on the religious shrines of the major oasis towns of Kucha, Qarashähär and Turpan. The German art historian A. Grünwedel divided the material recovered from this region (wood carvings, stucco sculptures, statues, wall paintings, portable art on fabric) into a series of broad art styles. The earliest were in the so-called Gandhara style with artistic motifs derived from the Kushan empire where a combination of Hellenistic, Iranian and Indic traditions all merged together. This style coincided broadly with the period of the Early Six Dynasties, the period in Chinese history between AD 220 and 386. It was followed by the so-called 'knights with long swords' (or 'Indo-Scythian' or 'Tocharian donor') style from *c.* 386 to the beginnings of the Tang dynasty in 618. It is the donor styles that interest us the most since so much of Buddhist art was broadly conventional no matter where it was produced. In contrast, portraits of local Buddhists bringing offerings to a shrine are of considerable ethnographic interest since they provide us with snapshots of the physical appearance, dress and other items of material culture of the

90. The cave shrines around Kucha have provided an enormously rich storehouse of both written documents and artistic relics.

native Buddhist populations. We will have good cause to return to these 'Tocharian donors' in a later chapter. The later styles coincide with Turkish (Uyghur) occupation of the northern Tarim.

The primary source of artistic representations, and certainly the most spectacular, are the numerous cave temples of the circum-Tarim, an architectural concept derived from India and represented in East Central Asia by more than a thousand sites. Two spectacular complexes were investigated in the vicinity of Kucha at Qumtura and Qizil. While traces of the Gandhara (and later Turkish) styles are present, the predominant representations are in the style of the 'knights with long swords'.

91. Sketch plan of Buddhist cave shrines at Qumtura by von Le Coq.

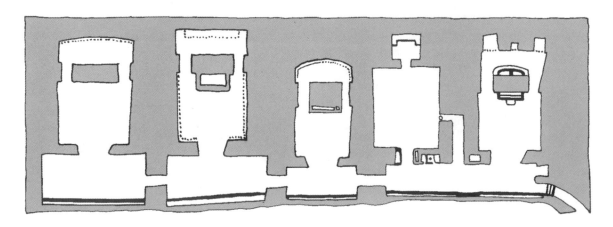

The cave shrines represent a warren of monastic life with not only shrines but also work-rooms and store-rooms, the last supplies of fruit, legumes and grain still preserved in their bins. The shrines comprise a series of chambers joined by a common passage with small windows confined to the monks' cells, all other rooms devoid of natural light. The typical chamber or cell has an entry gallery or porch and then a main chamber which may go back 20 m (65 ft 7 in) into the stone and carry a ceiling up to nearly 15 m (49 ft) in height. At the rear of the chamber would be the main cultic images of the Buddha, behind which a low corridor would be cut out to permit one to walk around the entire image. At the very rear is usually a statue of the Buddha in the reclining position, the *parinirvāṇa* ('perfect extinction'). The walls and ceiling would be painted with scenes from the Buddha's life and the presentation of gifts by benefactors.

The benefactors are depicted as Caucasoids with blond or red hair. The men wear long coats of brocades and a cape. Suspended on the left side of their chain-belts is a long sword with a cross-like pommel while a dagger hangs from the belt under the sword. The women wear tight bodices over a long flowing skirt . These frescoes date to about AD 700 and the figures are identified as the nobility of the people who left us the Tocharian documents. In some instances, Tocharian and Sanskrit instructions were written on the walls to indicate the positioning of stencils that provided the guides for the artists.

The other major oasis towns, Qarashähär and Turpan, have also produced a large quantity of cave shrines but here we find increasing representations of oriental types signalling the emergence of what Grünwedel described as the 'Old Turkish style' and the subsequent 'Late Turkish style'

92. Princes ('Tocharian donors') dressed in the Sassanian style, depicted on the walls of a cave shrine from Qizil. By this time the peoples of the region were Buddhists and cremated their dead.

Marc Aurel Stein

Sir Aurel Stein (1862–1943) was a Hungarian-born archaeologist and historian. A British subject from 1904, he was knighted in 1912. Stein's explorations in Central Asia were instrumental in revealing the fundamental importance of the region for Eurasian history. In 1892, as Principal of the Oriental College in Lahore, Punjab, Stein published the Sanskrit edition of Kalhaṇa's 12th-century *Rājataraṅgiṇī*, the only known extant ancient Indian historical work, and followed it in 1900 with his magisterial annotated English translation of the same work, *A Chronicle of the Kings of Kaśmīr*. Eager to supplement this meagre native historical tradition with knowledge gained by archaeological exploration, in that same year Stein embarked on the first of his four expeditions to Central Asia, journeying to Khotan. He meticulously mapped the early trade routes between China and the West and gathered a large quantity of invaluable documents and artifacts. He either carefully studied these himself or arranged for research to be done on them by the most highly qualified specialists.

Although Stein stumbled upon a number of ancient human remains in the Tarim Basin, he was basically uninterested in them because his main purpose was to elucidate classical history. Stein managed to convince Wang Yuanlu, the caretaker of the Dunhuang caves, that Stein's patron saint was the Buddhist pilgrim Xuanzang, even hinting that he himself was a reincarnation of the famous pilgrim. This gained Stein access to the caves where he was able to obtain precious manuscripts at ridiculously low prices; they are now housed in the British Library. Full reports of Stein's work during this period of his career were published in *Ancient Khotan*, 2 vols. (1907), *Serindia*, 5 vols. (1921), and *Innermost Asia*, 4 vols. (1928). These contributions would have been enough for a lifetime, but Stein went on to become Superintendent of the Indian Archaeological Survey (1910–1929), in which position he engaged in investigations of Alexander the Great's eastern campaigns and the identification of Graeco-Buddhist remains. Still not satisfied, Stein embarked on a study of ancient mounds in Iran and Baluchistan in an attempt to understand the relationship between the Mesopotamian and Indus civilizations. He also engaged in aerial photographic documentation of the Roman *limes* (frontier boundaries) in Iraq. When Stein was not in the field or doing research in museums or libraries, he was often ensconced in high mountain camps. Stein never married, devoting all of his attention to his research. He had a superabundance of energy and it was all channelled into finding out as much about ancient Asian history as possible. 'Furthermore, he was a ferocious writer of letters and dispatches. He had a positive mania for written communications and was known to have written between two and three thousand letters to a single correspondent. Stein thought nothing of marching thirty-five miles across country during the day, then pitching his tent and sitting up until four in the morning writing letters by the light of his portable lantern. As he penetrated deeper and deeper into unknown territory, he always took care to organize a complex system of runners and mail-carriers to maintain his postal links with his base, so that he was never out of touch with his sponsors; and he wrote so many notes and memoranda that one has the suspicion that Stein cowed officialdom by grinding it down, and defeating it at its own game.' (Severin, *Oriental Adventure*, p. 215). Approaching the age of 81, he finally received permission to carry out an expedition in Afghanistan but died while making preparations for it.

of the Uyghurs. This is particularly seen in the vicinity of Qarashähär and Turpan where pictorial representations of Asian physical features become far more frequent and the type of European figures encountered earlier at Kucha are few. We now find depictions of the new rulers of the Tarim Basin, the Uyghurs, who controlled much of the region from their capital at Khocho. But the local physical type still persisted. Adorning the walls of a temple at Bezäklik near Turpan as late as the 13th century we find, alongside the portraits of Turks, figures with the characteristic long noses, red or blond hair, blue or greenish-hazel eyes and the costume of the 'knights with long swords'. These are our most recent depictions of the physical type that we find across the Tarim Basin from 2000 BC onwards and it is now time to look the mummies in the face.

93. A female figure from one of the cave shrines (far left).

94. The artists of the cave shrines occasionally portrayed themselves at work (left).

CHAPTER FIVE

The Mummies Themselves

We have seen how Europeans and Chinese first learned of the lands of the Tarim mummies and we have briefly reviewed the evidence for the cultural history of the region and both the ethnic and linguistic groups known from our earliest historical sources. Now that we have established a context for our story, arranged the scenery and the lighting as it were, we can bring the main subjects of our book, the mummies themselves, back to centre stage. In this chapter we examine the reasons for their mummification, their numbers and their basic physical appearance while in the next two chapters we will consider the clothes they wove and wore, their possible genetic relations and their contributions to the modern population of the Tarim Basin.

How to Become a Mummy

The mummies of the Tarim Basin are primarily a product of nature rather than culture. It is the hot desiccating sands of the Täklimakan, the world's second largest desert, that mainly explain their remarkable preservation.

In most regions of the world when appropriate post-mortem steps have not been taken, death unleashes the digestive bacteria of the human gut which transform the corpse into a chemical factory producing gases and noxious fluids that flow out of the orifices, including the mouth and nose. The body can swell to two or three times its normal size, explosive pressures force the mouth open and the bloated tongue may protrude. The key problem, then, is the soft tissues, especially the entire digestive system, which must be removed to prevent rapid decomposition. Where we find artificial mummification, we usually find evidence for the removal of the guts, also often the brain, the remaining cavities might then be washed of blood and stuffed with some substance such as dried straw or, in the case of ancient Egypt, linen, to preserve the overall shape of the individual. The people of the Tarim Basin could have undertaken such remedies against decomposition had they wanted to: recall that at the site of Zaghunluq where some of the more spectacular mummies were recovered, those burying the deceased had removed the bone from the foreleg of a horse and stuffed the skin with reeds. But there is so far no evidence among the Tarim mummies for deliberate evisceration or removal of the brain.

Only two slight pieces of evidence suggest attempts to enhance the preservation of the deceased artificially. Multiple chambered tombs such as those at Zaghunluq positioned the deceased resting on wooden planks so that that the dry air could circulate over and under the entire body. This permitted more rapid evaporation of moisture and, generally speaking, there is a rough inverse correlation between depth of tomb or covering (amount of exposure to the dry air) and the level of preservation. At Qäwrighul, for example, the female and child whose remains were mummified had been buried at a depth of less than a metre while deeper graves yielded only skeletons. Moreover, traces of a fatty substance containing animal protein have been recovered from some of the best-preserved Zaghunluq and Subeshi mummies, as well as from the 'Beauty of Krorän'. Tian Lin, the conservator of the Ürümchi Museum, has suggested that this substance might have served as an anti-bacterial agent. The actual substance has not been identified but Elizabeth Barber recalls that a thin fish-paste was applied to some of the mummies of Peru (although here it may have served only as a binding for the thick mud paste that encased the body). The substance used to 'baste' some of the Zaghunluq mummies may have been ghee, a butter-like substance regularly employed in ancient India in ritual acts. It should be noted that the ethnic Chinese did employ artificial techniques of mummification in both the Han period and the much later Ming period (AD 1368–1644). Artificial mummies have been recovered from Hubei province (far to the east) and in Hunan (far to the southeast), where tombs were dug especially deep, densely sealed, lined and packed with charcoal, and chemicals such as mercury were applied to the bodies to prevent decay.

It is primarily, then, to the arid environment of the Täklimakan that we must look for preventing decomposition of the body. In a region where the annual average humidity is only about 5 per cent and it rains on average 35 mm per year, the production of bacteria is inhibited and putrefaction of the corpse ceases or is greatly retarded. The evidence for mummification indicates that the environment slowed down but in many cases could not instantly halt the natural processes of bloating. Mummies whose mouths are wide open and whose tongues protrude grotesquely are common enough. The people of the Tarim were well aware of this process and attempted to prevent the opening of the mouth with chin straps although, when made from an expandable material such as wool, they could not always be kept tense enough to hold the jaw in place against the swelling pressure exerted within the body. The need for holding the jaw shut might also explain why so many individuals are found wearing headgear, which often included a strap under their chins.

For the preservation of the flesh, Egyptian embalmers had recourse to natron, a hydrous sodium compound, i.e. a salt. Although it had originally been presumed that the bodies of the deceased had lain in a solution of natron, a sort of salty bath, it has since been proved that the natron was applied dry. How long precisely might vary but it fell well within the period of 70 days that historical sources suggest was required to produce a mummy. The curative properties of salt are, of course, well known and are also applied in the preservation of meat, which, from the viewpoint of a carnivore, is precisely what we humans represent. The ability of salt to dehydrate the body and retard bacterial growth is what helps prevent decomposition. In the Tarim Basin, such conditions could be found naturally, as the region is in essence an enormous dry sea-bed whose in-flowing rivers have deposited a tremendous quantity of salt. In the vicinity of Lopnur, the great salt marsh, are many deposits of salt and southwest of it we find the cemetery at Zaghunluq, now largely destroyed not only by treasure hunters but also by locals searching out deposits of rock salt. Thus, a combination of arid conditions and the high, at times almost pure, salt content of the soil has led to the preservation of the Tarim mummies. It might be noted that there are instances where it would seem that salt was the primary cause of mummification. Among the more recent discoveries of mummified remains (here of Mongoloid physical type), are two well-preserved dried-out bodies of gold miners of the Qing dynasty which were found in an abandoned mining shaft to the north of the Tängri Tagh. They had been tied with ropes, and their tools and even permission to pan for gold were found along with their clothing. Chinese archaeologists have suggested that a fight probably broke out over wages which led to the killings. Although the soil was wet, it contained sufficient salt to halt the growth of bacteria.

Time to Die?

There has been some debate among Chinese archaeologists as to whether there was also a seasonal factor in the preservation of the mummies. Wang Binghua, for example, has suggested that the freezing winter, which can drop to -30° C, might have inhibited the growth of bacteria in the mummies, hence the survival of some burials over others might be an indication of the season of their interment. He Dexiu, however, who excavated the more recent mummies from Zaghunluq, has suggested that it was the summer heat that would have been most effective as this would have provided conditions in which the mummies would have dried out all the faster. The fact that the Tarim Basin is dry *all* year round (at Zaghunluq the amount of evaporation is 135 times greater than the amount of precipitation) and that – as any forensic pathologist will tell you – one might expect the summer heat, when temperatures can reach +42° C, to accelerate rather than inhibit bacterial growth, provides better support for Wang's theory. In addition, if we employ clothing as circumstantial evidence for the season in which people were buried and preserved, we will see that quite a few of the better-preserved mummies appear to have been dressed for the winter cold (e.g. at Zaghunluq and Subeshi).

How Many Mummies?

Western publications have concentrated on a handful of the better-preserved, certainly better-dressed, mummies yet their numbers far exceed the small number that have graced the pages of the *National Geographic* or the Sunday supplements. For example, between 1959 and 1975 the Xinjiang Museum excavated 305 partially or well-preserved corpses from the cemetery at Astana near Khocho, the town that later became the Uyghur capital in the Turpan Basin. The graves date from the 3rd to 7th centuries AD and were apparently of Mongoloid extraction. Unfortunately, few of these have survived intact. Our two salt-preserved gold prospectors from the Qing (Manchu) dynasty of the 17th–19th centuries have also helped fill out the roster of mummies. A rough count based on an updated survey by Wang Binghua would suggest that about a dozen sites excavated over the past 40 years have yielded in various degrees of preservation something on the

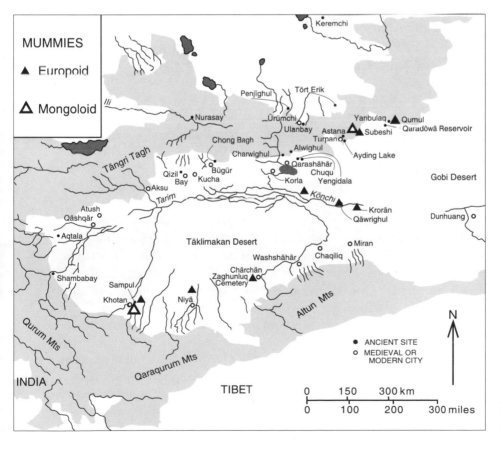

95. Distribution of the main concentrations of mummies in East Central Asia.

order of 500 mummies. To this we would have to add those reported in the expeditions in the earlier half of this century. These are occasionally depicted in the illustrated sections of the early reports but, as Folke Bergman relates, transportation difficulties rendered it impossible to bring the mummies back to Europe for scientific examination. Anyway, these numbers in many ways are still only a small proportion and readers sensitive to heritage issues may find what follows deeply disturbing.

The overwhelming majority of the Tarim mummies either have been or are currently in the process of being destroyed. In some instances, ripped from their graves and strewn over the ground like grotesque props from George Romero's *Dawn of the Dead*, literally hundreds of corpses could be found rotting in the sun at Ördek's necropolis or, more recently, at the cemeteries of Sampul and Subeshi. These are the human residue of treasure-seekers, salt-miners, farmers searching for fire-wood, and modern populations clearing ancient cemeteries of the heathen dead to bury the more recent and cherished 'believers'. Even if a mummy makes it past this first hurdle in its survival, the next, the lack of serious facilities for conservation, has radically reduced the number that actually reach environmentally protected museum cases. And the mummies hardly need look to the museums for sanctuary if they are to be unceremoniously dumped in the cellars to rot.

It is suspected that in some cases certain archaeologists and officials with their own political or racial agenda have been blatantly hostile to the discovery and preservation of these ancient 'foreign devils', especially when equally misguided Uyghur nationalists seize on them to demonstrate a more ancient claim to their territory than history allows. Now, before Western readers react with righteous outrage, they might peruse back issues of the letters column of the *Irish Times* when the major Viking settlement of Dublin was being threatened with obliteration and see how some correspondents shared a very similar attitude to the remains of 'pagan foreigners'. Far more explosive, indeed outright deadly, are the battles between Hindus and Muslims in India over whose tradition constitutes a national heritage worth protecting. As archaeology, originally defined as the study of the origins of peoples, by its very focus attracts so many racial or nationalistic agendas, we should hardly be surprised when *some* Chinese officials appear to prefer that the mummies of these troublesome foreigners dissolve under conditions of not-so-benign neglect. From their viewpoint, these were *hu*, 'barbarians', who contributed nothing to Chinese civilization in the past and represent an unnecessary distraction from its real achievements.

Sometimes the situation is so bizarre that it can only be true: access to an important set of mummified remains in the Xinjiang Museum in the provincial capital itself is blocked because the museum has let out half its space to a furniture store and has been forced to seal up its own storerooms with display cases! (Moreover, two-thirds of the parking lot in front of the museum has been leased to a truck and van dealer.) It fares no better with human skeletal remains: at the enormous multi-site cemetery of Charwighul, only about a hundred of the original thousand skeletons have been preserved for analysis and there are eye-witness accounts of the remains being tipped over the ridge on which the cemetery is located.

Altogether, we should probably be thinking in terms of at least several thousand mummies (not to mention tens of thousands of skeletons) that have already been uncovered in the Tarim Basin. Even with the enormous amount of destruction of human remains in Xinjiang, there still should be a very large sample of mummies calling for specialized study. What is so re-markable, however, is that apart from a few exceptions where Chinese scientists have undertaken admirably thorough examinations, there actually has been little analysis of these outstanding human relics. Only one or two have received the royal scientific treatment of Ötzi, the Tyrolean Iceman, or the bog bodies such as Lindow Man. If one is going to accede to the demands for scientific investigation and public education, hence admitting that there are legitimate reasons for removing the mummies from their graves rather than re-interring them, then there is clearly a responsibility to provide the highest standards of conservation and analysis. We will turn to those few about which something more can be illustrated and said.

The 'Beauty of Krorän'

The earliest Tarim mummies were those excavated at Qäwrighul cemetery and another site near the northern edge of Lopnur in 1979–1980. The dates run from *c.* 1800 BC down to the first centuries BC. Among the earliest, verified by radiocarbon dating, is a woman, popularly known in Uyghur as *Kirurän Güzäli* the 'Beauty of Krorän' (pl. IV) as she was found on the banks of the Töwän River in what later became the kingdom of Loulan (in Chinese) or, more properly, Krorän. She had blondish-brown hair and was dressed in wool and fur. Her hair, which was about 30 cm (1 ft) long, was rolled up within a distinctive headdress made of felt over a woven base and topped with two goose feathers. Scientific examination of the body indicated that she suffered considerably from head lice about her hair roots and pubic region and there were also traces of nits at the base of her eyelashes and eyebrows, so much so that the Chinese scientists who examined her wondered how they could have been tolerated by any living human being (of 18 mummies examined from the American Southwest, 8 also revealed head lice). Remains of one bed bug (*Cimex centicularis*) were also recovered. Her age was about 40–45 years and she measured 1.52 m (5 ft) which, taking into consideration some shrinkage, would suggest a live height of 1.56 m (*c.* 5 ft 2 in). Her dehydrated body weighs today but 10.7 kg or 23.5 lbs (the recommended 'live' weight for a small-framed woman of her height would be 47–52 kg or 104–115 lbs) which provides a graphic reminder of the extent to which human body mass consists of water (as a general rule the desiccated

96, 97. Reconstruction of the face of the 'Beauty of Krorän' (above), and the mummy herself (below).

weight of a mummy represents about 25–30 per cent of its live weight). Her skin was red-brown and smooth, and both the outer and inner layers of the skin were still in a very good state of preservation. An examination of her muscle tissue indicated that the level of preservation equalled if not excelled the level expected had she been preserved in formaldehyde; similar results were obtained from a large battery of scientific tests to which her skin, hair, muscles and internal organs were subjected. Examination of her lungs revealed a large quantity of charcoal and silicate dust: the combination of wind-blown sand and the smoke from indoor fireplaces did nothing to improve her health. She had been dressed in a woollen shroud and her feet were covered with leather boots, the fur turned inside. Accompanying her were a comb and a long, narrow straw basket. When discovered, her face and upper body were protected by a large woven winnowing basket. Above that was a 30-cm (1-ft) thick layer of branches, then a 10 cm (4 in) layer of reeds, then another 10 cm (4 in) layer of branches. The 'Beauty of Krorän' has become an icon of the Uyghur people who have claimed her (without any serious linguistic or cultural foundation but not without some genetic basis) as 'the mother of our nation' and her reconstructed face adorns national (Uyghur) posters.

Of equal antiquity, although not quite so well preserved, are the mummies of a woman and a child from the cemetery at Qäwrighul. The woman was about 20 years old. She had been wrapped in a woollen blanket and the only clothes she wore were a felt hat and fur shoes. Only her head is well preserved. Her hair and striking eyebrows are clearly blonde and red ochre had been applied sparingly to her face; particularly noticeable are two round dots on her forehead above her brows.

98. Young woman from
Qäwrighul cemetery
in situ.

Krorän

At site L.F. in his excavations in Krorän, Aurel Stein uncovered several burials compatible with those from Qäwrighul. The best-preserved was designated L.F.1, where a fence of planks marked a grave. At a depth of over a metre, Stein encountered the cow-hide covering of a coffin fashioned from the trunks of a toghrak tree. Within was the burial of a young man wrapped in a woollen shroud and wearing red leather moccasins. His hair was dark and wavy and there was a large cut over his left eye which may have been the cause of his death. Stein wrote:

99. Mummy of a man discovered by Aurel Stein at L.F.1.

It was not without a strange emotion that I looked down on a figure which, but for the parched skin and the deep-sunk eye cavities, seemed like that of a man asleep, and found myself thus suddenly brought face to face with a representative of the indigenous people who had inhabited, and no doubt had liked, this dreary Lop region in the early centuries of our era.

Stein compared him physically to the modern populations of the Hindu Kush and Pamirs (*Homo Alpinus*) while he was recently described as a 'Bohemian burgher' in a more popular archaeological magazine. The fact that his head was covered with a grain basket, and that he was wrapped in the same type of plain weave seen on the 'Beauty of Krorän' and accompanied by a bundle of ephedra renders him comparable with the other mummies of this region. The mummified remains of a young girl were uncovered at L.F.2 while a middle-aged man was found at L.F.4.

Now any of these mummies should have found coverage the equivalent of today's Sunday supplements yet they did not. Stein tells us why:

I greatly regret that the circumstances made it quite impossible to remove these mummified representatives of the old Lou-lan population. Even if we had disposed of sufficient time to improvise suitable cases from what ancient timber was at hand, no transport could have been spared to carry them with us to the land of the living. So I had to rest content with having the coffins carefully closed and the graves filled in again, putting blocks of clay on the top, to ward off as long as possible the ravages of wind-erosion.

Similarly, the feathered cap discovered with one of the burials (Nr. 36) from Folke Bergman's excavations in Krorän would also seem to belong to the same tradition as our 'Beauty'. Here an old woman was found in a hollowed-out log coffin and we can let the excavator himself describe her:

On the surface of the hill, particularly on the slopes, there were a lot of strange, curved, heavy planks and everywhere one stumbled across withered human bones, scattered skeletons, remains of dismembered mummies and rags of thick woven materials. Some of the mummies

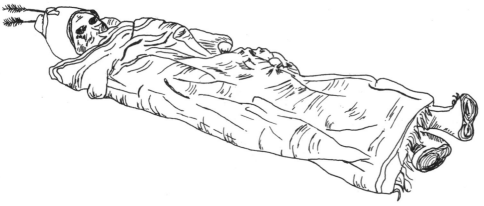

100. Woman from Folke Bergman's Burial Nr. 36.

had long, dark hair and incredibly well preserved faces, even an almost fair complexion. From others a ghastly-looking skull grinned out of a partly preserved blackened skin. I shall never forget the sublime expression on the face of a feminine mummy! On the dark flowing hair, parted in the middle, she wore a yellow pointed felt cap with red cords; her brow was high and noble, her eyes slightly closed, as if she were on the point of falling asleep; she had a fine aquiline nose and thin lips, slightly parted, and showing a glimpse of the teeth in a quiet timeless smile. How long had this 'Lady of the Inscrutable Smile' defied the roaring sandstorms of the desert, how often had she listened to the whistling of the wind in this 'Columned Hall of the Dead', how long was it since she closed her eyes forever to the dazzling and burning sunlight?

In his more prosaic description of the burial we find that Bergman had come across half a tree-trunk coffin that had been covered with ox hides rather than timber planks. Within was the mummy of an old woman whose long, grey hair had been parted in the middle. She was wrapped in a mantle of dark-brown wool and along the right side of the mantle, the fabric was tied up into three bags, each containing twigs of ephedra. The mantle was fastened by a series of wooden and bone pins. On her head was a cap of dark-brown felt with an outer cap of yellow felt decorated with two feathers. She wore raw-hide moccasins with lambskin soles. Among the grave

101. Young man from Bergman's Grave 5A. Note that the chest cavity has seen the greatest deterioration.

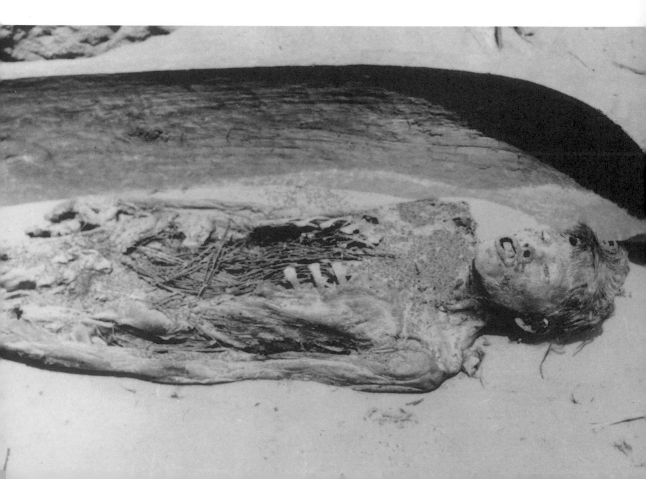

offerings was a wooden comb, a primitive 'rag doll', a ball of woollen yarn and a link of dark-brown hair.

Clearly related to these burials were those recovered from Ördek's necropolis, the surface of which was covered with 'withered human bones, scattered skeletons, remains of dismembered mummies, and rags of thick woollen materials.' The cemetery, numbered 5 in Bergman's system of reckoning, yielded the following mummies (indicated by letters).

Grave 5A, which comprised a mummy surrounded by the two sides of a split coffin, was that of a young man some 1.7 m (5 ft 9 in) tall. His hair was dark brown and tied back with a red string. His teeth were in good shape; not so his forehead where there was an obvious fracture. Although Bergman interpreted his wide grimace as a sign of his violent death, it is more likely to have been the result of post-mortem distortion of the facial features.

The young man wore a felt headdress with five feathers inserted into it, a loin cloth, mantle and ox-hide shoes, the last apparently never worn before. There was a small bag of wheat tied up in the top of the mantle near his head. A basket by his thigh contained millet porridge. There were calves' ears by his throat, grains of wheat and ephedra strewn down the decomposed centre of his body, and he clutched a tamarisk twig in his right hand. Under him were four arrowshafts without their heads.

The other human remains from this cemetery were in too poor a state to require description. All that remained of Grave 5E were the legs and feet

102. Woman with a well-preserved head from Grave 5K.

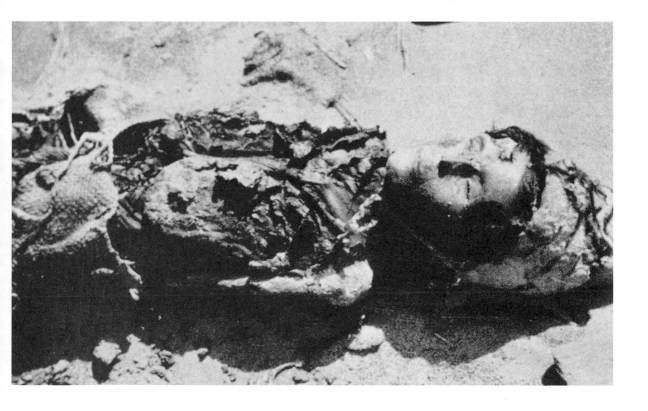

which were described as brown and hairy. The corpses in graves 5D and 5F had been dragged from their coffins by grave-robbers to decompose, and the latter was missing its head, but these other tombs all resembled Grave 5A. Among the human remains strewn on the hill were those of a young woman (from Grave 5K) whose head was still very well preserved (ill. 102). She had dark-brown hair, parted in the middle, and wore a headdress of yellow felt.

Qizilchoqa

This cemetery situated near Qumul (Hami) was excavated in 1978, 1986 and 1991 by the Xinjiang Institute of Archaeology. Of the 114 graves opened during this period, 11 have been regarded as complete corpses (mummies) and there are an additional 60 less well-preserved bodies. In 1995–1996 there were hurried excavations of additional graves, some of which did yield mummies, but there is neither word nor sign of their state of preservation. So far the range of radiocarbon dates suggests that the cemetery was in use during the period *c.* 1400–800 BC.

Among the best preserved of the mummies is that from Grave 24, dubbed here the 'Ravishing Redhead' because of her long red hair (actually, brownish-yellow and tied in a plait) but more mundanely known as the 'Hami Mummy' in Chinese scientific literature. She was curled up in the flexed position. She was about 35 years old and when alive would have stood about 1.6 m (5 ft 3 in) tall (her 'dead' height was 1.56 m or 5 ft 1 in). She has a narrow face, deep-set eyes, sharp nose and thin lips. Her hair is plaited in thick braids and trace-element analysis of her hair revealed remarkably large amounts of calcium. Possible reasons for this are many, including diseases such as hyperparathyroidism which decreases calcium in the bones while increasing it in the blood.

103. The best-known mummy from Qizilchoqa (often styled as the 'Hami Mummy').

A man, discovered in the late 1970s, is also on display in the Qumul Museum. His hair is reddish-brown, streaked with grey and piled on top of his head. He was about 40 years old, has a long, narrow head with deepset eyes and wears a bronze earring. His long fingernails attest that his was not a life of hard physical labour but that he was probably of noble birth. Like so many, he wears leather boots that go above the ankles.

Another mummy discovered in the late 1970s is that of a young female, about 18–20 years old. She has a rather flat face with high cheekbones and her hair, like that of the man, is reddish-blond. Her teeth show the pronounced overbite that is a European feature. She too has very long fingernails that had not been trimmed for a while, and even though account must be made for dehydration she still appears to have been extraordinarily emaciated, as though she had been ill for a long time.

Finally (and not on display but deposited in a storeroom) we come to the well-preserved mummy of a young woman in her twenties with dark hair. She stood under 1.5 m (5 ft) tall and her most distinctive feature is the elaborate blue tattoos on her right hand.

Zaghunluq

The mummies from Zaghunluq are dated *c*. 1000 BC, or possibly somewhat later to *c*. 600 BC, and are among the most spectacular recovered so far. We have already recounted the discovery of a male ('Ur-David'), several

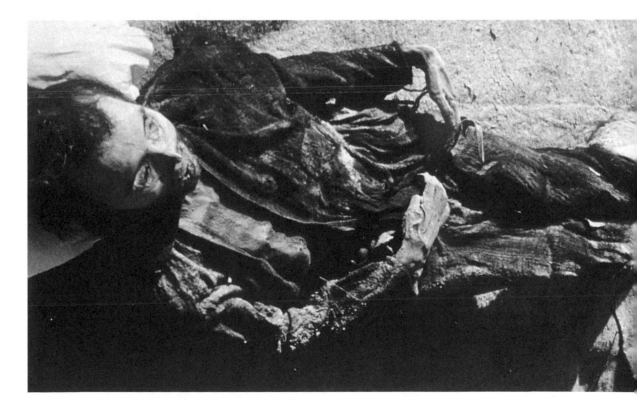

104. 'Ur-David' ('Chärchän Man') immediately after removal from his tomb.

females and a child in the same tomb. In his excavation report, the excavator claimed that the man stood close to 2 m (6 ft 7 in) in height, an observation that greatly impressed one of your authors. Unfortunately, this estimate would appear to have been considerably exaggerated unless the skeleton belongs to the 'incredible shrinking man', since the anthropological analysis of his stature indicates a 'dead' height of 1.76 m (5 ft 9 in); we can give him another inch or so when alive but no more. Well, how tall is tall anyway? While we may recall the report of the Singhalese trader to the Seres who described the people of the region as exceptionally tall, we should remember that this is purely relative and that, until the recent introduction of high-protein diets from infancy onwards, human stature had not increased markedly since the Neolithic (people were somewhat taller during the Palaeolithic). In Eileen Murphy's study of south Siberian (Caucasoid) steppe populations from the Scythian-Sarmatian period, where the number of burials provides a useful statistical sample, males averaged 169±3 cm, i.e. about two-thirds of all males ranged between 1.64 m (5 ft 5 in) and 1.78 m (5 ft 10 in) and the full range in males was 1.55 m (5 ft 1 in) to 1.8 m (5 ft 11 in). The human skeletal remains from 1,373 burials at the large cemetery in Shangma village (near Houma City in southwestern Shanxi Province) have been studied in detail by Chinese physical anthropologists. Since the dates of the Shangma cemetery are roughly contemporary with those from Zaghunluq and since the occupants of the cemetery consist of a combination of North Asian and East Asian Mongoloid types, data from this site offer

105. Blue and red cord around the wrists and five-coloured cord around the waist of 'Ur-David'. Note also the leather thong about the middle finger of the left hand.

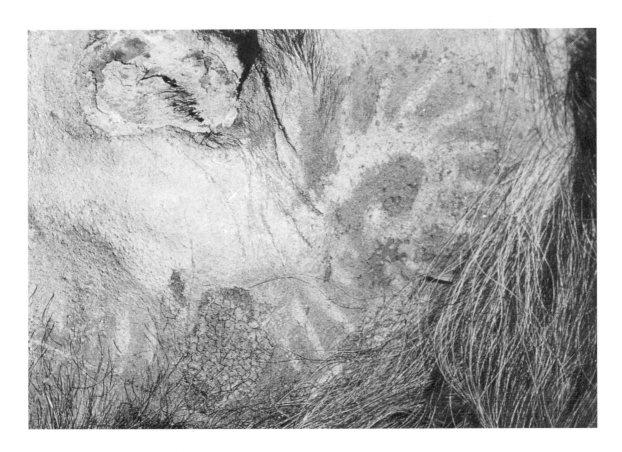

a valuable comparison with those from Zaghunluq. The average height of males from Shangma was approximately 1.65 m (5 ft 5 in) and they ranged from about 1.47 m (4 ft 9 in) to about 1.79 m (5 ft 10 in). 'Ur-David' would have been near the top of the scale for a North Chinese. 'Ur-David' stood 3–5 cm (1.2–2 in) taller than the average Bronze Age Irishman (1.73 m or 5 ft 8 in) and was taller than the largest of the Mediterranean Bronze Age people such as those from the royal shaft graves at Mycenae (averaging 1.72 m or 5 ft 7 in); contemporary Bronze Age males from Italy averaged about 1.68–1.69 m (5 ft 6 in). 'Ur-David' was on the tall side for his time but nowhere near the stature suggested by his excavator.

'Ur-David' lay extended on his back, his knees slightly bent and his hands lying across his abdomen, held in place by cords braided of red and blue strands of yarn that bound his wrists (pl. II, ill. 105). His hair was light brown streaked with occasional grey and he had a 2 in trimmed beard indicating that his society shaved, but hardly daily. In this he belonged to a similar tonsorial tradition to his male European counterpart, because it is also with the Middle and Late Bronze Age in Europe that we frequently find bronze razors on archaeological sites and accompanying graves. His hair was braided in two plaits (30 cm (1 ft) long and 5 cm (2 in) thick) that extended down his front. In an attempt to prevent his mouth from falling open, a woollen strap had been passed beneath his chin.

106. Ochre spirals ornament the forehead of 'Ur-David'.

His face had been painted with yellow ochre. Spirals were found on each temple and have been variously interpreted as sun-bursts (with even further extrapolation to sun worship typical of the early Iranians) or possibly schematic rams' horns, a very frequent motif in steppe art. The use of ochre in burials is a tradition which goes back to deepest antiquity and is found widely over Eurasia. Particularly prominent in the steppelands of the Ukraine and southern Russia, the major Copper Age culture, the Yamna culture, is also known as the 'Ochre-grave culture' as burials are frequently saturated in ochre. Interpretations of this practice are numerous (and invariably highly speculative), including suggestions that the colour of the ochre indicated life (red ochre is the colour of life-giving blood), death or the colour of the sun, or that the custom was a prophylactic against death (here obviously unsuccessful), a method of purification, or a means by which one might alter the appearance of the deceased through adornment to make them ready for the afterlife. Accumulations of ochre in the wrinkles about the eyes of 'Ur-David' might suggest that it was applied before he had died (and could screw up his eyes) but Paul Barber suggests that it is more likely that the ochre worked its way into the wrinkles during the post-mortem changes to his face before dehydration and total rigidity had set in. His grave was accompanied by two small bone spoons with a dish of ochre pigment, which would seem to indicate further that the ochre was applied after death. Other evidence for facial adornment is to be seen in the coloured strings of wool that apparently served as earrings.

Accompanying the main male burial were three females, one of which was also in an exceedingly fine state of preservation (pl. III). As with 'Ur-David', estimates of her height (1.9 m or 6 ft 4 in) by her excavator are wildly

107. The tattooed woman from the main chamber of the more recently excavated tomb at Zaghunluq.

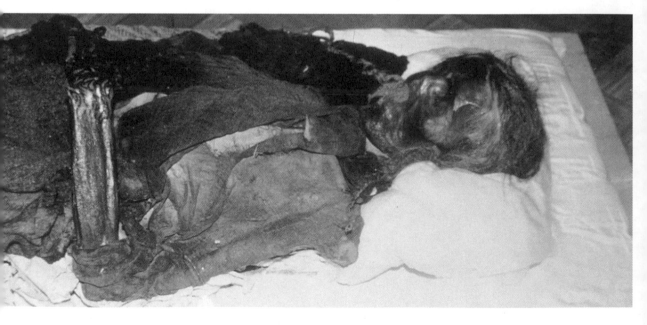

exaggerated and she is officially measured at 1.6 m (5 ft 3 in). Her height, then, would not have been exceptional and Eileen Murphy's study indicates that the average height of females in southern Siberia at this time was about 1.56 m (5 ft 1 in), i.e. 1.43 m (4 ft 8 in) to 1.54 m (5 ft 1 in) with the tallest woman set at 1.7 m (5 ft 7 in). If we wish to continue the comparisons that we made for males, then we could note that women in Bronze Age Ireland averaged 1.65 m (5 ft 5 in), Bronze and Iron Age Italian women averaged about 1.56–1.58 m (5 ft 1 in–5 ft 2 in), and the tallest of our Mycenaean 'princesses' was 1.61 m (5 ft 3 in). A woman of Mongoloid physical type and very delicate features, found buried in a Buddhist stupa near Subeshi (in Kucha district), has been claimed to have stood 1.9 m (6 ft 4 in) tall (incidentally, the *Guinness Book of Records* awards the tallest woman category to the Chinese Zeng Jinlian who measured 2.48 m or 8 ft 2 in).

The woman from Zaghunluq was about 55 years old. She had light-brown hair streaked with white. Her hair was parted into four braids, two of her own hair and two yellowish-brown braids that had clearly been obtained from another (and younger) woman; red wool had been woven into the ends of the braids. Her face was also painted, with a white stripe between her eyes and spirals on either side of her nose and even on her eyelids. Similar spiral motifs are to be found on other objects recovered from this cemetery, e.g. wooden spindlewhorls and on textiles. Like the male her hands were tied at the wrists as they lay on her stomach. Although her mouth had been strapped it had fallen open and her tongue protruded.

Of the two other women in the tomb, one had decomposed entirely into a skeleton while portions of the upper and lower parts of the third woman were still preserved.

The baby boy (known as 'Baby Blue') buried in a small pit a few feet away from the main tomb was aged no more than 3–6 months and was in remarkable condition, his tiny head with blond or light-brown hair peeking out from his blue woollen cap (pl. V). His nostrils had been stuffed with red wool. The doll-like appearance of the child is enhanced by the flesh-coloured paint that had been applied to his face. Most remarkable were the blue stones covering his eyes (Elizabeth Barber has suggested that these might indicate their colour). We might also keep in mind the practice of placing coins on the eyes of the deceased, a tradition in Central Asia that goes back at least to the Parthians and is also known in Mongolia. He was accompanied by what appears to be a sewn-up sheep's udder that served as a primitive baby-bottle and still preserved some milk solids.

The more recent (1989) excavations at Zaghunluq by He Dexiu uncovered what he has interpreted as a series of human sacrifices (adult women and a child) that were made to accompany a mature woman (pl. VII), who herself had been severed into several pieces (at the head and across the mid-section). She measured 1.7 m (5 ft 7 in) tall, with salt-and-pepper hair parted into two braids and tied up with red woollen string at the ends. Her thin black eyebrows appeared to have been recently painted. Her nostrils had been

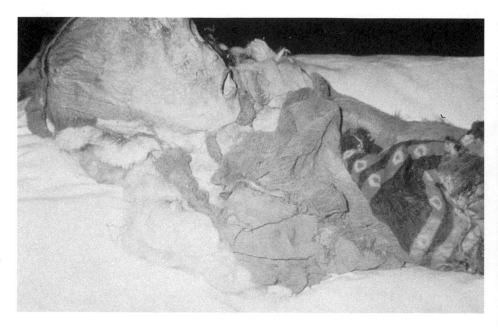

108. The infant who had been inserted head first into the chamber of the main tomb excavated in 1989.

plugged with tufts of wool to prevent post-mortem 'seepage'. Moon-shaped tattoos can be seen on her eyelids and oval tattoos on her forehead. Tattoos are also found covering the back and wrist of her left hand (pl. VIII). Her fingers appear to be exceptionally long.

Above her in the tomb, inserted face down, was the 'Scream Baby', a child probably over a year old (he had his lower incisors) who measured about 72 cm (2 ft 4 in). His blond hair included a very neatly woven braid on his head. To add to the gruesome tragedy, the child's chin had been strapped with a woollen band but it had failed in its task and the child's mouth was wide open. Equally poignant perhaps were the traces of tears and mucus on the infant's lower cheeks and below the nose. The open mouth and tears prompted the excavator to suggest that the baby had been inserted head first into the tomb of the older woman when he was still alive. But the open mouth, as we have already argued, could just as easily be explained by post-mortem changes and the tears and mucus might well have been produced by an ailing child before he died. He Dexiu's explanation is not one we would like to contemplate although it is still possible.

The woman who accompanied the burial was about 20–25 years old. She had long yellow-brown hair and her eyes had been gouged out. As her arms and legs were missing, she only measured some 80 cm (2 ft 7 in) long. Again we are confronted with different interpretations. The excavator prefers to see her as part of the interment, a form of human sacrifice, and there is certainly enough evidence for that across the steppelands during this same period. On the other hand, the mutilation – as was also the case with the main burial – may have been accomplished after burial. We know that throughout the Shang and Zhou periods, the desecration of the ancestors of one's enemy was a frequent pastime and this behaviour could well have extended to the

Tarim Basin where the preservation of the dead might also be seen as an ancestor cult (worth violating). Alternatively, the missing limbs might have a natural explanation; the deceased could have been buried elsewhere and only later removed to the tomb in which she was discovered, by which time her joints had decomposed and the limbs had been left behind (there were no chopping marks on her bones that might suggest deliberate removal of her limbs).

Subeshi

In the period 1991–1992 excavations were undertaken by the Xinjiang Institute of Archaeology at Subeshi where Lü Enguo is reported to have seen 23 corpses of which 7 were well preserved; of these, 14 reached the museum in Ürümchi but the lack of proper conservation represents a great danger to their continued survival. The remains date to about the 5th–4th centuries BC.

The mummies included a man who stood about 1.65 m (5 ft 5 in) tall. Capillary action, a normal process of decomposition, had forced his tongue to stick tightly against his upper teeth. His hands rested on his abdomen. Another male from Subeshi gives us a fine impression, both with respect to physical appearance and to accompaniment, of what a warrior looked like.

109. Male mummy from Subeshi; internal pressures have forced his tongue against his upper teeth.

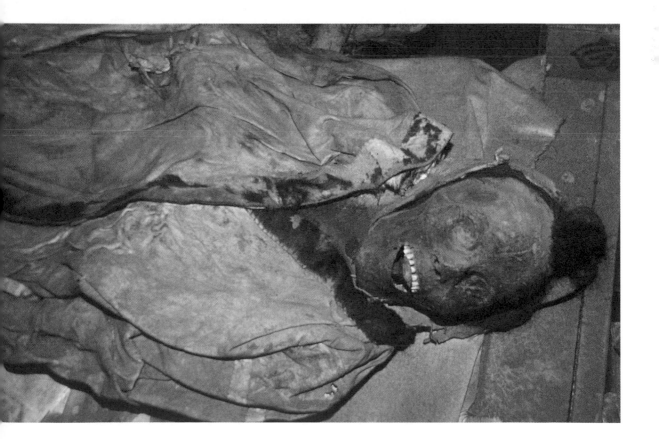

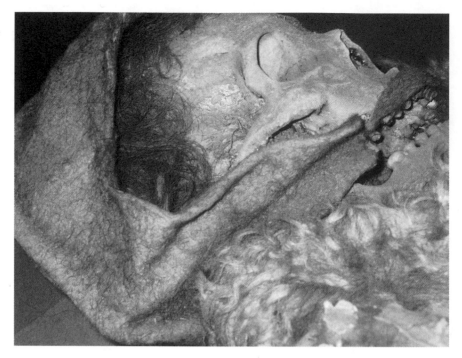

110. The 'Hero of Subeshi': a male warrior with a cap and fleece-covered coat.

Our 'Hero of Subeshi' was tough-looking, with light-brown hair beneath his felt helmet. He wore a very thick sheepskin coat (recall the arguments for winter burial, pp. 178–179) with the wool turned inside, and leather leggings. He was accompanied by a reflex bow in a leather case and arrows with wooden, bone, bronze and iron tips, the variety needed for different sorts of prey. There was also a woman 1.57 m (5 ft 2 in) tall, her hair in a net, wearing a woollen gown and white leather boots that covered her ankles.

Among the most spectacularly dressed of the mummies were three women who have been popularly identified as priestesses, although their headgear would mark them out as witches in Western society. The three women, tall and elegant, were crowned with enormous pointed hats. One possessed a double peak (which has prompted some local archaeologists to speculate that she had two husbands!) while another, recently relocated to the Ürümchi Museum, had a hat which was too tall to fit in her grave. Her hair was tied up in a hair net and the hat was removed and placed to the right of her chest. The peak was kept erect by sticks placed inside it. The woman was accompanied by a cosmetic kit (comb, etc.) which had been placed in a leather bag (ill. 112).

The preserved torso of another male (his body had been chopped in half by a bulldozer during road-building operations) was found with three curious surgical scars across his chest. The incisions, neatly placed and running horizontally for about 5 cm (2 in), had been sewn up with horse hair sutures but his wounds had not healed. Attached to his coat was a small bag with a brownish substance believed to be realgar (red orpiment) and in another

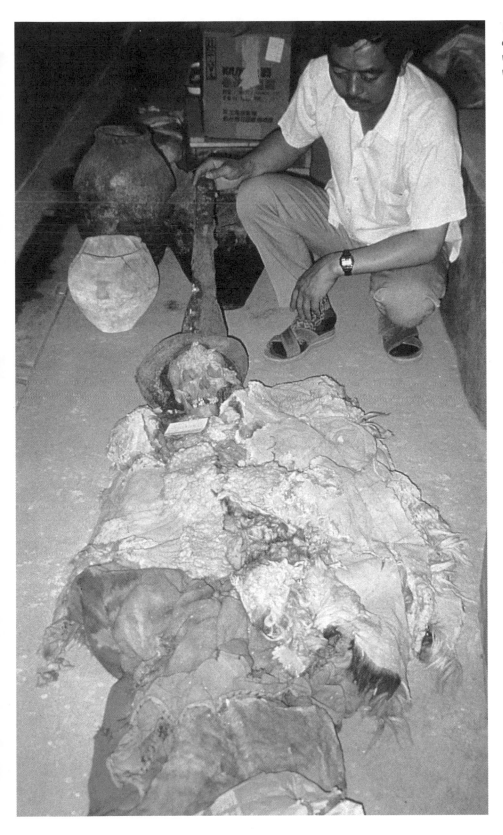

111. Lü Enguo, the excavator of Subeshi, with one of the 'witches' wearing a tall hat.

112. Subeshi cosmetic kit comprising whitener, rouge and a pointed stone for applying 'mascara'.

113. Torso of a man from Subeshi with surgical incisions sewn up with horsehair sutures.

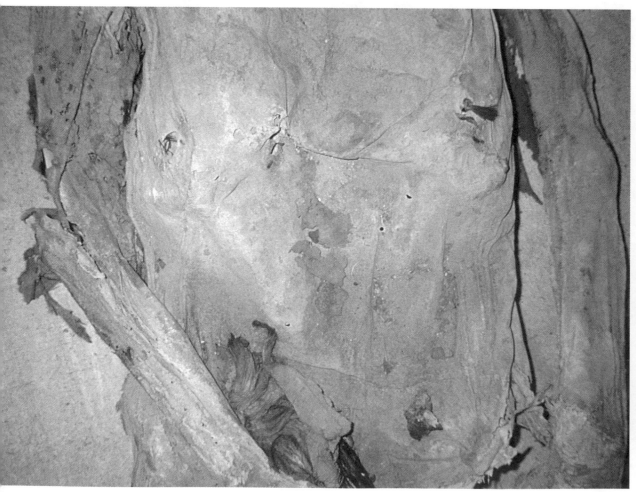

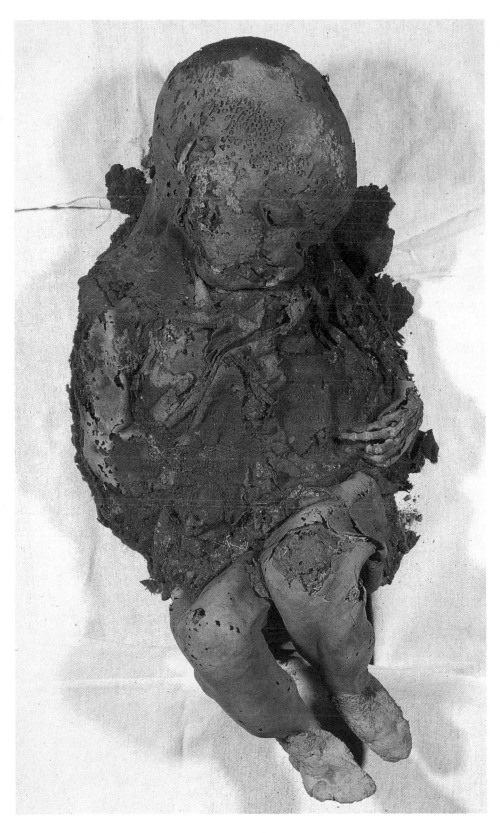

114. A 1½-year-old baby from Yanghe village in the Tuyuq Gorge (near Subeshi).

small bag were crushed plant remains, thought to be ephedra. These may have been two of the medicines he was treating himself with. Why the incisions in the chest region? We have no certain answer but, judging from the autopsies of other mummies, some form of pulmonary disease may have prompted the rather drastic (and apparently unsuccessful) operation.

Related to the people and culture of Subeshi was a little boy of 1½ years, whose body was found in Yanghe village in Pichan (Shanshan) County (ill. 114). He is said to date from around the 3rd century BC.

Imammusakazim

This site which lies within the region of Khotan and which dates to the period *c.* AD 420–589 yielded two Buddhist burials of women. The older of the two was about 30–35 years old, of Mongoloid extraction, and had brown hair with a black braid woven in. She wore a white patterned silk shroud. The younger individual was a girl of 10–12 years old who wore a red patterned silk shroud. Both women had silk bands to tie their mouths shut.

Lopnur Region: Grave 7

Grave 7 was located 7.5 km (4.7 miles) southwest of Grave 5. Here Folke Bergman discovered three or four graves, the best preserved of which was numbered 7A. The coffin was half of a hollowed-out tree-trunk which was sealed by two long boards and mounted on four wooden legs. The mummified remains of 'an elderly, stately gentleman with a small white beard, a thin moustache and white hair' had apparently been tipped out by plunderers (Bergman saw the hand of the ubiquitous Ördek in this). The nostrils of the 'high nose' had been stopped by plugs of wool covered with red silk, a far more elaborate affair than the simple woollen stoppers found in the earlier cemeteries. Bergman was impressed with the non-Mongolian features of the deceased and suspected that the mummified remains belonged to an Indian. Silk was employed in the clothing as well as the nose-plugs and there was a particularly elaborate collar which, Bergman conjectured, just might have been produced in a Persian workshop about the 3rd century AD. Somewhat similar material, including woollen and silk nose-plugs, were found in the other graves and a series of low poles were found at the top of the mound in which the graves had been inserted.

Among the graves excavated by Sven Hedin in the Lopnur region was Grave 35. Attracted by a standing tamarisk pole, Hedin's men dug down to uncover a wooden coffin fashioned from half of a hollowed-out log. Upon removal of the two boards that formed the lid, they found the remains of a young woman, 1.6 m (5 ft 3 in) in height. Her 'turban' and clothes were of silk and she was accompanied by a wooden drinking cup, a wooden food-tray, a sheep's skeleton and twigs of ephedra. Bergman conjectured that the tomb might date to the first centuries of our era.

115. The Yingpän mummy.

At Yarliq-köl, Bergman number-ed as Grave 10 a burial that he found near the southern bank of Qum-darya. Here a coffin, a hol-lowed-out poplar trunk some 2 m (6 ft 7 in) long, was found dis-lodged from a *yardang*, the ridges formed from wind action across the region. The coffin's interior had apparently been lined with thick felt. It contained the mumm-ified body of an old man (1.48 m (4 ft 10 in)). Behind the left ear his grey hair had been twisted into a knot. His teeth were generally in poor shape – the incisors were well worn and the lower molars were missing – although he still had 13 in his upper jaw.

Among the grave goods were the charred bones of a sheep's foreleg that had been covered by a piece of felt to imitate the flesh, and two fish vertebrae. Most unusual was that below his right hip and under his coat was a felt doll, apparently with feminine features painted on and hair in the pubic region, which Bergman interpreted as 'a symbol of a feminine companion'.

The only clue to the date of the burial was that the coat contained silk that measured 60.5 cm (2 ft) wide, 10 cm (4 in) wider than the standard in the Han and immed-iately post-Han period, thus setting it at the end of the floruit of the Kroränian kingdom.

Yingpän

Finally, we should add here notice of the most recent mummy to be discovered. The Chinese press announced in January 1998 that a new mummy had been uncovered in the Kroränian region at Yingpän, a cemetery that has yielded over 30 tombs and is situated to the west of Lopnur. The

116. *Mask of the man buried at Yingpän.*

remains belonged to a male, aged 25–30 years, who stood some 1.8 m (5 ft 11 in) tall and had been laid out in a wooden casket. He was wrapped in a red woollen robe with yellow embroidered designs and a satin sash was wound around his waist; to the sash was attached a perfume satchel. Grave goods included a necklace, a bow and arrows, a glass cup and a wooden comb. He has been dated to the Han–Jin period, i.e. probably about the 2nd–3rd centuries AD. The most striking feature of the new mummy is to be found on his head. Resting on a satin pillow (we are obviously talking about someone of considerable status, Chinese archaeologists suspect a rich merchant – Sogdian?), the deceased wears a mask over his face. The newspaper reports indicate that the mask is made of *má* which can mean hemp, jute, flax, ramie, and/or sisal. The wet 'hemp' was applied in layers over a wooden mould and allowed to dry; the mould was then removed and the hard cloth mask painted white. The forehead of the mask was adorned with a band of gold foil. This is not the only discovery of a masked individual, because in 1996 Wang Bo recovered from Zaghunluq a mummified head with a tightly fitting leather mask. The custom of masks, of course, may well derive from China, but we should not forget that one of the characteristics attributed to the population of Kucha was that dancers wore masks.

Pazyryk and Xinjiang

The spectacular remains from East Central Asia are not the only mummies known in Asia. The excavations of the royal tombs at Pazyryk in the Altai Mountains, some 960 km (600 miles) to the north of Turpan, also uncovered a series of mummified remains, attributed variously to Scythians, Yuezhi, Wusun, Xiongnu and the Arimaspians of Aristeas, to name but a few candidates. They date from about 300–250 BC and were found preserved in large timber chambers sealed by stone cairns. Unlike the Xinjiang mummies, preparation of the bodies for survival was deliberate, while the means by which it was achieved was accidental. We can partly thank the activities of ancient grave robbers for the preservation of the organic remains in the tombs because they breached the chambers in their lust to recover anything of value. This permitted the tombs to flood with water which, in the high Altai Mountains, froze: the stone cairns served to reflect sunlight and

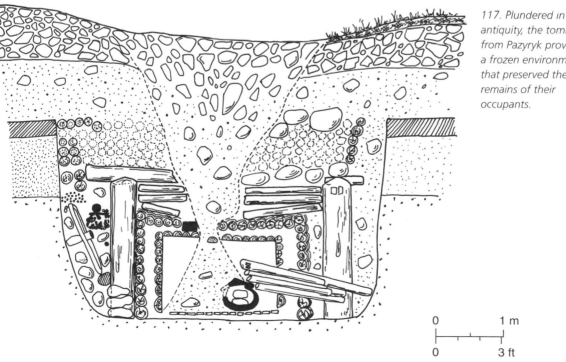

117. Plundered in antiquity, the tombs from Pazyryk provided a frozen environment that preserved the remains of their occupants.

0 ___ 1 m

0 ___ 3 ft

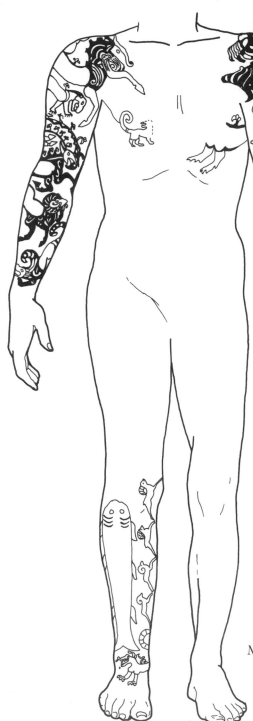

118. Tattoos on a
man from Pazyryk.

preserve the ground under them as a primitive ice box of frozen ground. The excavation of the mummies, which required heating water and slowly thawing out the remains, recovered artificially prepared human remains in which evisceration and removal of brains had been practised and the body cavities stuffed with straw before being sewn up with horsehair or tendon sutures.

Like the mummies of the Tarim Basin, hair had been artificially augmented: at Pazyryk a false beard was prepared for one of the mummies of Mongoloid extraction, who apparently required socially what his genetic background was unable to provide. Tattooing was also extremely important and the skin of one of the mummies provided an artistic tableau of mythical and real animals executed in the 'animal style' of the Eurasian steppe.

That there is a possible ethnic relationship between the Pazyryk mummies and those of the Tarim region is a fair inference although we cannot be too precise as to which ethnic groups (probably Iranian) may have been involved. But what of the origins of the mummification found at Pazyryk? The presumption held long ago by Grafton Elliot Smith that mummification was invented solely in Egypt and diffused from there to wherever else we encounter it is hardly tenable on a worldwide scale (for example, Peruvian mummies are the oldest in the world), and connections between ancient Egypt and the Altai Mountains are very difficult to contemplate. As to the origins of artificial mummification, there are (at least) two approaches.

Archaeologists working in the incredibly rich Minusinsk Basin region have suggested that mummification evolved slowly and out of the need to preserve bodies for longer periods as the construction of tombs became more elaborate and required more time. This, they suggest, can be seen in the Tagar culture, a contemporary of the Pazyryk tombs. Here we find the features of the deceased preserved in clay masks. The preparation of the burials required the removal of the soft tissue from the skeleton, the building of an interior mannikin with grass, the sculpting of a facial mask

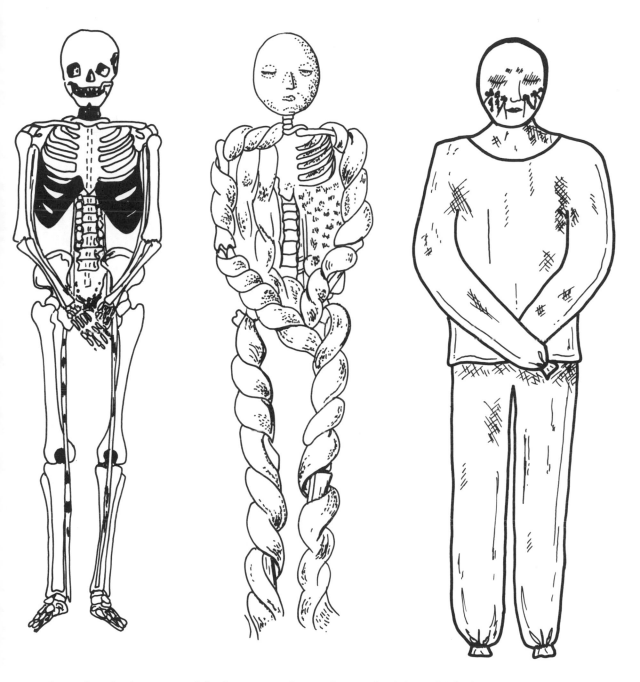

from clay, the fastening of the bones together to form a 'body' to which the head was then attached, and then the painting and dressing of the body. While elaborate, this is a far cry from the result achieved in natural or artificial mummification: it provides an effigy, not a fully preserved body. Those who regard mummification as a one-of-a-kind invention might ponder how these effigies are remarkably similar to the Chinchorro mummies (effigies) of southern Peru and northern Chile that date to *c.* 6000–2000 BC.

119. The preparation of a mannikin from the Minusinsk Basin involved defleshing the skeleton, reconstructing the figure with plant remains and then dressing it.

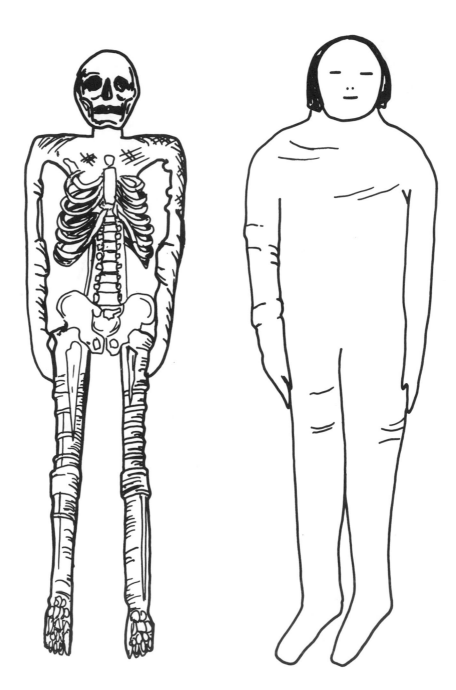

120. The preparation of a mannikin in Peru, which long antedates those found in Asia.

The second approach is to return to Egypt, not because the techniques of mummification diffused from there but rather because it might well provide one piece of the puzzle. Like the Tarim Basin, the arid sands of Egypt created suitable conditions for natural mummification and prior to the elaborate tombs of the dynastic period we do find well-preserved human remains buried in simple pits where their flesh has been in direct contact with the moisture-depriving sands. This may be satisfactory as long as you are content to bury your dead in shallow pits inserted into the desert sands. But as society became increasingly complex and hierarchical, there was a social drive to prepare increasingly more elaborate tombs, large brick chambers (ultimately pyramids) which separated the corpse from the dehydrating effects of sand and dry air. In some cases, we have mummies that were naturally desiccated and wrapped up without evisceration but, in general, if you wanted to retain the integrity of the deceased, artificial techniques were often required and it was these which resulted in our traditional concept of mummification.

While we have no direct evidence for such a transition in Asia, one can at least conjecture that in East Central Asia a similar process evolved. The naturally preserved remains that one would regularly encounter in the Tarim Basin had existed for nearly 2,000 years before we find evidence for deliberate mummification in either Han China or among the Iron Age steppe peoples. We have seen that pastoralists were in continuous contact with the populations of the Tarim Basin and could not have failed to observe the remarkable preservation of the local dead. Indeed, a distinction between some pastoral groups who wandered north of the Tängri Tagh and those resident in the Tarim Basin itself may be unwarranted. In this way, populations already imbued with either an ancestor cult, such as obtained in ancient China, or with a preoccupation with the integrity of the human form or facial features (for instance the inhabitants of the steppelands where clay masks first began in the 3rd millennium BC) may have stimulated others to achieve mummification of their own dead.

The Silence of the Mummies

The forensic scientists have laid out the 'Beauty of Krorän' on their dissecting table. They have weighed her internal organs, examined the integrity of her skin, retrieved nits from her body and tested her with a battery of other scientific techniques. But she still lies there, silent as ever and might just as well have a tag about her big toe, inscribed 'Jane Doe'. She cannot tell us where her ancestors originated, what language she spoke, what her settlement was like, nor who her descendants are. She is no longer articulate, but that does not mean that she has ceased to inform us. She and the other mummies all come to us clothed and, while we may not find a designer label, we may still recover quite a few clues to their identity from their garments.

CHAPTER SIX

Tartans in the Tarim

The Tarim and Turpan basins offer one of the largest collections of textiles in the ancient world. Their study has been primarily confined to Western scholars such as Vivi Sylwan who made detailed examinations of material uncovered in the earlier excavations of Sven Hedin, Folke Bergman and Aurel Stein. The more recent discoveries have seen enormous accumulations of new material in much better dated contexts and some useful descriptive work by Chinese specialists, but more detailed analysis has been limited to the work of Irene Good of the University of Pennsylvania and Elizabeth Barber of Occidental College, California, who were given partial access to some of the material (which provided a basis for Barber's fine book on the Xinjiang mummies and their textiles). Chinese archaeologists have been somewhat loath to surrender their material to foreigners for analysis. From their viewpoint, the archaeological treasures of China have been pillaged quite enough by Westerners and no one wants to defer to 'foreign experts' to interpret one's own heritage, especially when it concerns textiles, a field in which China has traditionally excelled. While this is understandable, it is frustrating to find the scientific reports which could place East Central Asia in the larger picture of the development of textiles in Eurasia so slow in coming. Textile production is not a mere adjunct to the cultural arsenal of a people: the materials employed and the technology involved in its production can be used to trace the course of cultural influences, possibly even migrations, while the decorative patterns employed in textiles or the cut of the material has long been known to be one of the more sensitive expressions of a culture's self-identity.

A Brief History of Twine

It is uncertain when humans began to clothe themselves although the circumstantial evidence of the freezing temperatures of the Ice Age coupled with the discovery of flint scrapers for cleaning hides would suggest that clothing (skin wraps at least) existed among the Neanderthals, i.e. even before the appearance of anatomically modern humans in Europe. By about 20,000 years ago we find in France what are interpreted as bone and antler needles that indicate the sewing of animal skins or textiles manufactured from plant and tree fibres, e.g. bast, a woody fibre derived from the linden and willow. Even earlier we have some evidence for nets about 26,000 years ago (from the Czech Republic) and a twisted cord of three-plied strands of spun vegetable (bast?) fibre that dates to about 15,000 BC. A massive amount of circumstantial evidence such as pendants, bead necklaces, etc., indicates the widespread use of string or cord both during and after the last glaciation.

Flint or other stone scrapers continue in abundance through the Neolithic and remind us that wrapping oneself in the skins of animals has always been an option. Textile finds across Eurasia from the earlier part of the Neolithic are almost uniformly of plant fibres, particularly flax and hemp. Flax, which provides linen, was probably the most widespread plant employed for clothing and, while we have no evidence for its domestication until *c.* 5000 BC, we do have evidence for linen textiles that precede such a date. This suggests either that people had domesticated the plant earlier than present evidence allows or that they used wild flax in linen manufacture. They also exploited hemp but, being coarser, it was more often used in the production of rope and sails. Hemp appears with reference to textiles by about the 5th millennium BC on Neolithic sites of the Yangshao culture in northern China but does not appear certainly as a material of textile production in the West until about the 1st millennium BC. Nettles could also be employed in the production of textile fibres although solid evidence for their use generally dates to no earlier than the 1st millennium BC.

Now what is most remarkable is that sheep and goat were already domesticated some 10,000 years ago, possibly earlier. In chronological terms, it means that across Eurasia for a period of several thousand years shepherds, themselves dressed in clothes of plant fibres, stood about tending their flocks of sheep and goats. Were they missing something obvious?

Not really. Although our image of a sheep may be that of a woolly quad-ruped (or for those who occasionally have to evict sheep from archaeological excavations, an incredibly stupid woolly quadruped), early Neolithic sheep were not at all woolly but covered with short, thick, coarse hairs or kemps. The coat on a sheep thus looked about as inviting for the production of woven textiles as that of a deer. The replacement of the coarse short kemps by a woolly coat was a process that apparently began about 5000 BC and woolly sheep did not become widespread in Eurasia until *c.* 3500 BC. The earliest appearance of woolly sheep is generally thought to have been in Iran and neighbouring territories from which it diffused east and west. In addition to the shift from kemps to wool, there was also a loss of pigmentation which would eventually result in purely white sheep (and wool). This provides a useful chronological marker in the history of dress: before *c.* 3500 BC we can normally expect and do encounter skins and plant-based fibres, and after this period we find increasingly greater quantities of woollen textiles. The archaeologist works to a three-age system: Stone, Bronze and Iron; for the history of textiles it is the same although the periods do not correlate with those of the archaeologist: Skin (?–5000 BC), Linen (6000–3500 BC) and Wool (3500 BC onwards).

The production of woollen fabric may be achieved by a variety of methods. Technologically, the simplest way is by felting. This only requires that one take the animal fibres, such as wool, and lay them out in the shape desired. Then you wet the fibres with warm water or whey, which enhances the ability of the scaly fibres to tangle with one another. Then apply pressure: repeated beatings, crushings, kneadings, whatever it takes to fuse the woollen fibres together into a coherent shape. If decoration is required, you can add small pieces of coloured material and subject it to the same rough treatment until it also has adhered. What you get is a textile that is water resistant and well insulated. Felt had many uses such as rugs, wall-coverings and tents, and hence it is very much associated with the pastoral peoples of the Eurasian steppelands. In terms of clothing, felt was typically employed in the manufacture of protective headgear and stockings.

When one considers the processes by which felt is made, there is a striking inevitability about the whole thing. Our earliest evidence dates to about 2600 BC, the date assigned to a felt rug discovered on the floor of a shrine at Beycesultan in Anatolia. Given the fact that sheep would have to be occasionally penned up and that they would naturally shed some of their coats, it would have only been a matter of time before they would accidentally trample some of their wool into a form that could occasionally be gathered in sheets to be fashioned into coverings such as hats, caps, small rugs, etc. Felt was an almost inevitable consequence of keeping woolly sheep.

121. Plan of plain weave.

122. Plan of twill.

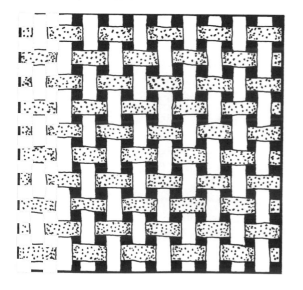

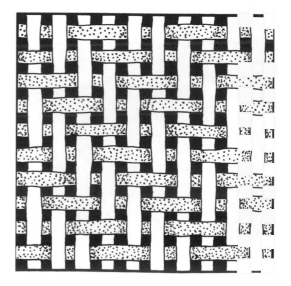

The main alternative to felting is weaving on a loom. This requires the weaver to set the threads into a fixed grid, thus forming the *warp* of the loom. Over and under these threads, in a variety of combinations, would run the threads of the *weft*. Among the enormous varieties of weaving patterns, there are two that we must pay particular attention to.

The simplest form of weaving, *plain weave*, or *tabby*, requires one only to pass the thread of the weft over and under each strand of the warp. Such a pattern is as old as the earliest evidence for the weaving of (plant-made) textiles around 7000 BC. A more complicated pattern can be obtained in the production of *twill*. This involves, ideally (there are variations on the theme), running the weft over two and under two of the strands of the warp but alternating the pattern in each row so that it is off-set one place. This results in a diagonal rib or alignment of the weave. The fabric is not simply visually different from plain weave but because the weft hops over two (or more) rows of the warp, it yields a denser fabric. Twill is almost invariably found associated with wool and not with linen. The earliest evidence for twill is from Anatolia and dates to the 4th millennium BC. This is followed by evidence from the Caucasus of the early 3rd millennium BC and then, after a considerable chronological gap, we recover evidence for twill in the Hallstatt culture in Austria (*c.* 1100–450 BC) and about the same time in Ferghana, the land of the 'blood-sweating horses', one of the western approaches to the Tarim Basin.

Silk and Cotton

The fabric synonymous with China, silk, derives from the silk worm (*Bombyx mori*), which is killed by heat within its cocoon so that the silk threads may be extracted before the moth breaks through the strands as it emerges from the cocoon. The earliest remains of such cocoons in an archaeological context come from the Yangshao, the north Chinese Neolithic culture, *c.* 5000 BC, but the earliest actual evidence for silk dates to *c.* 3300–2250 BC. When silk is first mentioned on an oracle bone from the later part of the Shang dynasty (*c.* 1200 BC) it seems to have become so abundant and well developed that one must presume a long tradition of prior evolution. The Chinese aristocracy kept the technique of its manufacture secret under penalty of death, yet silk is encountered in the West in Iron Age contexts dating to *c.* 600–500 BC and from Pazyryk in the Altai Mountains by about 300–250 BC. We have already seen how Han imperial policy employed silk as a bribe to hold off the depredations of the Xiongnu in the first centuries BC. The technique of boiling the cocoons to obtain the unbroken silk fibre from domesticated moths did not reach the West until the 6th century AD and the earlier discoveries of silk in the West, especially those prior to the opening of the Silk Road, can perhaps be explained by the exploitation of wild silkworms. A possible exception to all this is the development of silk in India, which may predate any putative contacts between it and China.

Finally, brief mention should be made of cotton which was domesticated earliest in India sometime in the 3rd millennium BC (or possibly the 4th according to more recent evidence). It is found in the Indus Valley or Harappan civilization which maintained trading links all over Central Asia and also with Mesopotamia. Nevertheless, the appearance of cotton outside India seems to be relatively late and it does not generally appear on archaeological sites or in literary references beyond its homeland until the 1st millennium BC.

Armed with some rudimentary knowledge of textiles, we can now turn to the evidence of the Tarim Basin. We might emphasize that the evidence for textiles is not limited to the mummies but that much of our evidence also derives from burials where only the skeletons have survived.

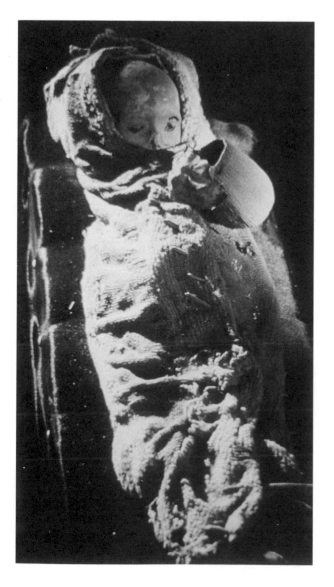

123. Baby from Qäwrighul.

Second Millennium BC: Qäwrighul

The earliest attested textile remains in Xinjiang were discovered at sites of the 2nd millennium BC such as the cemetery at Qäwrighul. As might be expected, the textiles from this period are the most primitive. There is no evidence for seams, piping, sleeves or trouser legs; dyeing is limited to very small areas of cloth. Generally, all woollen textiles are of felt or employ plain weave.

The 'Beauty of Kroran' from the Töwän River cemetery wore a woollen hood consisting of an underlay of two pieces of dark-brown woollen cloth covered by a weather-resistant felt overlay. Her mid-length skirt was made of leather with the fur turned to the inside for warmth and her cloak, which reached to her knees, was plain woven (with extra weft looped in) sheep's wool. Her boots were ankle-high moccasins. The other woman from the same period (*c.* 1800 BC) and the Könchi River region wore a similar felt hood and her cloak was a golden-brown woollen wrap consisting of two strips of plain weave that had been stitched together (the loom employed seems to have been incapable of producing a piece of cloth wide enough to cover the woman). The child from the same graveyard was wrapped in a brown and beige woollen blanket. The proud mother or grandmother who wove this blanket could almost be accused of showing off as it is a tour-de-force sampler of different weaves which changed every few inches.

The textiles from Qäwrighul are more than a fashion statement. We may recall that the range of the wild sheep does not extend as far east as China and the earliest evidence for sheep in China dates to the 2nd millennium BC. The presence of woollen textiles in the Tarim Basin indicates that by the early 2nd millennium BC domestic sheep from the west (along with domestic wheat, possibly barley) had been introduced to the Tarim Basin. Whether it was introduced by the direct ancestors of the Qäwrighul mummies or not is impossible to determine, although the association of a western physical type of humans with a (more) westerly domestic livestock suggests just such a conclusion.

While we cannot be certain of the date of a number of other mummies, some from the same general region may also be discussed here. The mummy discovered by Bergman at a site near Lopnur, which he numbered Grave 36, also had a double-layered felt cap, pegged with two feathers on the left side and with ear-flaps that could be tied under the chin. The old woman in this grave was enveloped in a large dark brown woollen cloak trimmed with a yellow and red border and fastened together with wooden (and one bone) pins. Around her waist was a string skirt of red and undyed woollen fringes. Her shoes were of rawhide with an inner sole of lambskin.

Male dress of this period is more difficult to discuss unless we presume that the burials excavated by Bergman at Ördek's necropolis date to approximately the same period on the basis of similar ritual and finds (they may actually be much later). Even here we will not get very far. The mummified young man from Grave 5A, the best preserved of the burials, wore a white felt cap with ear-flaps and five feathers mounted on pegs; it was

124. Hat from Grave 36 near Lopnur.

213

fastened around his chin with a cord. This at least indicates that the 'Robin Hood' style of headgear was worn by both males and females; whether there was a more subtle 'gender statement' being made in these hats we cannot tell without a greater sample. Certainly unsubtle was the fact that around his waist he wore a narrow loin-cloth (only 5 cm (2 in) wide) which had been anchored to his penis. It was made out of wool as was also the large mantle (2.1 m by 1.55 m (6 ft 10 in by 5 ft 1 in)) which was wrapped around him. This unfortunately is the only piece of male outer clothing from the area. As such a mantle may have served equally as a shroud, it is difficult to be certain how males actually dressed during this earlier period. Bergman did observe that the young man was shod with brand new moccasins of ox hide.

The 1st Millennium BC: Zaghunluq

The recently excavated mummies from Zaghunluq (near Chärchän) indicate new techniques that had appeared in East Central Asia by the 1st millennium BC. The quality of the weaving had improved and now included not only plain weave but twill. The quality of the wool was also superior: it was a fine wool with little evidence of kemps.

To fit out 'Ur-David', the gentleman from Zaghunluq, we can start with his array of caps and hats (he had ten altogether). A very stylish beret-like brown hat was made by the technique known as *nalbinding* ('needle binding' in the Scandinavian languages, made from a single piece of yarn), which gives the appearance of knitting. This is one of the earliest known examples of *nalbinding* in the world. Another brown beret from Qizilchoqa has been analyzed by Chinese textile specialists as having been knitted; this too would be the earliest example of that technique in the world. Another hat of white felt and a mid-seam had a rolled piece of felt in the front to form two 'horns' (like a cartoon viking) and there were two flaps with braided strings for fastening the hat to the chin. Still another hat was made by sewing together two pieces of thick brown felt with neat stitches of white thread to form a very high (32.7 cm (1 ft)), rakishly tilted peak with a turned-up brim that is also edged with the white decorative stitches. His shirt was crudely form-fitted: it consisted of two rectangular bolts of burgundy coloured wool that were draped over each shoulder to which were attached tubes to serve as sleeves; the fabric here was plain

125. Beret-type hat recovered from Zaghunluq.

weave with red piping along the seams. Also discovered in his tomb was a bulky, double-faced twill-weave sweater made of heavy cream-coloured threads; the sleeves would only have come down to the man's elbows and the low-cut, open neck was tied together with thread.

Below his waist the man wore a pair of woollen trousers and it might be noted that a pair of unaccompanied trousers were also recovered from else-where on the site. Seams as well as red piping were in evidence. He also wore a multicoloured belt (red, brown, blue, green and yellow) fashioned from woollen yarn. The concept of a five-coloured belt is reminiscent of the practice in India whereby brahmins wore and still wear a five-coloured (pañca-rūpa) thread over their shoulder. This belt, however, did not hold his trousers up but merely fastened the two sides of his upper garment. Deerskin boots rose to his knees but it was his stockings that really caught the eye. They were double layered with robin-egg-blue felt underneath for insulation and bright-red and yellow woollen strips wound around the outside to create the loudest socks known in the prehistoric world, although they would have been entirely covered by his boots.

One more garment is to be associated with his dress – an enormous outer coat made of extremely thick brown thread which was set about 80 cm (2 ft 7 in) from the surface of the grave and served to protect the lower chamber of the tomb (ill. 128). On top of it was a white felt blanket on which in turn were placed a leather saddle and a simple, round-based black jar. The saddle and trousers go together well: while Westerners may look to ancient Greece or Rome for the home of their philosophies, laws and literature they have adopted the costume of horse-riding barbarians who, for practical (and obvious) reasons, developed trousers. It might be noted that the ancient Greeks mocked the concept of trousers, suggesting that close-fitting pants repressed the sexual abilities of their northern neighbours!

126. 'Horned' hat made of white felt with chin strap; from Zaghunluq.

127. Tall peaked hat of brown felt with white stitching; from Zaghunluq.

128. The coat of 'Ur-David'.

The woman accompanying 'Ur-David' wore a finely woven twill robe of dark red that reached to her calves. This was a marvellous garment, so perfect that it almost had a sheen and would no doubt fetch a large sum if produced today. Under her knee-high boots of white deerskin her left foot was wrapped in red wool flannel and her right in yellow and sky blue, a possible fashion statement that now escapes us (of course, textiles were 'women's work' so we must presume she had quite a bit of say in what was worn). One of the other women in the tomb wore a dark-red dress and her legs were covered with a yellow- (or white?-) dyed woollen cloth with red spirals. The excavator also recovered a blue shawl of loosely spaced plain weave with red stripes.

The infant buried next to this tomb, 'Baby Blue', with the fluffy blue bonnet and blue stones over its eyes, wore a red-brown plain-weave shroud or baby blanket which was then wrapped in a white felt blanket. The same beautiful, rich shade, probably achieved by applying red dye to brown wool, was found on the man's dress. Moreover, the same kinds of thick strings of twisted blue and red strands that bound the hands of 'Ur-David' to his chest were used to bind up the baby's wraps. This seems to be a family whose clothing was made by the same woman who, not unexpectedly, produced colour-coordinated textiles for members of the same family.

In the more recently excavated 'sacrificial' burials at Zaghunluq (with the tripartite mature woman, the 'Scream Baby' and the mutilated younger woman), the mature woman wore a beautiful violet-purple upper garment and a coarsely woven greyish lower garment. The baby was dressed in an amazing brown shroud decorated with red strips on which were tie-dyed a series of yellow circles. A yellow woollen headband was employed to tie the baby's mouth shut (the family of 'Ur-David' used a burgundy strap).

Irene Good analyzed one additional piece of fabric from the Zaghunluq burials. The extremely fine thread suggests the possibility of cashmere on the site and Good points out that goat skulls are associated with one of the Zaghunluq burials. To this we might add a large quantity of spindlewhorls, some of which were ornamented with interlocking spirals.

Tartans at Qizilchoqa

Although dating to about the same period as Zaghunluq, the cemetery at Qizilchoqa to the northeast near Hami yielded different weaves for which far-reaching historical connections have been suggested. The precise date of the Qizilchoqa cemetery is problematic: the initial dates placed it at about 1200 BC, contemporary with the later period of the Yanbulaq culture, but a new radiocarbon date of *c.* 800–530 BC suggests that it belongs to the later Tört Erik (Sidaogou) culture. The abundant evidence for dress here revealed a variety of clothes, including woollen robes with coloured belt bands and fur coats (the fur turned inside) with integrated gloves, which fastened with wooden buttons (ill. 130). But our main story lies with the woollen textiles.

129. Robe from Qizilchoqa with a belt.

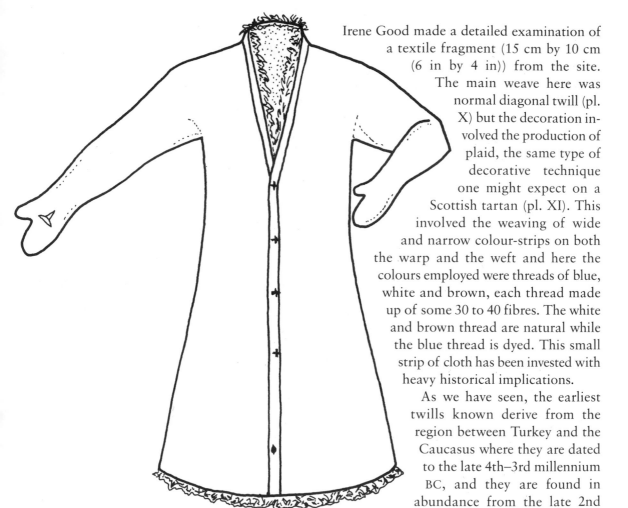

Irene Good made a detailed examination of a textile fragment (15 cm by 10 cm (6 in by 4 in)) from the site. The main weave here was normal diagonal twill (pl. X) but the decoration involved the production of plaid, the same type of decorative technique one might expect on a Scottish tartan (pl. XI). This involved the weaving of wide and narrow colour-strips on both the warp and the weft and here the colours employed were threads of blue, white and brown, each thread made up of some 30 to 40 fibres. The white and brown thread are natural while the blue thread is dyed. This small strip of cloth has been invested with heavy historical implications.

As we have seen, the earliest twills known derive from the region between Turkey and the Caucasus where they are dated to the late 4th–3rd millennium BC, and they are found in abundance from the late 2nd millennium BC in Europe, particul-

130. Fur coat (with the fur turned inwards) and integral gloves from Qizilchoqa.

arly at the site of Hallstatt. Here miners left residues of their clothing (and, occasionally themselves) in the protective environment of Austrian salt mines. As the Hallstatt culture occupied a territory which classical authors would associate with Celts only a few centuries later, it is generally presumed that the miners here (and the warriors and others buried in the neighbouring cemetery) were also Celts or Proto-Celts. The easternmost finds of twill, dating from the centuries around 1000 BC (or somewhat later), are the fragment from Qizilchoqa and many others like it from the same cemetery (some very Scottish looking); true twills are unknown in China until well into the 1st millennium AD. The Qizilchoqa twill is virtually identical to the textile fragments recovered from Hallstatt with respect to both style and technique (hence one of the arguments employed by the tabloid press for placing kilted Celts in the Tarim Basin). We are not talking simply of the diffusion of a particular weaving and colour pattern. As Elizabeth Barber writes: 'the regular combination of plaids and twills in the same cloth and the similar play of wides and narrows in the plaids move us into a border zone where it's harder to imagine the sum total as accidental'. There is also a similarity in the weight of cloth. Of course there are differences between the Hallstatt and Qizilchoqa materials, for example, Hallstatt employed only two colours while the Qizilchoqa plaids used from three to six colours. In addition, there are even differences among the Tarim plaids. Irene Good has noted that the weaving traditions of Zaghunluq and Qizilchoqa are themselves considerably different even though they both date to the period before the middle of the 1st millennium BC. The Qizilchoqa (Hami) fragment appears to derive from a hairy rather than woolly fleece and would seem to come from a different breed of sheep than that found at Zaghunluq; there are also differences in the crafting of the cloth, e.g. the Zaghunluq twill involved hopping over three stems of the warp rather than the more typical two as found at Qizilchoqa. In weighing the similarities between the European and East Central Asian material, Barber concludes that the two are related yet also makes it clear that neither is derived from the other. How do we connect the two textile traditions?

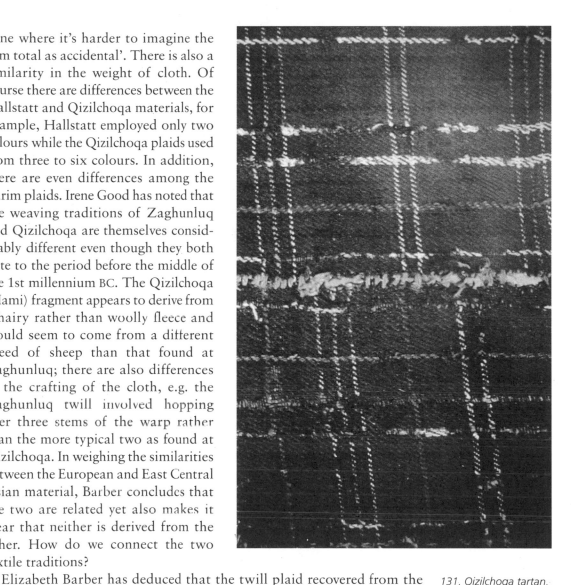

131. *Qizilchoqa tartan.*

Elizabeth Barber has deduced that the twill plaid recovered from the northern Tarim may be placed within the context of Indo-European migrations. As we have already recounted, one of the most popular theories of Indo-European origins would locate their homeland in the steppelands encompassing the Ukraine and southern Russia, a region which would have been in direct contact with the Caucasus whence we obtain some of our earliest evidence for twills. In this model, the earliest Indo-Europeans would have known plaid twill and carried it west into central and western Europe where it would later emerge among the Celts of the Hallstatt culture; it would also have been carried eastwards across the steppe where it would have been introduced by Indo-Europeans, here identified as the Tocharians, into the Tarim Basin.

The 'Witches of Subeshi'

The cemetery at Subeshi, dating to about the 4th or 3rd century BC, yielded the mummies of three elegant women. Their attire is so similar that description of one will suffice (pl. VI, ill. 132).

The woman wore a sheepskin coat that reached to her calves. As is so often the case, the waterproof hide is turned out leaving the warmer fleece inside. Although the cloak has sleeves, the excavators found that it was placed only over her shoulders, and it is possible that her arms were never intended to slip through the sleeves. The custom of wearing one's cloak over the shoulders was also widely known from Iran to China among the various nomadic tribes. Beneath the cloak was a kind of blouse, made from woven brown wool with long sleeves edged in red. Below this she wore a magnificent, eye-catching woollen skirt with horizontal stripes of yellow, red, blue and burgundy that reached to her ankles; it was fastened at the waist with a knotted cord of four colours (not unlike that found at Zaghunluq). Her feet were clad in leather slippers which had brown felt stockings attached. She wore a leather mitten on her left hand while her right was bare. But what attracts us most about her dress is her enormous funnel-shaped hat. Made of black felt, the hat rises a full 60 cm (2 ft) high and has a wide brim. Such an enormous pointed hat is, of course, quite in accord with the literary descriptions of those Saka who were distinguished by their large pointed hats, or Song Yun's description of the wives of the Hephthalite kings who wore 'a kind of horn 3 feet high'. From a Western perspective, the pointed hat looks uncannily like that worn by a witch (the witch's hat, the tall, peaked or steeple hat of felt or beaver, derives from 17th-century Puritan dress). The women are generally presumed to have been either priestesses or royalty (or both).

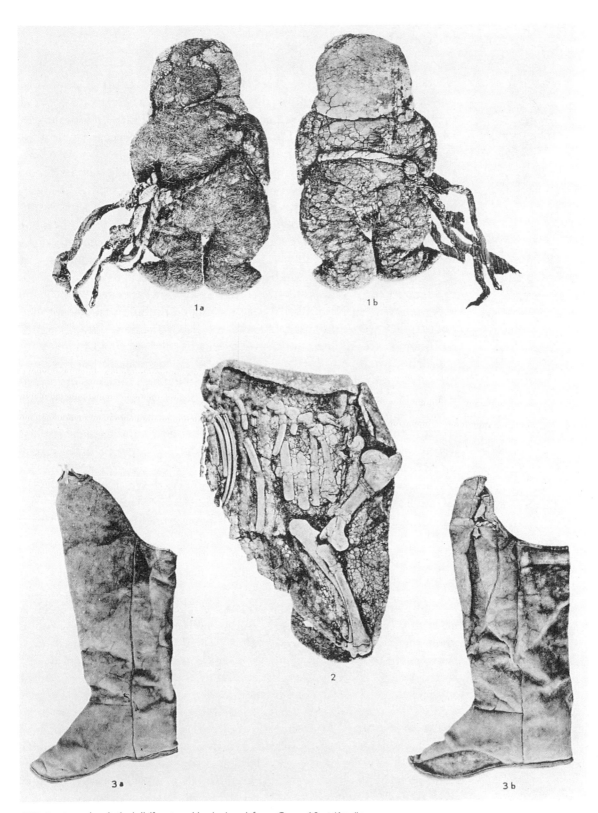

133. Boots and a cloth doll (front and back views) from Grave 10 at Krorän.

Historical Period

In order to round off this account of the apparel of the Xinjiang mummies, we will extend our survey briefly to the first few centuries of the 1st millennium AD. It is roughly to this period that we may assign a number of the burials excavated by Folke Bergman near Lopnur. Grave 10, for example, which contained the body of an old man, provided evidence for male dress in ancient Krorän in the centuries around AD 400. He wore a yellow-brown silk cloak with cotton trim; his sleeves were long, extending over his hands. His trousers were of sheepskin and reached down to just below the knees. Here were his leather boots, highest in the front and fastened with a strap that would be tied to the knee. Bergman observed that this was the same type of footwear depicted in murals of 'Tocharians' at Bezäklik. His socks were of felt. One of the most unusual objects, however, was a small painted felt doll of a woman that had been placed by his hip.

More recently an aristocratic couple have been excavated in the same grave (Grave 3) at Niyä. Buried together in a coffin built of thick wooden boards, they were accompanied by vessels, a bow, arrows, quivers, legs of lamb and textiles. They both wore exquisite silk robes and hoods with colourful, ornate patterns (pl. IX). The robes, fashioned from the same material, were meant to match, but whereas the man's robe was decorated with a checker-board pattern of blue and yellow squares, the woman wore a robe decorated with wavy yellow lines against a blue background.

From this brief survey of the evidence for the Tarim textiles we must admit that in terms of research, work has hardly begun. During rescue operations at Zaghunluq in 1996, Wang Bo recovered 40 large boxes of textiles for the Ürümchi Museum which will take years, if not decades, to examine and assess. As we cannot wait for the results of such examinations, we will see what light the evidence for language might shed on the Tarim textiles.

Schleicher's Sheep

We have already introduced the subject of language in our survey and it is helpful to consider at what stage in the development of textiles we might place the Indo-Europeans before they divided into their different stocks. With regard to sheep and wool, a convenient index of development can be seen in what is known in Indo-European circles as 'Schleicher's tale'. August Schleicher (1821–1868), one of the founders of historical linguistics, set himself an interesting exercise: he tried his hand at composing a short fable in the reconstructed Proto-Indo-European (PIE) language, a difficult task since it was not easy to find sufficient items of reconstructed PIE vocabulary with which to write a narrative. The plot of the tale was driven by whatever items of vocabulary were available and so in the year of his death Schleicher tried to deal himself as easy a hand as he could and stuck to some of the most widely attested words in the Indo-European lexicon. Below we tell the tale in Schleicher's original version, then an updated 'reconstruction' by D. Q. Adams based on more recent linguistic evidence, and, finally, an English translation for those whose Proto-Indo-European has become a bit rusty.

Schleicher's version (1868)

Avis, jasmin varnā na ā ast, dadarka akvams, tam, vāgham garum vaghantam, tam, bhāram magham, tam, manum āku bharantam. Avis akvabhjams ā vavakat: kard aghnutai mai vidanti manum akvams agantam.

Akvāsas ā vavakant: krudhi avai, kard aghnutai vividvant-svas: manus patis varnām avisāms karnauti svabhjam gharmam vastram avibhjams ka varnā na asti.

Tat kukruvants avis agram ā bhugat.

Adams' version (1997)

h₂óuis, kʷésio ulh₂néh₁ ne (h₁é) est, h₁ékuons spéket, h₁oinom ghe gʷrhₓúm uóǵhom uéǵhontṃ h₁oinom-kʷe méǵhₐm bhórom, h₁oinom-kʷe ǵhménṃ hₓóku bhérontṃ. h₂óuis tu h₁ekuoibh(i)os ueukʷét: 'ḱér hₐeghnutór moi h₁ékuons hₐéǵontṃ hₐnérṃ uidṇtbh(i)ós: h₁ékuōs tu ueukʷónt: 'ḱludhí, h₂óuei, ḱér ghe hₐeghnutór ṇsméi uidṇtbh(i)ós: hₐnér, pótis, h₂éuiom r ulh₂néhₐm sebhi kʷṛnéuti nu gʷhérmom uéstrom néǵhi h₂éuiom ulh₂néhₐ h₁ésti.'

Tód ḱekluuós h₂óuis hₐéǵrom bhugét.

English Translation

A sheep that had no wool saw horses – one pulling a heavy wagon, another one a great load, and another swiftly carrying a man. The sheep said to the horses: 'it pains my heart seeing a man driving horses'. The horses said to the sheep: 'listen sheep! it pains our hearts seeing man, the master, making a warm garment for himself from the wool of a sheep when the sheep has no wool for itself.'

On hearing this the sheep fled into the plain.

Ignoring for the moment that Schleicher's reconstruction presumes that a man rather than a woman, as ethnographic evidence generally suggests, was making the woollen garment, we can emphasize that Schleicher had no qualms about assigning 'sheep', 'wool' and a 'garment' to the Proto-Indo-Europeans. In other words, before the various Indo-European stocks had differentiated among themselves, the speakers of Indo-European shared a common vocabulary for sheep, wool and textiles. Let us try to establish how much the comparative linguistic evidence suggests they knew about textiles and how any of it might fit into the descriptions of the Tarim mummies.

Indo-European textiles

The sheep was known in Proto-Indo-European as a *h_2óụis* and reflexes of its name can be found in Celtic (e.g. Old Irish *oī* 'sheep'), Italic (Latin *ovis* 'sheep'), Germanic (e.g. Old Norse *ær* 'sheep', Old English *ēowu* 'sheep' (whence we gain our word *ewe*)), Baltic (e.g. Lithuanian *avìs* 'sheep'), Slavic (e.g. Old Church Slavonic *ovĭnŭ* 'sheep'), Greek *o(w)is* 'sheep', Armenian *hovi-w* 'shepherd', Anatolian (Luvian *hāwa/i* 'sheep'), Iranian (Wakhi *yobc* 'ewe'), Old Indic *ávi-* 'sheep', and Tocharian B *ā$_ụ$* 'sheep'. To a generic word for sheep, we could also add *h_2oụikéh$_a$-* 'ewe', *$h_1$er-* 'lamb', 'kid', possibly *(s)ķegos* 'sheep/goat'; from the Atlantic to Greece we have *$h_a$eg^{w}hnos* 'lamb' while from Greece to India we find *uṛh$_1$én* 'lamb'. Distinct textile associations can be seen in the reconstructed word *moisós* 'ram', 'sheep', 'fleece', 'skin' which is found in Baltic (e.g. Latvian *màiss* 'sack'), Slavic (e.g. Russian *mekh* 'skin', 'sack'), Iranian (e.g. Avestan *maēša-* 'ram') and Old Indic *meṣá-* 'ram', 'sheep', 'fleece', 'skin'. A derivative of this word is also known in Anatolian where Hittite *maista-* means something like a 'bale of wool'. The actual word for wool in Proto-Indo-European is *uĺh$_2$neh$_a$-* 'wool', which can be seen in Celtic (e.g. Welsh *gwlân*), Latin *lāna*, Germanic (e.g. Old English *wull(e)*, whence our modern English *wool*), Baltic (e.g. Lithuanian *vìlna*), Slavic (e.g. Russian *vólna*), Greek *lānos*, Hittite *hulana-*, Iranian (e.g. Avestan *varǝnā*), and Old Indic *úrṇā-*.

What we gain from these reconstructions is strong evidence that both sheep and wool were securely rooted in Proto-Indo-European culture and that of its daughter stocks. Given that sheep only begin to appear in China about the 3rd millennium BC and that they arrive from the west, it is at least suggestive that one of the vectors for their introduction may have been Indo-Europeans entering the Tarim Basin. The fact that the Indo-Europeans were also well acquainted with wool and that woolly sheep are largely a product of the 4th millennium BC suggests that the Indo-Europeans had not yet diverged linguistically from one another by that time. In other words, if we employ our textile-based three ages, then it is to the later Woollen Age (after *c.* 3500 BC) that we assign the Indo-Europeans. The one word that we have for 'linen' in Indo-European, *linom*, is confined to languages of the west and centre, i.e. Celtic, Latin, Germanic, Baltic, Slavic and Greek; it reveals no cognates among the Indo-European languages of Asia.

We know that the ancient Chinese must have received their domesticated sheep from the west; can we tell from whom? This is not at all easy – we have already seen some of the difficulties in working with ancient Chinese – but there is one possible linguistic argument to support this presumption. We have just seen that one of the Proto-Indo-European words for 'lamb' is *uṛh$_1$én*. Now the modern Chinese word for the sheep or goat is *yáng* and it occurs earliest in the Shang dynasty (1200 BC, roughly contemporary with the later Bronze Age occupation of the Tarim Basin) where the sign employed for 'sheep' looks like the head-on face of a sheep with its curved horns on top and pointed chin below. The character is also associated with a series of other characters conveying felicitous meanings, e.g. 'good', 'beautiful', an interesting association in that Chinese agriculture did not favour herbivores (lack of suitable pasture) and yet appears to have regarded sheep as a 'good' thing. Now *yáng* seems far removed from the Proto-Indo-European form but we should remember that the eastern Indo-European languages, such as Sogdian *wr'n* 'lamb', derive from an earlier Iranian form **varāna-* while the cognate Tocharian word *yrīye* 'lamb' would come from something like **w'är'än-*. And the earliest Chinese form that we can reconstruct for this word is **(γ)riang* which might just derive from some Iranian or Tocharian form for the word.

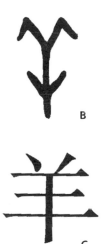

We have by no means exhausted our evidence for Indo-European clothing but rather than getting entangled in a web of linguistic forms, it is more convenient simply to list the different roots, their probable meanings, and their distribution, in a table (pp. 226–227).

Altogether we have about 42 roots or words that have a close association with textiles. Of these, 27 find cognates in the Asian languages of Iranian, Indic and Tocharian, the three language stocks also represented in East Central Asia. We need to keep our eye on these since it has long been observed that some words that are found among various Indo-European stocks cannot be assigned to the earliest periods of Indo-European antiquity. For example, we can see that the root **ruk-* is really only found among two language stocks, Celtic (actually Gallo-Roman) and Germanic, and is most likely a late regional term for a cloak or mantle in western Europe or a borrowing from some 'native' language; we would have no reason to suggest that any of the Tarim mummies used this root in describing their own clothing. Each word, depending on its distribution and shape, must pass some form of test concerning its antiquity. Although somewhat rough and ready, a widely accepted test is to demand that a cognate word appear in both a European and an Asiatic language.

So, what does our linguistic evidence tell us about what the Proto-Indo-Europeans knew about textiles (and they may have known quite a lot more even if we can't prove it from the linguistic evidence)? The chart indicates that the Indo-Europeans had combs, plucked/pulled out (wool), could make thread, could spin the threads and both plait/braid and sew. They could also clearly weave and dye, and had words for cloth. The word for 'clothes', 'cloak', **drap-*, seems to come from a root **drep-* 'split', 'tear off' which suggests that its antecedents rested with animal skins rather than weaving. This could be an old word and we might recall that among the earliest Tarim mummies, those recovered from Qäwrighul, cloaks of animal skins occur frequently enough. Cognates for getting dressed are well represented and the clothing could include both a belt and some form of headband. Cognates for the word for 'shoe' are confined to the centre and west of the Indo-European world. The root, **k̥rh₁pís*, is generally derived from the verbal

134. The hanzi for yáng 'sheep' imitates the image of a sheep's head (A). Here it is seen in its earliest representation in the Shang period (B) and its modern rendering (C).

Indo-European terms for textiles and clothing

Proto-Indo-European	Meaning	Celt	Ital	Gmc	Balt	Slav	Alb	Grk	Arm	Anat	Iran	Indic	Toch
THREAD													
*$dek̂$-	'thread', 'hair'	X*	-	X	-	-	-	-	-	-	X	X	X*
*$g^w hih_x(slo)$-	'sinew', 'thread'	X	X	-	X	X	-	-	X	X	-	-	-
*$t(e)rm$-	'warp-end'	-	-	X	-	-	-	X	-	-	-	-	-
*$pel/oth_a mo$-	'thread'	X	-	X	-	-	-	-	-	-	-	-	-
CLOTH													
*los-	'cloth'	-	-	X	X	X	-	-	-	-	X	X	-
*$p(e)h_2 no$-	'cloth', 'weft'	X	X	X	-	-	-	X	-	-	X	-	-
FELT													
*pil-so-/to-	'felt'	-	X	X	-	X	-	X	-	-	-	-	-
PLUCK AND COMB WOOL													
*$pek̂$-	'pull out', 'comb out'	-	X	X*	X	-	-	X	-	-	-	-	-
*$pleus$-	'(pluck) fleece/feathers'	-	X	X	X	-	-	-	-	-	-	-	-
*$reu(h_x)$-	'pull out'	X	-	X	X	X	-	-	-	-	X	X	X
*$kars$-	'scratch/comb (wool)'	-	X	X	X	X	-	-	-	-	-	X	-
*kes-	'comb'	X	-	X	X	X	-	X	-	X	-	-	-
PLAIT													
*$plek̂$-	'braid', 'plait'	-	X	X	-	X	-	X	-	-	X	X	-
*$resg$-	'plait', 'wattle'	-	X	X	X	X	-	-	-	-	X	X	-
*$u̯ei(h_x)$-	'plait', 'wattle'	X*	X	X	X	X	-	X*	-	-	X*	X	-
*$kert$-	'plait', 'twine'	-	X	X	X	-	-	X	-	-	-	X	-
*$mesg$-	'intertwine'	-	-	X	X	-	-	-	-	-	-	-	X
SPIN													
*$(s)neh_1(i)$-	'twist fibres together'	X	X	X	X	-	-	X	-	-	-	X	-
*$sneh_1 u$-	'twist fibres together'	-	X*	X	X	X	-	X*	X*	-	X*	X*	X*
*$(s)pen$-	'draw out', 'spin'	-	-	X	X	X	X	X	X	-	-	-	X
WEAVE													
*$h_{2/3}eu$-	'weave'	-	-	X	X	X	-	-	X	-	-	X	-
*$h_{2/3}u̯ebh$-	'weave'	-	-	X	-	-	X	X	-	X	X	X	X
*$u̯eg$-	'plait', 'weave'	X	X	X	-	-	-	-	-	-	-	X	-
*$krek$-	'beat the weft'	-	-	X	X	-	-	X	-	-	-	-	-

Proto-Indo-European	Meaning	Celt	Ital	Gmc	Balt	Slav	Alb	Grk	Arm	Anat	Iran	Indic	Toch
DYE													
*reg-	'dye'	-	-	-	-	-	-	X	-	-	X	X	-
FULL													
*knab(h)-	'pick at', 'tease out'	X	-	X	X	-	X	X	-	-	-	-	-
SEW													
*siuh$_1$-	'sew'	-	X	X	X	X	-	X	-	X*	-	X	X
*(s)ner-	'fasten with thread'	-	-	X	X	X	-	-	-	-	X	-	X
GET DRESSED													
*h$_1$eu-	'put on clothes'	X*	X	-	X	X	-	-	X	-	X*	-	X*
*ues-	'be dressed', 'dress'	-	X*	X	-	-	X	X	X	X	X	X	X
CLOTH, GARMENT													
*uospo-	'garment'	-	X	-	-	-	-	-	-	X	-	-	-
*bhru-	'(bolt of) cloth'	-	-	-	X	-	-	X	-	-	-	-	-
*drap-	'clothes', 'cloak'	X	-	X	X	-	-	-	-	-	-	X	-
*baitéh$_a$-	'cloak'	-	-	X	-	-	-	X	-	-	-	-	-
*kéntr/n-	'patch', 'patched garment'	-	X	X	-	-	-	X	X	-	-	X?	-
*lōp-	'strip of cloth'	-	-	X	X	X	-	X	-	-	-	-	-
*ruk-	'over-garment'	X	-	X	-	-	-	-	-	-	-	-	-
BELT													
*iéh$_3$s-	'gird', 'belt'	-	-	-	X	X	X	X	-	-	X	X	-
HEADBAND													
*puk-	'headband'	-	-	-	-	-	-	X	-	-	X	-	-
*déh$_1$mn̥	'headband'	-	-	-	-	-	-	X	-	-	-	X	-
SHOE													
*kr̥h$_1$pís	'shoe'	X	X?	-	X	X	-	X	-	-	-	-	-
Total cognates		14	20	35	26	19	6	26	7	7	15	21	11

root *(s)ker-'cut' and it is presumed that this indicates a shoe cut out from leather (as we find in the Tarim Basin) rather than one from tree bast (as worn by the Tyrolean 'Iceman').

What about knowledge of felting? The linguistic evidence here is not impressive and is largely confined to cognates in Latin (*pilleus*), Germanic (e.g. Old English *felt*), Slavic (*plŭstĭ*) and Greek (*pilos*). The word is clearly related to PIE *pulos* 'a single hair on the human body' and it may not have been PIE but reflect a somewhat later spread of a word and technique among Indo-Europeans in Europe. The only other word connected with felting is a verb (*nak-*) which is found in Greek as *násso* 'press', 'compress' and *tà naktá* 'felt shoes'. But in other languages such as Hittite it means 'weighty', 'important', i.e. 'pressing'. This suggests that the meaning of the word may have gravitated towards felting in Greek (and possibly Latin where *naccae* 'cloth-fullers' may be cognate if not derived from Greek) but that we really cannot claim that this was the original meaning in Proto-Indo-European. Given that felting probably preceded weaving as a technique, it seems odd that we cannot reconstruct a word for 'felt' in Proto-Indo-European. But the evidence for the proto-language is patchy, and terms for felting may have dropped out among many Indo-European groups. What is striking is our inability to obtain a cognate from Indo-Iranian although their probable steppe ancestors should have excelled in the production of felt and should have been one of the main vectors for bringing felt to the Tarim Basin.

While we have solid evidence that the Proto-Indo-Europeans knew weaving, the reconstructed vocabulary offers no additional evidence as to the appearance of the Indo-European loom; it may well have been a simple band loom, which can be hitched up wherever there are two convenient places to bind the ends. This would generally produce fairly narrow bands of cloth or belts (as we find associated with the earliest Tarim mummies). Our inability to reconstruct any form of loom contrasts with our knowledge of wheeled-vehicle parts whereby we can reconstruct words for 'wagon', 'wheel', 'nave' and 'thill' or 'pole'. This need not prove, however, that the Indo-Europeans lacked the loom although Elizabeth Barber has pointed out that all words associated with the warp-weighted loom in ancient Greek were either borrowed from another language or had to be recreated in Greek.

Drawing the Threads Together

If we take all of our evidence together, we can make the following observations:

On the basis of the linguistic evidence relating to textiles, the speakers of Proto-Indo-European, the language family presumably ancestral to the Bronze Age populations of the Tarim Basin, began to expand 1,000–2,000 years before our earliest evidence for Caucasoids in the Tarim Basin. The Tarim populations were not Proto-Indo-Europeans but could have belonged to some subsequent period of Indo-European linguistic evolution.

It is probable that Caucasoid populations, either across the steppe or through the Tarim Basin, introduced both sheep and wool to the region where they were adopted by the Chinese. It seems just possible that the Chinese might have borrowed their word for 'sheep' from some form of Iranian or Tocharian language.

Although we can broadly describe the vocabulary of textiles reconstructable in Proto-Indo-European, we cannot define the subsequent stages of textile development among the most easterly Indo-Europeans, the Tocharians and Indo-Iranians.

The earliest stages of textile development witnessed in the Tarim Basin are basically confined to headgear, shoes and some form of blanket or cloak; this may reflect the basic apparel of the population but it might also be governed entirely by ritual requirements (we seldom dress our own dead in trackshoes, swimming trunks, clown outfits, casual wear, etc.). One thing we can say about the clothes is that the dependence on woollen textiles conforms with a western or northern entry into the region.

Subsequently, about 1000 BC, we begin to find evidence for twills (a technique that, so far, our lexical evidence tells us nothing about). And by c. 800–500 BC we find plaids. We could follow Elizabeth Barber who suggests that twills began in the region between Anatolia and the north Caucasus and then spread east and west. But what about the specific correspondence between the European and Tarim plaids or tartans? Here we are in the embarrassing situation of suggesting that the extremes of our comparisons, Hallstatt and the Tarim Basin, are more similar in both production techniques and in final product than the areas in between. One is tempted to argue that only a direct historical connection (migration) between Europe and the Tarim Basin c. 1000 BC can possibly account for the similarities. Alternatively (and more circumspectly if we want to hang on to an academic reputation), we can admit that we simply do not know what types of textiles were worn in between these two distant outliers and be suspicious of any attempt to draw an arrow from Hallstatt to Qizilchoqa. New discoveries may support this thesis but the history of archaeology is full of cautionary tales where scholars, mesmerized, for example, by similar spirals found in Bronze Age Greece and elsewhere, had no difficulty sending Mycenaeans all over Eurasia to introduce their spirals and, more amazingly, sailing back several thousands of years to acquaint Neolithic populations with the motif (before radiocarbon dating you could get away with truly amazing theories). The evidence of textiles is particularly fragmentary – the discovery of cloth depends on very specific environmental conditions and so we have to take into account that our evidence is distributed unevenly in time and space. Barber's suggestion of a common source for both traditions at least splits the geographical distances involved and also places a distant origin on the cusp of two vast spheres of interaction. But if we want to get any closer to their origins we will have to strip the mummies not only of their clothes but also their skin and examine what their bodies can tell us of their origins.

CHAPTER SEVEN

Skulls, Genes and Knights with Long Swords

While the number of mummies from the Tarim Basin is impressive they are still only a small proportion of the human remains from prehistoric East Central Asia. They are also relatively unique, and without a chain of comparable mummies across Eurasia, they do not in themselves leave a trail that the archaeologist can easily follow. If we wish to trace the origins of the different peoples of the Tarim Basin we will have to make recourse to other evidence as well. For the prehistoric period we have the evidence of human skeletal remains and the new and developing field of 'molecular archaeology', the use of DNA in the study of ancient populations. Both of these help tell us where the mummies came from. We may also review the iconographic depictions of the historical populations of East Central Asia, particularly those produced before the Uyghurs absorbed the previous populations, in order to examine the appearance of the earliest historical descendants of the mummies in East Central Asia. Finally, we look to the modern population of the region to see if the genetic legacy of the mummies still survives.

Faces of the Past

The majority of mummies and human skeletal remains before the Han conquest of the Tarim Basin are of a Caucasoid physical type rather than Mongoloid or, as Chinese specialists might put it, they represent the 'minority' population of Xinjiang rather than the Han, the Chinese name for their own ethnic group. We have also seen how many of the mummies still retained their light-brown, reddish or even blond hair. But to take the description any further, we have to resort to the language of the physical anthropologist. The 'Beauty of Krorän', for example, whose hair was yellowish brown, possessed a face of 'medium flatness with prominent zygoma and high nasal bone', in other words, her face was relatively flat, her nose high and her cheek bones were prominent. In terms of her skull, her features exhibited 'mesocrany, euryprosopy leptorrhiny', i.e. the ratio between the length and breadth of her head fell in the middle (neither long-headed nor broad-headed), her face itself was broad and her nose was thin.

The best preserved of the mummies from Qizilchoqa, another reddish-brown-haired female (and clearly not of the Han), similarly had the prominent cheeks and high nose of the foreigners, i.e. Caucasoids. The shape of her skull, however, was dolichocranic, i.e. long headed, and mesocchine, i.e. she had medium sized orbits.

This, amazingly or disappointingly enough, is about as far as the physical appearance of the mummies goes in telling us of their ancestry or relationships. Unless there are populations similarly preserved over Eurasia, the mummies, no matter how well preserved, can tell us little of their origins. The irony is that their preservation actually obscures their more specific relationships: we may learn more when we undress them of their flesh.

Craniometry

The study of human skulls occupies a peculiar place in modern anthropological research. The rise in interest in human evolution and race in the 19th century prompted detailed analyses of the human skull. Like any object of biological study, it was seen that there were variations in the size and shape of the skull, some of which appeared to fall into a pattern with respect to time or geography. Particular interest concentrated on the overall relationship between the length and breadth of the skull. A ratio, the cranial index, involved dividing the length of the skull into the (obviously smaller) breadth of the skull and then multiplying by 100 (to remove the fraction). If the value was less than 75, the individual was determined to be 'long-headed' (i.e. dolichocephalic if living or dolichocranic if based on measurements of the fleshless skull) while a ratio of greater than 80 was labelled 'broad-headed' (brachycephalic/brachycranic). Individuals whose cranial index fell between 75 and 79.99 were classified as 'medium-headed' (mesocephalic/mesocranic). This permitted one to divide all human skulls into one of three categories (actually, you could also be a hyperbrachycephalic 'fat-head' when the ratio was greater than 85). Examination of modern populations or the excavation of various cemeteries revealed that these dimensions were not entirely arbitrary but that often a group of skulls from the same cemetery and period or modern population would be relatively homogeneous. It was, therefore, presumed that such measurements were an adequate reflection of sub-racial types and could be employed both to define and trace the ancestry of different populations.

Further refinements of such simple measurements were made where other characteristics were taken into consideration and this resulted in a more overtly ethnic classification of physical features and skulls into different types. Already in the late 18th century J. F. Blumenbach introduced the expression *Varietas Caucasia*, i.e. Caucasian, in the 3rd edition of his *De generis humani varietate nativa liber* (1795). He thought the people of the Caucasus to be the most beautiful subgroup of humans, the Caucasus to be the source of human origins and expansions, and that the skulls of the Georgians who occupied this region fell midway between those of the extremes, the Mongolians and the 'Aethiopians' of Africa. The Caucasian or Europoid could be defined by a whole suite of physical characteristics, e.g. small face with respect to size of brain case, long in proportion to breadth, small zygomatic bones, outer edges of orbits well demarcated, deep mandibular fossa of the temporal bone. The Caucasoids were subsequently divided into a series of more than a dozen subtypes, e.g. Nordic, Alpine and Mediterranean. Nordics were dolichocranic, their nose was leptorrhine (narrow) and male stature averaged 1.73 m (5 ft 8 in); Alpines were brachycranial, their noses were mesorrhine (medium-wide) and males averaged about 1.65 m (5 ft 5 in) in height. The Soviet leader Nikita Khrushchev was an Alpinid while Lord Kitchener, who graced so many British army enlistment posters of the First World War, was sternly and typically Nordic.

The problem with this approach became self-evident once the physical anthropologists undertaking such measurements came to draw historical conclusions. A single cemetery might reveal a variety of skull types and, while the archaeologists might find cultural uniformity across the cemetery, the physical anthropological report read like the description of a soirée at the UN. It appeared to archaeologists as if the skull measurements of the anthropologist were arbitrary and fixed categories that did not impart any particularly useful historical information. Imagine for a moment that human stature had been divided into three categories: tall = Watutsi, small = Pygmy, and medium = Syrian. When informed that analysis of the stature of 100 British burials resulted in 40 per cent Watutsi, 50 per cent Syrians and 10 per cent Pygmies, the archaeologist would be underwhelmed with the historical implications of such information. Suspicion that the physical anthropologist was not working with historically meaningful categories coupled with a general avoidance of anything that might smack of 'racism' since the Second World War resulted in a cleavage between archaeologists and those physical anthropologists who sought to identify sub-races of populations. This was considerably exacerbated by the attempts of anthropologists and geographers, the latter undergoing a phase of cartographical mania, to seek correlations between skull shape and just about anything else that might be measured or plotted on a map. For example, dolichocranics were shown to be more likely to divorce or commit suicide (not just in Sweden but even in France!), and various schools argued over the relative intelligence of the different physical subtypes.

If it were not for the atrocities perpetrated by 20th-century racists, the history of research concerning the cranial index and the Indo-Europeans would be a subject of pure amusement. Scientists argued violently through the 19th and early 20th centuries about whether the ancient Indo-Europeans were dolichocranic Nordics or brachycranic Alpines. The overtly racist George Vacher de Lapouge, for example, was able to boast that the dolichocephalic Indo-Europeans were cultivating wheat 'when those of the brachycephalics were probably still living like monkeys'. Alternatively, the Australian-based geographer, Griffith Taylor (1880–1964), found the cranial/cephalic index a sure guide to human evolution and the emergence of increasingly more progressive races and languages. With Taylor, one might read the cephalic index as an indicator of progress: the higher the index, the superior the brain. Hence, it was the Chinese with their brachycephalic heads who were the most progressive and spoke the most progressive language (not a clumsy, inflection-ridden Indo-European language!). Among the Indo-European languages, Taylor could also correlate the progressiveness of the language with its speakers' cephalic index. At the top end of the scale were the brachycephalic Indo-Iranians and Armenians and at the bottom were moored the least developed, the dolichocephalic Tocharians and the Celts (with Welsh scoring slightly more than Irish). With such egregious excesses, it is hardly surprising that the cephalic index became an object of ridicule and Colin Renfrew could write: 'Craniometry, the study and measurement of human skulls, has in recent years enjoyed about as much prestige in scientific circles as phrenology [i.e. the determination of a person's character on the basis of his or her skull shape].' Renfrew's statement is probably an accurate description of the attitudes of many archaeologists although it might be emphasized that archaeologists are as

Griffith-Taylor's cranial hierarchies

Group	Cephalic Index	Language
Centum	76?	Tocharian
(Dolichocephalic)	76	Gaelic
	77	Latin
	78?	(Oscan)
	78	Welsh
	78	Teuton
	79	Greek
Satem	80	Persian
(Brachycephalic)	81	Slavonic
	82	Lithuanian
	83?	(Sanskrit)
	84	Galcha
	85	Armenian

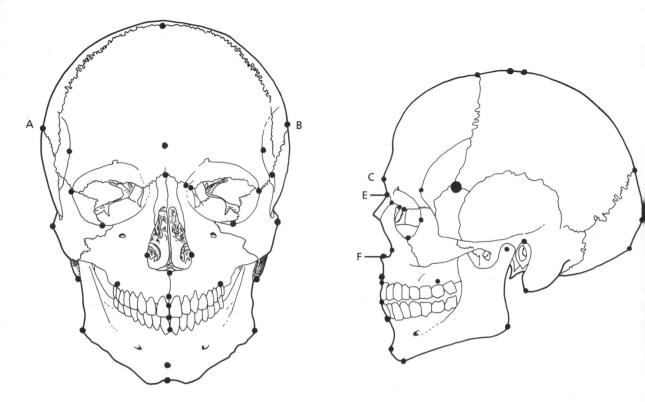

135. Examples of some of the Martin measurements: A–B indicates the breadth of a skull while C–D is the maximum length and E–F is the nasal height.

much subject to their own 'fashions' as people in any other discipline and many archaeologists are woefully ignorant of the current state of physical anthropology. But the cleavage has also occurred among physical anthropologists themselves who, on studying a cemetery may provide information on the sex, age, stature, demography, nutrition and pathology of the population but have no interest in what they regard as the arcane and suspect attempt to extract historical information out of the 21 separate bones that constitute the human skull. For many, R. S. Conway's conclusions at the beginning of this century – 'it appears the human cranium will not bear the weight of any ethnological deductions' – still holds true.

But this does not define all anthropologists and today there are many who would agree that, while there have been obvious and unfortunate (even criminal) excesses of interpretation in the past, if one increases the number of measurements and relates one's results to specific geographical populations, then meaningful results can be obtained. Analysis has often been drawn from an impressive list of about 100 possible measurements and ratios keyed against an internationally recognized list (for example, the Martin number, derived from Rudolph Martin's three-volume edition of his *Lehrbuch der Anthropologie*). The entire list is rarely if ever employed since it is a recipe book of possible measurements that one might make but the underlying reasons for making such precise measurements have never really been validated: they are just measurements. Some have sought to add new measurements which, they believe, are more sensitive to genetic factors, and there have been numerous investigations of living populations (comparisons between parents and children, between twinned and non-twinned siblings, etc.) that have attempted to isolate those facial features that are due to genetic inheritance from those that may depend on diet, environment or some other factor. Modern biological anthropologists have abandoned the approach of employing fixed subtypes for population genetics that accommodate the known evolutionary forces of natural selection, mutation, gene flow and genetic drift. Generally, any physical anthropologist engaged in assessing a population selects a series of measurements that he or she regards as most meaningful to a particular study.

The problem of verification is obviously difficult: the only way to determine whether skull measurements do provide useful genetic information is to trace skulls of known genetic relationships over a period of many generations. There are not many opportunities to do this; most modern populations tend to resent having their parents, grandparents, and so on exhumed in order to have their skulls measured. Fortunately, there are occasional situations where this is not such a problem. The village of Hallstatt in Austria which provided us with our evidence for ancient twill and early Celts, also practised an unusual way of disposing of their dead. Over a period of generations, the inhabitants of this mountain community exhumed the skulls and long bones of their relations, bleached their bones, and decorated the skulls with painted flowers before placing them in a charnel house. What is most important is that they not only decorated the

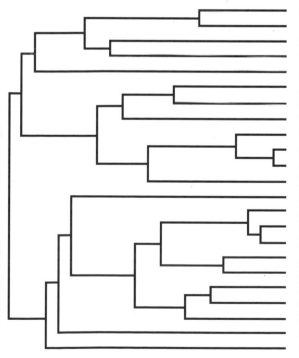

Norway, modern period
Faroe Islands, modern period
England, modern period
Ireland, modern period
Romano-British series
France, modern period
Czechoslovakia, modern period
Germany, modern period
Brittany, modern period
Switzerland, modern period
Gallo-Roman series
Denmark, modern period
England, Neolithic
England, Bronze Age
England, Iron Age
Denmark, Neolithic
Russia, Neolithic
Portugal, Neolithic
France, Neolithic
Sardinia, modern period
Etruscan series
Switzerland, Neolithic
Jericho, Bronze Age

136. Example of a dendrogram based on the craniometrics of both modern and ancient populations.

skulls but also inscribed them with their names which can then be related to parish registers to provide about five generations of individual families. Examination of these skulls, both with respect to absolute measurements and non-measurable surface features, has indicated that such techniques do correlate with the genetic relationships of the interred. Similar tests have been applied to other animals (mice and macaques) and good correlations between the evidence of physical anthropology and genetic relationships have again been observed.

Once a full array of measurements has been taken from each individual in a cemetery, the averages can be calculated and compared with those from other cemeteries or cultures. Statistical techniques then permit one to assess the relative affinity and differences among population samples. Such results can, at least, be intuitively plausible as may be seen from a recent dendrogram drawn up by Brace and Tracer (ill. 136). We should hardly be surprised that modern Norwegians and modern Faroese are closer together than to anyone else since they are also closely related geographically and linguistically. So also are the modern English and Irish, or modern Swiss and ancient Gallo-Romans. On the other hand, it also throws up relationships that simply will not do, e.g. the close relationship between Neolithic populations in Russia and Portugal makes absolutely no (pre-)historical sense at all. So, despite the impressive list of measurements and statistical techniques, it is still possible to obtain results that lack any historical meaning. With this caveat up front (and more to follow), we can look at the application of such techniques to the prehistoric populations of East Central Asia.

The Paths of the Skulls

Although some analysis was made of the skulls collected by Sven Hedin and other early explorers, only about 20 were examined employing the more archaic techniques of analysis that we have discussed above and, appropriately enough, with corresponding results, e.g. 11 skulls collected from the Lopnur region were separated into Chinese, Nordics and Alpines. The more recent excavations, however, have yielded much more material and now we have 302 skulls from more than nine cemeteries which have been examined in detail by Han Kangxin of the Institute of Archaeology in Beijing. We can summarize his results in tabular form (p. 237).

The Qäwrighul remains are relatively homogeneous and they exhibit features associated with a type known as Proto-Europoid, a rather robust Caucasoid, especially well represented in Northern Europe and the steppelands and forest-steppe of Russia and the Ukraine. Similar remains occur in the Bronze Age cemeteries of southern Siberia, Kazakhstan, Central Asia and the Lower Volga. Anthropologically, Han found the closest relatives of the Qäwrighul burials in the cemeteries of the Afanasevo culture (of the Yenisei and Altai region) and the Andronovo culture that spanned

Cemeteries and physical types according to Han Kangxin

Cemetery	Date	Total skulls	Type	Affiliations
Qäwrighul	1800 BC	18 (11 m, 7f)	Proto-Europoid	Bronze Age of southern Siberia, Kazakhstan, Central Asia, Lower Volga
Yanbulaq	1100–500 BC	29	Mongoloid (21) Proto-Europoid (8)	
Shambabay	800–500 BC	1	?Indo-Afghan	South Pamir (Saka)
Alwighul	700–1 BC	58 (33m, 25f)	Indo-Afghan Pamir-Ferghana Mongoloid	
Charwighul IV	500–1 BC	77 (50m, 27f)	*Proto-Europoid	
Monggul Kürä	400 BC–AD 200	13 (7m, 6f)	Pamir-Ferghana Mongoloid	Central Asia (Saka)
Sampul	200 BC	56	?Indo-Afghan	South Pamir (Saka)
Krorän	AD 200	6 (5m, 1f)	?Indo-Afghan (5) Mongoloid (1)	South Pamir (Saka)
Charwighul III	AD 200	11 (9m, 2f)	*Caucasian	

Kazakhstan and reached southwards into West Central Asia and the Altai. These comparisons are absolutely critical since they relate the earliest mummies to Bronze Age populations geographically proximate, whose own ancestry can be traced back earlier than that of the mummies.

The next oldest remains derive from the Yanbulaq cemetery near Qumul (Hami), situated to the northeast of Qäwrighul and the easternmost cemetery investigated. Here Han Kangxin identified 21 of the 29 complete skulls as Mongoloids and these are the earliest definite evidence of Mongoloids in East Central Asia. Their physical type, incidentally, was not that typical of the Han, the ethnic Chinese, but of the populations of eastern Tibet. The remaining skulls, however, belonged to Caucasoids who are closest to those from Qäwrighul and point to the same general direction for their origin, i.e. the steppelands to the north and west.

The single skull recovered from among the inhumation burials at Shambabay near Tashkurgan in the far west of the Tarim Basin has been compared with the type that spanned the Mediterranean across Central Asia; this type also includes the Saka tribes of the southern Pamirs.

A much larger sample of 58 skulls was recovered from one of the mass graves at Alwighul in the Tängri Tagh (Tian Shan). Here Han distinguishes

*Han Kangxin's analysis of 269 skulls recovered from 9 cemeteries. m = male, f = female, * = modified.*

137. The three types of human cranial variation in Xinjiang according to Han Kangxin.
1 = Proto-Europoid,
2 = Pamir-Ferghana and
3 = Indo-Afghan.

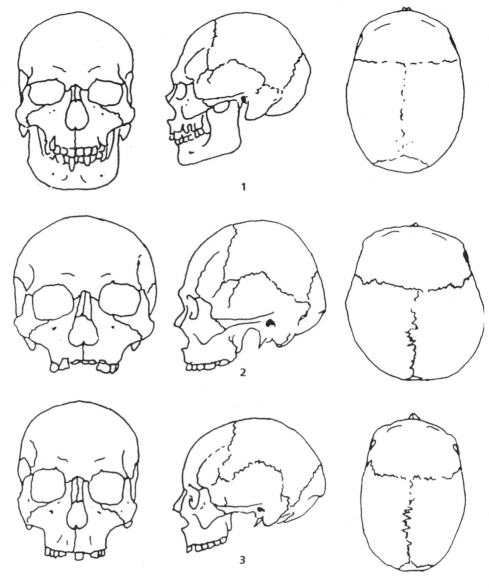

two Caucasoid types: the Eastern Mediterranean or Indo-Afghan type with their long and high skulls and the broader and rounder skulls of the Pamir-Ferghana type; Han also identified hybrids of these two subtypes as well as some evidence of Mongoloid admixture. By now, the attentive reader will know we owe another caveat: the three physical types employed by Han Kangxin – Proto-Europoids, Indo-Afghans and Pamir-Ferghanans – are largely relabelled Nordics, Mediterraneans and Alpines, terms that send shivers of apprehension down the spines of Western biological anthropologists. To be sure, Han is also working with a considerable suite of measurements but his typological approach or, at least, his terminology must admittedly be regarded as extremely old fashioned. But for the present, we will try to play the hand we are dealt.

Not too distant from the Alwighul cemetery and still along the southern slopes of the Tängri Tagh is the cemetery complex of Charwighul. At Cemetery IV the 77 skulls recovered were regarded as less robust forms of Proto-Europoids. Examination of the skulls also indicated widespread trepanation. This refers to the rather radical medical practice of drilling holes, here on the order of 1 to 2 cm wide, into the skulls. Such operations were performed on occasion several times, presumably to relieve the patient of physical pain or spiritual demons, and from traces of healing of the bone around the apertures, it is clear that, sometimes at least, people survived this widespread operation.

The burials recovered from Monggul Kürä, since they are located on the upper reaches of the Ili River and date to the centuries on either side of the Christian era, are generally identified with the Wusun and Saka. In so far as anyone can distinguish between these two historical groups archaeologically, 11 of the 13 skulls are assigned to Wusun burials and only two are Saka. There was variation between the skulls, among which two female skulls displayed definite Mongoloid features, but in general they could be assigned to the same Pamir-Ferghana type also seen at Alwighul.

The Sampul cemetery provides us with our only physical anthropological evidence of the southern Silk Road in the vicinity of Khotan. Although the cemetery contained various individual graves employing some form of log coffin, all the burials examined derive from the group graves which date to the first centuries BC. Han Kangxin has identified the remains as belonging to the same Indo-Afghan type that one encounters among the Saka of the southern Pamirs.

The half-dozen burials from a cemetery in Krorän provide interesting evidence for changes in the area around Lopnur where we earlier encountered the Proto-Europoids from Qäwrighul. Now, at this later period the physical features, like those from the Sampul cemetery to the west, are Indo-Afghan and again related to the Saka of the southern Pamirs.

Finally, the 11 burials from Charwighul III have been assigned by some scholars to the Xiongnu and date from the first centuries AD. They have been described only in the broadest terms as Caucasoid with some non-Caucasoid traits. Moreover, three of the skulls had been artificially deformed with markedly raised foreheads produced most likely by binding the skull at infancy until it had assumed its tall elongated shape. This practice was widely known among different populations of the Eurasian steppe: it probably defined the local group's concept of beauty and also marked them off ethnically from their neighbours. Artificial skull deformation is known in the steppelands from about 2000 BC among the late Yamna and Catacomb peoples north of the Black and Caspian seas where it can constitute up to 70 per cent of the skeletal populations of some regions. Skull deformation is widely known later in the Iron Age where it occurred among the Alans and Huns. As we have already recounted, skull deformation was also practised in Kucha during the 1st millennium AD.

Who's on First?

As no undisputed human remains have yet been uncovered from the Stone Age of East Central Asia, we can still say nothing about the original population of the Tarim Basin. We can only emphasize that so far the archaeology of the region admits certain evidence of extensive occupation in the Bronze Age but does not exclude the possibility of earlier settlement.

The variability of human remains recovered from Bronze and Iron Age cemeteries suggests, if one adheres to the typological approach employed by Chinese physical anthropologists, several different population groups in prehistoric Xinjiang. These groups have been posited to include three groups of Caucasoids: Proto-Europoids, Indo-Afghans, Pamir-Ferghanans; as well as two groups of Mongoloids: eastern Tibetan and Han (ethnic Chinese).

So far the earliest physical evidence has been identified as conforming to a rather robust 'Proto-European' type. Han Kangxin has recorded such traits from Qäwrighul, Yanbulaq, and Charwighul IV. He has also attempted to place the Qäwrighul population within the larger picture of Eurasian populations by comparing Qäwrighul males and females separately with 24 other populations on the basis of a ratio derived from cranial and facial indices. The results obtained by Han Kangxin are of considerable interest. Among males the ratio provided by these indices produces a tight cluster of samples possessing similar values. Members of this cluster include

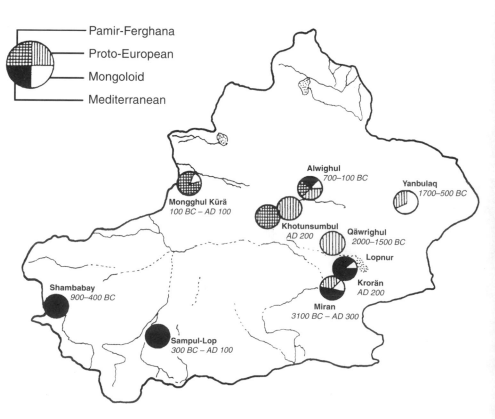

138. The distribution of physical types in Xinjiang according to Han Kangxin.

Pamir-Ferghana
Proto-European
Mongoloid
Mediterranean

Alwighul
700–100 BC

Yanbulaq
1700–500 BC

Mongghul Kürä
100 BC – AD 100

Khotunsumbul
AD 200

Qäwrighul
2000–1500 BC

Lopnur

Krorän
AD 200

Miran
3100 BC – AD 300

Shambabay
900–400 BC

Sampul-Lop
300 BC – AD 100

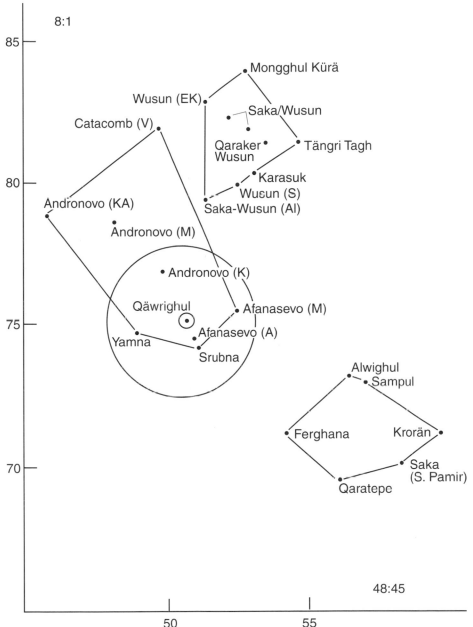

139. A plot of the cranial (8:1) against the facial (48:45) indices finds the Qäwrighul skulls most closely related to those of the Eurasian steppelands. (A) = Altai, (Al) = Alai (EK) = Eastern Kazakhstan, (K) = Kazakhstan, (KA) = Kazakhstan-Altai, (M) = Minusinsk Basin, (S) – Semirechye, (V) = Volga.

Qäwrighul males, males of the Afanasevo culture of the Minusinsk Basin and the Altai Mountains, and males from the Yamna and Srubna cultures of the Russian steppelands. Before the excavations at Qäwrighul, these last cultures were long regarded as a closely related unit to which one might also add the Sredny Stog culture of the Dnieper-Don region. The relationship had its difficulties. Not with the Sredny Stog, Yamna and Srubna cultures that represented a succession of cultures between the Dnieper and Volga *c.* 4500–1200 BC, but with the inclusion of the Afanasevo culture. For the

Afanasevo culture occurs at an enormous distance (*c.* 1500 km (931 miles)) to the east. Nevertheless, it was generally presumed, on the basis of the evidence of physical anthropology and an impressive suite of economic and cultural features, that the Afanasevo culture represented an eastern outlier of the European steppe cultures that expanded to the east sometime during the 4th to early 3rd millennia BC. That this movement may not have halted at the Altai but extended southwards into the Tarim Basin had been previously suggested on the most fragmentary of archaeological evidence (surface finds of pottery recovered by Aurel Stein that bore vague similarities to Afanasevo pottery). Han's suggestion that there was an intrusion of human populations from the north into the eastern Tarim would seem to be the most economical solution if indeed the males recovered from Qäwrighul may be identified as the earliest Europeans in Xinjiang. That the physical remains from Qäwrighul and Charwighul IV remain unmixed with Mongoloids suggests that these robust Caucasoids were the first to arrive in the Tarim; Mongoloid populations lay still farther east and only begin to appear in the later 2nd millennium or early 1st millennium BC at sites such as Yanbulaq, predictably enough the easternmost of our Xinjiang cemeteries. It is difficult to say whether the Mongoloid settlement of the eastern Tarim represented an actual push of Mongoloid populations into East Central Asia or whether they had been established there long before. We have already seen that all the physical remains from neighbouring Gansu have been Mongoloid. Han Kangxin emphasizes that of the 302 skulls assembled for

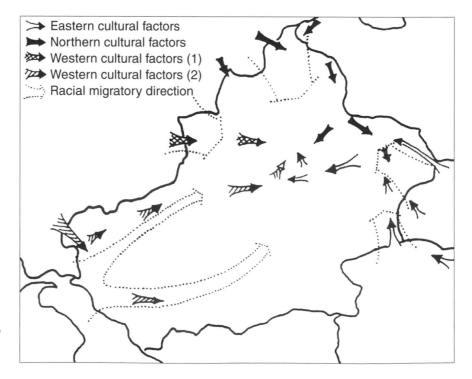

140. Han Kangxin's map of cultural and biological influences on the populations of Xinjiang.

his survey of the prehistoric burials of Xinjiang, only 11 per cent belonged to Mongoloids, the major movement of Mongoloids into the Tarim Basin dating to the Qin and Han periods which coincides roughly with our historical evidence for Chinese expansion. Of the later Caucasoid types, we find that the Indo-Afghan or Eastern Mediterranean physical type appeared in the last millennium BC at a series of sites stretching from the southern Pamirs (Shambabay) along the southern Silk Road to Khotan (Sampul) and then on into the Lopnur territory where Proto-Europoids were previously attested. This physical type is closest to that of the southern Saka whose remains have been identified in the southern Pamirs since about the 6th century BC. It has more distant ties with the agricultural populations of Central Asia (inferred from archaeological evidence but to date unsupported by biological testing).

The third group of Caucasoids is the Pamir-Ferghana type whose greatest similarities lie among populations to the north of the Indo-Afghans, i.e. the northern Pamirs and Ferghana. Their remains are largely concentrated along the southern border of the Tängri Tagh (Alwighul, Monggul Kürä) or in the upland regions of the Ili River. While one may point to probable ancestors of the Indo-Afghan type, it is not so clear with the Pamir-Ferghana. Some scholars consider them to be a mixture of Proto-Europoids with the Indo-Afghan type. As we have seen, the two types do come together in the cemetery at Alwighul.

Following the most recent analysis of Han Kangxin, the general picture then suggests an initial colonization of East Central Asia from the northern steppelands by Proto-Europoids with a later push westwards by Mongoloid populations. A second movement of Caucasoids of the Indo-Afghan type can be traced along the route from the Pamirs across the southern route of the Tarim Basin as far as Lopnur. This type is also found in some sites to the north where we encounter the Pamir-Ferghana type in the late 1st millennium BC.

We have described the results of Han Kangxin's analyses as an economical explanation as to what happened in the Tarim Basin, but is this model entirely justified? As we observed above, the typological approach that discusses population movements in terms of fixed sub-racial types is dismissed by the majority of biological anthropologists in the West who require that their results be supported by more rigorous statistical procedures. In a perfect world we would expect that any attempt to trace the relationships of the Tarim populations would employ the analysis of a larger number of pre-selected measurements and that these would include a much wider range of populations than was employed in Han's study. For example, the figure that places Qäwrighul in a cluster of steppe populations should be tested against a larger number of potential 'relations' (we should not be overly surprised if Qäwrighul is closer to the steppe populations when many of the foreign samples being compared belong to steppe populations). We need to open the analysis up and employ a much wider range of 'Caucasoid' populations from the neighbouring regions and a greater number of measurements and then put them through more robust statistical scrutiny. The absence of comparable measurements across a large number of samples makes this impossible at the present but at least a start has been made.

For the past four years Brian Hemphill of Vanderbilt University has been examining the population dynamics of societies in West Central Asia and the Indus region, two of the areas that potentially could have populated the Tarim Basin with a Caucasoid physical type. He has only recently expanded his studies to include several of the samples from the Tarim Basin, specifically the sites of Qäwrighul, Alwighul and Kroran. Here nine measurements were employed (less than what one would hope for but all that could be assembled from the available data) to compare the Tarim samples with samples obtained from 21 sites comprising territories extending from the steppelands across Central Asia and as far south as the Indus Valley. In some respects his preliminary (and unpublished) results support those of Han. For example, both Alwighul and especially the later burials from Kroran manifest closest affinities with Bronze Age Bactrian populations, especially the earliest sample from Sapalli Tepe (c. 2200–2000 BC). But what about Qäwrighul, our earliest cemetery of Caucasoids in the Tarim Basin?

In Han's study, the closest affinities with Qäwrighul were shared by Bronze Age steppe populations. Hemphill included much the same series of steppe cultures in his own study, including several Afanasevo and Andronovo populations. But not one of five different statistical tests yielded the expected placement of Qäwrighul in the cluster of steppe populations. Rather, the results obtained from his series of multivariate statistical analyses resoundingly rejected any connection between Qäwrighul and steppe populations to the west. These analyses repeatedly identified Qäwrighul as an outlier that exhibits no close affinities to any other samples. To be sure, a distant and peripheral association was indicated between Qäwrighul and populations in the Swat Valley of Pakistan, but it is more likely that the Qäwrighul people are simply so different, so peripheral, from their contemporary neighbours that at the present we cannot determine the ultimate origins of this population with any degree of certainty. Nevertheless, one possibility raised by these results is that the ancestors of the Qäwrighul people may have entered the Tarim Basin in small numbers some centuries or more before the skeletal remains we have discovered. Once settled, the Qäwrighul population may have experienced a significant degree of genetic drift that served to set them apart from their parent and any contemporary neighbouring population. Nevertheless, it is quite clear from the results obtained by Hemphill that any explanation which seeks to account for the origins of the Qäwrighul people by suggesting that they stemmed from a massive migration of Caucasoid steppe populations is not supported by the biological evidence currently available. Hence, until we have more measurements and more evidence of neighbouring populations, the origins of the Qäwrighul people, at least from the perspective of biological anthropology, remain a mystery.

Universal Donors

At present, the most precise source of information on the origin of the European populations in East Central Asia rests with the skeletal remains but future analysis may lie elsewhere. The mummies, like any cadaver stretched out on the coroner's table, can be made to reveal something of their identity. Chinese scientists have examined several of the best-preserved mummies and have provided us, for example, with information concerning their blood types. This, incidentally, was not gained directly from the blood itself but from samples of hair and rib. Although our data is extremely restricted, so far it suggests that prehistoric Xinjiang was a good area for a transfusion: all the mummies so far examined have been revealed as universal donors, i.e. type O. Blood typing has been carried out on the 'Beauty of Kroran' from the cemetery on the Töwän River and three of the female mummies from Qizilchoqa also possessed blood type O. The sample here, however, has been extremely small and is incapable of providing us with much in the way of useful information concerning the origins of the mummy population.

In addition to blood type, the 'Beauty of Kroran' was examined by the Immunological Laboratory at the Shanghai Institute of Blood Transfusion. Here the scientists were interested in retrieving evidence for what is known as human lymphocyte antigens or HLA; these are proteins that form on the white blood cells and are part of the body's immune system. As there is great diversity in the immune response of individuals, examination of HLA subtypes has become of considerable interest to those tracing the migrations of people, or at least their genes, since the variation within HLA samples provides markers of one's genetic ancestry. The 'Beauty of Kroran', for example, possessed the following antigens: HLA-A2, A9, A11, B5, B40 and Bw22. There is nothing startling about such a combination of antigens since they all occur among native populations of China. What might be observed, however, is that two of them (HLA-A9 and HLA-B40) both show distinct associations with northern Eurasia and their frequency diminishes the farther one moves south. The HLA evidence can accommodate the hypothesis that there was movement of some populations from the north into the Tarim Basin although it hardly secures such a conclusion.

Genetic Fingerprints

Another approach to the ancestry of the Tarim mummies is genetics. It should be emphasized that public expectation that the study of DNA will resolve all major issues of the origins and migrations of peoples far outstrips what we can say with any degree of confidence at the present time. Statements that the closest living relative to some genetically fingerprinted mummy is an estate agent in South London might make good press but are of little historical value when we know so little about the DNA of all the peoples across Eurasia. Both the available sample size of modern populations and our knowledge of past populations must be extended enormously before we can make the type of pronouncements that many mistakenly assume are already within our grasp. Yet there is still a consensus that DNA will eventually be one of the most powerful tools in the arsenal of the prehistorian.

Those 'molecular archaeologists' interested in tracing the origins and relationships of past communities have concentrated on the genetic trails exhibited by mitochondrial DNA (mtDNA). Unlike cellular DNA, the chains of genes that are a product of both our parents and that reside in the nucleus of a cell, mtDNA is to be found in the mitochondria, the chemical powerpacks of cells, whose genetic contribution derives entirely from the mother's side. The genetic information encoded in mtDNA is then passed from one generation of mothers to the next and in the current most widely accepted hypothesis, this trail leads ultimately to the female ancestor of *Homo sapiens sapiens* who has been nicknamed 'African Eve'. This trail extends back to something on the order of 130,000 years ago. Following the trail of the mtDNA is far easier than chasing after one's DNA inheritance because mtDNA possesses 37 genes arranged in 16,569 base pairs while that of cellular DNA itself possesses hundreds of thousands of genes in 3 billion base pairs: if one is looking for a needle in a haystack it is best to keep the haystack as small as possible.

In terms of 'racial' divisions, the course of mtDNA suggests that modern humans evolved earliest in Africa whence they emerged and began expanding sometime around 100,000 years ago, eventually replacing earlier forms of hominids such as the Neanderthals of Europe. Within Eurasia itself a split later developed between the Caucasians and the Asians who, in turn, divided between the Northeast Asians and the American Indians.

In the more refined study of the population relationships among northern Eurasians, geneticists have usually concentrated on two segments of the mtDNA chain of chemicals known as the control zones, each consisting of about 400 base pairs. Mutations that accumulate in these regions, especially that designated region I, provide historical data on the ancestry of the individual, and scientists are now trying to establish which mutations in these particular regions may reflect a specific historical path.

It was his drive to know the results of DNA analysis on the mummies that first prompted Victor's involvement in the prehistory of Xinjiang. As part of the initial project, Paolo Francalacci from the University of Sassari obtained tissue samples from 11 mummies from Qizilchoqa and from mummies housed in the museums at Ürümchi and Korla, as well as at the Institute of Archaeology in Ürümchi. Although he sampled 11 mummies, the Chinese authorities permitted Paolo to carry off samples from only two of them and the DNA in one of these was too damaged for analysis. At present the genetic history of the mummies rests with but a single individual.

Paolo discovered that the DNA of one of the mummies belonged to what is known as Haplogroup H, one of the nine subtypes of mitochondrial lineages that are largely associated with European populations. Haplogroup H is the commonest marker of European populations and occurs in about 40 per cent of Europeans (but also in about 15 per cent of people from the Near East), while haplogroups A through G are more typically 'Asian'. As it may be found among people of such diverse ancestry as Swedes, Finns, Tuscans, Corsicans and Sardinians, it cannot so far relate the mummies yet to any specific European subgroup; it merely emphasizes once again that the Xinjiang mummies find their closest genetic relations among Europeans. As for Victor's original quest: the relationship between the Tarim mummies and the Tyrolean 'Iceman', the latest results on the latter show him to belong to Haplogroup K, a widespread European haplotype which occurs in about 10 per cent of the population of Europe. Paolo is convinced that if he were able to recover more tissue samples from other Tarim Basin mummies, they would probably reveal other European and Asian haplogroups.

For the present, 'molecular archaeology' is more a hope than a solution to our problem. If the procedures can be extended to the analysis of ancient populations such as those presented in our survey of human skeletal remains,

141. Paolo Francalacci extracting samples for DNA analysis from an exhumed mummy at Qizilchoqa.

e.g. Afanasevo, Andronovo and Saka, then DNA may ultimately provide us with the types of answers we are looking for.

Knights with Long Swords

As we have already seen, the Caucasoid physical type continued to flourish in East Central Asia through to the early historical period. This is clearly attested both in the written descriptions of various populations such as the Wusun but also in the splendid frescoes associated with Buddhist shrines in the northern Tarim region near Kucha, specifically at the cave shrines at Qumtura and Qizil. The shrines depict stylized deities, guardian figures and, most important from the perspective of physical type, those in the style known as the 'knights with long swords' or 'Tocharian donors' which date to about the 6th and 7th centuries AD (pl. XII). Dressed in the Sassanian style of Iran with long coats, long swords and daggers, the features of the individuals painted are clearly European. Their hair is usually light brown or red which could alternatively be interpreted in terms of their natural hair colour (blond or red) or of deliberate dyeing as the use of henna to redden

142. Bearded Europoid figures from Qizil.

hair is known up until the present time in Xinjiang. Either way they make a reasonable match with our earlier mummies, e.g. the 'Ravishing Redhead' of Qizilchoqa. The eye colour of the individuals is difficult to determine – they have often been deliberately defaced – although in those instances where some colour remains it would appear to be light (grey, green or blue). In these portrayals, one has the impression that we are dealing with local artists depicting their own people. Another perspective perhaps can be seen farther east at Khocho in the Turpan region, the later Uyghur capital, where we find paintings of both oriental monks and Caucasoid ones. The combination of green eyes and red hair with the poorly shaven face seen, for example, in the portrayal of a 'local' monk beside a Chinese monk, establishes a very marked contrast (pl. XIII). Another monk from Khocho boasts massive brow-ridges and round eyes, again characteristic of a 'foreigner', at least through the eyes of a Chinese artist. The *Youyang zazu*, a document dating to the Tang dynasty (AD 618–906) attributes the exotic appearance of people with blond hair, green eyes and red beards to their being the issue of an ancestral spirit and a cow.

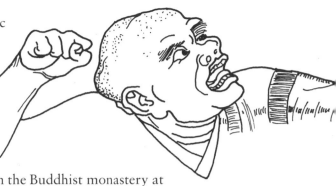

143. Portrayal, if not caricature, of a Caucasoid 'foreigner' from Khocho in the Turpan Basin. The original reveals greenish-blue irises.

Another site to offer major evidence of the appearance of Caucasoids is Temple 9 from the Buddhist monastery at Bezäklik. Here we again have donors but also monks, the European monks dressed differently from their Mongoloid counterparts; the Caucasoid monks also always have their heads shaven unlike the Mongoloid monks. The monks are depicted with reddish-brown and black hair and light-coloured (blue, green) or less frequently brown eyes. The rugged European physical type has commonly been assumed to reflect Tocharian speakers. In addition to the monks, we also have two Caucasoid-looking merchants. One had reddish-brown hair and green eyes; the other black hair and brown eyes. The dress here, complete with hats, has been identified as that of Sogdian merchants.

144. Sogdian merchant from the Buddhist monastery at Bezäklik.

The Modern Population

Ethnically, modern China defines itself as a country of 56 nationalities (the number is growing as additional groups apply for this coveted status which brings with it special consideration) among whom the overwhelming majority (over 93 per cent) belong to the Han. Many of the minorities also belong to Mongoloid groups but some retain features characteristic of Caucasian groups, specifically those occupying the northwest of China, i.e. the Kazakh, Dongxiang, Hui and the Uyghur of East Central Asia. Other than obvious physical differences between populations – which may be obvious but difficult to quantify – there are also biological differences between the world's major population groups. One of these occurs in what is known as immunoglobulin Gm which appears in 'racially' specific variants or allotypes. For example Gm f;b is associated with Caucasoids, Gm a;bst occurs specifically in Mongoloids and other types of Gm are found among peoples of African descent. Additional differences can be found in the Rh factor where about

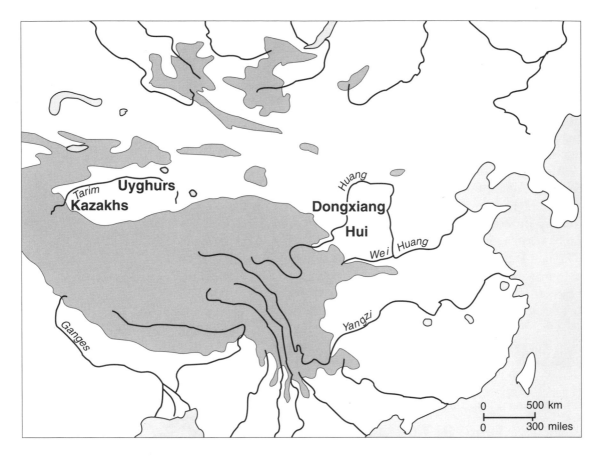

145. Distribution in China of major groups with Europoid related genes.

15 per cent of Caucasoids possess the relevant gene for Rh negative while the frequency among most Chinese nationalities ranges from only about 0.1 per cent to 0.4 per cent. There are further genetic differences as well.

Chinese scientists have measured these various gene frequencies across the modern populations of their country and these measurements provide the basis for estimating the contribution of various Caucasoid-related genes to the four minority groups in which we find them. Among the Uyghurs, 'Caucasian genes' have been estimated at as much as 54 per cent while the Kazakhs, who also occupy parts of Xinjiang, reveal about 34 per cent. To the east in Gansu we find the Dongxiangs with 25 per cent and still farther east in Ningxia are the Hui whose Caucasian admixture is set at about 11–14 per cent. From these figures, the trajectory of Caucasian genetic influence in East Central Asia and East Asia seems quite clear: it originates in the west and diminishes toward the east.

How and when this admixture took place is not entirely clear as we can never be entirely certain whether or not the Uyghurs, before settling in East Central Asia, were already intermarrying with Caucasian populations or, indeed, whether their ancestors had done so when they were living farther to the northeast. What we suspect is that upon their arrival in East Central Asia and the establishment of their own empire there, they engaged in

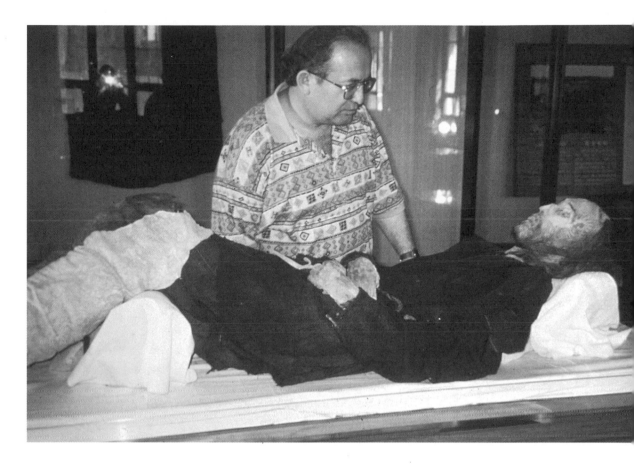

substantial intermarriage with Caucasian populations whose own ancestors may be traced back in the region to the beginnings of the Bronze Age. The blood of the Xinjiang mummies runs through the veins of the current population of the region.

146. Ultimately related? The Uyghur archaeologist Dolkun Kamberi and 'Ur-David' whom he excavated.

CHAPTER EIGHT

The Usual Suspects: The Indo-Iranians

At the head of the list of usual suspects are the ubiquitous Indo-Iranians. In one guise or another Indo-Iranian languages were spoken across the entire area of East Central Asia and apart from Chinese in the east and Tibetan to the southeast, and Turkic and Mongol to the northeast, almost all other approaches to the Tarim Basin carried one through lands which were at one time or another historically attributed to the Indo-Iranians. Moreover, if one imagines that archaeology may serve as circumstantial evidence for the distribution of a prehistoric language (this is admittedly a very big 'if'), then the Andronovo culture, which is widely credited with having stimulated cultural change in East Central Asia, is generally associated with the early Indo-Iranians.

We have already reviewed the general linguistic landscape of the approaches to East Central Asia and briefly surveyed the discovery of the various Indo-Iranian languages of the region. It is now time to examine how they fit together, where they originated and whether they can be identified among the *prehistoric* populations of the Tarim and Turpan basins.

The Indic Overlay

If we attempted to peel off the layers of Indo-Iranian languages in East Central Asia, we would look to the Indic or Indo-Aryan languages as one of the topmost layers. We have seen that the Indo-Aryan languages attested in East Central Asia come basically in two varieties. One of these is subdivided into Sanskrit and Buddhist Hybrid Sanskrit which were the literary languages employed by Buddhists in East Central Asia. Consequently, they are reasonably well distributed over the Tarim Basin wherever we find remains of Buddhist monasteries, and they are also languages upon which translations were made into other languages such as Chinese or Tocharian. Sanskrit as found in East Central Asia occurred only as a written language and almost exclusively in Buddhist contexts. Buddhist Hybrid Sanskrit is essentially a Prākrit (vernacular) that was 'Sanskritized' in order to serve the needs of Buddhist literature, hence its antiquity can be no greater than Buddhism itself. For this reason, while it is widely attested, the date of its arrival in the Tarim Basin can be no earlier than the spread of Buddhism, possibly as early as the first centuries BC, and the language itself is attested in documents no earlier than the 4th century AD. As it was a liturgical language that was not specific to any ethnic group, it cannot be regarded as a serious contender for one of the vernacular languages of the Tarim Basin. Moreover, the Buddhist content and artificial character disqualifies it as a language that might have been spoken by the prehistoric populations of the Tarim who have left mummified remains.

The second type of Indo-Aryan language embraces Indic vernaculars, specifically what are known as Prākrits. While Buddhist monks may have employed Sanskrit and Buddhist Hybrid Sanskrit in their literature and liturgy, we have seen that the administrative language of much of East Central Asia in the first centuries of our era would appear to have been a Prākrit. A comparison here might be made between the situation in East Central Asia and that of the Catholic Church which, until relatively recently, employed Church Latin as the language of liturgy while its central administration in Rome used Italian on a day-to-day basis.

We have recounted how Aurel Stein discovered large quantities of Prākrit documents in his excavation at the site of Niyä and these date to about the 3rd century AD. The earliest evidence for a form of Prakrit in the Tarim derives from a translation of the *Dhammapada* which was found in Khotan. This document dates back to about the 1st century AD. Now as the earliest evidence for the Prākrits in India itself only dates to about the 3rd century BC and Prākrits in the Tarim Basin are again exclusively associated with the Kushans (2nd century BC and later), they too make poor candidates for the languages of the prehistoric populations. Moreover, some Prākrit documents recovered from the site of Niyä contain Iranian words which suggests either that a Prākrit was superimposed on a population that spoke an Iranian language or, more likely, that it arrived in the Tarim after absorbing Iranian loanwords along the way, i.e. as it passed through Bactria, one of the cultural and religious gateways to East Central Asia. Either way, we have good reason to regard Indo-Aryan as a weak contender for the language of any of the prehistoric mummies although a native Indic speaker might possibly be identified with some of the mummies from the region of Krorän that date to the Han or a later period. But we'll find some better candidates among the much more diverse set of Iranian languages.

Sogdian

Although Sogdian was widely employed in the Tarim Basin, it is not one of our prime suspects. Even more than the Indo-Aryan languages, Sogdian, could be cast in the role of a late interloper in East Central Asia, albeit an extremely important one. Surely the most eclectic of the Iranian languages, Sogdian served as a vehicle for recording the documents of not only the Buddhists but also of the Manicheans and Christians in the Tarim and Turpan basins. In addition, it was employed to record secular documents, which is not at all surprising since Sogdian served as the *lingua franca* of the northern half of the Silk Road. Most documents written in Sogdian date to the 7th to 9th centuries although they occur from at least the 4th century AD and there are inscriptions on coins in Sogdiana that date to a few centuries earlier. Although Sogdian itself has become extinct, it is survived by Yaghnobi, a language spoken by a community of less than 2,000 people in Tadjikistan.

For the purposes of our survey, the expansion of Sogdian into East Central Asia must be regarded as a relatively recent phenomenon. The centre of Sogdian speech was Sogdiana with its centre in the Samarkand-Bukhara region and its core area was confined to Uzbekistan. It is from there that the language was carried eastwards into the Tarim Basin by Sogdian traders who controlled the caravans' transit around the northern and southern rims of the Täklimakan Desert. There is no reason then to see in Sogdian anything other than a language that entered the Tarim region with the opening of the Silk Road; there are no grounds to associate it with the earlier prehistoric populations of Xinjiang.

Saka

The best-attested Iranian language of East Central Asia is Saka or Khotanese Saka which serves as a reminder that the manuscripts of this language were found primarily in the territory of ancient Khotan on the southern branch of the Silk Road. The language is attested both in literary documents, essentially translations of Buddhist literature, and in secular documents. The script used to convey the language was the Brāhmī script that was imported from India and employed in the production of the Buddhist originals that were translated into Saka.

Other documents in a Saka language have been recovered from the northern branch of the Silk Road at Maralbashi and Tumshuq. In addition, pre-Islamic Qāshqär is also assigned to Saka speakers. The datable Saka documents begin in about the 7th century AD and continue through to the 10th century, by which time Uyghur was replacing all the earlier languages of the Tarim Basin. Saka documents were apparently carried eastwards from their native territory into the region around Turpan and farther into Gansu, since Khotanese manuscripts were found at Dunhuang.

From a geographical perspective, the Saka dialects were originally confined to the western part of the Tarim Basin and, at least in documentary form, only moved eastwards after they had been long established in the western Tarim.

The Saka, as we have already seen, constituted an ethnic group that occupied an enormous area which, according to ancient historians, spanned the European and much of the Asian steppe – if one wishes to include both the Scythians and the people whom the ancient Iranians called Saka in a single linguistic entity. We have also seen that they expanded to rule briefly in both Bactria and northern India. It is ironic then that most of our linguistic evidence derives from their easternmost outpost in East Central Asia; where they dominated in Bactria or northern India, the evidence is largely confined to personal names of rulers. It is as if the French language were known primarily from the documents written in Corsica rather than in France itself.

The trajectory of the Saka languages in Xinjiang would appear to have been from west (or northwest) to east and, although they became extinct in East Central Asia, dialects related to the earlier languages of the Saka have survived in the western Pamirs. Some of these languages such as Sarikoli can be found near Tashkurgan in Xinjiang itself, although linguists regard this as the result of the relatively recent movement of Shugni immigrants, speakers of another Saka-related language situated in the Pamirs. Wakhi is spoken in the ancient territory of Wakhan in the southern Pamirs. In general, these languages, related most closely to that of the ancient Saka, are located in those valleys through which one must pass if one wishes to link up with the western ends of either the northern or southern routes along the Silk Road through the Tarim Basin.

For us the critical question is how long the Saka language was spoken in the Tarim Basin. Here, unlike the other languages, we are not dealing with an essentially religious or trade language but rather one that also provided a vernacular for established populations. Moreover, we are dealing with an historical entity, the Saka, who were attested by name in historical documents by the end of the 6th century BC, at a time preceding the development of Buddhism and the Silk Road. To all this we might add the evidence of physical anthropology which relates many groups of ancient Tarim populations, ranging from the Ili River in the north southwards to Tashkurgan and Sampul near Khotan, with population types known from the Pamirs or Ferghana, two territories historically occupied by Saka tribes. To explore how early Saka-speaking populations may have entered Xinjiang, we need to widen or linguistic picture and work our way back to the emergence and dispersals of the Iranian languages.

Eastern Iranians

Linguists are fond of drawing family trees of languages which provide a simplified genealogy of a language's development and relationships. The Saka language and its descendants belong to the northeastern group of Eastern Iranian languages. These are the languages that spanned both the region of the Eurasian steppe in antiquity (i.e. the languages spoken by the Scythians and the Saka) and the languages of Central Asia that were evidently affected by movements from the steppelands southwards (e.g. Choresmian, Sogdian and Bactrian). In some instances, the steppeland languages penetrated mountain retreats, e.g. Ossetic in the Caucasus and the Iranian languages of the Pamirs. All of these are more closely related to one another than they are to the West Iranian languages that moved to take up positions south of the Caspian, e.g. Median, Parthian, Old Persian and their descendants.

The earliest attested of the Iranian languages is Avestan (assuming its composition date is earlier than the Old Persian inscriptions), the liturgical language of the Zoroastrian religion. We have already seen that setting an absolute date for the Avestan language is problematic but a date of about 1000 BC would probably not be too far wrong. We have also seen that historical attestations of other East Iranian languages or, at least, ethnic groups date from about 600 BC. There is, therefore, nothing that would violate the linguistic plausibility of a movement of Saka speakers into the Tarim Basin some time within the 1st millennium BC, i.e. at a time by which we already have considerable evidence for Caucasoid mummies. How much earlier carries us into the chronological relationships between Iranian and Indo-Aryan.

Indo-Iranians

Within the Indo-European language family, the most closely related language stocks are those of the Iranians and Indo-Aryans, which, as we have seen earlier, are so closely related that we can reconstruct a common Proto-Indo-Iranian language. The date of separation between the Iranian and Indo-Aryan languages obviously marks the lower threshold for the date of any Iranian language. In other words, the intrusion of East Iranian Saka speakers into East Central Asia can hardly be earlier than the separation of the Iranian branch from Indo-Iranian. To what extent can we fix a date for this process?

Iranian languages

	Ancient	Modern
Northeastern	Scythian/Saka	Ossetic, Wakhi
	Sogdian	Yaghnobi
	Bactrian	Pashto, Yidgha-Munji, etc.
	Avestan	
	Choresmian	
Southeastern	?	Parachi, Ormuri
Northwestern	Median, Parthian	Baluchi, Kurdish, etc.
Southwestern	Persian	Persian, Tadjiki, etc.

Table of Iranian languages. The modern languages are not necessarily direct descendants of the ancient languages.

256

The earliest evidence that such a split between the Indo-Iranian languages occurred dates to about 1500 BC and is to be found in those archives of the Hittite empire that relate to the region between the Zagros Mountains and northern Mesopotamia. Here we discover the existence of a state historically known as Mitanni. The Mitannians spoke the local non-Indo-European language, Hurrian, which is known in this region from the 3rd millennium BC onwards. But although their language was Hurrian, they also left traces of an Indo-Aryan language. When they concluded a treaty with the Hittites, for example, they swore not only by the Hurrian and any other local deities but also by the gods Indara, Mitraśil, Naśatianna and Uruvanaśśil, who correspond neatly to the gods of the *Ṛgveda*, named in the ancient hymns of the Indo-Aryans as Indra, Mitra, Nāsatya and Varuṇa. We also find Indo-Aryan words used to describe the number of turns a chariot does about the course and the colours of the horses of a chariot team. This association between Indo-Aryan and chariotry is very close and, as we will soon see, absolutely critical. Among the texts in the Hittite language is a manual for training horses written by Kikkuli 'the Mitannian' which also includes such Indo-Aryan loanwords.

In order to explain this Indo-Aryan element among the Mitannians, it is generally presumed that Indo-Aryan charioteers may have superimposed themselves briefly as rulers of Mitanni and, although they were absorbed into the local population and adopted the local Hurrian language, they left traces of their origins in the names of their gods, in some of their personal names and in the vocabulary of their chariotry. The archaeological evidence can accommodate the linguistic evidence since it is in about 1500 BC that we find evidence for both the horse and chariot in the area southeast of the Caspian. Moreover, artistic motifs from this area depict figures that appear to be among the earliest 'animal style' art motifs known across Eurasia, and we have already seen that this style is typical of the populations of the Indo-Iranian steppelands. Ritual paraphernalia, similar to those employed later in India, are also encountered. Furthermore, it is to about 1500 BC that one tends to date the arrival of the Indo-Aryans in northwest India (although demonstrating this archaeologically is another thing altogether). In any event, by *c.* 1500 BC, the Indo-Aryan language would already seem to have evolved from Proto-Indo-Iranian and taken on an independent identity.

In about 1500 BC we have historical evidence suggesting that a split between Indo-Aryan and the rest of the Indo-Iranian languages had occurred; we do not know how much earlier it *might* have occurred. Unfortunately, beyond historical records, the dating of a linguistic event becomes increasingly conjectural with time. We do, however, have several kinds of circumstantial evidence. First, as we have already seen, the languages employed in both the *Avesta* and the *Ṛgveda*, the two central religious texts of the Iranians and Indo-Aryans respectively, are so close that linguists do not believe they could have long been separated, certainly by no more than 500 years. The dating of neither text is secure, but on the widely held presumption that the Ṛgveda dates to about 1200 BC, possibly somewhat earlier, we would still be talking about a date of separation this side of 2000 BC. Secondly, if we consider the question of chariotry, the vocabulary of which is found in the Indo-Iranian languages and, more specifically, in documents from Mitanni, some of the earliest evidence for the spoke-wheeled chariot dates to about 2000 BC where chariots are found at the site of Sintashta in the southern Urals. If we must look for the earliest Indo-Iranians, they should be sought somewhere before 1500 BC and, admitting that the antiquity of any item of material culture may be pushed back somewhat earlier than our existing knowledge allows, after 2500 BC. What all this permits (suggests would be far too strong a word) is that Eastern Iranian, the language grouping which appears right across the steppelands and in East Central Asia, might have existed as early as the 2nd millennium BC, and although it might be pushing it a bit, we cannot really exclude the possibility that Eastern Iranians could have existed at the same time that Caucasoid populations began entering the Tarim Basin. Where might they have come from?

The Indo-Iranian Enigma

The search for the origin and dispersal of the Indo-Iranians takes us into one of the great puzzles of Indo-European studies since the evidence could not be more contradictory (the spice of intellectual enigmas). Let us lay out the ground rules and see where they get us.

We begin with two observations. First, the Indo-Iranians are a major branch of the Indo-European language family and so they must be genetically related to their Indo-European sister branches, in particular,

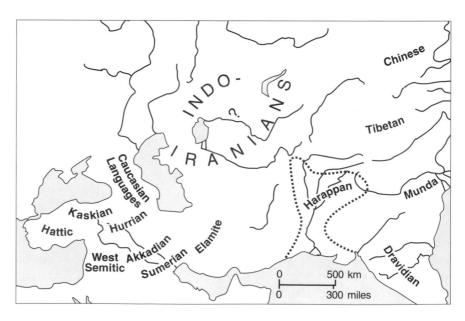

147. The distribution of non-Indo-European languages in western and eastern Asia suggests that the Indo-Iranians must have come from somewhere to the north.

their closest relations the Slavs, Balts and, perhaps more distantly, the Armenians and Greeks. We cannot start the Indo-Iranians off somewhere in Eurasia on their own as if they had an independent story to tell; they are merely part of the larger story of Indo-European expansions. Any 'solution' to the puzzle of Indo-Iranian origins that neglects this point is an illusion.

Secondly, when we first meet the Indo-Iranians, they are in motion and moving over territories where we have excellent or at least good circumstantial evidence that the previous occupants were non-Indo-Europeans. We have already seen that the earliest Indo-Aryans managed to superimpose themselves or at least heavily influence a non-Indo-European people, the Mitannians, in the Hurrian territory west of the southern Caspian. Persians pushed south through Iran to superimpose themselves on the territories of Elam which preserved its own native language long enough to require the Persian kings of the 6th–5th centuries BC to employ Elamite, along with Old Persian and Akkadian, in their inscriptions. The Persians, of course, occupied territories previously held by the Assyrians and are only mentioned in Assyrian records from the 9th century BC onwards. The linguistic situation in northern India is difficult to reconstruct on primary evidence. The Harappan culture or Indus Valley civilization (*c.* 2700–1900 BC) had its own script but we know too little about it to translate it with any great confidence, although the work of Finnish linguists such as Asko Parpola, who have proposed decipherments employing a Dravidian key, would certainly seem to offer the best bet. The Dravidians still occupy the southern third of India and with pockets of Dravidian speakers farther north and Dravidian loanwords in the earliest Indo-Aryan texts, this all suggests that they were once spread over much more of India and have been subsequently pushed southwards by the Indo-Aryans. In fact, some argue that Dravidian is closely related to Elamite, the native language of southern Iran, and that this linguistic continuum (Elamo-Dravidian) was shattered by Iranians in the west and Indo-Aryans in the east.

The conclusion that one draws from all this is that the Iranian language did not begin in Iran and the Indo-Aryan language did not derive from the Indian subcontinent. They both had to come from elsewhere. A quick glance at the map of Eurasia with its various linguistic entities in mind tells us where to look. The Indo-Iranians could not have come from China or Tibet since this was the homeland of a very different language family. To the south and to the west we have the Elamite, Sumerian, Semitic and Hurrian civilizations – all non-Indo-European families. The Indo-Iranians must have been intruders from the north.

Intruders from the North

In the 1920s Harold Peake and Herbert Fleure published a marvellous series of small books entitled *Corridors of Time*. One of the volumes was *The Steppe and the Sown*; it contrasted the development of pastoral nomadic

148. Reconstruction of a house from the Andronovo culture.

societies on the Eurasian steppe with their agricultural neighbours, and while the book is now naturally out-of-date, its title and central focus still encapsulate the major issue of Indo-Iranian origins. We have already recounted at some length the peoples of the steppelands, the Scythians, Sarmatians, Alans and, most importantly, Saka, and seen that they all belong to the northeastern branch of the Iranian group of languages. Our earliest historical testimony of their existence dates back to the mid-1st millennium BC, the Iron Age of the Eurasian steppe when we learn from historical sources such as Herodotus that the steppelands were occupied by various groups of pastoral nomads. At this time our archaeological evidence is overwhelmingly derived from burials such as the Scythian tombs of the Ukraine or the royal burials at Pazyryk in the Altai Mountains.

We can follow the archaeological trail of Eurasian nomads back into the Bronze Age. The Andronovo culture, in actual fact a blanket term for a number of regional cultures, occupied the entire West Asiatic steppe from the Ural River east to the Yenisei in the period *c.* 2000–900 BC. There is evidence of both settlement and burial. The Andronovans occupied small villages, generally with a few up to about twenty houses, situated in a row along a river. The houses were relatively large in dimension (80–300 sq. m (860–3,230 sq. ft)), semi-subterranean, i.e. dug partially into the ground (one of the old Iranian words for 'house' or 'room' is *kata-* which is usually taken to mean originally 'dug out'), and roofed with timber beams. The economy was based primarily on stockbreeding with abundant evidence of cattle, sheep/goat and horse, and occasionally even camel; the pig, a sure indicator of a permanent settled form of life, is conspicuous by its absence. Everything points to a relatively mobile economy or, at least, one which included a mobile component. The deceased were buried in timber or stone-lined chambers which were covered by barrows, or, to use the Russian word, *kurgans*, a feature of steppeland burials that is encountered on the European steppe at least since the 4th millennium BC. They were accompanied by animal offerings, including horses, cheek-pieces indicating horsemanship, wheeled vehicles, ceramics, and metallic weapons and ornaments. One of the predecessors of the Andronovo culture is the Sintashta culture (*c.* 2300–1900 BC) of the southeast Urals which is represented by both fortified settlements

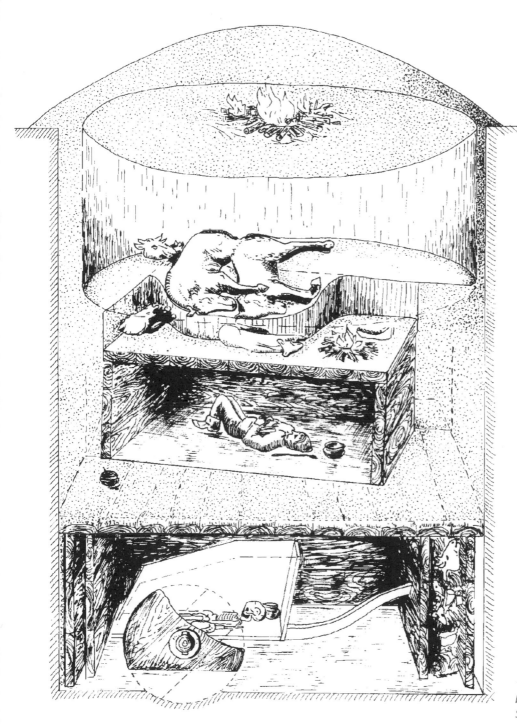

149. A chariot
burial from
Sintashta.

and royal burials that included some of the earliest evidence for chariots in
Eurasia. There are few, if any, archaeologists who would doubt that Sintashta
and Andronovo represent the prehistoric Iranians or Indo-Iranians of the
Eurasian steppe. Conclusion: the Indo-Iranians were clearly the preponder-
ant pastoralists of the West Asiatic steppe.

South of the Aral Sea in the territory of ancient Bactria and Margiana we find at the same time a series of agricultural settlements attested by complexes of fortified citadels, both rectangular and circular. The economy was based on mixed agriculture, the use of irrigation providing the basis of a cereal economy. The primary domestic animal appears to have been sheep/goat followed by cattle; there is so far no certain evidence for horse. The settlements, which date to *c.* 2200–1700 BC, also contain elaborate ritual complexes. In these multi-roomed structures there is clear evidence of both fire altars and rooms for the preparation and consumption of hallucinogenic beverages. The fire altars with their accompanying ash pits closely match the descriptions of the fire cult found in the later religious literature of the Zoroastrians of Iran and the Vedic Indians (and Chinese historical documents for some of the populations of East Central Asia). The temples also exhibit rooms which contain all the necessary apparatus for the preparation of drinks extracted from poppy, hemp and ephedra. One of the central cults of the ancient Indo-Aryans and Iranians involved the consumption of the hallucinogenic compound (a liquid form of ephedra) known as *soma* in India and *haoma* in Iran (or **sauma* in the ancestral Proto-Indo-Iranian language) and we find its use attested earliest in the ritual centres of what is now known as the Bactria-Margiana Archaeological Complex (BMAC). The art of this culture has also been interpreted in the light of the religious motifs depicted in the sacred writings of the Indo-Aryans and Iranians. Burials containing BMAC material are subsequently found farther to the south on the main approaches to northern India as one might predict for the immediate ancestors of the Indo-Aryans. It is clear then that the prehistoric Indo-Iranians were the occupants of these agricultural citadels. Conclusion: the Indo-Iranians originated in the agricultural oases of Central Asia.

How do we reconcile deriving the Indo-Iranians from both the 'steppe' and the 'sown'? This is not easy since the origins of the two cultural worlds are very different. The BMAC and its antecedent cultures can be traced back to the earliest farming communities of the southeast Caspian. Here,

150. A citadel of the Bactria-Margiana Archaeological Complex.

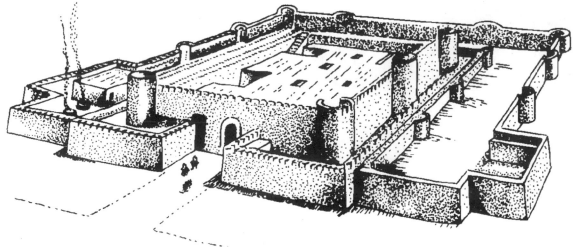

colonists pushed northwards from highland Iran and Iraq to establish farming villages by the 6th millennium BC. The development of irrigation agriculture permitted farmers to expand eastwards into the oases of Bactria and Margiana. Most of the cultural influences that we find in the Central Asian agricultural settlements derive from neighbouring cultures of the south and west. In a very crude way, the Early Bronze Age oasis citadels of Central Asia reflect a push northeastwards of cultures whose roots lie in the Near East.

On the other hand, the steppe cultures of the Sintashta and Andronovo cultures look westwards for their antecedents. Increasingly mobile economies based on stockbreeding had emerged by the 5th and 4th millennia on the European steppe between the Dnieper and the Ural rivers. It is here that we find the evolution of wheeled vehicles (in the steppe region at least) from the 4th millennium BC onwards. Direct cultural antecedents of Sintashta-Andronovo can be found in the Early Bronze Age cultures between the Volga and Ural. And as the Andronovo culture emerged in Kazakhstan, so also did its sister culture, the Timber-grave or Srubna culture, appear on the European steppe where it provides archaeological antecedents for peoples like the Scythians of the western steppe.

It is evident then that there is no way we can construct a common origin for the steppe tribes (whose origins lie between the Dnieper and Ural) and those who occupied the oases of Central Asia (whose origins lie south and west of the Caspian). By extension, there is no way we can find in the two cultural regions grounds to identify a common linguistic ancestor. The odds of two totally different and independent cultural worlds simultaneously developing the same Indo-Iranian language are about the same as the hordes of simian typists successfully completing *Hamlet*. We are going to get nowhere in reconciling the two different cultural traditions by looking to their roots; we must look elsewhere.

Contact

While the Andronovo culture and that of the oasis-dwellers of Central Asia were not genetically related, they were most certainly aware of each other's existence and came into frequent and quite close contact. This is indicated by three types of evidence.

The characteristic Andronovo pottery provides a trail of its contacts as this hand-made ware is fundamentally different from the wheel-thrown ceramics manufactured in the semi-urban oasis complexes. Yet it can be found in varying amounts in BMAC settlements which indicates some form of interaction, presumably direct, between the peoples of the steppe and those of the sown. The presence of Andronovo material on BMAC sites suggests that Andronovo tribes may have traded with the semi-urban settlements, and the presence of such pottery in the very cult centres indicates that they may also have participated in the religious rituals of these centres.

The second hint of an Andronovo presence in Central Asia is even more concrete. In the area immediately south of the Aral Sea we find the Tazabagyab culture (*c.* 1500 BC) which itself is regarded as a variant of the Andronovo cultural horizon. But unlike their northern kinfolk, here they settled to engage in small-scale irrigation agriculture. There are some 50 or so small Tazabagyab villages known with their distinctive semi-subterranean houses measuring about 10 by 10 m (33 by 33 ft) or more in size. Their metal artifacts and ceramics show their derivation from the steppelands, and here we also find remains of horse as well as the other domestic livestock. In their burials, males are interred on their right sides while females are placed on their left, a practice seen in other areas of Eurasia. This purportedly reflects a gender-symbolic view of the world where males were associated with the right, and here we not only mean the direction and right hand, but as in English usage, 'being right', straight, open, healthy, strong. Females, in

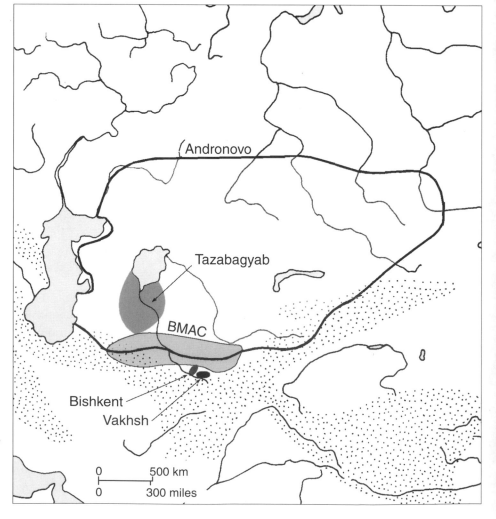

151. Generalized distribution of the Andronovo culture and the cultures sometimes linked with it; note that the Andronovo culture came into contact with that of the Bactria-Margiana Archaeological Complex (BMAC). Mountain ranges are indicated by the dotted area.

this (obviously male-biased) system are associated with the left, the unpropitious direction in Indo-European thought, and one that is associated with a host of negatively charged ideas – unhealthy, crooked, devious – or, as with the word for 'left' in Latin, sinister.

The third hint of steppe pastoralists in the region is a series of independent cultures contemporary with the BMAC but which could in no way be regarded as proto-urban. In southern Tadjikistan, for example, we find the Bishkent culture (*c.* 1700–1500 BC), which is known primarily from the cemeteries of mobile pastoralists. The ceramics are apparently a mixture of local, BMAC and Andronovo styles while the metalwork is clearly Andronovo-derived. At the cemetery of Tulkhar there were found about 80 burials with the same sexual marking of position as we saw in the Tazabagyab culture. Moreover, here there were other hints of Indo-Iranian practices. The burials of the different sexes were accompanied not only by the usual grave-goods but also by hearths. Males were provided with small rectangular hearths, reminiscent of the rectangular fire hearths (*āhavanīya*) of the Indo-Aryan male priest while the women were given small round hearths, a shape ascribed in Indo-Aryan belief to the *gārhapatya*, the domestic hearth usually associated with women. In the same region along the middle and lower reaches of the Vakhsh River (which, for those who enjoy such trivia, is the location of the highest dam in the world) is a culture of that name which is contemporary with the Bishkent culture. Here there is some slight evidence that the population lived a more settled way

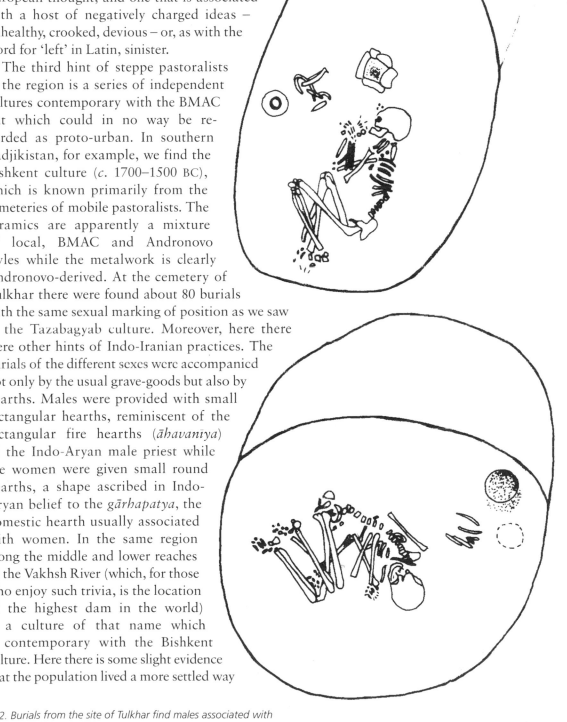

152. Burials from the site of Tulkhar find males associated with rectangular hearths and females with round hearths, a pattern later suggested in Vedic religion.

of life (houses of stone and mud brick), and engaged in mixed agriculture (barley, wheat, cattle, sheep/goat, horse, donkey and camel). Burials include graves with small catacomb niches and the placement of small stones in a swastika arrangement.

All of this suggests that in the period between *c.* 2000 and 1500 BC, steppe tribes penetrated West Central Asia and were actively engaged in exchange with the more settled oasis communities. It also demonstrates the capacity of these earlier nomadic tribes to absorb material culture and probably behaviour from their more settled neighbours. In some instances, there is clear evidence that they were able to settle and exploit the region as irrigation agriculturalists as well. We are dealing with a highly adaptable society that could adjust to circumstances and opportunities. It hardly needs emphasizing that these are precisely the same types of skills and economies that would prepare communities to move off the steppe and settle in the oases of East Central Asia where we find our earliest mummies. The central question now, however, is linguistic: in the meeting of the steppe and the sown, whose language predominated?

Whose Language?

The answer to the question of whose language eventually won is based on evidence that is circumstantial but nevertheless fairly persuasive. Let us perform an experiment and consider what happens if we assume that the Indo-Iranian languages did originate among the oasis-dwellers of Central Asia, a theory that has some vigorous proponents. In this model, the (Indo-Iranian) language of the oasis-dwellers (BMAC) would have to have spread to the Andronovans of the Asiatic steppe. Since we have evidence for Iranians in the European steppe as well, the Andronovans would have been required to carry their language into southern Russia and the Ukraine. Although there is no solid archaeological evidence for such a movement at the time required, we can also maintain that there is no archaeological evidence to contradict this. But when we consider that Indo-Iranian is merely one branch of the Indo-European language family, then the entire edifice of this proposition crumbles. Where were all the other Indo-European stocks when the Indo-Iranian languages were evolving? We have already seen that they could not have lain to the east, south or immediate west of Central Asia, since these territories were all occupied by non-Indo-European language families. The only direction left is north but the model we have just proposed has presumed that the north was occupied by something else (Andronovans?) before it became Iranian. What happens to the Slavs, Balts, Greeks, Italics, Celts, Germans and other Indo-European groups? There is just no room in this model to place Indo-Iranian in the context of the other Indo-European languages, particularly those of Europe. As we have seen, no solution to Indo-Iranian origins can be regarded as adequate unless it can also be accommodated within the general framework of Indo-European movements.

An indigenous Central Asian origin for the Indo-Iranians falls at the first hurdle.

The alternative is to presume that the Indo-Iranians are to be associated with the steppeland cultures. This can at least be fitted into most solutions to Indo-European dispersals that see the Indo-Iranians emerging from the easternmost development of European steppe cultures during the 3rd millennium BC. The other Indo-Europeans lay to the west, either by virtue of having occupied eastern Europe (beyond the steppe) since the beginning of the Neolithic or because earlier steppeland peoples, beginning in the 5th and 4th millennia BC, had spread westwards into the Danube basin and superimposed their earlier forms of Indo-European in that region.

When it comes to the interface between the steppe and the sown in West Central Asia itself, this second model depends on the social organization of the steppe cultures as a possible explanation for the spread of their language. We have already seen that they were capable of producing fortress-dwelling and chariot-driving aristocracies by c. 2000 BC. They also exploited and controlled a vast system of metallurgical extraction, production and exchange that extended from the west European steppe as far east as the Yenisei. The more mobile populations were, as we have suggested above, the internet and social glue that connected a vast region of Eurasia. According to this model, the Andronovans would have come into contact with the oasis-dwellers, adopted items of their material culture, some of their religious beliefs and cultural practices (such as the fire cult and consumption of the hallucinogenic *sauma*), but not the language of the oasis-dwellers. Rather, the language of the steppe-dwellers would have operated as the *lingua franca* of exchange between regions, then perhaps within the settlements themselves until some variety of Indo-Iranian had become the main language of West Central Asia (perhaps in the same way as Uyghur came to dominate in East Central Asia).

As we have noted, evidence for the BMAC is not limited to West Central Asia but is also found farther south on the main approaches to northwest India where it would appear to be intrusive wherever we find it. It is possible then that during the period of the BMAC, the linguistic stage of Indo-Iranian would find the BMAC and its southern spread associated with the separation of the Indo-Aryans from the Iranians of the north. The linguistic difference between Indo-Aryan and Iranian is slight enough that those changes that distinguish Iranian from Indo-Aryan could then have spread through the northern regions after the collapse of the BMAC.

And the Mummies?

Let us review what we think we can say about the Iranian languages of East Central Asia. All the Iranian languages attested across the territory belong to the group of East Iranian languages and at least some of them still survive along the western periphery of the Tarim Basin, particularly in the Pamirs.

All these languages would also seem to have home territories farther to the west in Central Asia or the Asiatic steppe. Both of these statements have some additional significance. We should emphasize that there is no evidence of an Iranian language that belongs to a different subgroup of Iranian and, more importantly, we have no evidence of some 'earlier' form of Iranian or Indo-Iranian language in East Central Asia. So far we have treated the Indo-Iranian languages as a double (Indo-Aryan and Iranian) block of languages to keep things as simple as possible, but now we need to mention that a third 'branch' of the group exists – the Nuristani languages of the Hindu Kush. Attested only in recent times and over a small region, the Nuristani languages belong specifically to neither the Indo-Aryan nor the Iranian branch but are generally treated as having divided at such an early period from the Indo-Iranian continuum that they should be treated as a separate mini-branch (although they may be more closely related to Indo-Aryan). Such an early separation tells us that we may be dealing with a linguistic remnant that survived during the original spread of the Indo-Iranian languages *c*. 2000–1500 BC, i.e. Nuristani represents a residual branch of Indo-Iranian which attests to the presence of Indo-Iranians near the southwestern approach to East Central Asia. But we have no evidence that Nuristani or indeed any similar 'early branch' of Indo-Aryan or Iranian was spoken in the Tarim Basin. We are left only with the more recently attested northeast Iranian languages. This may, obviously enough, be accounted for by two hypotheses. First, a very early form of Indo-Iranian language may have entered the Tarim Basin between *c*. 2000 and 1500 BC and may have been spoken by the Bronze Age 'mummy cultures'; this language (attested in no later written sources) was then subsequently replaced by a specifically northeastern Iranian language. Alternatively, the earliest Iranians in the Tarim may only have arrived after the dispersal of the Iranian languages across the Eurasian steppe and Central Asia. This would accommodate a later arrival of the Iranians in the Tarim.

If we reflect back on the picture gained from the evidence of physical anthropology – be it the admittedly suspect 'typological' approach or Brian Hemphill's more robust multivariate statistical approach – then we have at least two, possibly three, waves of Indo-European population groups penetrating the Tarim Basin. Where the earliest emerges from is still disputed but the later intrusion, cast either in terms of Indo-Afghan and Pamir-Ferghana physical types or simply the grouping that finds a close affinity between Alwighul and Krorän on the one hand and Bronze Age Bactrians on the other, can support the thesis of later population movements from the west (the direction of Bactria). This is, at least, suggestive that the earliest Iranian populations in East Central Asia entered in the 1st millennium BC carrying a variety of northeastern Iranian dialects eastwards. This would permit us to assign some of the mummies from the 1st millennium BC to the Iranians. Could Iranians be identified with still earlier populations in the Tarim region?

Here we should recall that, in our review of the archaeology of East Central Asia, we have seen how the basic subsistence economy from *c.* 2000 BC onwards must have derived from the west. Wheat, barley, domestic sheep, domestic horse, domestic camel, bronze working and wheeled vehicles would all have come either from the northern steppelands or from the agricultural communities of West Central Asia. We have also already noted how the use of ephedra in the Qäwrighul culture, where it was deposited with burials, might be linked to its use in the BMAC religious shrines where it was consumed in liquid form as *sauma*. Moreover, the BMAC blazed the trail of oasis-dwelling cultures to the east and would have possessed the knowledge necessary to initiate irrigation agriculture in the Tarim Basin. In short, if we could fly BMAC colonists from Bactria into the Tarim oases they would make a very strong theoretical candidate for the earliest agricultural settlers in the Tarim Basin. But we can only talk of them theoretically in the 2nd millennium BC since we have no clear evidence of transplanted BMAC populations in East Central Asia. We may find BMAC graves over a wide area of West Central Asia but they are not so far directly attested in East Central Asia. It may be that our knowledge of the Bronze Age of Xinjiang is still so woefully inadequate that we have not yet discovered concrete evidence for Bactrian immigrants. There are, to be sure, seals from the Ordos region of China (centred in Inner Mongolia) that have parallels among the Bactrian seals but these need not indicate anything more than distant exchange relations that never involved transit through the Tarim Basin itself. It may also have been that the mountain passes of the Pamirs proved too much of a melting pot for Bactrian colonists to preserve their material culture in their journey into the Tarim Basin. Fortunately, in our attempt to establish the ethnic identity of the earliest mummies we still have one more suspect.

CHAPTER NINE

Tocharian Trekkers

Of all the major well-attested Indo-European language stocks, Tocharian is the most intriguing. The two Tocharian languages are among the most recent of the Indo-European languages to have been discovered; they were used along the Silk Road, the easternmost of all the Indo-Europeans; their texts, largely translations, reveal excruciatingly little about their speakers; they are the only language stock to be found exclusively in East Central Asia; and, according to a sizeable body of linguistic opinion, Tocharian's relationship with the rest of its language family makes its location on the extreme east of the Indo-European world totally incongruous. For most of this century we have been able to look at the texts and gaze into the faces of the 'knights with long swords' in Buddhist shrines but still have not the faintest idea who the Tocharians were, what their culture was like, or how they came to be here in the oases of the Tarim Basin. We had the remains of disembodied languages but not their speakers. In this chapter we will present briefly the nature of the Tocharian languages, the basis of our knowledge about them, their position within the Indo-European language family, whatever clues they might themselves offer as to their origins, and why they they are so crucial to our understanding of the prehistoric mummies of East Central Asia.

The Discovery of Tocharian

The first Tocharian document to be published was a page containing lines of a hymn to the Buddha which was extracted from a collection of manuscripts held by the Russian consul to Qäshqär. It appeared in 1892 although it would not be read until years later. One of the most recent discoveries of the language was in 1974 when farmers accidentally came across 44 fragments of Tocharian documents at a Buddhist site near Qarashähär (Yanqi). Altogether the number of Tocharian documents known runs to ⋅ 3,640 pages or fragments of Tocharian texts of which the majority are held in Paris (about 2,000), then Berlin (1,170) and the rest in London, St Petersburg, Kyoto, Ürümchi and Beijing. To these may be added about 70 additional inscriptions found on walls or other objects (graffiti). We should not be overly impressed with the number of documents since the great majority are fragmentary, possessing less than a single full line of text. The number of Tocharian words known is in the order of 4,500–5,000. This too is less impressive than it might seem since the figure comprises the vocabulary of two languages – Tocharian A and Tocharian B – both of which have borrowed heavily from Indic for their religious terms; essentially, the size of our vocabulary for each Tocharian language is not much larger than that possessed by a 7- or 8-year-old child (although the choice of vocabulary is radically different). Nevertheless, there was at least ample evidence to indicate that we were dealing with Indo-European languages.

The contents of the manuscripts are overwhelmingly Buddhist and largely translations of texts from Sanskrit or other languages employed in Buddhism. The texts detail the rules of monastic existence, recite the doctrine and law of Buddhism, relate the life of the Buddha in straight narrative form and in translations of Indian plays, and present poetry or even magic spells. In some cases we have bilingual texts in Sanskrit and Tocharian. It is worth emphasizing that the context of discovery of most of our texts is shrines and monasteries, which helps to account for the

English	Tocharian B	Old Irish	Latin	Old English	Greek
father	*pācer*	*athair*	*pater*	*fæder*	*patér*
mother	*mācer*	*māthair*	*māter*	*mōdor*	*métēr*
brother	*procer*	*brāthair*	*frāter*	*brōðor*	*phrātér*
sister	*ṣer*	*siur*	*soror*	*sweostor*	*éor*
sheep	*āᵤ*	*oī*	*ovis*	*ēowu*	*ó(w)ïs*
cow	*keᵤ*	*bō*	*bōs*	*cū*	*boûs*
horse	*yakwe*	*ech*	*equus*	*eoh*	*híppos*

Tocharian compared with other Indo-European languages.

Tocharian greatly simplified the Indo-European sounds, particularly the consonants. Note, for example, that while the Tocharian words for 'father' and 'brother' both begin with the same sound (*p*), the other Indo-European languages indicate two different sounds. In simple terms, Tocharian did not distinguish between a *p* and a *b* nor between a *k* and a *g*.

Sanskrit	*yathā hy agāraṃ ducchannaṃ vṛṣṭiḥ samatibhindati*
	evaṃ hy abhāvitaṃ cittaṃ rāgaḥ samatibhindati
Tocharian	*mäkte ostä pakwārem aiposä swese olypotse kauṣäṃ*
	mant ra mā yairoṣ palsko no kauṣn eṅkl olypotse
	as the rain lashes over a poorly-roofed house
	so passion lashes over an unpurified spirit.

A Sanskrit-Tocharian bilingual text shows how markedly different were the two languages.

overwhelming religious bias. Try to imagine what our knowledge of the Romans would be like if we were furnished solely with fragmentary excerpts from the Christian liturgy and had no idea of the existence of Caesar, Cicero, Virgil or any other classical author. Although we find Tocharian employed in certain secular contexts, e.g. caravan passes, some suggest that the secular language of greatest currency in the north Tarim was the same as that found over a broad area of the south, i.e. a form of Prākrit.

We have given enough public lectures about the Tarim mummies to know that among the most frequently asked questions are 'Who were the Tocharians?' and 'What were the Tocharians like?' How can one answer that? One way is to refer the reader back to Chapter Two and our account of the oasis state of Kucha as this was one of the major centres of the Tocharians. But this account was based exclusively on Chinese documents that did not recognize the existence of a Tocharian language or people, nor did it isolate specific ethnic identities in the multicultural Tocharian-speaking oases. The evidence of language is our last, albeit imperfect, route to answering the question: 'Who were the Tocharians?'

How did linguists first crack the code and decipher these previously unknown languages? The original decipherment of Tocharian texts depended essentially on the fact that Tocharian employed a script (Brāhmī) that was well known from other languages and that the Tocharian texts themselves were almost exclusively translations of documents that were known in some other language (Sanskrit, Prākrit, Khotanese Saka, Chinese, Tibetan); these provided a ready guide to their contents and a key to the meanings of the words. Occasionally, we find Tocharian translations of Buddhist texts which are not known in the original language of their composition. Manichean is the only other religion to be represented in a single bilingual text in Tocharian and Turkish that dates from the 10th century and was recovered at Turpan. There are also a number of other genres such as grammar, astronomy, medicine and history. Purely secular 'literature' has so far found but a single text, a touching love poem (see opposite). Finally, we have administrative texts concerning the running of monasteries, legal affairs and, as mentioned above, caravan passes. These are extremely useful in that they may also carry dates; the one absolutely securely dated Tocharian text comes from AD 642. The earliest of our texts would date to the 6th, possibly as early as the 5th century AD when the statelets of the Tarim Basin could act independently. They continued into the period of the Tang dynasty (AD 618–907) when the Chinese first regained the Tarim Basin and then lost it in the face of Tibetan and, subsequently, Turkish incursions.

Milestones of the 'death' of Tocharian come in a variety of forms. The last mention of the ruling house of Bo 'White', which may serve as a rough designation for the ruling Kuchean-speaking aristocracy, occurs in Chinese sources for the year AD 787 and the Uyghurs were already predominant in a number of northern oasis towns by 800. Chinese sources are largely silent

Tocharian Love Poem

[mā] ñ[i ci]sa noṣ / śomo ñ[e]m [wno]lme / [l]āre tāka,
mā ra postaṃ / cisa lāre mäsketär-ñ.
ciṣṣe laraumñe / ciṣṣe ārtañye / pelke kaltta[r]r śolämpa ṣṣe /
mā t(e) ställe śol wärñai.
taisyu pälskanoym: /sanai ṣaryompa / śāyau karttse[ś] śaulu
wärñai / snai tserekwa snai nāne.
yāmorñīkte ṣe / cau ñī palskañe / śarsa.
tusa ysaly ersate, / ciṣy araś ñi sälkāte.
wāya ci lauke, / tsyāra ñiś wetke, / klyautka-ñ pāke po läklentas./
ciṣe tsārwo sampā[te-ñ].

There has never been any person dearer to me than you
and there never will be any dearer.
The love for you, the delight in you is breath together with life.
This should not change for life.
Thus I used to think: with a single beloved will I live well
lifelong without deceit, without pretence.
The god Karman alone knew this my thought.
Therefore, he caused dissension and tore from me the heart that belongs to
* you.*
He led you away, separated me and had me partake of all sorrows.
The joy I had in you he took away from me.

Portion of a Tocharian caravan pass (literal translation by D. Q. Adams)

ṣletaś piṅkäṃ yuṣaiśco twe	[the] mountain commander writes to Yuṣai: thou
ñī yaitkorsa maṃt pyām kuce kaṣake pu-	my command-by thus do that [the] Qäshqärian Bhu-
ttamitre parra yaṃ caumpa śāmna i-	ddhamitra outside goes: him-with twen-
käṃ kercapaṃ treya yakwe ṣe te	ty: asses three: horse one: this
parra tārka tentsa auṣap mā tärka-	outside permit: than-this more not per-
nat ṣa[k] kṣ(u)ṃntsa śtarce memne	mit ten[th year] regnal-period-of: fourth month-in

on the Tarim Basin for the period of the 9th and 10th centuries and by the 11th century we find at least the northern oases, especially the Turpan Basin, clearly under Uyghur rule. We have sufficient evidence of Tocharian texts with either glosses in Turkish or with indications that their copying had been commissioned by Turkish speakers that we can imagine that Turkish spread first as a vernacular, replacing the languages of the earlier Tocharians, until Tocharian survived only as a liturgical language which then itself gradually disappeared as the population abandoned it in favour of Uyghur; eventually, the population also adopted the Islamic religion.

The Tocharian Languages

We have seen that written documents reveal the existence of two Tocharian languages, commonly designated Tocharian A and Tocharian B. The texts themselves are found across the northern route of the Tarim Basin from Maralbeshi (Bachu) on the west as far east as Bezäklik on the east which helps us define the known limits of the Tocharian world. The specific sites of Tocharian A documents are confined to the east where they are found at the religious sanctuaries of Shorchuq near Qarashähär, the ancient kingdom of Agni, and hence Tocharian A is also known as Agnean or East Tocharian. Documents in Tocharian A are also found farther east in Buddhist sites in the vicinity of Turpan such as Qarakhoja and Khocho, and at Tuyuq, Sängim and Bezäklik, all excavated as part of the German expeditions at the beginning of this century. Tocharian B documents are found across the entire region. They have been recovered from Maralbeshi, in various religious establishments near Kucha, i.e. Duldur Aqur, Qumtura, Subeshi and Qizil. It is for this reason that Tocharian B is also known as Kuchean or West

153. General distribution of sites with evidence of the Tocharian languages.

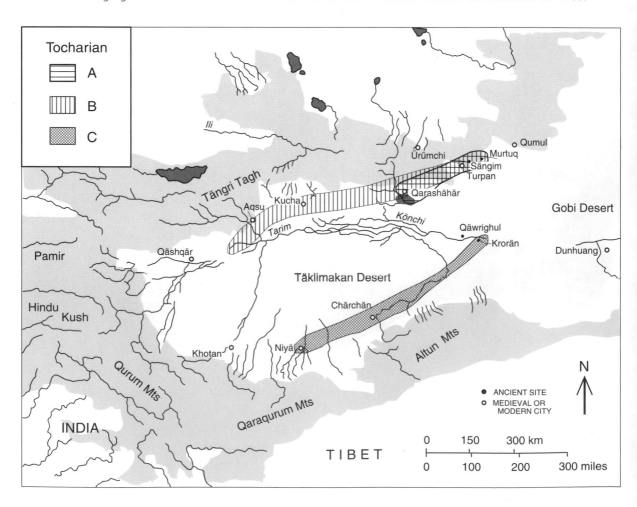

Tocharian, but the latter is something of a misnomer since Tocharian B documents are also known across the east, generally in the same sites as Tocharian A, i.e. Qarashähär, Turpan, Khocho, Tuyuq, Sängim and exclusively at Murtuq.

How great is the difference between Tocharian A and Tocharian B? Substantial enough in vocabulary and grammar that it is doubtful that they were mutually intelligible languages at the time they were committed to writing, although one can always find identical or extremely similar words between the two. Donald Ringe suggested that the two Tocharian languages were about as similar as Old English and Old High German (D. Q. Adams prefers the contrast between Italian and Romanian). Let us give both these comparisons a brief run by first counting to ten and then listing some basic kinship words in the two Tocharian languages and the languages cited by

Comparison of cognate words between Tocharian, Germanic and Romance languages.

English	TochA	TochB	Old Eng	Old High German	Italian	Romanian
one	*sas*	*ṣe*	*ān*	*ein*	*uno*	*unu*
two	*wu*	*wi*	*twā*	*zwā*	*due*	*doi*
three	*tre*	*trai*	*þrīe*	*drī*	*tre*	*trei*
four	*śtwar*	*śtwer*	*fēower*	*fior*	*quattro*	*patru*
five	*päñ*	*piś*	*fīf*	*fimf*	*cinque*	*cinci*
six	*ṣäk*	*ṣkas*	*siex*	*sëhs*	*sei*	*şase*
seven	*ṣpät*	*ṣukt*	*seofon*	*sibun*	*sette*	*şapte*
eight	*okät*	*okt*	*eahta*	*ahto*	*otto*	*opt*
nine	*ñu*	*ñu*	*nigon*	*niun*	*nove*	*nouă*
ten	*śäk*	*śak*	*tīen*	*zehan*	*dieci*	*zece*
father	*pācar*	*pācer*	*fæder*	*fater*	*padre*	*tată*
mother	*mācar*	*mācer*	*mōdor*	*muoter*	*madre*	*mamă*
brother	*pracar*	*procer*	*brōðor*	*bruoder*	*fratello*	*frate*
sister	*ṣar*	*ṣer*	*sweostor*	*swestar*	*sorella*	*soră*

Ringe and Adams (the Tocharian numerals can be given both in a masculine and a feminine form, but only the masculine will be given here).

In most of these cases, the words in the different languages are cognate with one another, i.e. they come from the same ultimate Proto-Indo-European origin (Romanian employs the children's forms for 'father' and

Comparison of non-cognate words in the Tocharian languages with examples from Germanic and Romance languages.

English	TochA	TochB	Old Eng	Old High German	Italian	Romanian
head	*mrāc*	*āśce*	*hēafod*	*houbit*	*testa*	*ţeastă*
hair	*śāku*	*matsi*	*hǣr*	*haar*	*capelli*	*păr*
right	*pāccās*	*saiwai*	*riht*	*reht*	*destro*	*drept*
meat	*śwal*	*mīsa*	*flǣsc*	*fleisc*	*carne*	*carne*
friend	*naṣu*	*waṣamo*	*frēond*	*friunt*	*amico*	*amic*
man	*napeṃ*	*śaumo*	*mann*	*mann*	*uomo*	*bărbat*
root	*tsmār*	*witsako*	*rōt*	*wurzala*	*radice*	*rădăcină*
now	*tāpärk*	*ñake*	*nū*	*nū*	*adesso*	*acum*

'mother' which could be paralleled in the other languages). On the other hand, there are also differences in vocabulary, at least where we have the texts for the words, between the two Tocharian languages, even in some fairly 'basic' vocabulary. Here are a few examples with the comparative words alongside for good measure (foot of previous page).

And when we come to the grammar of the two languages, here too we find marked differences. We can take the word for 'horse' (c.f. Latin *equus*) as an example.

Case forms for the word for 'horse' in the Tocharian languages.

Case	TochA	TochB
Nominative	*yuk*	*yakwe*
Oblique	*yuk*	*yakwe*
Instrumental	*yukyo*	–
Perlative	*yukā*	*yakwesa*
Genitive	*yukes*	*yākwentse*

In short, we are not dealing with two dialects that closely resemble each other, but something more on the order of two different languages. This is an important point because it suggests that these languages had been separated from one another for a considerable period, estimated by linguists as possibly somewhere between 500 years and a millennium, before our earliest texts. This would indicate a lower date for the break-up of Proto-Tocharian, the language ancestral to Tocharian A and B, at very roughly 500 BC.

A second major difference between the two languages is their geographical situation. We find Tocharian B texts across the entire northern rim of the Tarim Basin (about 1,100 km or 700 miles) while Tocharian A seems to have been confined to the area between Qarashähär and Bezäklik, a linear distance of only 300 km (200 miles). In the case of Tocharian B, regional differences have suggested the existence of three dialects: the first (western) in Kucha and the area surrounding it, the central dialect of the Qarashähär region and, finally, the eastern dialect of the Turpan oasis (in the east). Werner Winter has proposed that the central dialect, best represented by texts from Shorchuq, was the prestige dialect of the monastery of Yurpāṣka which eclipsed Kucha after it fell in the mid-7th century.

The third, and one of the most critical distinctions between the Tocharian languages, is the context in which they were used. While both languages were employed in the translation of Buddhist documents, only Tocharian B occurs in secular and administrative contexts as well. This has led to the well-supported supposition that what we have of Tocharian A is the remains of a liturgical language, probably a dead liturgical language at that, while Tocharian B was the only living language in the period from which we draw our texts. We find instances, for example, where a monk, copying out a Tocharian A text, would come across words that would be unfamiliar to him, and feel the need to write their definitions in his own language

(Tocharian B). This was a widespread practice in the Middle Ages and we could just as well point to instances where Irish monks, confronted with a section of tricky Latin text, scribbled the meanings in Old Irish in the margins of their manuscripts or immediately above the difficult words. We also find accounts of the history of Kucha, the centre of the western language and also of Buddhist learning in the Tarim region, recorded in Tocharian B as far east as Murtuq, in an area where we otherwise find Tocharian A texts. And at Sängim, again in the east, we discover a text instructing the novice in Sanskrit where the words are glossed in Tocharian B.

One of the ironies of the Tocharian languages is that the living and the dead language do not behave as expected: Tocharian B, the 'living' language, was on the whole the more conservative of the two languages. Although both Tocharian languages have seen fairly brusque losses of their earlier endings, Tocharian A reveals far greater loss of syllables and endings, e.g. Tocharian A *yuk* 'horse', *känt* 'hundred', and *kukäl* 'wagon' but Tocharian B *yakwe*, *kante*, and *kokale*. In crude terms, there is unexpectedly more left over of the Proto-Tocharian forms in the 'living' Tocharian B than in 'dead' Tocharian A.

We have then two languages, considerably different from one another, one of which may have been purely a liturgical language. Explaining their geographical context becomes all the more complicated when one considers that the distance between Kucha and Qarashähär is only about 300 km (200 miles). How could two languages which were geographically so close have diverged so much from one another? Werner Winter has argued that Tocharian A did not actually develop in the region in which we find it used, but that it was merely the language of the Buddhist mission to the Turks. The Tocharian A manuscripts were prepared under the auspices of the Turks who settled in the eastern part of the Tarim Basin in territories that were occupied by Tocharian B speakers. This would suggest that Tocharian A, when it was at home, was situated somewhere between the Tocharian B speakers of the north Tarim and the early Turks to their north and east. This, of course, would imply that the Tocharian languages were once far more widespread than their surviving manuscripts reveal. This is no surprise and one can imagine that the A and B languages are merely the two surviving languages of a whole chain in which the intermediate languages had died out. This hypothesis will become useful when we are searching for the linguistic identity of some of the mummies.

Tocharian C?

While Tocharian documents are well attested in the northern part of the Tarim Basin, no Tocharian documents have been discovered along the southern Silk Road. Here, as we have already seen, we find documents largely in Prākrit, a Middle Indic language, that served both as a liturgical and administrative language, and in Khotanese Saka, an Iranian language. A sizeable group of documents was uncovered in the ancient territory of Kroraïn (Kroraina, Loulan, later Shanshan). These were among the 'treasures' recovered from the highly productive site of Niyä, excavated by Aurel Stein, which lay on the borders of Khotan, while other documents were discovered at Ändir and in the vicinity of Kroraïn itself. The Prākrit documents, however, revealed various strata of vocabulary. Although written in a language of northwest India, their authors had frequent occasion to use words in a different language. About 40 of these 'foreign' words are borrowed from Iranian and many of the proper names are Indic but there remain about an additional 100 words and 1,000 personal and place names that cannot be explained as either Indic or Iranian. These exotic words fill out many semantic categories ranging from agriculture, land use, textiles, material culture, transportation and social organization. That the words fill so many semantic categories and that they also include so many local place and personal names suggests that these words derive from the 'natives' of Kroraïn and, therefore, we can refer to this segment of the vocabulary as Kroränian.

What was Kroränian? Thomas Burrow examined these peculiar words in the 1930s and came to a conclusion that still finds general support today – that the native vocabulary is best explained as some form of Tocharian. One has to be vague here since the linguists are really in difficulty when it comes to the Kroränian vocabulary. The problem is that the Prākrit documents (and Kroränian words) are administrative texts but we simply do not find corresponding texts that deal with the same things in Tocharian A or B. It is something like being given a handful of pages ripped from an automobile manual detailing the repair of a carburettor and told to use it as a key to translating Shakespeare's sonnets. Unsurprisingly then, only a handful of words have been compared so far between Kroränian and the two Tocharian languages. The local Kroränian word for 'district' *kilme* is certainly to be compared with Tocharian A *kälyme* 'direction'. Much less certain are some of the other words proposed. Referring to a camel, the Prākrit text describes one as *amklatsa*, which Burrow compared with the Tocharian (A and B) word *aknatsa* 'ignorant', i.e. an untrained camel. Among the names of agricultural products, the author had to resort to a local word, *oĝana*, which was compared with Tocharian A (borrowed from Tocharian B) *oko* 'fruit'. Less plausibly, *maka* 'some commodity that could

Examples of Kroränian words

Textiles	Camels	Crops	Objects
akiṣḍha	pungebha	oĝana	ḍhipu (bow)
arnavaji	vaghu	aḍini	taravacena (cutting)
avalika	sukri	phalitaga	arohaga (saddle)

be sent a long distance as a tax' was set beside Tocharian *malke* 'milk' (although one would be a bit surprised to see such generic terms turning to the local patois; nor can one readily imagine a long-distance milk shipment in the Tarim Basin).

Far more convincing is the fact that the exotic words tend to reflect the Tocharian phonetic system and contain what would appear to be Tocharian suffixes. For example, in Tocharian A, one of the ways of forming an adjective is to add the suffix *-ñci*, e.g. *ātäl* 'man' but *ātläñci* 'belonging to the man, male'. In the Prākrit documents we find a similar suffix *-e(ṃ)ci* as in *kilme* 'district' but *kilme(ṃ)ci* 'belonging to the district' or *Kroraiṃci* 'Kroränian'. In short, it is as if one stumbled across a document in English which read that 'Brothers *Schwalbe* and *Schwenter* behaved *äffisch* and *schweinisch* during their morning prayers'. The two proper names and one of the 'strange' adverbs all begin with a *schw*, which is not admitted in English (except in German loanwords), while the two adverbs, even if we didn't know their meaning ('apish' and 'swinish'), have the same non-English *-isch* suffix which, were we to know German, we would be able to identify easily enough.

Burrow concluded that in the southern Tarim there existed traces of a Tocharian language. Although the hard evidence was meagre enough, Burrow also suggested that it reflected a different dialect than that found in the northern Tarim Basin (we would need to know much more about this language before we could pronounce definitively on this), which we might call Kroränian or Tocharian C. What is most interesting is that the Prākrit documents date from the 3rd century AD i.e. they are about 300 years older than any of our other Tocharian documents. That they are replete with what are taken to be Tocharian personal and place names and what are apparently local names for agricultural commodities suggests that they reflect the language of the natives of the region who had converted to Buddhism as it spread along the southern route through East Central Asia. This places Tocharian C in the region earlier than the Buddhist mission to the Tarim Basin. That the documents contain so few Iranian loanwords (which, as Burrow suggests, are more likely to have been picked up en route from India to the Tarim Basin) indicates that Tocharians may have also preceded Iranians in their occupation of the central and western regions of the southern Tarim Basin. It might be added that analysis of loanwords specifically associated with Buddhism in the other two Tocharian languages (Tocharian A and B) suggests that the Saka were the earliest agents for the spread of Buddhism here. The Tocharians, in short, make a case for a people or, at least, a language that preceded the Buddhist mission, the Indo-Aryans and, more importantly, probably the Iranians into the southeast of the Tarim Basin. And of still greater interest, it places the earliest evidence for Tocharian in the same region where we find the earliest evidence for Caucasoid settlement of East Central Asia as well as many of our earliest and best-preserved mummies.

By Any Other Name?

What did the people who left the Tocharian documents call themselves? On the one hand, this is a fairly easy question; on the other, it presents one of the goriest academic battlefields imaginable and, so as not to sicken the general reader, we have set much of our discussion in an extended note at the end of this book where the braver members of our audience, those who sit at the back of lecture halls and torment speakers with questions about the jumble of names that constitutes the 'Tocharian problems', may sate their lust. Let us start with what we know.

Tocharian B documents make it explicit that at least some of the people who wrote them regarded themselves as Kucheans. The name of the state was Kuci (or *Kuśi) which is rendered today in Mandarin as Qiuci (in the early medieval period this would have been pronounced *kuw-dzi). The adjective was kuśiññe and we even have a document with the phrase kuśiññ oroccepi lānte yaitkorsa 'by the order of the great king of Kucha'; the same appellation is provided in a Sanskrit document which refers to the Kuci-mahārāja 'great king of Kucha'.

As we have seen above, the region of Qarashähär where Tocharian A texts have been recovered was known in Sanskrit documents as Agni and in Chinese as Yanqi (Middle Chinese *ian-gji or *iän-g'ji). The name is also well represented in other languages, e.g. Khotanese Argi and Buddhist Hybrid Sanskrit Agnideśa ('Agni-country'). Some have maintained that both names were derived from words meaning 'white' or 'silver', i.e. both Kucheans and Agneans regarded themselves as 'the brilliant ones', but there are sufficient reasons to be wary of such claims and pursuing them gets us no closer to their identities.

Now it would be convenient to leave things as they stand, i.e. designating the western language as Kuchean and the eastern as Agnean, were it not for several other texts which lead us into a labyrinth of linguistic and historical arguments. The attentive reader will by now have already seen at least one of the problems: if the speakers of the two languages called themselves Kucheans and Agneans, then why do we call them Tocharians? And haven't we already mentioned the Tocharians with respect to the Yuezhi conquest of Bactria and the establishment of the Kushan empire? Are all these the same people, i.e. were the Yuezhi speakers of Tocharian languages who carried their language into Bactria in the 2nd century BC? We will set out the problem so that the reader can understand the ultimate implications of such equations. In order to do this we will have to engage in some wordplay and, until further notice, we will refer to the languages attested in the north Tarim basin as KA (Kuchean-Agnean) rather than Tocharian.

As we have seen, the latest of the KA texts were prepared under the auspices of the Uyghurs whose own Turkic language ultimately replaced that of the earlier inhabitants of the region. About AD 800 an Uyghur translation of a Sanskrit drama was prepared and in the colophon (that part of a manuscript referring to the circumstances of its creation), one reads in Uyghur: 'The sacred book *Maitreyasamiti*, which was composed by the Bodhisattva *guru ācarya* Aryacandra, native of Agnideśa, in the *toχri* language from the Sanskrit language, and which has been translated by the *guru ācarya* Prajñārakṣita, native of Il-baliq (the Uyghur capital of Khocho), from the *toχri* language into the Turkic language'. In a nutshell, the colophon tells us that a Sanskrit drama was first translated from Sanskrit into the *toχri* language of Agnideśa (and we know that this means the Agnean kingdom) and then from *toχri* into the Turkish language of Il-baliq by two learned gurus. Armed with this equation, in 1908 E. Sieg and F. W. K. Müller reasoned that the apparent Uyghur designation of Agnean, *toχri*, was very close to the name of the well-known ethnic group *Tókharoi* (in Greek), Latin *Tochari*, Sanskrit *Tukhāra* or Chinese *Tuhuoluo*, the name applied in ancient sources to Bactria, i.e. Tokharistan. It has been further suggested that the same name can be found in other ancient sources; e.g. Ptolemy's gazetteer of the known world, dated to the 2nd century AD, lists a *Thaugouroi* in Gansu, a *Takoriaioi* north of the Imaus (Himalayas) and a *Taguouraioi* in the vicinity of Issyk-kul. Peoples with a name sounding like 'Tocharian' seemed to be everywhere from the borders of Gansu to Bactria. To give an idea of where such observations can lead, consider as examples the following two proposals by A. K. Narain and W. B. Henning.

As we have just mentioned, the people who emerge as Tocharians in Western sources are often equated with a branch of the Yuezhi of Chinese sources who were driven first from the Gansu borderlands by the Xiongnu, then farther west by the Wusun, arriving at the Oxus, and going on to conquer Bactria and establish the Kushan empire. Narain argues that once one accepts the equation Tocharian = Yuezhi, then one is forced to follow both the Chinese historical sources (which for him would propel the Yuezhi back to at least the 7th century BC) and the geographical reference of their first cited historical location (Gansu) to the conclusion that they have lived there 'from times immemorial'. Narain infers that they had been there at least since the Qijia culture of *c.* 2000 BC and probably even earlier in the Yangshao culture of the Neolithic. This would render the Tocharians as virtually native to Gansu (and earlier than the putative spread of the Neolithic to Xinjiang) and Narain goes so far as to argue that the Indo-Europeans themselves originally dispersed from this area westwards. Seldom has a tail so small wagged a dog so large.

Rather than starting from the east, Henning found the origin of the Tocharians to lie in the west. He picked up their historical trail on the western borders of Babylon where, *c.* 2100 BC, the kingdom of the Akkadians was being harassed by the barbarian Guti 'whose language is queer' and whose neighbours included the Tukriš. Henning speculated that both of these peoples had probably come from farther north, south Russia to be precise, by way of the Caucasus very much in the same manner that the later Cimmerians and Scythians poured down into the Middle East in the

1st millennium BC. Why they should be associated with the peoples of the Tarim Basin rested on several lines of evidence. First and foremost was the apparent similarity of these names with those found 2,000 years later in the Tarim. At that time, according to Henning, the pronunciation of the Chinese morphosyllables that are now pronounced Yuezhi should have then been approximately *Gu(t)-t'i, which would provide a perfect phonological correspondence. In the KA language, Guti would have been rendered Kuči, and hence be equivalent to Kuchean. As for the *toχri* mentioned in the Uyghur colophon, Henning believed one need look no further than the name of the Tukriš who had been neighbours of the Guti in western Persia and hence had given their name to both the toχri of the northern Tarim and the Tocharians of Bactria.

The presumption that there was a connection between two names found in Akkadian documents and names encountered over two millennia later in the Tarim Basin did not elicit widespread support. Henning suggested that the variation in endings found among the names of Gutian kings might be explained as case endings which themselves might be compared with those employed in Tocharian documents some two and a half thousand years later, an enterprise of extreme dubiousness. He also made passing reference to similarities between ceramics found in Iran and in the Tarim Basin, although these currently play no part in discussions of the prehistory of the Tarim Basin, and the maintenance of ceramics, especially painted wares, among supposedly nomadic peoples wandering from Persia into the Tarim would be regarded as exceptional indeed on every count. Of greater detriment to such a theory is that Henning accepted a reconstructed Chinese pronunciation of Yuezhi as *Gu(t)-t'i when, in fact, it is commonly reconstructed now as *ngiwăt-tiĕg which makes it a far less transparent correspondence.

How one interprets these various references to Tocharians and words similar to Tocharians does make an obvious difference to how one interprets the ethnic history of East Central Asia. But any conclusions are so tentative that we will cut to the chase and try to present the main kinds of alternative conclusions in terms relevant to our search for the identification of the Tarim mummies.

The first type of result we can call the Iranian hypothesis. It begins with the observation that there is no evidence whatsoever that the historical Tocharians, who are associated with the conquest of Bactria, and who included in their number the people who were later to be called the Kushans, ever spoke a language similar to KA; all the evidence of the Kushan empire indicates that those who administered it employed an Iranian language (or Prākrit). As for the Yuezhi, there is no firm evidence from any Chinese source as to the language that they spoke. Prior to the Xiongnu political dominance of the Tarim Basin, the region may have been under Yuezhi control but this did not entail any linguistic domination, although it may have been yet another vehicle for Iranian loanwords into the KA languages. The basic urban population, or at least their ruling classes, remained KA speakers irrespective of whether they were ruled by Yuezhi, Xiongnu or Chinese; only the Uyghur, who actually settled in the region and occupied towns themselves, were able to effect the linguistic assimilation of the KA speakers. This hypothesis receives some coincidental support from descriptions of the Greater Yuezhi which indicate that they, like other Iranian-speaking peoples described in ancient literature, permitted women to hold high-status positions. Moreover, they are regarded as the same as the Iranian-speaking Parthians with respect to land, customs, produce and coins, and it has been suggested that their success in bringing the region under their own power was due to the fact that they shared a similar ethnic perspective and language. While it is not greatly important to us what language was carried into Bactria by the Yuezhi, this theory suggests that the eastern part of East Central Asia was dominated by Iranian speakers during the last centuries BC, possibly earlier. This hypothesis receives additional support from the evidence for cultural borrowing during the Bronze Age between Iranians and Chinese which would require very early direct contacts between the two populations.

We can refer to the second hypothesis as the Tocharian gambit. It runs something like this. The Yuezhi, who occupied the area from Gansu west to the Tarim Basin, spoke KA languages. By the time those who migrated west arrived in the Oxus, they had shed KA for an Iranian language or simply took up the expedient course of many foreign rulers and employed the local Iranian language for their administration. From our own particular perspective, this would mean that both the nomads of the eastern border of East Central Asia and the oasis-dwellers of the Tarim and Turpan basins and the Lopnur region spoke a KA language, at least by the first centuries BC (we can imagine here a situation something like the Arabs who may be either settled farmers or nomadic Bedouins). As we also have some Tocharian loanwords in Chinese that date to about the 3rd century BC (possibly much earlier but that cannot be easily demonstrated), we can have a Tocharian rather than an Iranian world adjoining the Han.

No matter how these hypotheses develop, the starting point is the Yuezhi on the borders of Gansu (and it may be that their location 'between Dunhuang and the Qilian Mountains' actually indicated that they were situated farther to the northwest, i.e. between Dunhuang and the Tängri Tagh). So which, if any, of our mummies belonged to the Yuezhi, whose language we are most uncertain about in the first place? It is time to introduce an admittedly jaundiced archaeological spin to the whole affair. The Yuezhi of the Gansu corridor have an historical existence, not an archaeological presence, i.e. there is so far absolutely no evidence for the camps or burials of the more than 400,000 Yuezhi recorded in Chinese texts anywhere that historians have positioned them. While we may not expect much from pastoral nomads, we should remember that the Saka and Wusun are both identified by their burials in the Ili River region and we also cannot dismiss the Gansu corridor as a terra incognita, as here we find the settlements and cemeteries of the Siba culture, an Early Bronze Age culture whose physical type would appear to be Mongoloid, in the same territory where we would later expect the Yuezhi. The only way we can discuss Yuezhi is to extend the name over much broader areas of the Tarim and Turpan basins than the historical records allow. We are engaged in moving names across a map without any evidence of the people. If the Chinese histories had never mentioned the Yuezhi on the borders of China, no archaeologist would have had the slightest reason to postulate their existence. The Yuezhi are 'ghosts', summoned up by historians to torment archaeologists. We have no need to look for ghosts; we have the remains of real people with at least some evidence of their material culture.

Linguistic Prehistory

Embedded in any language is evidence of its past. The preceding sentence of nine words contains five words which are derived from Germanic (*in, any, is, of, its*), three which derive from Latin via French (*language, evidence, past*) and one which combines a Latin prefix with a Germanic root (*embedded*). That the most basic verbs, articles and prepositions are all Germanic would suggest a relative chronology in which English was originally a Germanic language that was later heavily influenced by a Romance language.

An examination of the Tocharian languages (we can now come up for air and revert to this designation rather than KA) also reveals something of their past although we cannot work back too far here. Curiously enough, the impact of Chinese on Tocharian is not very significant (e.g. Tocharian B *cāne* 'price' derives from the Chinese word for 'money', the (modern) *qián* with the medieval pronunciation **dz'iän*; also measurements of capacity, and, as D. Q. Adams has recently indicated, the word for 'rice') nor does Turkish provide a significant source of Tocharian vocabulary. On the other hand, Middle Iranian languages current in the Tarim Basin and surrounding areas in the 1st millennium AD provided a major and predictable source of loanwords to the Tocharian languages. From Khotanese Saka, the language of the southern Tarim Basin, we find loanwords such as *āṣaṇa-* 'worthy' borrowed as Tocharian B *aṣāṃ* 'worthy', while the Sogdians who acted as one of the principal middlemen in the transportation of goods along the Silk Road contributed the word *mwδ* 'wine' (cognate with our English *mead*) which was taken up as Tocharian B *mot* 'alcohol'. Somewhat earlier contacts with Iranian languages can be seen in words such as *tsain*, 'arrow', which was apparently borrowed from a northeast Iranian language such as Avestan (*zaēna-* 'weapon'). Not all borrowings came by way of Iranian since there is also evidence of Indic borrowings (as well as the direct importation of Sanskrit in Tocharian religious literature). These terms refer to aspects of Buddhist life which would have been foreign to the pre-Buddhist Tocharians, e.g. Tocharian B *aśiya* 'nun', *aśari* 'teacher' and *ṣamāne* 'monk' which all find their origins in words from Gāndhārī (the language of Aśoka's inscriptions) of the 2nd century BC to the 4th century AD.

Tocharian specialists are generally reluctant to admit that there was any flow of Indo-Iranian vocabulary into Tocharian earlier than the 1st millennium BC, a time when words such as Tocharian A *porat*, Tocharian B *peret* 'axe' may have been borrowed from some Iranian language (we find Ossetic *färät* 'axe'). Tocharian also employs a word for 'iron' (A *añcu*, B *eñcuwo*) which some compare with similar words such as Ossetic *andan* 'steel'. While such evidence can only be employed positively, i.e. it cannot demonstrate that contacts did not exist, there have been few to suggest that the ancestors of the Tocharians were in close contact with their Indo-Iranian neighbours before *c.* 1000–500 BC. To go back any earlier takes us into one of the most disputed areas of Tocharian studies.

Real 'Europeans'?

The relationship between Tocharian and the other Indo-European stocks or subfamilies and the issue of how 'European' the Tocharian languages actually are has dogged Tocharian studies since its inception. If we reflect again on the various Indo-European language stocks, we see that that which embraces the Indic (and Nuristani) and Iranian languages is the most certain higher-order group in Indo-European. By this we mean that we can reconstruct a linguistic stage between the development of Iranian and Indo-Aryan on the one hand, and Proto-Indo-European on the other, namely, Proto-Indo-Iranian. In short, we get from Proto-Indo-European to Sanskrit or Avestan only by way of Proto-Indo-Iranian, and any discussion of Indo-Aryan or Iranian origins will include the geographical staging area of Proto-Indo-Iranian. The majority of, although not all, Indo-Europeanists would also accept a Balto-Slavic stage before the independent development of the Baltic and Slavic languages. Now both these subgroups of Indo-European are satem languages (i.e. they changed a 'hard' *g* or *k* to *j, z* or *s*) and the existence of other unique linguistic features shared between these satem languages suggests some degree of proximity between the two groups, i.e. in some way there was a continuum of Balto-Slavic-Indo-Iranian which experienced a number of common innovations not experienced by the other Indo-European stocks. Tocharian, as we have seen in Chapter Three, belongs to the centum languages which are defined by their hard pronunciation of what we reconstruct as palatal velars ($*\hat{g}, *\hat{k}$, etc.). It is generally, although not universally, presumed that the centum languages did not participate in the innovations experienced by the satem languages; being a centum language, however, does not tell you any more about its prehistoric relations. For that, linguists have sought other criteria among the various centum languages to determine their correct positions on the Indo-European family tree. And it is a truly amazing array of models that they have proposed. We list their putative relationships below on a west to east axis.

1. Tocharian is most closely related to Italo-Celtic, i.e. its closest linguistic relatives are to be found in the far west of Europe. There were those who claimed that it was specifically closest to Celtic and one scholar even wanted to lump it together with the 'other' Celtic languages (which, despite the tartans, it emphatically is not). Geographically, this theory places the pre-Tocharians somewhere on the eastern fringe of the early Celtic world, i.e. central Europe.

2. Tocharian is most closely related to Germanic. Geographically, this normally sets the pre-Tocharians somewhere to the south and east of the early Germanic languages of northern Europe.

3. Tocharian is most closely related to Italo-Celtic, Germanic and Balto-Slavic, i.e, it was one of the languages of the so-called 'Northwest European group'. This theory places the pre-Tocharians somewhere on the southeastern margin of these other languages.

4. Tocharian is related most closely to Balto-Slavic or it falls somewhere between Balto-Slavic and Greek, i.e. it was a language whose closest relations are to be sought in central and eastern Europe.

5. Tocharian is most closely related to Greek (or established later relationships with Greek after earlier relationships with languages farther to the northwest). This relationship need not be geographically translated into a Greek origin since many would presume that pre-Greeks entered Greece from the north; a southeast European origin should do in this case.

6. Tocharian is most closely related to Thracian (a Balkan language) and Phrygian (employed in Anatolia). Here again, a southeast

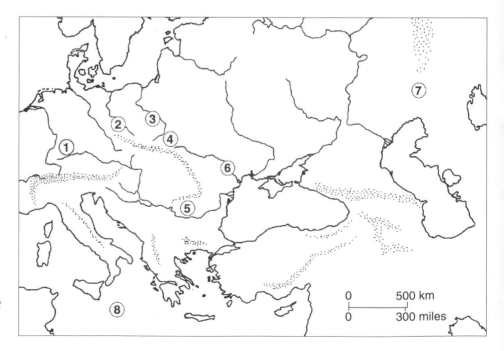

154. Map of Tocharian proposed relationships (numbers keyed against the various hypotheses mentioned in the text).

European origin, possibly one that found the pre-Tocharians on the northwest corner of the Black Sea, may be envisaged. It might be added that both these languages are so poorly known that this hypothesis is barely discussable.

7. Tocharian belongs to the Indo-European peripheral languages which comprise Celtic, Italic, Phrygian, Anatolian and Tocharian, i.e. the expansion of the Indo-European languages was centrifugal from a centre that found the Tocharians on the outer eastern rim of language expansion. Here, Tocharian's relationship with Italic and Celtic, for example, does not have geographical connotations other than that they all were on the outer rim of the Indo-European world.

8. Tocharian is a relatively independent language stock not closely related to any other stock. Generally, such a conclusion presumes that Tocharian departed early (after Anatolian) from the continuum of late Indo-European dialects, thereby it shares few if any innovations with other Indo-European stocks. Such a model is geographically non-specific provided that at an early date the pre-Tocharians take themselves away from the other Indo-European stocks.

The Measure of a Language

To some degree, all these theories for Tocharian's relations are still very much alive and kicking, so much so that hardly a subsequent sentence in this chapter could not be vigorously challenged by a competent Tocharian specialist or Indo-Europeanist. How can this be? The answer lies partly in the nature of the evidence and partly in the methods by which linguists seek to establish the proximity of one genetically related stock with another. The hard linguistic 'facts' are the comparative descriptions of the phonology (sounds), morphology (grammar) and vocabulary of Tocharian with other Indo-European languages. Two languages, genetically related, may share a common feature because 1) they have both inherited it from the proto-language (even if all the other languages have lost it); 2) they have both created the feature independently in their own language; 3) the immediate linguistic ancestor of both created the feature at some time after the dissolution of the proto-language; and 4) one language innovated and passed the new feature on to a geographically contiguous language. We have, in effect, already investigated situation 4 where we have found late loans between the Indo-Iranian languages and Tocharian. We now need to look briefly at the other situations.

Let us propose that Tocharian and Celtic are especially closely related as a 'straw dog' to see how these different principles work. We can see that a similarity between two stocks that is determined by situation 1 is of no geographical utility because the two languages are, like all the other members of the same language family, only related by way of the proto-language itself. That Tocharian A *yuk* 'horse' is cognate with Old Irish *ech* 'horse' tells us nothing of a common geographical origin since cognates for the same word for 'horse' can be found in almost all other Indo-European languages (e.g. Old English *eoh*, Latin *equus*, Greek *híppos*, Sanskrit *áśva*); it only shows that they all derive from a common proto-form, not that there is any special relationship between, say, Irish and Tocharian.

This is easily understood, but how do we distinguish between this situation and that described in situation 3 where the two languages in question were the only languages that shared a particular set of cognate words or grammatical forms? This is one of the grounds on which linguists have sought to demonstrate that Tocharian has a more exclusive or unique relationship with some rather than other Indo-European languages. Some of the evidence of vocabulary shared exclusively between Tocharian and other languages has been assembled by both A. J. Van Windekens and Douglas Adams.

What do these lists convey? They at least illustrate the reason why we may find some linguists attempting to locate the ancestors of the Tocharians somewhere, say, between the Germans, the Balts and the Greeks (and some of the others such as Celtic look far less impressive), but do they offer sufficient grounds for any conclusion? Even Douglas Adams admits that one cannot tweak these figures into what might pass for statistical probability, and they seem to throw up as many problems as they try to resolve. For example, why should Tocharian share about half as many isoglosses with Iranian as Indo-Aryan when the shared vocabulary should have occurred before the collapse of Proto-Indo-Iranian? The probable answer is that we have preserved for us a vastly larger Indo-Aryan vocabulary than we have for early Iranian and hence a far better chance of finding cognates. The same would go for Greek and Germanic, the first with a truly enormous early vocabulary, and the second with an impressive number of

	Van Windekens general**	Adams	Adams revised	Adams exclusive dyads***
Celtic	6	34	76	2
Italic	30	35	74	2
Germanic	77	96	143	16
Baltic	34*	65	120	4
Greek	69	73	121	8
Armenian	4	2	?	0
Anatolian	5	11	?	2
Indo-Aryan	65	63	129	4
Iranian	34	34	103	0

Proposed correspondences between Tocharian and other Indo-European languages according to Van Windekens and Adams.

*Van Windekens distinguishes between common Balto-Slavic, Baltic and Slavic and Indo-Iranian, Indo-Aryan and Iranian; in both cases the common number found in Balto-Slavic and Indo-Iranian have been added to the numbers found exclusively in each stock. **Adams scores 3 points for complete morphological identity, 1 for only a root identity, and 2 for something in between. ***His dyads represent words shared between Tocharian and *only* one other Indo-European stock.

well-attested and well-studied languages. The only rule evident here is that the greater the overall preserved vocabulary, the greater the chance of finding cognate 'hits' between Tocharian and some other language. Douglas Adams has attempted to rectify this situation by recomputing the figures as if each language were an equal contributor to our reconstructed Proto-Indo-European vocabulary (his 'revised' computations above). But the results will almost invariably be contradictory. For example, there is a unique Tocharian-Germanic isogloss in that Tocharian A *koläm* 'boat' and Tocharian B *kolmo* 'boat' would appear to be cognate with Old High German *skalm* 'boat'. Fine, we move the pre-Tocharians somewhere towards northern Europe. On the other hand, when we look at the outcome for the cognate sets for the word for 'tear (drop)', we find that Tocharian (A *ākär* 'tear', B *akrūna* 'tears') aligns itself with Baltic (Lithuanian *ašarâ*), and Indo-Iranian (Avestan *asrū-*, Sanskrit *áśru-*) and does not participate in the prefixing of this word with a *d*-sound found in Celtic (Old Irish *dēr*), Italic (Old Latin *dacruma*), Germanic (Old English *tēar*), and Greek (*dákru*). Here it is peripheral perhaps and certainly nowhere near the early Germans.

It may be argued that comparison of grammatical and phonological traits should be of greater value in that we generally have enough of any major language stock to evaluate these features on an equal basis. Douglas Adams incorporated the Tocharian data into an earlier study that utilized 30 phonological and 44 morphological traits to examine the similarities among the various Indo-European dialects. His data revealed that Tocharian shares features in order of frequency with Greek, Armenian, Germanic, Italic, Balto-Slavic and Celtic (while showing negative correlations with Indo-Iranian). But these similarities embrace a wide variety of types: many may be shared retentions of features rather than common innovations and, what we take as innovations may be independent as well as shared. It is, therefore, the *nature* of the evidence rather than the *quantity* that counts in establishing a relationship between two stocks, and unfortunately there is simply too little consensus here to make much of a case for any special *geographical* relationship between Tocharian and another Indo-European language stock. As anyone familiar with clustering techniques is aware, just about any body of data will permit itself to be clustered no matter how meaningless it is. We could prepare a tree-diagram that would show how Beethoven was 'closer' to Haydn than Bach; adding Hoagy Carmichael, Scott Joplin and Elton John to the same tree is always possible but what would the results mean? Does it matter anyway? It certainly does and the 'jaundiced archaeologist' gambit is not going to get us out of this mess.

The Flight of the Arrow

The most powerful weapon in the arsenal of anyone attempting to establish the origins and dispersion of an ethnic or linguistic group is a felt-tipped pen, preferably red (but a black one will do at a pinch). Consider for a moment

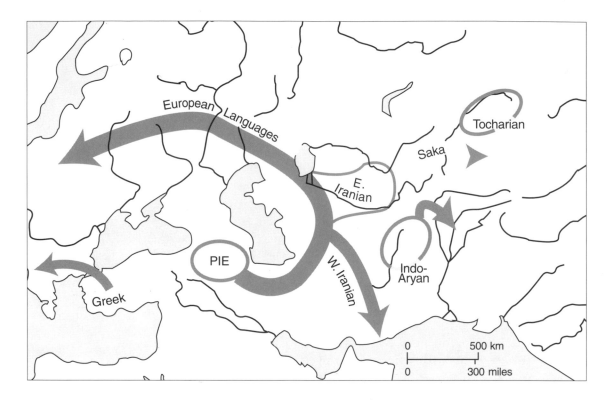

155. Indo-European expansions according to the recent account by Tomas Gamkrelidze and Vyacheslav Ivanov in their Indo-European and Indo-Europeans. *Note that the Tocharians are not shown to derive from anywhere specifically but just occupy their historical region.*

how the problem of Tocharian origins has been resolved over the past century. We know that the Tocharians ended up in the Tarim Basin so we have one of two choices. We can admit our ignorance, draw a ring around Tocharian territory and pretend that they grew out of the ground while all the other Indo-European groups arrive in their historical homes on the tips of arrows. This, of course, would explain nothing about the origins of the Tocharians. Alternatively, we can draw an arrow with our red felt-tipped pen. We know where to put the point – in the Tarim Basin. But where do we place the base of the shaft of the arrow? Where do we set it into flight? So far this depends solely, it would seem, on where one finds its closest linguistic neighbours. If this is, for example, Celtic, then we have an incredibly long arrow that stretches from Central Europe all the way to the Tarim Basin (generally this is held to be visually too 'extreme' and so the flight of the arrow is frequently truncated: we only get a shorter arrow arching its way out of Central Europe in an easterly direction). There are no cultural or archaeological arguments for these arrows: they represent felt-tipped pen archaeology.

A Brief History of Tocharian Time

Now those who have sought to employ dialectal arguments to position the pre-Tocharians in space have often (though not always) ignored the temporal problems involved in any such claims. For example, if one were to accept that

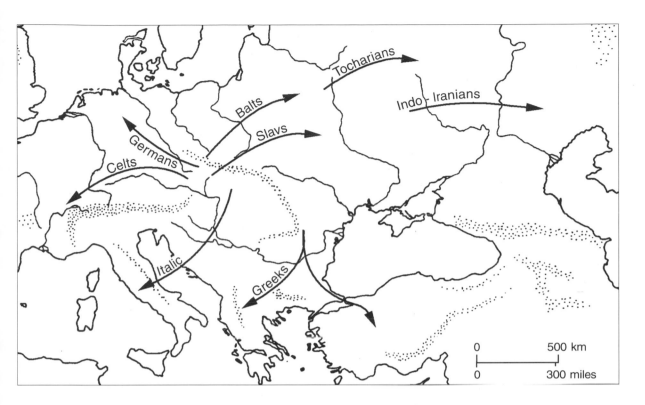

there was a particularly close association between Tocharian and Celtic or Germanic, what does that mean in terms of both real time and real space? Invariably, Tocharian seems to finish a poor second and the linguist begins to draw his or her arrow of Tocharian migrations from the eastern margin of whoever is lucky enough to be chosen as its partner. It is with very few exceptions the Tocharians who are required to take the long walk (or ride) while the Celts (or Germans) get to sit in their historically attested seats of central and western Europe. Why? As the relationships under discussion supposedly occurred before the formation of Proto-Celtic and Proto-Tocharian, neither need have achieved their historical seats at the time of their proposed relationship.

Knowing when such relationships should have developed is absolutely critical since space, at least in our four-dimensional universe, has no meaning without time. And here we must face the frequently ignored asymmetry of the Indo-European space-time continuum. The dates that have been estimated for the emergence of the various European proto-languages, i.e. Celtic, Italic, Germanic, Baltic and Slavic, all of which have been partnered with Tocharian, is generally set broadly within the period *c.* 1500–500 BC (we have also seen that Tocharian might be dated to this period). Before this time we seem to be dealing with some ill-defined period of Late Indo-European during which pre-Celtic, pre-Germanic, etc. linguistic tendencies were coming into being. This would not be of such great importance if it were not also apparent that Greek, Anatolian and the Indo-

156. Map showing Indo-European expansions from a study by Giacomo Devoto in his Origini Indeuropee. *Here the Tocharians are given a more westerly origin to accommodate their affinities with other Indo-European speakers.*

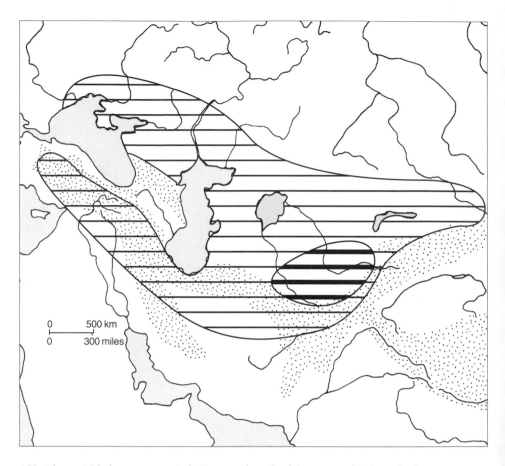

157. Johanna Nichols proposes an Indo-European homeland that emerged in Central Asia (indicated by heavy shading). According to her, this area was the centre of linguistic innovations that spread through the range of related Proto-Indo-European dialects (lighter shading). Such a position for an Indo-European homeland (for which archaeological evidence is wholly lacking) would place the ancestors of the Tocharian languages very close to their later historical home.

Iranian proto-languages must have all emerged by or before *c.* 2000 BC. There are a number of consequences to all this.

If the pre-Tocharians were in any form of specific relationship with the northwest languages (Celtic, Italic, Germanic, Baltic, Slavic), it could have been at any period from *c.* 4000 to 500 BC. Where these relations may have taken place depends largely on *when* they are imagined to have occurred and *where* one wants to locate the Indo-European homeland in the first place. The earlier the connections, the less the need to translate such a linguistic relationship into a geographical one that approximates the historical positions of the various European languages. For example, if pre-Tocharian and pre-northwest European connections occurred at *c.* 4000 BC and one wanted to place the homeland in the steppe region of the Don and Volga rivers, then that is also where the pre-Tocharians might have been sitting at the time. If one prefers a very late relationship between pre-

Tocharian and northwest European, say in the 1st millennium BC, then this would certainly drag the pre-Tocharians much farther west since we can be fairly confident of where the immediate predecessors of the northwest European proto-languages were sitting after 1000 BC. If we accept some form of northwest orientation for Tocharian, can we provide any evidence for its date?

Strictly speaking, the answer is probably 'no' but there is some circumstantial evidence to suggest that any putative connections must be earlier rather than later. There is considerable evidence that Germanic, Baltic and Slavic once formed some type of linguistic continuum that experienced innovations in both morphology and vocabulary. The latter offers some vague indices of dating since it includes cultural terms such as 'gold', 'silver', 'rye' and 'oats', all of which are unlikely to have been adopted across northwestern Europe prior to c. 2000 BC. Tocharian participates in none of this particular shared cultural vocabulary (we have no idea what, if any, were the Tocharian words for 'rye' and 'oats' but we do know the words for 'gold' and 'silver') and so if it indeed does share certain unique forms with this area, it is more likely to have been earlier when the geographical implications of such a relationship would be ambiguous at best.

Those who have attempted to associate Tocharian with other Indo-European language stocks appear to be in agreement that there are no grounds whatsoever for seeing a special genetic relationship with Indo-Iranian. Taken in the light of the probable date of loanwords from the Indo-Iranian languages, this provides us with some interesting parameters for locating the ancestors of the Tocharians in both space and time. We generally imagine that the Indo-Iranian language stock formed sometime around 2500–2000 BC somewhere in the east European or west Asiatic steppe, i.e. between the Ukraine and western Kazakhstan; and wherever the ancestors of the Tocharian language lived, they should not have been part of the nucleus of the Indo-Iranians at this time.

Those who argue that the Tocharians cannot be closely associated with any other Indo-European stock would appear to be noncommittal about the geographical position of the pre-Tocharians except for the spatial constraints required by no evident relationships, i.e. where we find the other Indo-European groups would not appear to be the best place to look for the pre-Tocharians. Implicit in this is the belief that pre-Tocharian was separated from the Indo-European linguistic continuum at a quite early date before other dialectal relationships developed. This, incidentally, does not demand that the Tocharians were necessarily only a small group of speakers who wandered off from the rest; they may have been a major group which, by the time they entered the historical record, had been whittled down to those surviving in the Tarim Basin (in the same way that the distribution of Celtic languages has declined to a few pockets in Atlantic Europe). On the other hand, had they occupied a larger area of Eurasia, one might have expected, after their absorption by other Indo-European stocks, particularly

Indo-Iranian, that some traces of their language might have been borrowed into these other languages. So far the evidence here is wanting. It is also possible that where they once existed was later occupied by non-Indo-European languages. For example, the (Proto-)Tocharians may once have covered most of Kazakhstan and although their territory was later occupied by Iranians we would still have no evidence that the Tocharians were once there since Turkish has since swept over and filled this entire region.

Tocharians and Afanasevo

With so many possibilities, it is difficult to make logical demands on where we should expect to find the prehistoric Tocharians. Nevertheless, there are aspects of Tocharian origins that more easily accommodate one sort of solution than others. The type of solution that would best fit the linguistic evidence is one that derives the Proto-Tocharians from somewhere that was not in obvious or close contact with the prehistoric ancestors of the Indo-Iranians and that permitted them to enter their historical seats before the arrival of the Iranians. Such an origin would permit them to evolve linguistically without sharing the innovations, e.g. satemization, experienced by the Balto-Slavic-Indo-Iranians. As this would appear to have reflected a continuum that spanned the region from eastern Europe to Kazakhstan, we might look for the Tocharians on either side of this continuum. In this way, they could develop in isolation before their arrival in the Tarim Basin. There is one archaeological culture that might just fit the bill.

The Andronovo culture, which we have already seen to be widely associated with some stage in the development of the Indo-Iranian languages, was not the first culture to practise stockraising on the Asiatic steppe. Before the expansions of Andronovo tribes, there were the Afanasevo communities of the eastern steppe in the region between the Minusinsk Basin of the Yenisei River and the Altai Mountains. Dating to the period *c.* 3500–2500 BC, the Afanasevo culture represents an archaeological enigma as its closest cultural relations appear to lie 1,500 km (930 miles) to its west in the European steppe.

Most of our evidence derives from burials which were deposited in stone-walled enclosures, rectangular or circular, which might then be capped with stone slabs. The deceased were extended on their backs but with their legs flexed, a rather rare burial position attested primarily on the European steppe in the Yamna (Pit-grave) culture. Like the Yamna culture ochre was also employed in the burials. The pottery included round- and pointed-based vessels, similar in a generic sense to the pottery of the Yamna culture. Specifically more closely related to the Yamna and later Catacomb cultures of the European steppe were the ceramic 'censers', small legged bowls which are believed to have held some form of aromatic substance (one from Romania contained traces of hemp which we know was later utilized in rituals of the Iron Age steppe nomads). There are also traces of horse

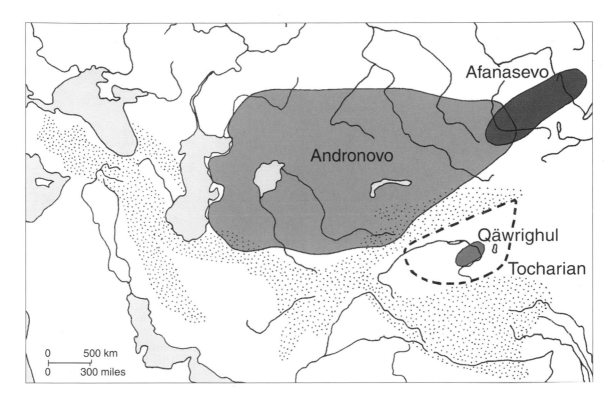

(whether wild or domesticated is not determined), metallurgy employing copper and silver, and possibly wheeled vehicles which are depicted on stone slabs. Finally, the physical type of the Afanasevo culture is Caucasoid and has been most closely related to that of the European steppe populations.

It is still very difficult to explain the origins of the Afanasevo culture since it appears so far east of its European cousins and there is a stark absence of intermediate sites excepting a handful of Afanasevo-type burials. The current working hypothesis would explain them as one of the earliest food-producing cultures to emerge out of the European steppe which, for reasons that still elude us, pushed far to the east. The territory between the Volga-Ural and the Yenisei is archaeologically poorly known and it is hoped that the filling of the gaps that might underwrite this model will be accomplished eventually.

From a linguistic point of view, the Afanasevo culture provides us with the opportunity to fit a culture to the type of linguistic development that we have suggested for the Tocharians. Here is a culture that was linked to developments in Europe but isolated far to the east. Moreover, when the Andronovo culture emerged, the culture most closely associated with the Indo-Iranians of the steppelands, the Afanasevo culture had already disappeared. If Tocharian documents had been found in the Minusinsk Basin or in the Altai Mountains, we would not have had any great difficulty explaining their origins. But this is not where we discover our written evidence for the Tocharians but rather in the Tarim and Turpan basins.

158. The distribution of the Afanasevo and Andronovo cultures compared with that of the Qäwrighul culture and the general distribution of the Tocharian languages.

Although the centre of the Afanasevo culture lies far to the north of the Tarim, there is some evidence that it spilled southwards and Afanasevo sites have been claimed for both Mongolia and northern China. Some suggest that we may look even farther south, right into the heartland of the mummies of East Central Asia.

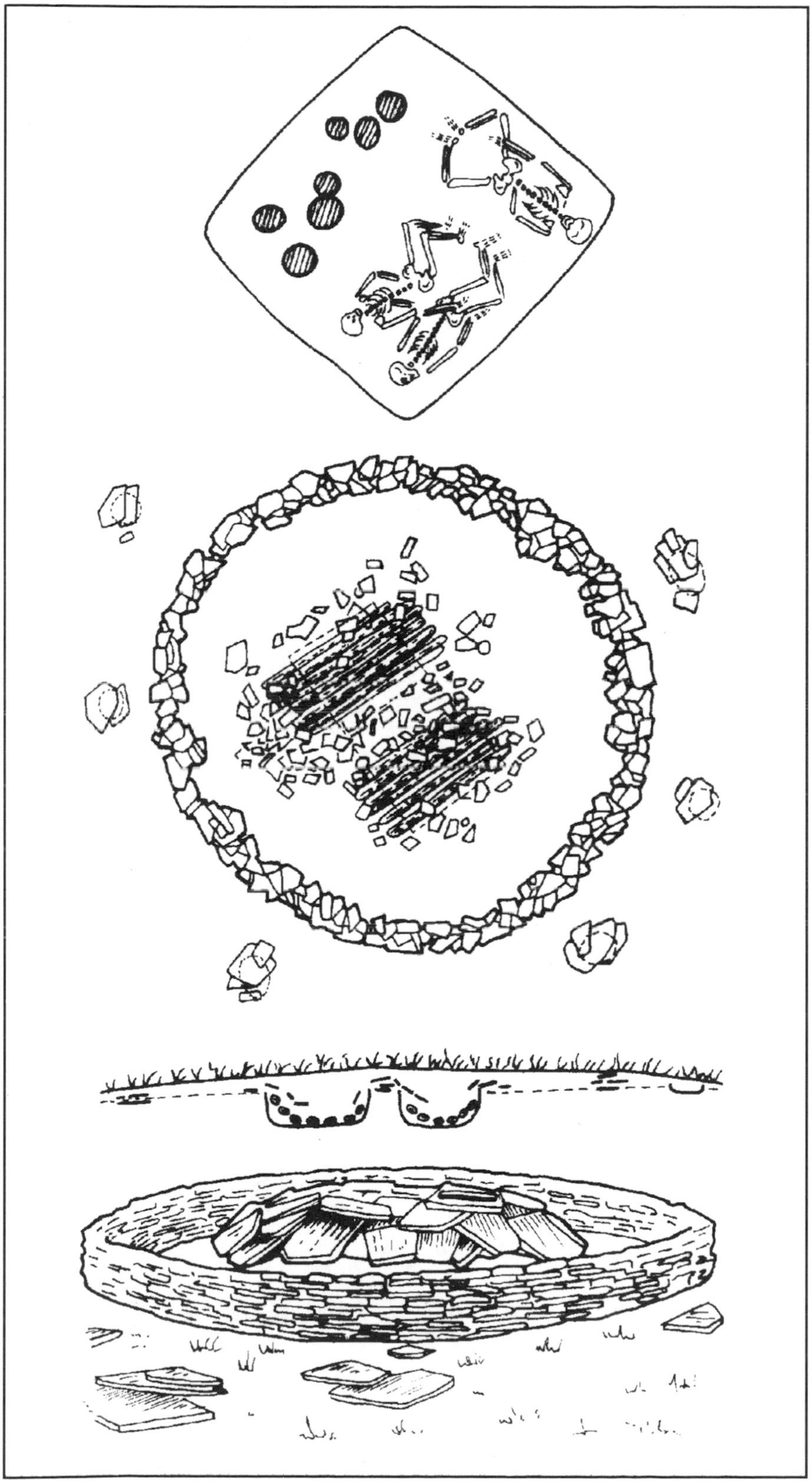

159. Afanasevo burials employed stone enclosures.

CHAPTER TEN

Who Were the Mummies?

I t should be abundantly evident by now that our attempt to reconstruct the ethnic prehistory of East Central Asia will require quite a feat of both archaeological and linguistic legerdemain. From a period comprising ethnically-anonymous and poorly-known prehistoric cultures, which provide the cultural context for the Xinjiang mummies, we must navigate through a period of ambivalent parahistorical references to populations of East Central Asia dating primarily from the Han and later dynasties and, somehow, tie these into the evidence of the myriad languages of our still more recent written documents. We would do well, then, to keep our assumptions in mind, not so much to guarantee the validity of any of our conclusions as to ensure the integrity of our speculations. Here are a few of the more obvious.

The mummies and the populations from which they were drawn need not have belonged to a single ethno-linguistic group but may have spoken a number of different languages. This possibility is enhanced by the differences between the prehistoric populations with respect to their date of deposition, geographical distribution and human physical type. It is quite possible, then, that there is no single answer to the question: who were the Xinjiang mummies?

Although it is more likely that people from a single cemetery at a single time were themselves linguistically related, this too is an assumption. The nature of the tribal confederations of the steppe suggest considerable linguistic mixing and the documentary evidence of the Tarim oases in the historical period suggests that bilingualism was probably the norm rather than the exception with multiple language groups occupying any given centre. In short, we are not asking what language the mummies may have spoken but what language they spoke at home?

The language(s) spoken by some or all of the prehistoric mummies may be totally unknown, i.e. did not survive to be reflected in the documentary record of the Tarim and Turpan basins. Instances of the near disappearance of a language are frequent enough to make this a genuine rather than a merely theoretical possibility. From Europe, we have only very meagre written evidence for the Pictish language of Scotland, the Tartessian and Iberian languages of Spain and Portugal, Iron Age Balkan languages such as Thracian, Dacian and Illyrian, Etruscan and other non-Latin languages in Italy, languages from along the western coasts of Anatolia, etc. In all these cases and many others, had the written record arrived more than a few centuries later than it did, we might well have been deprived entirely of the evidence that such languages were once spoken in their respective regions. In some cases, traces of an extinct language are also recoverable from the place names of a region, e.g. Gaulish names underlie the names of many a French town. But here in East Central Asia, the recovery of earlier linguistic horizons is likely to be extremely hazardous since it is often difficult enough recognizing 'Western' personal or place names in their Chinese transcriptions, much less reconstructing the phonetic shapes of non-Chinese place names purely from their citation in early Chinese texts. The great scholar of Saka studies, Harold Bailey, listed a large number of personal names from the Khotanese documents which did not appear to him to be Iranian, Chinese or Tibetan in origin; Douglas Adams examined them and added Tocharian to the list. If Khotanese phonological changes have not totally obscured loanwords from more familiar languages, it is possible that we may be dealing with some unknown substrate language (or the elusive Burushaski?) in the southwest part of the Tarim Basin.

Finally, we have made it clear that the mummies themselves are only the accidental residue of the prehistoric inhabitants of East Central Asia. Pinning an ethno-linguistic name on any particular group of mummies is by no means the same as reconstructing the complete prehistory of the populations of ancient Xinjiang. For example, our evidence for mummies along the northern Tarim Basin is negligible, yet this would become the major northern route of the Silk Road. On the other hand, attempting to assign specific ethnic identities to the mummies is probably as good an introduction as any to the wider problem of reconstructing the ethnic prehistory of East Central Asia.

Identifying the Mummies

Focusing our attention on those *prehistoric* mummies whose physical type has been labelled 'Caucasoid', we can divide them into four broad groups:

1. The Chärchän group comprises those mummies so far recovered from the cemetery at Zaghunluq.
2. The Lopnur group provides the earliest and most diverse assemblage of mummies from the excavations of Aurel Stein, Sven Hedin, Folke Bergman and the more recent excavations at Qäwrighul and the Töwän River. All these fall within the general region of the ancient kingdom of Krorän.

3. The Qumul group comprises the mummies found near Qumul (Hami) east of the Turpan Basin.
4. The Turpan group is represented by the cemetery of Subeshi (here also are the later Mongoloid mummies from Astana).

We shall not discuss here the recently unearthed mummies from the south-central and southwestern sites of Niyä and cemeteries such as Sampul in the vicinity of Khotan, even though they are Caucasoid, because many of them date after the Early Iron Age (post Han dynasty), our cut-off point for trying to understand the movements and positioning of the peoples of East Central Asia; most of them have not been adequately conserved or even preserved, but have been left in pieces in their original sites (this is sadly often true of mummies discovered elsewhere in the Tarim Basin and surrounding areas); and of these few have been brought from the field into the museums or archaeological research units or have yet been made available for study.

Can we blithely leap from the distribution of the mummies to the later evidence of language? Let us consider what would happen if we attempted to assign an ethno-linguistic identity to a Bronze Age burial in England. Extrapolation would lead us to identify it as English (or Anglo-Saxon) which, as we know with historical hindsight, it simply could not be. Are we likely to make the same type of mistake if we adopt this approach in assigning identities to the Tarim mummies? It will be up to the reader to judge the validity of our logic.

From a purely geographical and temporal perspective, the Lopnur (Krorän) group falls within a territory that later provides us with Kharoṣṭhī Prākrit as its administrative language. We can be certain that this was not the language of its pre-Han inhabitants because this particular Prākrit language, derived from northwest India, did not even exist until the latter part of the 1st millennium BC, and reflects a relatively late phenomenon of the region, associated with the spread of Buddhism and Buddhist monks no earlier than the first centuries BC and presumably somewhat later. And we have also seen that the Prākrit documents retain traces of another, presumably earlier substrate language that might be termed Kroränian (it includes Saka loanwords as well). On the basis of its personal names, some of its vocabulary, and principally its grammatical forms, we have seen in the last chapter how this Kroränian may be set alongside the other Tocharian languages as 'Tocharian C'. Since we find ourselves faced with but two choices – Prākrit or Kroränian – as the language of the earliest mummies of this region, then Kroränian is the clear favourite.

While Kroränian was apparently the earlier vernacular language of Krorän, the fact that the majority of the documents with Tocharian C material derived from the site of Niyä far to the west may indicate that much of the southeastern Silk Road, at least that between Niyä and Krorän, was once occupied by Tocharian C-speaking populations as well. If one

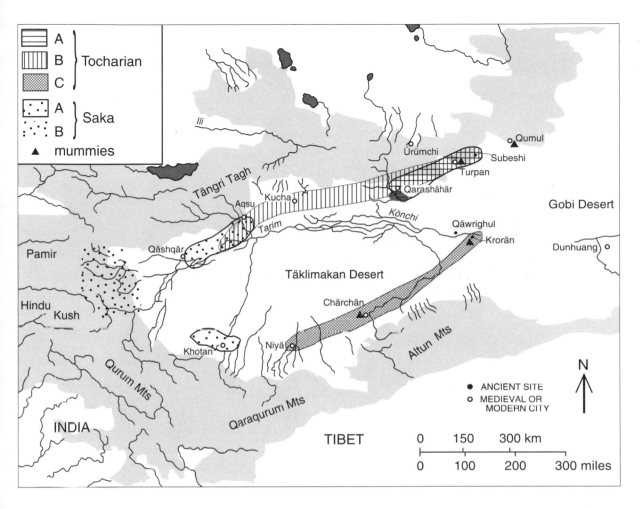

160. Distribution of four major Europoid mummy groups plotted against different languages from the historical period.

accepts this then the simple observation that the Chärchän group is situated between Niyä and Krorän invites us to assign these mummies also to Tocharian C.

But before we can assign our first two groups of mummies to the Proto-Tocharians, we should recall the evidence of Chinese physical anthropologists who propose the movement of at least *two* Caucasoid physical types into the region: an earlier Proto-Europoid at Qäwrighul and a later Indo-Afghan type at Krorän. Both of these are earlier than our earliest Prākrit documents from the region which date to about the 3rd century AD. If we accept these divisions can we say which, if any, of these two 'waves' spoke Kroränian, the language of the Tocharian C substrate? Any attempt to secure a tight relationship between physical type and language is highly suspect and here we will regard physical type as merely circumstantial evidence for geography rather than direct evidence for a particular language. We know that the direction from which the Prākrit language must have come was the west, i.e. northern India via Bactria. As the Saka were widespread across the steppe and also penetrated Bactria and even northern India, they could enter the Tarim Basin from either the west or the north. Of these two potential sources the west is surely the preferred option because the main source of Saka texts is Khotan on the southern Silk Road, which was not readily approachable directly from the north other than along a desert road. We have also seen that the physical evidence along the entire southern route of the Silk Road back into Bactria appears to be marked by the same general physical type. The trajectory of this Indo-Afghan type, therefore, is most easily assigned to those who carried Indic or Iranian (Saka) languages from the west, and this is further confirmed by the survival of Saka's closest linguistic relations in the Pamirs. Thus, by a crude process of elimination, this leaves the earlier attested Proto-Europoids (or Hemphill's peripheral Qäwrighul people) as the more likely candidates to be identified with the Tocharian C substrate. There is, admittedly, a chronological gap between the latest mummies and Kroränian texts but we should recall that the mummies from, for example, Zaghunluq ('Ur-David', the baby in the blue bonnet, the tripartite woman, the 'Scream Baby', etc.) date to c. 600 BC and we are only suggesting that they be associated with a linguistic substrate that must have been established before the 3rd century AD. As Tocharian loanwords are attested in Chinese a few centuries before the Kroränian documents, we can perhaps narrow the gap still further between the prehistoric mummies and the Tocharian languages.

The Turpan group with its burials dating to about the 5th or 4th centuries BC falls within a territory where historical evidence reveals both Tocharian A and B documents. While it is difficult to know how far back we can extrapolate either of these languages as the vernacular language of the region, Tocharian at least supplies a plausible candidate for the Turpan group of mummies since we have no other language in this region that offers a credible alternative. In terms of general physical type, here too the Proto-Europoid type appears but alongside the Indo-Afghan type, with the Pamir-Ferghana type apparently the most recent.

Mummy groups, languages and background physical types

The table indicates the four major groups of mummies, the later historically attested (or in the case of the Qumul group – conjectured) languages, and the broad physical types reconstructed from non-mummified remains in the various regions.

Group	Language	Physical Type
Chärchän	Prākrit Kroränian	undetermined
Lopnur	Kroränian Prākrit	Proto-Europoid/Qäwrighul isolate Indo-Afghan
Qumul	?Tocharian A	Proto-Europoid
Turpan	Tocharian A Tocharian B	Proto-Europoid Indo-Afghan Pamir-Ferghana

Finally, although the Qumul mummies lie beyond our documentary evidence for the vernacular languages of East Central Asia, we still have a few hints as to what language they may have spoken. We do, for example, have Tocharian documents a mere 150 km (93 miles) to the west. We might also now recall Werner Winter's suggestion that the language which emerged in written sources as Tocharian A may have been spoken farther to the northeast, i.e. in the direction of the later Turkish penetration of East Central Asia, before it had been taken up as a 'dead' liturgical language. When we examine the general physical type of the more easterly populations such as those from Yanbulaq, it is the same as that found at Qäwrighul. The chronological gap between the Qumul mummies, dated to about 1000 BC, and Tocharian texts of about the 7th century AD is indeed great but here we may recall that with respect to Tocharian A we are dealing with an already dead language which should have preceded its historical attestation in this region by a matter of centuries, thus narrowing the gap between the mummies and our language horizon. Here too then one might propose a north–south movement of early Tocharians.

The evidence of a crude slash from Occam's razor would seem to suggest that the majority of our earliest prehistoric mummies may be regarded as ancestors of the later Tocharians. These conclusions should, however, be tempered with the observation that, except on the basis of medieval wall paintings, we cannot speak of the physical type of those populations who occupied the territory most closely associated with our Tocharian B documents, i.e. around Kucha. In other words, we cannot easily relate the Bronze Age populations with the later oasis states mentioned in Han documents that produced the Tocharian documents of the historical period. What we have proposed is merely that on the evidence of physical typology and geographical distribution, the Tocharians would appear to derive from the north and the Indo-Iranians largely from the west: how robust are such conclusions when we add into the equation the evidence of archaeology?

The First Farmers

We have seen how our earliest archaeological evidence for human occupation of East Central Asia is extremely meagre and it is impossible to determine with any certainty from which direction the Tarim and neighbouring regions were initially settled if colonization preceded the Bronze Age, i.e. *c.* 2000 BC. From the beginnings of the Bronze Age itself the circumstantial evidence that we have surveyed would render it more likely that it was settled from either the north or the west rather than the south or east. The paucity of a Mongoloid physical type among the earliest human remains and its confinement to the far east of East Central Asia suggests that Mongoloid populations entered late and from the east and southeast. Furthermore, we have a good idea of the settlements and cemeteries of the Neolithic Yangshao culture of northern China which expanded westwards into neighbouring

Gansu and yet we lack any such evidence for typically Chinese Neolithic settlements and cemeteries in East Central Asia. Nor, given our knowledge of the subsistence economies of the early farmers of northern China, is it likely that they would have found settlement east of the Jade Gate viable, much less attractive.

If the east is excluded, what about the southwest, i.e. greater India? Here we have a Neolithic culture in Kashmir by the middle of the 3rd millennium BC which itself appears unrelated to developments elsewhere in India. But other than the occasional employment of ochre in burials and the later adoption of mud brick in building, there is very little archaeological evidence to tie Kashmir with the earliest inhabitants of the Tarim Basin or those who introduced the agricultural economy to the region.

The earliest Bronze Age cultural remains are still assigned to the Qäwrighul culture which was situated near Lopnur. All the other earlier Bronze Age cultures (i.e. Yanbulaq, Ayding Lake, Yengidala (Xintala)) are localized in the northeast or northwest (e.g. Qaradöng (Haladun)) of the Tarim Basin. These are the cultures that provide the initial context for the Xinjiang mummies and if we can exclude the east and south as their probable area of origin, we must then face the two most probable *archaeological* solutions to the origins of the Xinjiang mummies – the western (Bactrian) and northern (Steppe) hypotheses.

The Bactrian Solution

Early farming villages appeared southeast of the Caspian by the 6th millennium BC and began a gradual expansion eastwards. By *c.* 2000 BC we have seen how the Bactria-Margiana Archaeological Complex (BMAC) was employing irrigation agriculture to exploit the oases of Margiana and Bactria, the latter of which had not seen the introduction of agriculture (other than that associated with the site of Shortugai in the northeast of Bactria which had served as a trade outpost of the Harappan civilization) prior to the BMAC. One might then be tempted to propose that the BMAC not only spread subsistence agriculture into Bactria but that its farmers continued much farther east, perhaps through Ferghana, to enter the Tarim Basin. There are a number of factors in favour of this proposition.

Since the earliest agriculturalists of the Qäwrighul culture do not seem to appear until after 2000 BC, a time after which the BMAC had already formed and begun to expand, there is no great temporal difficulty in deriving agriculture from the BMAC, although the distance involved is formidable and so far unbridged by intermediate sites. Also, western crops such as wheat, and livestock such as sheep entered China from the west and both of these were possessed by the BMAC. More importantly, the BMAC had successfully mastered the techniques of exploiting oases with irrigation agriculture and so it would have possessed the technological prerequisites for exploiting the particular environment of the Tarim Basin.

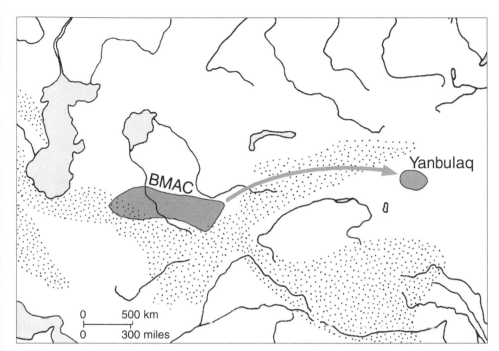

161. The Central Asian hypothesis: here one may imagine that oasis-dwellers of the Bactria-Margiana Archaeological Complex crossed through Ferghana into the Turpan Basin to settle at Yanbulaq.

In addition to its subsistence basis, there are a few other features in favour of the BMAC. We have mentioned how its use of mud brick in domestic architecture finds some parallels in the Yanbulaq culture where we also found mud brick in both the tombs and domestic architecture. And we have also seen how the BMAC reveals striking evidence for the consumption of stimulants and hallucinogens in religious rituals, i.e. the ritual preparation of poppy, hemp and ephedra. It is tempting to tie this to burials in the Lopnur region that reveal the widespread use of ephedra. Finally, the BMAC provides a strong candidate for the culture of early Indo-Iranians and, there-fore, can be related to one of the major language groups that we encounter in the Tarim Basin.

A case, then, can be made for an extension of West Central Asian culture eastwards into the Tarim Basin. But the evidence is still hardly compelling. While BMAC burials may be found far from Bactria-Margiana in, for example, Baluchistan, there are no actual BMAC burials nor ceramics in East Central Asia. On the other hand, the successful exploitation of oases and the use of mud brick (absent from neighbouring Bronze Age Gansu) do suggest western contacts of some form. But these are seen most clearly in the Yanbulaq culture rather than the Qäwrighul culture which still appears to be the earliest of the East Central Asian Bronze Age cultures. Moreover, despite the presence of West Central Asian 'influences', Chinese archae-ologists attribute much of the Yanbulaq culture to local populations who employed a material culture similar to that of the Qäwrighul culture. Finally, the evidence of the human physical type at Yanbulaq, i.e. primarily Mongoloid but with some Proto-Europoids, is incongruent with the type of populations we find in Bronze Age Bactria-Margiana where a more gracile form of Caucasoid predominates. It is difficult then to imagine that the human vector that provides us with our earliest Bronze Age populations, including most of our prehistoric mummified remains, came from Bactria.

The Steppe Solution

The second major hypothesis emphasizes connections between Qäwrighul and other early cultures with those of the steppelands to the north (and northwest), specifically the Afanasevo and Andronovo cultures. It might be noted that contacts with the steppelands were not a single event but a protracted process which did not cease until the Uyghur conquest of East Central Asia. What does the Steppe hypothesis have going for it?

162. Hemp-smoking apparatus from Pazyryk: the tripod held up a tent in which one inhaled smoke from hemp heated on a brazier.

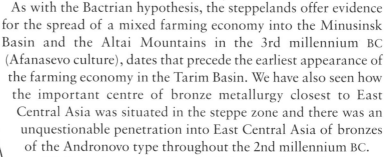

As with the Bactrian hypothesis, the steppelands offer evidence for the spread of a mixed farming economy into the Minusinsk Basin and the Altai Mountains in the 3rd millennium BC (Afanasevo culture), dates that precede the earliest appearance of the farming economy in the Tarim Basin. We have also seen how the important centre of bronze metallurgy closest to East Central Asia was situated in the steppe zone and there was an unquestionable penetration into East Central Asia of bronzes of the Andronovo type throughout the 2nd millennium BC.

While we have no evidence of the use of ephedra among the steppe tribes, we have already seen that they did share in the cultic use of hemp, a practice that ranged from Romania east to the Yenisei River from at least the 3rd millennium BC onwards where its use was later encountered in the form of apparatus for smoking hemp found at Pazyryk.

Elena Kuzmina, one of the foremost authorities on the peoples of the eastern steppelands, has noted a number of specific similarities between the Qäwrighul and steppe (Afanasevo, Andronovo and later) burials:

a) use of enclosures such as fences, stone circles and radial features;

b) use of timber or bark roofs (or floors) for chambers, often lined with felt or pelts on the inside;

c) inclusion of animal sacrifice with burial;

d) use of ochre in burials;

e) similar clothing, i.e. leather boots, felt caps.

As with the Bactrian hypothesis, the evidence does not permit a firm conclusion in the sense that we can describe the Qäwrighul culture as a regional variant of the Afanasevo or Andronovo culture. Ceramics, which were abundant in both the Bactrian and steppe burials, were not found in those of the Qäwrighul culture (we have no idea what type of pottery they employed or whether they even utilized ceramics – the lack of local clays may have largely precluded their manufacture in some of the southern sites) nor did the Qäwrighul culture reproduce the stone enclosures that surrounded the Afanasevo burials.

If the Afanasevo or early Andronovo culture had penetrated southwards into Xinjiang, we should expect to find their monuments initially in the Jungghar (Yarish or Dzungarian) Basin which was midway, both in geography and environment, between the Yenisei-Altai and the Tarim Basin. Do we have an intermediate culture in this region? Here we recall the remains of the Keremchi (Ke'ermuqi) culture which was situated along the northern foothills of the Jungghar Basin. On the debit side, this culture lacks radiocarbon dates and most of its tombs have been plundered so its precise chronological position remains highly problematic. On the plus side, however, it may offer some evidence for a 'missing link' between the Afanasevo and Qäwrighul cultures. The Keremchi cemeteries employ stone-built enclosures, erect anthropomorphic stone figures, and exhibit round-based primitive clay vessels decorated with incised ornament that are reminiscent of Afanasevo pottery. There are also ceramic parallels with the early Andronovo culture. Without precise dates for this culture, conclusions must be speculative and, as was the case with the Qäwrighul culture, we may be dealing with a very long-lived phenomenon in the first place.

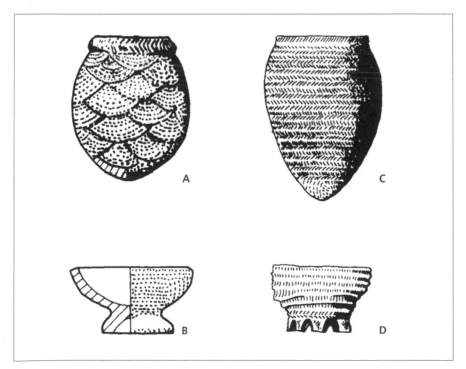

163. A pot (A) and footed bowl (B) from Keremchi, and a typical pot (C) and censer (D) from the Afanasevo culture.

Nevertheless, if the similarities with the Afanasevo and subsequent cultures can be translated into dates, the evidence provides additional support for the expansion of a steppe-derived culture into East Central Asia by the 2nd millennium BC. Keremchi burials are found also in the southern Altai and as far south as Ürümchi and the Yanbulaq culture.

Splitting the Differences

We must reconcile ourselves to the fact that the earliest Bronze Age culture, possibly the earliest farmers, in East Central Asia were representatives neither of the Afanasevo culture nor of the BMAC per se. Of the two cultures, the Afanasevo boasts earlier dates and more mobile antecedents. So far it reflects the earliest evidence for the exploitation of domestic animals in the steppelands far east of the Urals. To connect the earliest Bronze Age settlement of East Central Asia with the Afanasevo culture would seem to require one of the following models.

One might propose that there was an earlier common source for both the Afanasevo and Qäwrighul cultures that spread across Kazakhstan eastwards to the Yenisei and southeastwards into the Tarim Basin. How early such a phenomenon might be is constrained by the fact that the earliest Afanasevo dates would carry this culture back to *c.* 3500 BC (already embarrassingly early given its supposed antecedents in the west) and so we would have to envisage a spread of stockkeepers eastwards during the first half of the 4th millennium BC. This is not impossible but evidence for such an agricultural expansion is not supported by archaeological data and we know of cultures east of the Urals that date to the 4th millennium BC that are

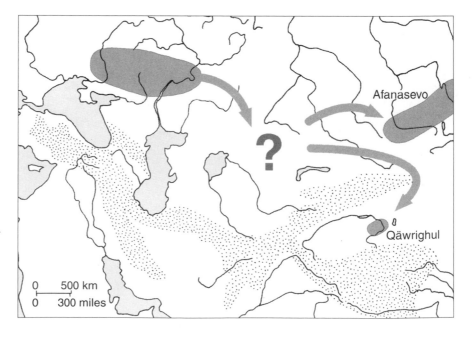

164. Hypothesis of a common source for both the Afanasevo and Qäwrighul cultures. The common source would ultimately lie west of the Urals but a staging area for both cultures in Kazakhstan is purely conjectural.

clearly *non*-agricultural. Unless the archaeological picture of Kazakhstan alters radically (a possibility since there is still so much unknown) an earlier common source for both the Afanasevo and Qäwrighul cultures is probably not the preferred option.

Alternatively, the spread of agriculture and stockbreeding to the east which is indicated by the Afanasevo culture may have also seen a subsequent movement south into East Central Asia. If this were the case, then populations such as the Qäwrighul culture would either have had to have abandoned the deposition of pottery in graves (as is well known in the Afanasevo and later Andronovo cultures) or possibly to have neglected the manufacture of pottery altogether and replaced it by organic containers (basketry is highly developed at Qäwrighul). This latter situation is not unheard of and is encountered, for example, at the transition to the Iron Age in Ireland and western Britain. But neither settlement of the steppelands of the Minusinsk Basin nor the uplands of the Altai should have prepared such newcomers for the environmental regime of the Tarim Basin: how could mixed stockkeepers and farmers from the north have successfully developed the irrigation agriculture required to exploit the oases of East Central Asia?

It is this need to develop an irrigation-based economy that turns our attention westwards back to West Central Asia, specifically Bactria and Margiana, where we have seen that a very successful oasis economy was developed by *c.* 2000 BC. But we have also seen that so far there is no question of a direct import of the BMAC into the Tarim Basin and the parallels tend to be general rather than specific. The case for external influences improves markedly between the Tarim Basin and the west, specifically between the Tarim Basin and Ferghana, in the later 2nd millennium BC, a time after the initial settlement of the Tarim by Bronze Age farmers. For this reason we have an incongruity between a burial rite and material culture that may be derived from the steppelands and an irrigation economy that should derive from the agricultural oases of Central Asia. How can these two very different components be reconciled?

Our most obvious recourse is the structure of relationships between the steppe populations and those of the oasis communities. We have already seen in West Central Asia that steppe tribes could settle and adopt irrigation agriculture. But in West Central Asia, where we witness such phenomena, this symbiosis always occurs where we have prior agricultural settlement. This is not a model that we can easily transfer to East Central Asia since we have no substantial evidence for agricultural settlements prior to the establishment of the Bronze Age, nor can we demonstrate that the physical type associated with such an intrusion of farmers predates those from the northern steppelands. To prepare a 'northern steppe culture' for life in the Tarim Basin, we might expect that it first came into contact with one of the existing West Central Asian oasis-based cultures before it arrived in East Central Asia. Some linguistic evidence may support just such a hypothesis.

The Linguistic Stratigraphy of Tocharian

We have seen in the preceding sections that one of the critical issues is the correct ordering of our evidence, be it that of populations or archaeological influences. The problem before us now is arranging in correct chronological order the different *prehistoric* languages spoken in the Tarim Basin. Various degrees of difficulty accompany such an exercise but from our perspective the primary goal is to arrange correctly the relationship between the Tocharian and Iranian languages as these are the languages most likely to have served as the vernaculars of its prehistoric populations.

As we have already seen, every language contains something of its own cultural history in its vocabulary. Some of the vocabulary will be inherited from Proto-Indo-European, some will be new words created from older inherited elements. These do not hold the same interest for us here that loanwords do, since borrowed vocabulary, particularly diacritic cultural vocabulary, may point to the time and place of foreign contacts.

As we have remarked before, Chinese appears to have had a very minimal impact on the Tocharian language. To be sure, we have the odd loanword, e.g. Tocharian *klu* 'rice' from Old Sinitic **gləw* (modern Chinese *dao*) and names for units of measurement, e.g. *ṣank, tow* (= 10 *ṣank*) and *cāk* (= 10 *tow*), all transparently from Chinese. But the impact here is minimal, culturally predictable and comparatively recent. Otherwise, there is no evidence that the Tocharians gained their vocabulary for the native flora and fauna of the Tarim Basin from earlier Chinese inhabitants, nor do they appear to have gained their agricultural vocabulary from this source. This lends additional support to the argument that the Chinese were both latecomers into the Tarim Basin and did not have a significant impact until relatively late in the easternmost regions.

Now many of the other loanwords found in Tocharian are connected with the religious and social life associated with Buddhism and hence the sources here are Buddhist Hybrid Sanskrit, Prākrits and other Indic languages, occasionally perhaps filtered through Iranian intermediaries. These may be easily enough associated with the relatively late spread of Buddhism among already established populations, both Tocharian and Iranian-speaking.

By far the greatest number of loanwords in Tocharian would appear to derive from Saka or some other East Iranian language and these fill out a larger semantic range. In some instances they appear to have been loanwords associated with exchange, e.g. Tocharian B *pito* 'price' may derive from Saka *pīha-* 'price', and Tocharian A *pare*, Tocharian B *peri* 'debt' would be derived from Saka *pīra-* 'that which is to be paid'. There are other words which might also be assigned to the general realm of commerce, e.g. units of weight and measure. Iranian military terms also had an impact on Tocharian and when one considers depictions in Buddhist temples of Tocharian knights kitted out like Sassanians with long swords, one might recall that the

Tocharian B word for sword, *kertte*, is derived from some East Iranian language, e.g. Avestan *karəta-* 'dagger'. Bactrian also supplied loanwords filling out similar political contexts, e.g. *kamirdo* 'head', 'chief' (god) gives Tocharian A *kākmärtik* 'ruler'. It is also important to note that the Tocharian word for 'iron' (Tocharian *eñcuwo* or *añcu*) would appear to be related in some way to Iranian (Ossetic). In some instances the loanwords are connected with exotic animals, e.g. Tocharian B *mewiyo* 'tiger' from Saka *muya-* 'tiger', or Tocharian B *ekṣinek-* 'pigeon' which seems related to Saka *aṣṣänaka-* 'pigeon'. By and large, however, it would be exceedingly difficult linguistically to make any case for the temporal priority of Saka in the Tarim Basin with respect to Tocharian. Of the approximately 25 or 30 loanwords, most could be easily explained as later borrowings passed between communities along the Silk Road connected with the rise of urban or Buddhist institutions. Most importantly, there is no evidence that the vocabulary of agriculture in the Tarim Basin specifically derives from Saka.

Asses, Canals and Bricks

Although Saka and Sogdian are the earliest of the Iranian languages directly attested in the Tarim Basin, there are some Iranian loanwords in Tocharian that may derive from a still earlier period. Two of these have only recently come to light in the form of a Tocharian B text that documents the transfer of an estate. Within the text there is reference to the *orotsa newiya* 'great canal' and the *ārte*, some form of watercourse that can serve as an estate boundary. Douglas Adams has recently suggested that both of these words are early loans from an East Iranian language (or proto-language) and, while there are a number of ways to explain how these loans could have taken place, only one is not problematic. As irrigation agriculture is the only type of agriculture that one can practise in the Tarim Basin, it is difficult to see how the Tocharians could have eked out a living there before they knew of irrigation. It is also unlikely that the Iranians and Tocharians both arrived at precisely the same time, the Iranians passing onto the Tocharians the technology of agriculture before the latter had starved to death. The simplest explanation would be to place the Iranians in position first and then have the Tocharians, largely pastoralists, wander in and adopt agriculture; this is precisely the type of pattern we have earlier encountered in West Central Asia where steppe pastoralists moved into the oases and adopted the agricultural techniques of the earlier inhabitants. But, as we have already seen, we do not really have typically West Central Asian BMAC farmers occupying the Tarim Basin, nor does our review of the physical evidence suggest that populations from West Central Asia arrived in the Tarim and Turpan basins earlier than those from the north. None of our usual models will do.

Adams suggests that the most convenient explanation would involve the adoption of irrigation techniques and East Iranian terminology by the

Tocharians *en route* to their historical seats. This model would fit nicely for those archaeologists who have noted that while there is no evidence for the BMAC in East Central Asia, certain similarities between the Yanbulaq culture and that of the BMAC do suggest some form of mediating culture, presumably a more mobile pastoral culture of the Andronovo type. We may suggest then that Tocharian populations moved from the steppe, through the Altai and Tängri Tagh, and south into the Jungghar, Tarim and Turpan basins, settling in the oases of the latter two to engage in irrigation agriculture.

It might be objected that no one entering the Tarim and Turpan basins who had to make their way through the surrounding mountain passes is likely to have carried the techniques and vocabulary of irrigation agriculture with them. This is not a serious objection as the underlying East Iranian word for 'irrigation canal' that we find borrowed into Tocharian may also be found in mountainous regions where it is known in Sarikoli, one of the Pamir languages related to Saka, and cognates are also known in the far northwest of India in the Nuristani and Dardic languages. That common words connected with irrigation can be found on the western mountainous approaches to East Central Asia at least suggests the possibility that Tocharian speakers passing through this region could have adopted such terms and techniques. Of course, a western entry would not really solve the problem before us but if East Iranians were in occupation in Ferghana and perhaps present in the Altai as well, it might provide a plausible route for northern steppe peoples southwards into East Central Asia.

Another instructive piece of evidence is the Tocharian word for the ass, Tocharian B *kercapo* which is universally agreed to be related to Old Indic *gardabhá-*. If this is a borrowing, it is a very early one when the underlying form in Proto-Indic and Proto-Tocharian was something like **gordebhós*. Now such a form could just as well be Proto-Indo-European and so we are not dealing with some word borrowed from the period of Buddhist expansion in East Central Asia; a word **gordebhós* should have been circulating among peoples in the 2nd millennium BC or earlier. We are uncertain as to whether the original word referred to the domestic ass or the wild onager, and was then transferred to the domestic ass. The ass was originally domesticated in North Africa and then expanded into Mesopotamia by the 4th millennium BC, spreading from there both northwards and eastwards; its first appearance in northwest India is around 2000 BC. On the other hand, the so-called 'half-ass' or onager ranged across the entire steppe and south into Central Asia and northern India. Whatever the original meaning of the word, the linguistic evidence suggests some form of contact between Tocharians and Indo-Iranians long before the opening of the Silk Road and the spread of Buddhism.

We have already seen that one of the cultural features that tends to link the prehistory of East Central Asia with that of West Central Asia is to be seen in the use of mud bricks in domestic and funerary architecture. Of interest then is the fact that Tocharian *iścem* 'clay' would appear to be related to Avestan *ištyam* 'brick', *zəmōištva-* 'clay-tile', Old Indic *iṣṭakā* 'brick', and Khowar (a northeast Indo-Aryan language) *uštú* 'sun-dried brick', 'large clod of earth'. This would again point to either a loan from a very early stage of Indo-Iranian or the mutual inheritance by both language stocks of a common eastern Indo-European proto-form **isti-* 'clay', 'brick'.

So far the linguistic evidence is hardly overwhelming, but it does hint at contacts between Tocharians and Indo-Iranians prior to the spread of Buddhism in East Central Asia. These contacts need not have been particularly intense and we would be giving a very mistaken impression if we were to portray the Proto-Tocharians as wandering nomads who only learned their agriculture from settled Proto-Indo-Iranians. To be sure, they entered the Tarim Basin with their livestock whose Indo-European names were retained, e.g. Tocharian B *ke$_u$*, *okso*, *ā$_u$* and *suwo* are cognate with the English words 'cow', 'ox', 'ewe' and 'sow' respectively. They also retained at least one of the inherited Indo-European words for 'grain' (Tocharian B *tāno* from a late Proto-Indo-European **dhoh$_x$néh$_a$-*), and words for the basic agricultural pursuits of ploughing, sowing, threshing and grinding. The ancestors of the Tocharians were already mixed farmers (agropastoralists) and were not ignorant of cereals before they entered the Tarim Basin, nor did they require contact with Indo-Iranians to learn about farming. One curious word, Tocharian B *kanti* 'some form of bread' is possibly related to Indo-Iranian words for 'wheat' (e.g. Avestan *gantuma-*, Khotanese Saka *ganama*) and Hittite *kant-* 'wheat'. Although this may have been a common word in the eastern Indo-European world, it is generally taken to be a loanword from some Near Eastern language that spread through Asia. Finally, one other feature should be noted: there is no evidence of the Indo-Iranian languages adopting Tocharian words; our loanwords only seem to go in one direction.

So far then we have found recurring evidence that north = steppe = (?)Proto-Europoid (if one follows the typological school) = Tocharian; and west = oasis = Indo-Afghan/Pamir-Ferghanoid (or Hemphill's Bactrian-Alwighul-Krorän group) = Indo-Iranian. Before we pat ourselves on the back it is about time we get a grip on things and have an 'assumption alert'.

The logic of all this hangs on our identification of the northern intruders as Proto-Tocharians and not some form of Indo-Iranians. But we have already seen that the BMAC is not the only culture to which we assign an early Indo-Iranian identity; the Andronovo culture and some of its western neighbours on the European steppe are also widely regarded as Indo-Iranian. Indeed, we have given strong reasons to believe that the Indo-Iranians were originally steppe peoples themselves who came to dominate the oasis culture of West Central Asia. And we have also seen that the Qäwrighul physical type might be related to that of the Andronovo culture. One is at perfect liberty to propose the equation: north = steppe (Andronovo) = Proto-Europoid = Indo-Iranian. The Occam's razor we employed earlier to separate Tocharians and Indo-Iranians has suddenly become a very dull instrument indeed. It is time we played the Afanasevo card.

The Afanasevo Card: The Short Trek

We have worked our way into a logical corner but at least we have some notion of what type of device it is going to take to extract us from our predicament. We have the Tocharians in the northern and, accepting the Kroränian evidence, southeastern part of the Tarim Basin by the first half of the 1st millennium AD. We have set out arguments to indicate that they should have been there at least by the 1st millennium BC (before the spread of Buddhism) and we have seen why it is easier to derive them from the north than from any other direction (although we must admit that Iranians might also have come from this same direction). Furthermore, we know from our examination of the separation of the various Indo-European stocks that there are no particular reasons to associate Tocharian genetically more closely with Indo-Iranian than with any other stock. We have already reviewed the linguistic evidence and seen that opinion tends to be split between assigning Tocharian its closest relations among various European stocks (Germanic, Greek, etc.) and arguing that it separated from the other Indo-European stocks at such an early date that there are no grounds to presume it was a close neighbour of any other Indo-European group during a large part of its early development. Either way, the Tocharians are clearly not part of the greater Indo-Iranian superstock and so, for linguistic reasons, we will prefer any model that keeps some distance between them and the other stocks throughout a considerable part of their early evolution. On the other hand, they did come into contact with the Indo-Iranians when they had already emerged as an independent stock, presumably sometime after 2500–2000 BC. It is most likely that it was during the early part of the 2nd millennium BC that Proto-Tocharians came into contact with already settled Indo-Iranians and borrowed a few terms and techniques relating to irrigation agriculture, brickwork and possibly the domestic ass.

From an archaeological perspective, one way to accommodate all these demands is to regard the Proto-Tocharians as an offshoot of the Afanasevo culture of the Altai-Yenisei region. As we have already seen, it displays genetic connections with the cultures of the European steppelands (and hence might represent the eastern extreme of an Indo-European linguistic continuum) but it was also isolated from the other steppe cultures with the later Andronovo culture filling the gap between the European steppe and the Yenisei River and then replacing it. If an offshoot of the Afanasevo culture moved southwards into East Central Asia in the centuries around 2000 BC, it could hardly have avoided contact with Indo-Iranians of some sort just to its west and it may thus have adopted the rudiments and some of the vocabulary of irrigation agriculture from them. It would then have moved into the northern and southeastern Tarim Basins where it established itself, with marked cultural change and adaptations, and continued until the historical expansion of the Uyghurs.

In this model the Proto-Tocharians moved south from the Altai region in about 2000 BC to settle in the northern Tarim and the southeast (Kroränian). Subsequent movements of populations from the north may have carried Iranian speakers into the Tarim Basin as well but they never achieved linguistic ascendancy in the north and east. The Saka, however, entered the Tarim from the west during the 1st millennium BC and established themselves in the northwest of the Tarim and in the south at Khotan. How does such a model work geographically?

If we look at the map of the approaches to the Tarim Basin then the natural route would be from the northwest towards the southeast, i.e. from territories that may have once been part of the Indo-Iranian chain of languages of West Central Asia to the Altai southeast into the land of our earliest mummies. To this day, the best passes for entering the Jungghar Basin from the north are along its northwest side where one can skirt the forbidding centre of the basin and move along the southwestern mountain slopes to the south. This would bring northern immigrants through a funnel

165. Northern approaches to East Central Asia lead one into the eastern end of the Tarim Basin. A movement from the Afanasevo culture would carry one through lands occupied (later) by the Andronovo culture before arriving in the Tarim region.

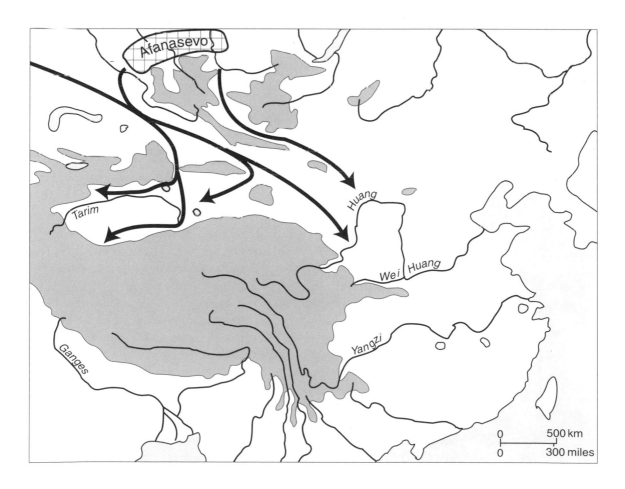

that disgorges near Ürümchi and the major pass south through the Tängri Tagh into the Turpan Basin and then the eastern portion of the Tarim Basin. Potential immigrants from the Afanasevo culture thus would have been forced first to veer west where they may have come into contact with Andronovans (Indo-Iranians) on their path to the south.

The model presented here is the most efficient in terms of geography, linguistics and archaeology (the evidence of physical anthropology remains moot). It requires the least distance for the Tocharians to journey into their historical seats and it provides them with a staging area which is, on the one hand, distant from the rest of the steppe continuum to account for the independent evolution of a Tocharian stock of languages while also permitting them to come into contact with Indo-Iranians during their move south into East Central Asia. It also places them in that part of East Central Asia which is most closely associated with the steppelands to the north. If we suggest an alternative and attempt to pin Tocharian origins on a west–east migration across the Pamirs into East Central Asia, we will find it difficult to explain why it is the Saka who predominated in the western part of the Tarim. To argue that the Tocharians were the earliest colonizers from the west who were subsequently pushed eastwards by Iranians such as the Saka would leave the early Proto-Europoid/peripheral Qäwrighul physical type in what would become later the Tocharian-speaking territories entirely anonymous. Moreover, there is no evidence in the Saka vocabulary that they absorbed the earlier vocabulary of already settled Tocharian farmers.

The European Card: The Long Trek

While the Afanasevo model may have much to recommend it, there are those who would reject its underlying linguistic premise: that the Tocharian language stock was somehow peripheral to the other Indo-European stocks. As we have seen, there are a considerable number of linguists who would regard Tocharian as a 'western' Indo-European language and insist that its origins cannot be on the outer edge of the Indo-European continuum of dialects but rather that it must start farther to the west. Specifically, this means beginning the Proto-Tocharian movement from somewhere west of the Indo-Iranians, e.g. in eastern Europe (northwest of the Black Sea). Support for this model might be found in some of the textile evidence that relates the use of twills and plaids among the populations of East Central Asia with those of West Central Europe. Such a model then requires the ancestors of the Tocharians to move through the territories in which the Indo-Iranians were dispersing in order to arrive, again from the north, in the Tarim Basin. How robust is this model?

From an archaeological standpoint this renders the Proto-Tocharians archaeologically invisible until they emerge in the Tarim Basin. By this we mean that 1) there is no archaeological culture that makes a west to east trajectory during the 2nd or 1st millennium BC that we could conveniently associate with a Tocharian migration and 2) if the Proto-Tocharians are to be associated with one of the existing archaeological cultures, e.g. a phase or regional grouping of the Andronovo or other steppe culture, then they are indistinguishable from archaeological cultures to which we would assign an Indo-Iranian linguistic identity. To this it might be added that the basic trajectory of the steppe populations from at least the 1st millennium BC onwards was from east to west, carrying Cimmerians and Scythians into contact with farmers northwest of the Black Sea; a western origin for the Tocharians requires them to move upstream of the current of population movement. The only way this objection could be mitigated is by proposing a long trek to the east during a narrow window of opportunity in the centuries just before the general westward movement of steppe populations that began around the 8th century BC. Such a migration would have had to be quick and clean – so clean that it left no deep archaeological traces such as burials, settlements, etc.; we may find parallels between the textiles of Central Europe and the Tarim Basin but, so far, these do not include flying carpets!

There are linguistic problems with this model as well. A western origin for the Tocharians requires them historically to move across the face of prehistoric Indo-Iranians and to do so over a protracted period in their move towards the east. If such a movement had actually occurred, we might expect a far greater impact of Indo-Iranian on Tocharian than we find and those cultural loanwords which we do encounter borrowed from Indo-Iranian into Tocharian, i.e. words associated with irrigation agriculture, would be inexplicable.

The model of an origin of the Tocharians to the west of the Indo-Iranians, whatever its linguistic merits, is by far the weaker of the two models proposed. It is not that it can be shown to be impossible – archaeological evidence cannot be used in such a way – but it is archaeologically undetectable.

Conclusions

We may now offer as a working hypothesis the following model of ethno-linguistic development in East Central Asia.

1. The earliest Bronze Age settlers of the Tarim and Turpan basins originated from the steppelands and highlands immediately north of East Central Asia.

2. These colonists were related to the Afanasevo culture which exploited both open steppelands and upland environments employing a mixed agricultural economy.

3. The Afanasevo culture formed the eastern linguistic periphery of the Indo-European continuum of languages whose centre of expansion lay much farther to the west, north of the Black and Caspian seas. This periphery was ancestral to the historical Tocharian languages.

4. By about 2000 BC the Afanasevo culture, which was at that time being absorbed by the Andronovo culture from its west and other cultures in the Yenisei region, pushed southwards and came into contact with settled Indo-Iranians to the northwest of the Tarim Basin. Here they gained both the rudiments of irrigation agriculture and some of the Indo-Iranian terminology associated with it before they entered the Turpan and Tarim basins as the Proto-Tocharians.

5. Many of the Bronze Age mummies preserved in the archaeological record of East Central Asia may be assigned a probable (Proto-) Tocharian identity.

6. The descendants of these earliest Bronze Age colonists occupied the northern and eastern portions of the Tarim Basin and survived in their oasis settlements to emerge later as the occupants of Kucha, Qarashähär and Turpan, leaving a residual linguistic legacy in Krorän.

7. Subsequent movements from the steppelands carried other peoples into the Tarim Basin. Those who settled in oases occupied by the Tocharians or in their vicinity were linguistically absorbed by them, while those who maintained a nomadic social structure moved with their herds around the peripheries of the Tarim and Turpan basins to be recorded in Han documents as Yuezhi, Wusun and other possibly nomadic peoples. These were at least in part Iranian-speaking populations, although remnants of and combinations with the initial colonization by Tocharians may also have been part of these societies. It is entirely possible that the ancestors of some of the mummies derived from these later intrusions.

8. Throughout the 1st millennium BC other Iranian populations, historically ancestral to the Saka languages, entered the Tarim Basin from the west and ensured that the western and southwestern portions of the Silk Road were Iranian-speaking. This population maintained its mobility and secured the spread of Iranian loanwords throughout East Central Asia which were adopted by the earlier Tocharians. This can be seen most clearly in the vocabulary of commerce and warfare.

These movements of both Tocharians and Iranians into East Central Asia were not a mere footnote in the history of China but, as we are about to see, were part of a much wider picture involving the very foundations of the world's oldest surviving civilization.

CHAPTER ELEVEN

Legacy

In the early 17th century Viscount Saint Alban, Baron of Verulam, or, as we usually encounter him in the history of literature, philosophy and science, Francis Bacon, wrote that the three most significant inventions in the history of humankind were printing, gunpowder and the magnetic compass. For him, the origins of all three inventions were 'obscure and inglorious'; for us, their origins lay, along with a host of other important discoveries, in China. In some cases, the Chinese were simply first with their inventions, taking chronological priority over developments in the West. For example, the Chinese were the first to utilize iron ploughs for clearing wet and heavy soils while people in the West independently manufactured their own iron ploughs somewhat later. In other instances the list of Chinese improvements in the technology of the plough, particularly the curved mould board that permits a vastly more efficient turning of the soil, had a direct impact on the West. Brought from China in the 17th century by Dutch sailors and then conveyed to England where the Dutch were employed to drain the East Anglian fens and Somerset moors, the Chinese plough became the model design for the subsequent European and American ploughs. By a similar route, 18th-century Europeans began to replace their winnowing

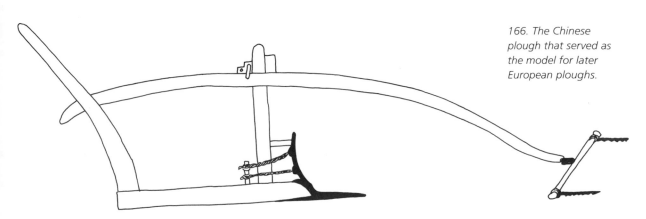

166. The Chinese plough that served as the model for later European ploughs.

baskets for separating the grain from the chaff with the rotary winnowing fan (here the Chinese were some 2,000 years ahead of the West!). Dutch informants also carried back to the West accounts of Chinese deep-drilling apparatus, designed in China to extract brine for salt manufacture or natural gas to heat the salt pans (the Chinese were exploiting natural gas for heat and light by the first centuries BC). By 1834 Europeans were employing Chinese drills for extracting salt brine and less than a decade later they were also recovering oil.

167. Ceramic figurine of a Chinese horseman with a stirrup; 7th–9th century BC. The introduction of the stirrup into European society from Eurasian steppe tribes is said not only to have revolutionized early medieval warfare but also to have helped to create the distinctly European feudal system.

The long-distance sea contacts between China and the West were not the only route that carried Chinese inventions to Europe. Another route was the major information and population highway of the steppelands, and hence inventions such as the trace harness and stirrup were carried westwards by steppe populations such as the Avars, often identified with the Ruanruan who dominated East Central Asia in the 4th–6th centuries AD, and who entered Europe from the east in the 6th century AD. Sometimes the Europeans obtained the information more directly as when Italians in overland contact with China brought back the spinning wheel in the 13th century (the Chinese had already developed the belt drive by the 1st century BC). And sometimes the route of Chinese ingenuity to the West was even more direct. The Chinese, who had invented the earliest cast iron, had also developed techniques for manufacturing steel from cast iron (by the 2nd century BC). In 1845, William Kelly of Kentucky employed four Chinese experts in steel casting to develop the production techniques which we know today as the Bessemer steel process.

Paper and Printing

What about the three inventions cited by Bacon? Paper was invented by the Chinese by at least the 2nd century BC. The earliest paper, a sediment formed from rotting fibres in a mould, was made from hemp, as was the earliest paper employed in Europe. The other main source was the bark of the mulberry tree. Early Chinese paper had a wide variety of uses – clothes, hats, belts, armour, packing material, paper handkerchiefs, toilet paper, wallpaper, kites, currency (9th-century), cards, umbrellas, etc. – and the Chinese were invariably the earliest to utilize them. The oldest archaeological find of paper employed as a medium for writing dates to about AD 110 and our major source of early paper documents is, not surprisingly, the desiccating sands of the Tarim Basin. The establishment of trade and religious links with the Buddhist world led to the spread of paper first to India and then into the Arab world where the secret of its manufacture was guarded for centuries (the Europeans, dependent on either papyrus or vellum, had to buy paper from the Arabs). The earliest manufacture of paper in Europe was in the 12th century.

The combination of paper and a means of printing came gradually. Anticipating various printing processes, the early Chinese employed seals to make impressions of

168. Playing card dated c. AD 1400 from Turpan.

names on materials both soft (paper) and hard (clay moulds for bronzes). They became masters of stone rubbing, preparing a template of a text on stone, so that it could be 'lifted' on paper with ink. Stencils were also supplied and the driving force behind this was the desire to disseminate copies of religious scriptures, particularly Buddhist. Woodblocks were carved largely from pear, the jujube tree or boxwood, and printing production was enormous. The earliest known printed book, a Chinese translation of the Buddhist *Diamond Sutra*, was discovered by Aurel Stein at Dunhuang; it dated to AD 868. The route west was the Silk Road through Turpan (movable type worked far more easily with the limited character set of the Uyghurs than the enormous set of characters required to print in Chinese), and then on into Persia and farther west. Some suggest that when Johannes Gutenberg 'invented' movable type in the 15th century, he did so with the help of a copy of an eastern publication before him.

Gunpowder

Chinese alchemists in the 9th century, searching for the elixir of immortality, discovered instead one of the major means by which modern populations hasten their own mortality. One of the ingredients of gunpowder, saltpetre (potassium nitrate) was already employed in the 2nd century BC to dissolve minerals. Sulphur, the second major ingredient in gunpowder, was being purified for pharmaceutical uses by the 2nd century AD and alchemists were combining the two by the 4th century. The third element is some form of carbonaceous material and we find Chinese texts of AD 850 indicating the full recipe for the explosive substance.

Gunpowder was put to use in projectile weapons by the 10th century. Beginning with the fire-lance, which ejected both fire and any objects placed into the tube, it evolved into the fully fledged gun by at least the 13th century (the rocket was invented a century earlier). The fire-lance and the gun both reached Europe by the 14th century, with gunpowder preceding it by a century. The route was overland (or river) and carried west by either Christian missionaries or traders who dealt with the Mongol rulers of China at that time. The similarity between the earliest European cannon and those of China are so great that it is suspected that Chinese cannon were imported wholesale to provide the models for European weapons.

Compass

The third of the inventions that Bacon cited is the magnetic compass which may have been developed independently in different parts of the world. The earliest citation in Chinese literature ostensibly goes back to the 4th century AD where the *Guiguzi* (*Book of the Devil Valley Master*) reports how some people, on jade-collecting expeditions, take along compasses to ensure that they can find their way back. Chinese compasses pointed south rather than north. Early pointers were in the shape of spoons, modelled after the shape of the Big Dipper (or Plough), or in the shape of fish. Arab texts mention the use of fish-shaped compasses for navigating at sea in the 13th century (providing cinema buffs with a nice anachronism for the film *The Vikings* where a former African slave guides Tony Curtis and his followers through the Norse fog to 9th-century Northumbria with the help of a fish-shaped compass). The earliest mention of a compass in European literature dates to the late 12th century.

Full Circle: Wheelbarrows and Bicycles

To recount the number of Chinese inventions, or the comparable technological developments where China long preceded Europe, not only dispels Western chauvinism but is perfectly capable of inducing a profound inferiority complex among all societies of the 'First World'. Throughout a period of nearly 2,000 years, the West lagged behind China technologically. The technological and scientific legacy of China is so massive that, in some instances at least, one marvels not so much at the precociousness of the Chinese as the slowness of the Europeans.

Wheelbarrows, for example, were invented in China by the 1st century BC. Their initial use was military and they provided the means of supplying armies in the field; in addition, they provided a mobile obstruction to break cavalry charges. The Chinese invented numerous types of wheelbarrow capable of carrying the heaviest of loads over the narrowest of surfaces with ease. They took their wheelbarrow technology seriously and fitted the design to the task – a fact appreciated by any archaeologist who has seen generations of workers on an excavation topple their loads *before* they reached the spoil heap or worse, back into the excavation trench. The earliest wheelbarrow known in the West is depicted in a window in Chartres Cathedral and dates to about 1220.

On the other hand, let us consider the bicycle whose riders swarm the streets of any Asian town and which provides the main form of transportation in China today. The earliest four-wheeler dates from the 17th century (France) and the earliest two-wheeler was exhibited in Paris in 1818 after which technological improvements have continued steadily to provide the most efficient human-based form of propulsion in the world. This is clearly not a Chinese invention and the Chinese are inheritors of the West. But the reason for the bicycle's efficiency is its chain drive, for whose invention the Chinese do have a prior claim. Adapted from the chain-pump, the chain-drive was invented to run mechanical clocks in AD 976 (the inventor was Zhang Sixun). The first chain-drive in the West appeared only in

169. *The earliest illustration of the chain-drive, from Su Song's* Xin yixiang fayao *(New Description of an Armillary Clock); c. 1092.*

1770 and was applied to bicycle propulsion in 1869. The relationship between China and the West was not *entirely* a one-way street, then. This can be seen when we consider the swiftest wheeled vehicle of the Bronze Age.

Chariots: East and West

One of the major characteristics of the Shang (*c.* 1558–1041 BC), China's first historically attested dynasty, was its royal burials where, as with most of the world's early civilizations and many stratified 'uncivilized' cultures (such as the Scythians), the burial of the aristocracy was accompanied conspicuously by humans, animals and metallic wealth. Among the primary features of the Shang tombs was the burial of chariots, teams of horses and charioteers near the royal tombs. The chariot, the primary vehicle of aristocratic warfare, reflected both the military and social organization of the Shang and later Zhou dynasties. Edward Shaughnessy has argued that the chariot, which appeared in China around 1200 BC in an already fully developed form, was initially employed by the Shang as a prestige vehicle, a command platform in battle and for riding to the hunt. It was only in the succeeding Zhou dynasty that massed chariot warfare is recorded and Shaughnessy has suggested that it may well have been the use of the chariot that permitted the Zhou dynasty to overthrow the Shang in *c.* 1041 BC. At this time it was used initially to assault infantry but later was employed in mass chariot assaults on opposing chariot units. Finally, the chariot was replaced by cavalry under pressure of the nomadic tribes to the north in the first centuries BC.

There is no history of wheeled vehicles of any form in China prior to the emergence of the chariot in the Shang period. For the evolution of vehicles we must look to the West where by the 4th millennium BC four-wheeled wagons and two-wheeled carts had dispersed from

170. Chariot from the royal Shang burials at Anyang.

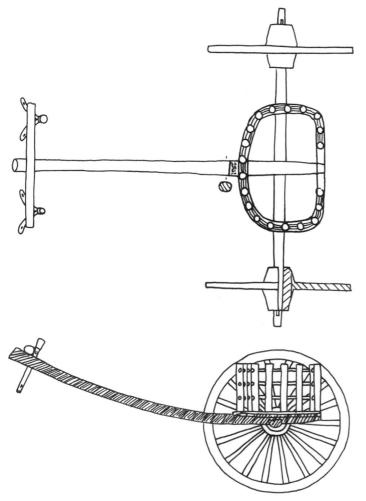

Mesopotamia to eastern Europe. The earliest chariot would appear to date to about 2000 BC and while there may be debate as to precisely where the chariot, a light spoke-wheeled vehicle, was first invented, there is no doubt that it was being employed by 2000 BC between the Volga and east of the Urals. The deposition of chariots is one of the major features of the steppe burials at Sintashta, a predecessor of the Andronovo culture of the eastern steppelands. The priority of the chariot in the West is indisputable and we have also seen traces of the spread of wheeled vehicles into East Central Asia where disc wheels and hubs, derived from heavier carts or wagons, were recovered from the cemetery at Qizilchoqa (c. 1350–1000 BC).

It is from the same direction that we derive the propulsion of the chariot, the domestic horse. The earliest evidence of the widescale employment of the domestic horse is in the European steppelands between the Dnieper and the Ural rivers where the horse was domesticated by the 4th millennium BC in the Yamna culture and perhaps its immediate predecessors. The chariot burials are also accompanied by so-called bow-shaped instruments that were presumably associated with driving the chariots, and knives with either a ring or an animal at the end of the hilt – both features of the steppe cultures of the period.

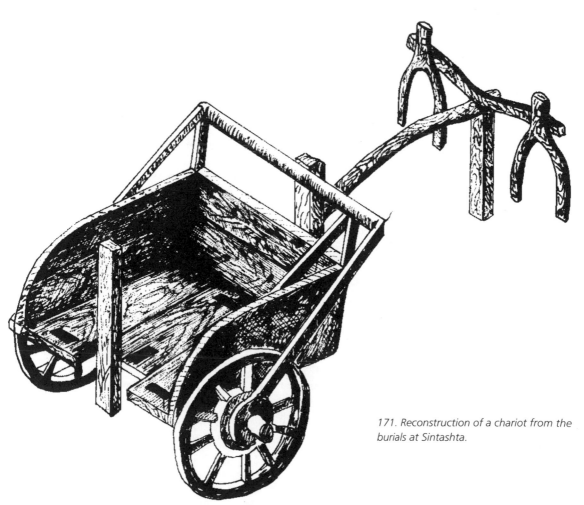

171. Reconstruction of a chariot from the burials at Sintashta.

If the chariot came from the West, what about the name for the vehicle? Here there is some linguistic evidence to support such a movement. The Chinese word for chariot, the modern Mandarin *ch'e*, would have been articulated roughly as *$kl^y ag$* during the Shang dynasty, and this word bears a certain resemblance to one of the Proto-Indo-European words for 'wheel' (*$k^w \acute{e} k^w lo$*) which provided the base for the word for vehicle in Tocharian, i.e. Tocharian A *kukäl* and Tocharian B *kokale*. Rather than a direct Tocharian source, it has been suggested that the underlying form may have been some form of early Iranian language. This would hardly be surprising in that the Indo-Iranians perfected chariot warfare and either introduced it or, at least, were so proficient in it that they were the acknowledged masters of chariotry in the Near East. It seems probable, then, that Bronze Age Iranians or Tocharians came into contact with peoples of western China in the 2nd millennium BC and introduced the chariot to the Shang. The venue of the meeting of these two worlds was, naturally, the modern province of Xinjiang and the area just to its northeast. Once introduced, the Chinese began to work their own special technological magic on any western loan. But the West was not only supplying them with vehicles, it was also sending something of its own magic into the very courts of the Shang.

Wise Men From the West

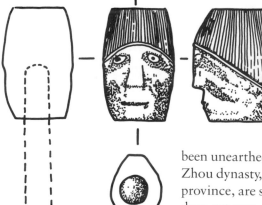

172. Image of a Westerner, fashioned from a clam shell. Note that the symbol on the figure's head was known both in China and the West to indicate a mage or wizard.

In addition to technology we can look to an Iranian source for the name of the royal magicians or fortune-tellers of the Shang and Zhou courts. The modern Mandarin word for such a magician is *wu* but this would earlier have been pronounced something close to *$m^y ag$* or *mag* which suggests that it may have been borrowed from Iranian, e.g. Old Persian *maguš*. In ancient Iran, the role of the *maguš* was that of the court priest who performed whatever religious duty was required: telling the future, offering prayers, making sacrifices and preparing astrological calculations. The linguistic evidence suggests that long before three of these Magi journeyed west to present their gifts at Bethlehem, Iranian priests had entered the courtly world of the Shang and subsequent Zhou dynasties. That people of a Caucasoid physical type became priest-magicians to the nascent Chinese state finds support from unexpected quarters. Several figures depicting what are widely regarded as Caucasoid physical types have been unearthed in both Shang and Zhou contexts. The two from the Zhou dynasty, recovered from the excavations of a palace in Shaanxi province, are small heads carved from shell. They display large and deep-set eyes, wide mouths, thin lips, large noses and narrow faces, all of which would tend to mark out a Europoid or Caucasoid physical type. Their conical headgear has also been compared with that of some of the steppe tribes. On top of one of them is the cruciform Chinese character for 'mage', a symbol which is also reprised in Western art to indicate a magician. So here we find the image of a European physical type in an early Zhou palace and designated with the Chinese word for a 'magician-priest', a word believed to derive from the earlier Iranian word of the same meaning. All of this suggests that Iranian priests were journeying along what would later become the Silk Road long before our earliest historical references in East Central Asia to the fire altars and the worship of a sky god, two of the elements of the Zoroastrian religion. With Western priests in the court and Western chariots on the field of battle, perhaps it is time to consider to what extent the development of Chinese civilization itself was stimulated by Western 'barbarians'.

Metallurgy

Connections between China and the steppe zone to the northwest can be seen clearly in the earliest metallurgy that emerges in China. Prior to *c.* 2000 BC, finds of metal artifacts in China are exceedingly few, simple and, puzzlingly, already made of alloyed copper (and hence questionable). Archaeologists have noted that in a number of instances the earliest metal objects known from China find distant parallels in West Central Asia. In the centuries after 2000 BC, however, we see a remarkable explosion of

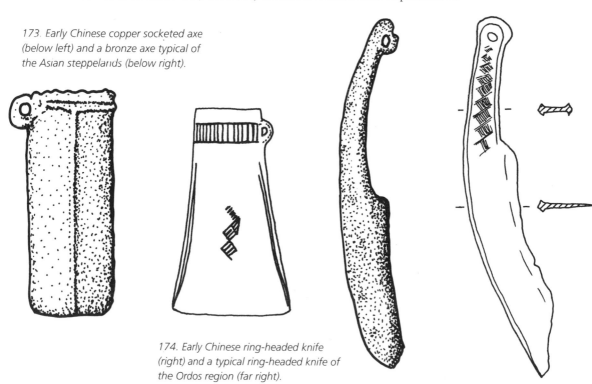

173. Early Chinese copper socketed axe (below left) and a bronze axe typical of the Asian steppelands (below right).

174. Early Chinese ring-headed knife (right) and a typical ring-headed knife of the Ordos region (far right).

metallurgy in the Erlitou culture that precedes the Shang. The route west from the pre-Shang territory of the Central Plains led through Gansu where we have already described the Qijia culture of the Early Bronze Age. This culture, itself indigenous, provides us nevertheless with evidence that it was in contact with Western cultures. This can be seen, for example, in the local production of a copper socketed axe reminiscent in its form of the bronze axes that are characteristic of the Altai-Minusinsk region (ill. 173). The presence here of ring-pommelled knives also shows Western contacts (ill. 174); to this we can add the discovery of some evidence for both the horse and the donkey, again gifts of the West.

For generations it was assumed that metallurgy (along with agriculture) first entered China from the West. Over the past several decades, however, Chinese archaeologists have mounted counter arguments, based on more recent excavations, to demonstrate that China underwent its own Neolithic Revolution, i.e. transition to a settled agricultural economy. On the other hand, the argument that metallurgy was entirely indigenous to China does not seem so robust as once thought and the scholarly gradient now inclines to accept that the earliest bronze metallurgy in China was stimulated by contacts with western steppe cultures. We can follow the path of bronze metallurgy in general from the steppelands and Central Asia east through Xinjiang (or southeast via the Ordos) into Gansu and then into the Central Plains where bronze metallurgy suddenly appears in the Erlitou culture. A similar path for iron smelting, which again appears earlier in the West, has been proposed for the introduction of iron into China. The wastes of the Western Regions, the land of our mummies, from which the Shang may have later acquired its jade, may have earlier supplied it with bronze metallurgy, one of the prerequisites of Chinese civilization.

Horsemen in the South?

The province of Yunnan is situated in the southwest of modern China, the region of the upper Mekong and upper Salween rivers. In antiquity, Chinese historians describe it as populated by both indigenous and foreign populations, one of which has been identified as descendants of the Saka or, as the Chinese called them, Sai (Old Sinitic *Sək). Zhang Zengqi, a Chinese archaeologist with over 30 years of experience in Yunnan, has noted figures on bronzes from this region with 'high-bridged noses and deep-set eyes' which he would identify with the Xi of Chinese sources, a name he believes is simply a local transcription of Sai. To demonstrate that Eurasian nomads actually penetrated so far south, he cites evidence of art in northern Yunnan which depicts fighting animals that are reminiscent of the 'animal style' of the Eurasian steppelands, horsemen riding to the hunt with lances as also depicted in steppe art, and drinking horns. There are artistic sources and the accounts of Herodotus and other authors that relate how among the Scythians, two men become blood brothers by drinking from the same horn,

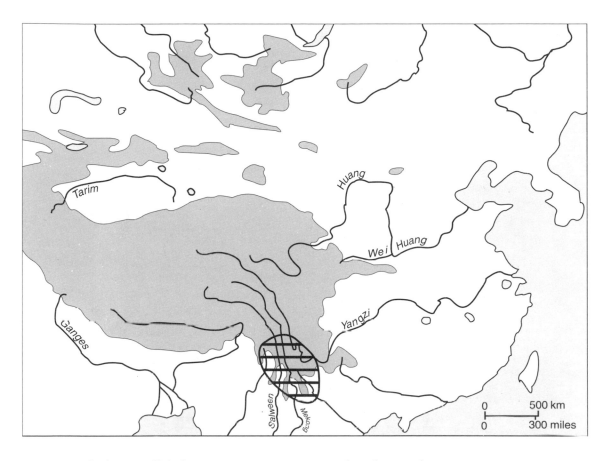

a practice which is paralleled in Yunnan to some extent where host and guest display their close relationship by drinking from the same horn. Tzehuey Chiou-Peng, the Chinese-American art historian, has provided additional support for identifying some of the horsemen of Yunnan with the steppe culture. She notes that, in the artistic representations of the horsemen, we can observe that they have braided hair as is seen in the steppelands and which, as we have already seen, is typical among a number of the mummies, e.g. our 'Ur-David' from Zaghunluq. Many of the figures depicted in the art of the prehistoric Dian civilization of Yunnan, furthermore, have Caucasoid features and wear clothing that is virtually identical with that worn by steppe nomads or Tarim mummies of the 1st millennium BC. Zhang argues that when the Yuezhi displaced the Saka (Sai), some moved south in the first centuries BC to settle in Yunnan. Tzehuey Chiou-Peng suggests that such movements to the south began even earlier, before 1000 BC, and can be traced in the erection of cist graves and some metallurgical features such as daggers typical of the Eurasian steppe.

Farther to the east and some centuries later, there is evidence of gold belt-plaques with 'Scythian' 'animal style' art, greaves, barrows and other indications of the penetration of steppe cultures south of the Yangzi before the Han period. This should not be in the least surprising, since we have

175. The distribution of putatively Saka material in southern China.

176. 'Animal-combat style' belt-plaque from northern Yunnan (above) compared with an example from the Eurasian steppe.

already seen that nomadic influences were already present in the royal Shang burials a thousand years earlier, most conspicuously in the form of bronze knives and adzes/celts which have obvious counterparts in Transbaikal, the Minusinsk Basin, and other regions of the 'Northern Zone' that were archaeologically linked to the mummies of East Central Asia. As for the hundreds of jades that have been chemically assayed to have come from East Central Asia, these may well have been supplied to the Shang royal family by the mummy people themselves. With such massive infiltration of technology and culture from the northwest into the very capital of the first Chinese dynasty, it would seem likely that ideas and concepts would have percolated over far wider areas in succeeding centuries.

Mythology and Economy

We are already familiar with 'Heavenly Horses' (*Tian ma*) and 'Heavenly Mountains' (*Tian shan*). Now it is time to acquaint ourselves with the enigmatic literary text known as the 'Heavenly Questions' (*Tian wen*). This work, quite long for a Chinese poem, consists almost entirely of questions; it is attributed to Qu Yuan (340?–278 BC), the first Chinese poet known by name and a member of the royal family of the southern kingdom of Chu. Although 'Heavenly Questions' is maddeningly frustrating because it only asks questions and cruelly refuses to answer them, the poem is extremely valuable because it gives clues (often the only ones available) to the most ancient body of Chinese mythology, which is notoriously fragmented. Now one of the most intriguing myths alluded to in this obscure poem has to do with the loss and retrieval of cattle and sheep. The poem asks why Hai (one of the predecessors of the Yin, the royal line of the Shang dynasty) was murdered 'where he pastured his cattle and sheep'. Hai, said to be the first herdsman, loses his livestock. This is not the sort of myth that one would expect of the agriculturally oriented Chinese who to this day drink little milk (unlike most Europeans they are intolerant of lactose), wear few woollens and seldom eat beef or mutton. Sheep, as we know, came to China from the west across East Central Asia and so also might this myth of pastoralists. Such a myth is reminiscent of the traditions about cattle-raids and cattle-stealing that are found in many Indo-European stocks, including those of the Indo-Aryan, Iranian, Celtic and Germanic groups.

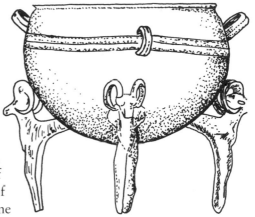

The 'Heavenly Questions' mentions another motif widely found in both Chinese and Indo-European mythology – the tripod. During the Eastern Zhou and Han periods, a common mythological motif was the search for the 'divine tripod' as a symbol of central political power and the ruler's virtue. The 'divine tripod' was actually a bronze cauldron with two loop handles attached to the rim. Similar bronze cauldrons (sometimes with three legs but more often on a circular pedestal) have been unearthed from sites in East Central Asia and are frequently encountered in the 1st millennium BC across the Eurasian steppe in association with nomadic people. The magic cauldron is an essential theme in both Ossetic (East Iranian) and Celtic mythology and is regarded as the prototype for the 'Holy Grail' stories. That the sacred cauldrons of the Indo-Europeans and Chinese may be related is suggested by the fact that the Old Sinitic word for 'earthen vessel', 'cooking pot' is *guō* in modern Mandarin and is probably cognate with the homonymous modern term for 'metal cooking pot'. Now the ancient pronunciation of *guō* was *kwar* and this is so close to Proto-Indo-European *$k^w erus$ 'large cooking pot', 'cauldron' that we may again suspect some ancient contact between Indo-Europeans and the Chinese.

Finally, the very form of the 'Heavenly Questions' is reminiscent of the type of Indo-European riddle texts, catechisms if you will, that characterize parts of the literary tradition of India (the *Vedas*), Iran (*Avesta*) and the early Norse (the *Edda*).

177. The cauldron-tripod occupied a central place in both belief and metallurgy from China across the Eurasian steppe.

The Meaning of the Mummies

The Tarim Basin has been the arena for contacts between the East and West for some 4,000 years. Not only silk passed along its trade routes but also many of the inventions and ideas of the East. But it was not a one-way road and it also provided a conduit for plants, animals, technology and ideas to the East. Its earliest farmers brought the domestic sheep and wheat into the world of ancient China. From 2000 BC onwards we see the introduction of bronze metallurgy, wheeled vehicles and the domestic horse either directly from the Eurasian steppelands or mediated through the settlements of East Central Asia. By the late 1st millennium BC, the flow of commodities, natural and intellectual, had accelerated. 'Blood-sweating' and 'heavenly' horses together with the alfalfa that foddered them served to secure Chinese civilization against incursions from northern tribes. The domestic grape provided wine for the Han and later aristocracies, while Buddhism passed along the trade routes of the Tarim Basin to flower in China. As might be expected in a culture so accustomed to innovation, the Chinese invariably reshaped whatever they took from the West to make it uniquely their own and, on occasion, pass what was once Western back to its place of origin but much improved.

Through this entire history of East–West exchanges, the mediators between these two worlds were the Western populations who first settled East Central Asia in the Bronze Age. They carried into a harsh world of barren wastes and occasional oases their Western livestock, textile traditions and metallurgy; from the West they also brought their languages, Tocharian and Iranian, and they were open to the religions and wisdom of the West as much as of the East. But it is in their burials, where ritual and an arid climate conspired to preserve them as mummies, that the ancient people of East Central Asia, perhaps more than any prehistoric people on earth, have left us the clearest expression of their own physical identities. Geographical chauvinism may place them on the extreme eastern periphery of the West or the western wastelands of the East; in the more considered cultural history of all Eurasia, they were people very much at the centre.

APPENDIX ONE

On the Tocharian Problems

These notes on the Tocharian problems outline the nature of some of the issues associated with calling the people and languages of the kingdoms of Kucha and Agni (KA) 'Tocharian'. In order not to crush the reader with arcane minutiae, we limit our survey to 2,000 words.

Discussion begins with the colophon on the Uyghur translation (AD 800) of the *Maitreyasamiti* setting up the equation: language of Agnideśa = *toχri*: language of the Uyghurs = Turkic. On this basis, Sieg and Siegling (1908) and Müller and Sieg (1916) suggested that the similarity between *toχri* and 'Tocharian' was such that they may be equated, i.e. the people of former Bactria/north India identified in Greek, Latin, Indic and Chinese documents as Tocharians (Greek *Tókharoi* = Latin *Tochari* = Sanskrit *Tukhāra* = Chinese *Tuhuoluo*) = those leaving Tocharian A documents .

A more recent centrepiece of discussion is a badly damaged fragment of a Kuchean text which is housed in St Petersburg. Here the Sanskrit word *tokharika* 'a Tocharian woman' is followed immediately by what is presumed to be its KA equivalent *kucaññe iṣcake*. This has been variously interpreted as a 'Kuchean woman' (if *iṣcake* is related to Sanskrit *iṣṭikā*) or a 'Kuchean member of a Brahmin family (*iṣṭaka*)' and whatever the second element, the first has been regarded as equivalent to *kuśiññe* 'Kuchean' thus securing, in the Kuchean language itself, the equation between Sanskrit *tokharika*, i.e. a 'real' Tocharian (of Bactria), and a Kuchean. We also have a Tocharian B text that glosses 'Tocharian' with 'Kuchean', thus providing evidence from Kuchean and Agnean that they both regarded themselves as 'Tocharian'.

To these equations we may add that (1) 'Tocharian' was widely used before and after our Kuchean-Agnean (KA) documents for peoples and places in East Central Asia (and not just Bactria), and (2) if we follow the Chinese equation and usage of Yuezhi for Tocharian (of Bactria), there is persistent evidence for

the Yuezhi (= Tocharians) in East Central Asia *after* the Great Yuezhi's historically attested departure in the Han period. Ptolemy's citation of a *Thaugouroi* in Gansu, a *Takoriaioi* north of the Imaus (Himalayas) and a *Taguouraioi* in the Issyk-kul vicinity, for example, provides 'Tocharianoid' names from *c.* AD 100. At the other end of the temporal scale, the Tibetan '*Dzam-gling-rgyas-bshad* of Bla-ma Btsan-po (1820) informs us: 'As for the River Si-ta (Tarim), it rises from a mountain range to the northwest of the Snow-mountain Ti-se and after traversing the country of Yer-khen (Yarkand) and others, it flows into the lake called Tska-mtsho (Lopnur), which is in the Thur-phan (Turpan) region of Tho-dkhar (Tokhara)' (Wylie 1962: 58). Thus, a Tibetan source referred to the entire Tarim Basin as Tokhara (generally it was limited to the southwest region of the Tarim, north of Gilgit; Wylie 1962: 122, n. 70).

With reference to the Chinese equation: Yuezhi = Tocharian, we find evidence for Tocharians living or remaining in East Central Asia. Xu Wenkan (1996) relates how hundreds of Buddhists, identified as Greater Yuezhi from Kushan (Tocharia), settled in Chang'an and other areas in the 2nd–5th century AD, taking the surname Zhi, which is short for Yuezhi, i.e. the Kushans identified themselves as Yuezhi (just as the Chinese identified them). Accepting that the Chinese word for 'Buddha' derives from a proto-form **but*, he notes a bronze statue of Buddha recovered from Chang'an, inscribed *buca* (where *t > c* in the Krorän document). According to him this confirms that the source of the word was Tocharian (KA) and as Chinese historical tradition derives Buddhism from the Yuezhi (Kushans), this further secures the equation Yuezhi = Kushan = Tocharian (KA) language.

We should note here the issue of the political entity of the Tarim Basin known as 'the four Tuγaristān' (e.g. Persian *čahār tuγaristān*, Sogdian (adj.) *čtβ'r*

twγr'kč'ny). At Qarabalgasun, the old Uyghur capital in Mongolia, there was erected a stela that carried an inscription which celebrated the Uyghur conquest of 'The Four Twγr' between AD 808 and 821. This provides us with another political term bearing a 'Tocharianoid' name. A Turkish reference to the *tört küsän* 'four Kushans' may also be equivalent. Moreover, these four 'twgr' may refer to four towns mentioned in Central Asian Sanskrit texts (Hecyka, Bharuka, Kucha and Agni) which are arguably Tocharian-speaking (D. Q. Adams, pers. com.)

This edifice of cross-equations that would render the Tocharians of Bactria (the Kushans) the ethnic and linguistic siblings of both the Yuezhi of easternmost Central Asia and of the people (or at least languages) that are commonly called 'Tocharian' (KA) has been assaulted on almost all fronts. The main arguments against such equations are:

1. There is no definite association between *toχri* in the Uyghur colophon and the classical 'Tocharians'; these names may fortuitously resemble one another.

2. The text making this equation is Turkish and tells us only what the Turks (Uyghurs) called the language of Agnideśa, not what the natives called it (or themselves). It is possible, for example, that the Indic original of the *Maitreyasamiti* was first translated into **toχri* (some Iranian language) and only then translated into Tocharian A and Turkic (Winter, pers. com).

3. As for the St Petersburg document, *kucaññe* reveals an *a* where we would expect *i*, i.e. *kᵘśiññe* 'Kuchean', therefore, there are grounds to doubt that the *kucaññe* = Kuchean (Winter suggests that the referent here may be 'Kushan' although this requires one to explain why the Uyghurs were interested in a people who had existed a millennium before). More importantly, the Sanskrit word clearly refers to a 'Tocharian woman', and yet the Tocharian equivalent *iṣcake* is either a

masculine or neuter noun, i.e. it frustrates any attempt to translate the word as 'woman'.

4. While we cannot be absolutely certain what 'the four Tuɣaristān' refers to, there is some evidence that it may be equated with the 'Four Garrisons' of the Tang dynasty and as these included Qäshqär and Khotan, both of which would have spoken an Iranian rather than a KA language, it is difficult to see how this reference supports the equation of Tocharian = KA in the Tarim Basin.

The argument of many of the objections concerns either the rejection of phonological equations as spurious, or the imprecision of any ethnic term regarding Kushan, Yuezhi, etc., because these words were regularly re-applied exocentrically by the Chinese and Turks, and may have made any number of logical interpositions. For example, Kucheans were Buddhists and Buddhism came from the Tocharians/ Kushans, therefore the Kucheans were Tocharians/ Kushans, or Kushans in East Central Asia adopted the name 'Yuezhi' because this equation already existed in Chinese tradition (and not because the Kushans felt themselves ethnically or linguistically 'Yuezhi', whatever that meant). A document from Dunhuang, dating to AD 966, indicates, for example, that the state between Khocho and Kucha, i.e. the state centred on the town of Yanqi (Agni), was known also as Yuezhi. One can then argue that the Yuezhi held on to this territory even after the departure of the Greater Yuezhi and thereby associate the Yuezhi with territory in which we later recover KA manuscripts. Or this could merely reflect the tendency of the Chinese to label ethnic minorities whose cultures had been heavily influenced by Buddhism as Yuezhi. The claims and counter-claims concerning the equation Tocharian = KA continue with no clear sign of major agreement.

Two additional problems, the self-designation of the Kucheans and Agneans, require comment as well.

What did the Kucheans call themselves? We have seen that the name of the state was Kuci (or *Kuśi, in Tocharian B $k^u ci$) = MSM Qiuci = early medieval *kuw-dzi. The adjective is kuśiññe, e.g. kuśiññ oroccepi länte yaitkorsa 'by the order of the great king of Kucha'. As the Chinese name for the royal house of the Kucheans was Bo 'white', linguists have sought to derive $k^u ci$ from a nominative plural *kwiteyes which is cognate with

both Sanskrit śviti- and Avestan spiti- 'white', 'brilliant', i.e. $k^u ci$ = 'the brilliant ones', cf. the Iranian royal family who were expected to possess solar brilliance, the Avestan $x^v arənah$-. The equation is phonologically possible but there are serious problems: (1) a root *kwiti- is not attested in the Tocharian languages although there are several other words for 'white' or 'brilliant'; (2) the genitive of Kuci is Kuciñ indicating that the word is singular rather than plural, i.e. Kuci cannot refer to 'the bright ones'; (3) while 'the brilliant ones' makes sense as an ethnonym, it does not as a place name; and (4) although the Chinese referred to the royal house of Kucha as 'Bo', the recurrent element of the Kuchean royal names was Sanskrit Suvarṇa 'gold', i.e. Tocharian B Ysāṣṣe. In other words, the tie-in should be with 'gold' and not 'white'.

What did the Agneans call themselves? Some propose that the native name for Agni (Chinese Yanqi), the region of Qarashähär where Tocharian A texts have been recovered, is Ārśi and that this word also indicates 'shining ones'. A Tocharian A text refers to ārśi-käntw-ā, literally 'in the Arsi-tongue'. Some linguists derive ārśi from an earlier *arĝeyes which is built on the same root that provides Sanskrit árjuna- and Latin argentum 'silver'. Two Old Turkish inscriptions from Mongolia (Kül-Tegin and Bilgä Qayan) from stelae that date to the period around AD 732–735 both refer to the toquz ärsin 'the nine Ärsin' which, the stelae suggest, were located just where we would expect the Ārśi, in the vicinity of Qarashähär.

Although this equation is phonologically possible, almost all the points proposed can be challenged because (1) thc underlying form is not attested in either Tocharian language (although extensions of the same root underlie Tocharian A ārki 'white' and Tocharian B ārkwi); (2) it is possible that the Tocharian word is singular rather than plural as the interpretation seems to demand and, if so, it fails for the same reasons given in our discussion of Kucha; (3) all external references to the Agnean kingdom show a hard velar (k/g) (i.e. Khotanese Argi, Buddhist Hybrid Sanskrit Agnideśa) and never the ś demanded by the proposed equation with ārśi; and (4) the assumption that the ārśi-tongue refers to Tocharian A is rejected by most Tocharian specialists who see it as a translation of Buddhist Hybrid Sanskrit ārya- in the meaning of

'religious mendicant' and when modifying a language it refers to Sanskrit and not Tocharian A.

According to D. Q. Adams, it is more likely that the Agneans called themselves what all our other sources call them, something like *ākñi which could derive from a Proto-Tocharian *āke 'end', 'limit', i.e. the people occupying the area of Qarashähär were the 'borderers', 'marchers', the type of ethnonym which we find elsewhere in Europe, e.g. Ukraine ('beyond the borders') or Old English Mercia ('the Marches').

Further Reading

Bailey, H. W., 1970 'Tokharika', Journal of the Royal Asiatic Society, 121–122.

Bailey, H. W., 1936 'Ttaugara', BSOS 8, 883–921.

Haloun, G. 1937 'Zur Üe-tṣī-Frage', ZDMG 91, 243–318.

Henning, W. B., 1938 'Argi and the "Tocharians"', BSOS 9, 3, 545–571.

Henning, W. B., 1949 'The name of the "Tokharian" language', Asia Major 1, 158–163.

Henning, W. B., 1978 'The first Indo-Europeans in history', In Society and History, Essays in Honor of Karl August Wittfogel, ed. G. L. Ulmen, 215–230. The Hague, Mouton.

Konow, S., 1933 'War "Tocharisch" die Sprache der Tocharer?', Asia Major 9, 455–466.

Müller, F. W. K., 1918 'Toχri und Kuišan (Küšän)', SBAW, 566–586.

Müller, F. W. K. and E. Sieg., 1916 'Maitrisimit und "Tocharisch"', SBAW, 395–417.

Narain, A. K., 1987 'On the "first" Indo-Europeans: The Tokharian-Yüezhi and their Chinese homeland', Papers on Inner Asia, No. 2, Bloomington, Indian, 1–28.

Pelliot, P., 1934 'Tokharien et koutchéen', Journal Asiatique 224, 23–106.

Sieg, E., 1918 'Ein einheimischer Name für Toχri', SBAW, 560–565.

Sieg, E., 1937 'Und dennoch "Tocharisch"', SBAW, 130–139.

Sieg, E. and W. Siegling., 1908 'Tocharisch, die Sprache der Indoskythen', SBAW, 915–932.

Thomas, W., 1981 'Zu skt. tokharika und seiner Entsprechung im Tocharischen', KZ 95, 126–133.

Winter, W., 1984 'Zur tocharischen Entsprechung von skt. tokharika'. KZ 97, 131–133.

Wylie, T. V., 1962 The Geography of Tibet according to the 'Dzam-Glind-Rgyas-Bshad. Serie Orientale Roma 25, Rome, Istituto Italiano per il medio ed estremo oriente.

Xu Wenkan 1996 'The Tocharians and Buddhism', Studies in Central and East Asian Religions 9: 1–17.

Radiocarbon Dates From Selected Sites

All dates are calibrated according to Radiocarbon Calibration Program Rev 4.1.2, Stuiver, M. and P. J. Reimer, 1993, *Radiocarbon 35*: 215–230; and based on data sets of Stuiver, Reimer et al, 1998, *Radiocarbon 40*: 1041–1083. Dates are calibrated to 95% probability employing a laboratory error factor of 1.

Location	Lab. No.	Material	Date BP	Cal BC	Location	Lab. No.	Material	Date BP	Cal BC
ALWIGHUL (ALAGOU)					III M13	ZK-2045	wood	1890±70	41–AD 321
M1	WB77-14	wood	2410±80	792–262	III M14	ZK-2046	wood	1830±70	AD 27–384
M3	WB78-24	wood	2360±90	782–202	III M15B	ZK-2047	wood	1870±90	46–AD 383
M4	WB77-21	wood	2260±65	406–169	III M16	ZK-2048	wood	1800±70	AD 68–409
M21	WB77-27	wood	2140±80	391–AD 47	III M19	ZK-2049	wood	2050±95	360–AD 131
M28	WB77-26	wood	2490±130	900–234					
M30	WB77-25	wood	2260±65	406–169	**CHONG BAGH (QUNBAKE)**				
M32	WB77-24	wood	2350±80	762–204	I M1	ZK-2113	wood	2500±70	804–401
					I M2	ZK-2114	wood	2720±100	1185–673
CHARWIGHUL (CHAWUHUGOUKOU)					I M3	ZK-2115	reed	2600±90	919–411
M4	ZK-1328	wood	2600±80	903–414	I M3	ZK-2116	wood	2620±75	913–541
I M6	ZK-1329	wood	2610±75	903–522	I M4	ZK-2117	wood	2420±80	794–264
I M20	ZK-1330	wood	2580±75	894–412	I M9	ZK-2143	wood	2190±80	400–2
I M25	ZK-1331	wood	2750±80	1125–796	I M10	ZK-2144	wood	2480±95	824–386
I M29	ZK-1332	wood	2670±75	995–672	I M27	ZK-2145	wood	2550±80	833–406
I M31	ZK-1333	wood	2690±90	1015–600	I M34A	ZK-2146	wood	2380±75	765–233
I M32	ZK-1334	wood	2550±90	894–403	II M4	ZK-2288	wood	2570±80	894–409
I M59	ZK-1335	wood	2530±75	827–404	II M7	ZK-2289	wood	2600±75	900–519
I M60	ZK-1336	wood	2450±80	799–386	II M10	ZK-2290	wood	2440±75	796–386
I M06B	ZK-2031	wood	2150±75	391–AD 17	II M12	ZK-2291	wood	2530±75	827–404
I M09	ZK-2033	wood	2740±90	1185–788	II M18	ZK-2292	wood	2230±90	410–45
I M025	ZK-2036	wood	2460±75	799–392					
I M030	ZK-2037	wood	2720±90	1108–765	**LOPNUR (LUOBUBO)**				
1 M035	ZK-2038	wood	2930±80	1389–904	MA2	WB80-24	wood	2010±75	199–AD 131
1 M043	ZK-2039	wood	2550±70	829–409	MB1	WB80-25	wood	1870±80	41–AD 376
1 M045	ZK-2040	wood	2640±70	919–562					
II M2	ZK-2110	wood	2510±80	824–400	**NURASAY COPPER MINE (NULASAI)**				
II M6	ZK-2111	wood	2380±70	764–259	Mine	BK77001	charcoal	2580±170	1185–260
II M15	ZK-2112	wood	2330±75	759–202	Mine	WB82-51	wood	2340±70	759–206
III M13	ZK-2043	wood	1870±75	38–AD 339					
III M12	ZK-2044	wood	2090±70	357–AD 64					

Location	Lab. No.	Material	Date BP	Cal BC

QĀWRIGHUL (GUMUGOU)

Location	Lab. No.	Material	Date BP	Cal BC
II M38	BK81042	wool	3390±100	1939–1441
II M38	BK81043	sheepskin	3510±170	2295–1431
II M38	BK81044	wood	3430±70	1918–1596
M4	BK81045	wood	3560±80	2137–1688
M12	WB81-28	wood	4140±80	2902–2471
II M23	ZK-1003(1)	wood	3550±60	2106–1694
II M23	ZK-1003(2)	wool	2120±105	397–AD 116

QIZILCHOQA (WUPU)

Location	Lab. No.	Material	Date BP	Cal BC
M19	WB79-12	wood	2990±65	1408–1004
(2)M4	WB79-13	wood	2760±80	1185–797
M26	WB79-14	wood	3010±85	1436–999
M101	WB79-15	wood	3030±85	1491–1004

SAMPUL (SHANPULA)

Location	Lab. No.	Material	Date BP	Cal BC
M02	WB84-11	reed	2780±90	1210–797
M6	WB84-12	reed	1720±95	AD 81–540
M01	WB84-14	reed	2050±65	345–AD 80
M02	WB84-15	wood	1940±75	105–AD241
M2	WB84-17	wood	2140±75	388–AD 22
M02	WB84-19	charcoal	2230±65	402–111

SHAMBABAY (XIANGBAOBAO)

Location	Lab. No.	Material	Date BP	Cal BC
M13	BK 77002	wood	2370±70	762–233
M13	WB77-19	wood	2400±70	783–263
M40	WB78-01	wood	4270±90	3096–2584
M17	WB78-12	wood	2539±65	824–409
M21	WB78-13	wood	2670±65	969–765

SUBESHI (SUBASHI)

Location	Lab. No.	Material	Date BP	Cal BC
M3	WB81-61	wood	2160±70	391–1
M8	WB82-05	wood	3060±75	1495–1053

TÖMÜRLÜK (TIEMULIKE)

Location	Lab. No.	Material	Date BP	Cal BC
M2	BK82107	wood	2470±60	796–399
M4	BK82108	wood	2140±60	378–1

TÖRT ERIK (SIDAOGOU)

Location	Lab. No.	Material	Date BP	Cal BC
T5(3)H50	WB77-29	charcoal	2260±80	480–112
T4(3)	WB77-30	charcoal	2400±65	775–379
T3(3)	WB77-31	charcoal	2270±80	504–119
T1(4)	WB77-32	charcoal	2360±65	760–233
T1(4)H44	WB77-33	charcoal	2320±65	537–203
T2(5)	WB77-34	charcoal	2800±70	1206–810
H4	WB77-35	charcoal	2510±80	824–400
T6	WB78-27	charcoal	1990±60	164–AD 130
M2	ZK-1052	wood	1480±70	AD 424–670

TÖWAN RIVER (TIEBANHE)

Location	Lab. No.	Material	Date BP	Cal BC
'Beauty'	ZK-1001	sheepskin	3480±70	2009–1621
F4	WB80-23	wood	1860±75	36- AD 376

YANBULAQ (YANBULAKE)

Location	Lab. No.	Material	Date BP	Cal BC
M64	ZK-2186	wood	2970±55	1386–1004
M70	ZK-2187	wood	3300±75	1743–1413
M45	ZK-2188	wood	3130±65	1521–1219
M54	ZK-2189	wood	2580±55	829–541
M20	ZK-2194	wood	3610±55	2137–1777
M14	ZK-2195	reed	2410±80	792–262
M7	ZK-2196	wood	3250±90	1739–1319
M64	ZK-2197	wood	2600±85	910–412

YEWIRGHUL (YU'ERGOU) = ALWIGHUL CULTURE

Location	Lab. No.	Material	Date BP	Cal BC
M67	WB78-21	wood	2580±85	898–408
M37	WB78-14	wood	2570±65	831–414
M42	WB78-20	wood	2370±85	782–206
M58	WB78-40	wood	2300±130	789–4
M55	WB78-19	wood	2100±65	357–AD 51
M81	WB78-23	wood	2060±80	355–AD 123
M30	WB78-02	wood	2010±80	201–AD 133
M47	WB78-22	wood	1890±60	36–AD 316

ZAGHUNLUQ (ZAHONGLUKE)

No published dates but He Dexiu indicates there are five dates in the range c. 3200–2700 BP, i.e., c. 1500–850 BC.

Bibliography

Abbreviations

JIES – Journal of Indo European Studies

General

Barber, Elizabeth, 1999 *The Mummies of Ürümchi*. New York: W. W. Norton; London: Macmillan.

Frank, A. G., 1992 *The Centrality of Central Asia*. Amsterdam: VU University Press.

Frye, R. N., 1996 *The Heritage of Central Asia: From Antiquity to the Turkish Expansion*. Princeton: Markus Wiener.

von Gabain, A., 1979 *Einführung in die Zentralasienkunde*. Darmstadt: Wissenschaftliche Buchgesellschaft.

Grousset, R., 1970 *The Empire of the Steppes: A History of Central Asia*. New Brunswick: Rutgers University Press.

Harmatta, J. ed., 1994 *History of Civilizations of Central Asia, Vol. 2: The Development of Sedentary and Nomadic Civilizations: 700 BC to AD 250*. Paris: UNESCO.

Litvinsky, B. A. ed., 1986 *Vostochny Turkestan i Srednyaya Aziya*. Moscow: Nauka.

Mair, V. H. ed., 1998 *The Bronze Age and Early Iron Age Peoples of Eastern Central Asia*. 2 vols. Washington and Philadelphia: *JIES* Monograph 26.

Reid, Howard, 1999 *In Search of the Immortals: Mummies, Death and the Afterlife*. London: Headline.

Samolin, W., 1964 *East Turkestan to the Twelfth Century: A Brief Political Survey*. The Hague: Mouton.

Sinor, D. ed., 1969 *Inner Asia: History, Civilization, Languages*. Bloomington: Indiana University.

———,1990 *The Cambridge History of Early Inner Asia*. Cambridge: Cambridge University Press.

Tikhvinsky, S. L. and B. A. Litvinsky eds., 1988 *Vostochny Turkestan v Drevnosti i Rannem Srednevekov'ye*. Moscow: Nauka.

Yu Taishan ed., 1996 *Xiyu tongshi* [Comprehensive History of the Western Regions]. Zhengzhou: Zhongzhou guji chubanshe.

CHAPTER ONE
Beyond the Centres: Tarim Between East and West

Birrell, Anne trs. and annot., 1999 *The Classic of Mountains and Seas*. Harmondsworth: Penguin.

Bolton, J. D. P., 1962 *Aristeas of Proconnesus*. Oxford: Clarendon.

Bunbury, E. H., 1879 *A History of Ancient Geography*. 2 vols. London: John Murray.

Dabbs, J. A., 1963 *History of the Discovery and Exploration of Chinese Turkestan*. The Hague: Mouton.

Davis-Kimball, J., V. A. Bashilov and L. T. Yablonsky, eds., 1995 *Nomads of the Eurasian Steppes in the Early Iron Age*. Berkeley: Zinat Press.

Drège, Jean-Pierre and Emil M. Bührer, 1989 *The Silk Road Saga*. New York, Oxford: Facts on File.

Gardiner-Garden, J. R., 1987 *Apollodoros of Artemita and the Central Asian Skythians*. Papers on Inner Asia No. 3. Bloomington: Indiana University.

Harley, J. B. and D. Woodward, 1987 *The History of Cartography. Vol. 1: Cartography in Prehistoric, Ancient, and Medieval Europe and the Mediterranean*. Chicago: University of Chicago Press.

———, 1994 *The History of Cartography. Vol. 2, Book 2: Cartography in the Traditional East and Southeast Asian Societies*. Chicago: University of Chicago Press.

Hudson, G. F., 1931 *Europe and China: A Survey of their Relations from the Earliest Times to 1800*. London: Edward Arnold.

Hulsewé, A. F. P., 1979 *China in Central Asia: The Early Stage: 125 BC–AD 23*. Leiden: Brill.

Knauer, E. R., 1998 *The Camel's Load in Life and Death: Iconography and Ideology of Chinese Pottery Figurines from Han to T'ang and Their Relevance to Trade along the Silk Routes*. Zürich: Akanthus.

Levi, M. A., 1989 *I Nomadi alla frontiera*. Rome: 'L'Erma' di Bretschneider.

Litvinsky, B. A. and A. P. Terent'ev-Katansky, 1988 'Puteshestviya, ekspeditsii, arkheologicheskiye raskopki [Journeys, expeditions, archaeological excavations].' *Vostochny Turkestan v Drevnosti i Rannem Srednevekov'ye*, eds. S. L. Tikhvinsky and B. A. Litvinsky, 17–82. Moscow: Nauka.

Mathieu, R., 1978 *Le Mu Tianzi zhuan: traduction annote, ètude critique*. Paris: Collège de France, Institut des hautes ètudes chinoises.

———, 1983 *Étude sur la mythologie et l'ethnologie de la Chine ancienne*. Paris: Collège de France.

Ma Yong and Wang Binghua, 1994 'A'ertai yu Ou-Ya caoyuan sichou zhi lu [The Altai and the Eurasian Steppe Silk Road].' *Caoyuan sichou zhi lu yu Zhongya wenming*, ed. Zhang Zhiyao, N.p.: Xinjiang meishu sheying chubanshe, 1–8.

McNeill, W. H., 1987 'The eccentricity of wheels, or Eurasian transportation in historical perspective.' *American Historical Review* 92: 1111–1126.

Phillips, E. D., 1955 'The legend of Aristeas: fact and fancy in early Greek notions of East Russia, Siberia, and Inner Asia.' *Artibus Asiae* 18, 2: 161–177.

P'yankov, I. V., 1986 'Vostochny Turkestan v svete antichnykh istochnikov.' *Vostochny Turkestan i Srednyaya Aziya*, ed. B. A. Litvinsky, 6–23. Moscow: Nauka.

Rolle, R., 1989 *The World of the Scythians*. Berkeley: University of California Press; London: Batsford.

Romm, J. S., 1989 'Herodotus and mythic geography: the case of the Hyperboreans.' *Transactions of the American Philological Association* 119: 97–113.

———, 1992 *The Edges of the Earth in Ancient Thought*. Princeton: Princeton University Press.

Shiratori, K., 1957 'On the Ts'ung-ling traffic route described by C. Ptolemaeus.' *Memoirs of the Research Department of the Tokyo Bunko*, 1–34.

Thomson, J. O., 1948 *History of Ancient Geography*. Cambridge: Cambridge University Press.

CHAPTER TWO
East Central Asia: Players at the Centre of the Board

Brough, J., 1965 'Comments on third-century Shan-shan and the history of Buddhism.' *Bulletin of the School of Oriental and African Studies* 28: 582–612.

Chen Chien-wen, 1998 'Further studies on the racial, cultural, and ethnic affinities of the Yuezhi.' *The Bronze Age and Early Iron Age Peoples of Eastern Central Asia*, ed. V. Mair, 767–834. Washington and Philadelphia: *JIES* Monograph 26.

Daffinà, P., 1982 *Il nomadismo centrasiatico*. Rome: Istituto degli Studi dell'India e dell'Asia Orientale.

Di Cosmo, N., 1994 'Ancient Inner Asian nomads: Their economic basis and its significance in Chinese history.' *Journal of Asian Studies* 53.4: 1092–1126.

Enoki, K., 1963 'The location of the capital of Lou-lan and the date of the Kharoṣṭhī inscriptions.'

The Memoirs of the Research Department of the Tokyo Bunko 22: 125–171.

Enoki, K., G. A. Koshelenko and Z. Haidary, 1994 'The Yüeh-chih and their migrations.' *History of Civilizations of Central Asia, Vol. 2: The development of sedentary and nomadic civilizations: 700 BC to AD 250*, ed. J. Harmatta, 171–189. Paris: UNESCO.

Erdélyi, I., 1994 'The settlements of the Xiognu[sic].' *The Archaeology of the Steppes: Methods and Strategies*, ed. B. Genito, 553–563. Napoli: Istituto Universitario Orientale.

von Gabain, A., 1961 *Das Uigurische Königreich von Chotscho 850–1250*. Berlin: Akademie-Verlag.

de Groot, J. J. M., 1921 *Die Hunnen der vorchristlichen Zeit*. Berlin and Leipzig: Walter de Gruyter.

Haloun, G., 1926 *Seit wann kannten die Chinesen die Tocharer oder Indogermanen überhaupt. Erster teil*. Leipzig: Asia Major.

———, 1937 'Zur Üe-tṣï-Frage.' *Zeitschrift der Deutschen Morgenländischen Gesellschaft* 91: 243–318.

Hikata, R., 1992 'The peoples and their religions of Central Asia before the 9th century.' *Studies in Buddhism and Buddhist Culture*, 21–55. Monograph Series of Naritasan Institute for Buddhist Studies.

Hulsewé, A. F. P., 1979 *China in Central Asia*. Leiden: Brill.

Jenner, W. J. F., 1981 *Memories of Loyang: Yang Hsüan-chih and the lost capital (493–534)*. Oxford: Clarendon Press.

Kumar, B., 1973 *The Early Kuṣāṇas*. New Delhi: Sterling.

Litvinsky, B. A., 1996 *History of Civilizations of Central Asia, Vol. 3: The crossroads of civilizations: AD 250 to 750*. Paris: UNESCO.

Liu, Mau-tsai, 1969 *Kutshca und seine Beziehungen zu China vom 2. Jh. v. bis zum 6. Jh. n. Chr* [= *Asiatische Forschungen, Band 27*]. Wiesbaden: Otto Harrassowitz.

van Lohuizen-de Leeuw, J. E., 1949 *The 'Scythian' Period*. Leiden: Brill.

Maenchen-Helfen, O., 1945 'The Yüeh-chih problem re-examined.' *Journal of the American Oriental*

Society 1945: 71–81.

Menges, K. H. 1968 *The Turkic Languages and Peoples*. Wiesbaden: Otto Harrassowitz.

Mirsky, J., 1964 *The Great Chinese Travelers: An Anthology*. New York: Pantheon.

Prušek, J., 1971 *Chinese Statelets and the Northern Barbarians in the Period 1400–300 BC*. Dordrecht: D. Reidel.

Sima Qian, 1993. *Records of the Grand Historian*. 3 vols. Hong Kong and New York: Renditions and Columbia University Press. Translated by Burton Watson.

Ssu-ma Ch'ien, 1961 *Records of the Grand Historian of China* (translated by Burton Watson). New York and London: Columbia University Press.

Stein, M. A., 1907 *Ancient Khotan*. 2 vols. Oxford, Clarendon Press reprinted 1975, New York: Hacker Art Books.

———, 1921 *Serindia*. 4 vols. Oxford: Clarendon Press.

Wright, D. C., 1997 'The Hsiung-nu–Hun equation revisited.' *Eurasian Studies Yearbook* 69: 77–112.

Yu Taishan, 1992 *Saizhong shi yanjiu* [Studies on the History of the Sakas]. Beijing: Zhongguo shehui kexue chubanshe; complete English translation in *Sino-Platonic Papers*, 80 (1998).

Yü, Ying-Shih, 1990 'The Hsiung-nu.' *The Cambridge History of Early Inner Asia*, ed. D. Sinor, 118–149. Cambridge: Cambridge University Press.

Zürcher, E., 1968 'The Yüeh-chih and Kaniṣka in the Chinese sources.' *Papers on the Date of Kaniṣka*, ed. A. L. Basham, 346–390. Leiden: Brill.

CHAPTER THREE
The Linguistic Landscape

Cardona, G., 1986 *Storia Universale della Scrittura*. Milan: Mondadori.

Daniels, P. T. and W. Bright, 1996 *The World's Writing Systems*. New York and Oxford: Oxford University Press.

Gardiner-Garden, J. R., 1987 'Ktesias on Early Central Asian History and Ethnography.' *Papers on Inner Asia*, No. 6. Bloomington: Indiana University.

Harmatta, J., 1994 'Languages and scripts in Graeco-Bactria and the Saka kingdoms.' *History of Civilizations of Central Asia, Vol. 2*, ed. J. Harmatta, 397–416. Paris: UNESCO, .

———, 1994 'Languages and literature in the Kushan empire,' *History of Civilizations of Central Asia, Vol. 2*, ed. J. Harmatta, 417–440. Paris: UNESCO.

Mallory, J. P., 1989 *In Search of the Indo-Europeans*. London and New York: Thames and Hudson.

Mallory, J. P. and D. Q. Adams, 1997 *Encyclopedia of Indo-European Culture*. London and Chicago: Fitzroy Dearborn.

CHAPTER FOUR
The Testimony of the Hoe

An Zhimin, 1992 'Neolithic communities in eastern parts of Central Asia.' *History of the Civilizations of Central Asia, Vol. 1, The Dawn of Civilization: Earliest Times to 700 BC*, eds. A. H. Dani and V. M. Masson, 153–168. Paris: UNESCO.

———, 1992 'The Bronze Age in eastern parts of Central Asia.' *History of the Civilizations of Central Asia, Vol. 1, The Dawn of Civilization: Earliest Times to 700 BC*, eds. A. H. Dani and V. M. Masson, 319–336. Paris: UNESCO.

Bayinguoleng Menggu Zizhi Zhou Wenguansuo, 1992 'Qiemo xian Zahongluke gumuzang 1989 nian qingli jianbao [Preliminary report on the 1989 excavations of an ancient grave at Zaghunluq in Chärchän County].' *Xinjiang wenwu* 2: 1–14.

Chen Ge, 1985 'Guanyu Xinjiang yuangu wenhua de ji ge wenti [On several questions concerning the cultures of remote antiquity in Xinjiang].' *Xinjiang wenwu* 1: 27–38.

———, 1991 'Lue lun Yanbulake wenhua [A brief discussion on the Yanbulaq culture].' *Xiyu yanjiu* 1: 81–96.

———, 1995 'Xinjiang yuangu wenhua chulun [A preliminary study of the ancient culture in Xinjiang].' *Zhongya xuekan* 4: 5–72.

Chen Kwang-tzuu and F. Hiebert, 1995 'The late prehistory of Xinjiang in relation to its neighbors.' *Journal of World Prehistory* 9: 243–300.

Debaine-Francfort, C., 1988 'Archéologie du Xinjiang des origines aux Han: première partie.' *Paléorient* 14: 5–29.

———, 1989 'Archéologie du Xinjiang des origines aux Han: deuxième partie.' *Paléorient* 15: 183–213.

———, 1990 'Les Saka du Xinjiang avant les Han.' *Nomades et sédentaires en Asie centrale, Apports de l'archéologie et de l'ethnologie*, 81–95. Paris: Editions du C.N.R.S.

———, 1995 *Du néolithique à l'âge du bronze en Chine du nord-ouest: La culture de Qijia et ses connexions*. Paris, Éditions Recherche sur les Civilisations.

Fitzgerald-Huber, L. G., 1995 'Qijia and Erlitou: The question of contacts with distant cultures.' *Early China* 20: 17–67.

Han Kangxin, 1994 'The study of ancient human skeletons from Xinjiang, China.' *Sino Platonic Papers* 51, Philadelphia: University of Pennsylvania.

Hiebert, F. and N. Di Cosmo, 1996 *Between Lapis and Jade: Ancient Cultures of Central Asia* (*Anthropology and Archeology of Eurasia* 3.4).

Horvath, I. and Du Yaxiong, 1995 'Xinjiang's population of the pre-Turkic age in light of Chinese archeology and historical sources.' *Eurasian Studies Yearbook* 67: 95–108.

Hou Can, 1985 'The rise and fall of Loulan.' *Social Sciences in China*, Spring, 1985: 156–178.

Kamberi, Dolkun, 1994 'The three thousand year old Chärchän man preserved at Zaghunluq.' *Sino-Platonic Papers* 44, Philadelphia: University of Pennsylvania.

Lin Meicun, 1995 *Xiyu wenming: kaogu, minzu, yuyan he zhongjiao xinlun* [The Serindian Civilization: New Studies on Archaeology, Ethnology, Languages, and Religions]. Beijing: Dongfang chubanshe.

Li Wenying, 1997 'New archaeological finds from the ancient city of

Jiaohe (Yarkhoto).' *Circle of Inner Asian Art Newsletter* 6:4–6.

Mair, V. H., 1998 'Priorities.' *The Bronze Age and Early Iron Age Peoples of Eastern Central Asia*, ed. V. H. Mair, 4–41. Washington and Philadelphia: *JIES* Monograph 26.

Ma Yong and Sun Yutang, 1994 'The western regions under the Hsiung-nu and the Han.' *History of Civilizations of Central Asia: Vol. 2*, ed. J. Harmatta, 227–246. Paris: UNESCO.

Ma Yong and Wang Binghua, 1994 'The culture of the Xinjiang region.' *History of Civilizations of Central Asia: Vol. 2*, ed. J. Harmatta, 209–225. Paris: UNESCO.

Mu Shunying, Qi Xiaoshan and Zhang Ping eds., 1994 *Zhongguo Xinjiang gudai yishu* [The Ancient Art in Xinjiang, China]. Ürümchi: The Xinjiang Art and Photography Press.

Mu Shunying and Zhang Ping eds., 1995 *Loulan wenhua yanjiu lunji* [Collected Papers on Krorän Culture]. Ürümchi: Xinjiang renmin chubanshe.

Nagasawa Kazutoshi and Wang Binghua eds., 1992 *Rōran ōkoku to yūkyū no bijo* [The Kingdom of Krorän and the Eternal Beauty]. Tokyo: Asahi shinbunsha.

Samolin, W., 1958–58 'Ethnographic aspects of the archaeology of the Tarim basin.' *Central Asiatic Journal* 4: 45–67.

Tikhvinsky, S. L. and B. A. Litvinsky, 1988 *Vostochny Turkestan v Drevnosti i Rannem Srednevekov'ye*. Moscow: Nauka.

Wang Binghua, 1996 'A preliminary analysis of the archeological cultures of the Bronze Age in the region of Xinjiang.' *Anthropology and Archeology of Eurasia* 34, 4: 87–101.

Wang Bo and Qin Dahai, 1990 'Hami Yanbulake muzang de fenqi wenti [Questions about the periodization of the graves at Yanbulaq, Qumul].' *Xinjiang wenwu* 3: 30–38.

Yu Taishan, Chen Gaohua and Xie Fang eds., 1996 *Xinjiang ge zu lishi wenhua cidian* [Dictionary of the History and Cultures of the Various Peoples of Xinjiang]. Beijing: Zhonghua shuju.

Xinjiang Shehui Kexueyuan Kaogu Yanjiusuo ed., 1983 *Xinjiang kaogu sanshi nian* [Thirty Years of Xinjiang Archeology]. Ürümchi: Xinjiang renmin chubanshe.

Xinjiang Weiwuer Zizhiqu Bowuguan ed., 1991, *Xinjiang Weiwuer Zizhiqu Bowuguan* [Museum of the Xinjiang Autonomous Region]. Beijing and Tokyo: Wenwu chubanshe and Kodansha.

Xinjiang Weiwuer Zizhiqu Shehui Kexueyuan Kaogu Yanjiusuo, 1985 *Xinjiang gudai minzu wenwu* [Cultural Relics of the Ancient Peoples of Xinjiang]. Beijing: Wenwu chubanshe.

Xinjiang Weiwuer Zizhiqu Silu kaogu zhenpin [Archaeological Treasures of the Silk Road in Xinjiang Uyghur Autonomous Region]. 1998 Shanghai: Shanghai Translation Publishing House.

Xinjiang Wenwu Kaogu Yanjiusuo ed., 1995 *Xinjiang wenwu kaogu xin shouhuo (1979–1989)* [New Achievements in Archaeological Research in Xinjiang during the Time Span 1979–1989]. Ürümchi: Xinjiang renmin chubanshe.

Xinjiang Wenwu Kaogu Yanjiusuo and Xinjiang Weiwuer Zizhiqu Bowuguan eds., 1998 *Xinjiang wenwu kaogu xin shouhuo, xu (1990–1996)* [New Achievements in Archaeological Research in Xinjiang during the Time Span 1990–1996]. Ürümchi: Xinjiang meishu sheying chubanshe.

Zhang Guangda, 1996 'The city-states of the Tarim Basin.' *History of Civilizations of Central Asia, Vol. 3: The Crossroads of Civilizations: AD 250 to 750*, ed. B. A. Litvinsky, 281–301. Paris: UNESCO.

CHAPTER FIVE
The Mummies Themselves

Angel, J. L., 1973 'Human skeletons from grave circles at Mycena.' *O Taphikos Kyklos B ton Mykenon*, ed. G. Mylonas, 379–397. Athens.

Barber, P. T., 1995 'Mummification in the Tarim Basin.' *JIES* 23: 309–318.

Bergman, F., 1935 'Newly discovered graves in the Lop-nor desert.' *Hyllningsskrift Tillägnad Sven Hedin*. Geografiska Annaler 1935: 44–61.

———, 1939 *Archaeological Researches in Sinkiang*. Stockholm: Bokförlags Aktiebolaget Thule.

Bokovenko, N. A., 1995 'The Tagar culture in the Minusinsk Basin.' *Nomads of the Eurasian Steppes in the Early Iron Age*, eds. J. Davis-Kimball, V. A. Bashilov and L. T. Yablonsky, 299–314. Berkeley: Zinat Press.

Borgognini Tarli, S. M., 1992 'Aspetti antropoligici e paleodemografici dal Paleolitico superiore alla prima età del ferro.' *Italia Preistoria*, eds. A. Guidi and M. Piperno, 238–273.

Cockburn, A., E. Cockburn and T. Reyman, 1998 *Mummies, Disease and Ancient Cultures*. 2nd ed. Cambridge: Cambridge University Press.

Hadingham, E., 1994 'The mummies of Xinjiang.' *Discover* 15: 68–77.

He Dexiu, 1998 'A brief report on the mummies from Zaghunluq site in Chärchän county.' *The Bronze Age and Early Iron Age Peoples of Eastern Central Asia*, ed. V. H. Mair, 169–174. Washington and Philadelphia: *JIES* Monograph 26.

Kamberi, Dolkun, 1994 'The three thousand year old Chärchän man preserved at Zaghunluq.' *Sino-Platonic Papers* 44.

Kuz'min, N. Ju. and O. B. Varlamov, 1988 'Osobennosti pogrebal'nogo obryada plemen Minusinskoy kotloviny na rubezhe nashey ery.' *Metodocheskie Problemy Arkheologii Sibiri*, ed. R. S. Vasil'evsky, 146–155. Novosibirsk: Nauka.

Mair, Victor H., 1995 'Mummies of the Tarim Basin.' *Archaeology* 48 (March/April): 28–35.

———, 1995 'Prehistoric Caucasoid corpses of the Tarim Basin.' *JIES* 23: 281–307.

Mallory, J. P., 1995 'Speculations on the Xinjiang mummies.' *JIES* 23: 371–384.

Nagasawa Kazutoshi and Wang Binghua, 1992 *Rōran ōkoku to yūkyū no bijo* [The Kingdom of Krorän and the Eternal Beauty]. Tokyo: Asahi shinbunsha.

Power, C., 1993 'Reconstructing patterns of health and dietary change in Irish prehistoric populations.' *Ulster Journal of Archaeology* 56: 9–17.

Reid, Howard, 1999 *In Search of the Immortals: Mummies, Death and the Afterlife*. London: Headline.

Shao Xingzhou and Wang Bo, 1989 'Zhahongluke er hao mu liang ju gushi de chubu yanjiu [Preliminary research on two ancient mummies from tomb 2 at Zaghunluq].' *Xinjiang wenwu* 4: 72–77.

Stein, Sir Aurel, 1928 *Innermost Asia*. 3 vols. Oxford: Clarendon Press.

Wang Binghua, 1992 'Xinjiang gushi fajue ji chubu yanjiu [The excavation of mummies in Xinjiang and their preliminary study].' *Xinjiang wenwu* 4: 80–88.

———, 1996 'Excavation and preliminary studies of the ancient mummies of Xiniang in China.' *Human Mummies: A global survey of their status and the techniques of conservation*, eds. K. Spindler, H. Wilfing, E. Rastbichler-Zissernig, D. zur Nedden, and H. Nothdurfter, 59–69. Vienna and New York: Springer.

Yu Zhiyong, 1995 'Xinjiang diqu kaogu faxian de huishen he wenshen [The painting on the body and tattooing found archaeologically in Xinjiang].' *Xiyu yanjiu* 3: 98–104.

Zhang Yuzhong, 1992 'Xinjiang gudai ganshi de kaogu faxian he yanjiu zongshu [A summary account about the finding and studies of Xinjiang mummies].' *Xinjiang wenwu* 4: 89–96.

CHAPTER SIX
Tartans in the Tarim

Barber, E. J. W., 1991 *Prehistoric Textiles*. Princeton: Princeton University Press.

———, 1995 'A weaver's-eye view of the second millennium Tarim Basin finds.' *JIES* 23: 347–355.

Good, Irene, 1995 'Notes on a Bronze Age textile fragment from Hami, Xinjiang with comments on the significance of twill.' *JIES* 23: 319–345.

———, 1995 'On the question of silk in pre-Han Eurasia.' *Antiquity* 69: 959–968.

———, 1998 'Bronze Age cloth and clothing of the Tarim Basin: The Chärchän evidence.' *The Bronze Age and Early Iron Age Peoples of*

Eastern Central Asia, ed. V. H. Mair, 656–668. Washington and Philadelphia: *JIES* Monograph 26.

Sylwan, Vivi, 1941 *Woollen Textiles of the Lou-lan People*. Stockholm: Tryckeri Aktiebolaget Thule.

CHAPTER SEVEN
Skulls, Genes and Knights with Long Swords

Baker, J., 1974 *Race*. London: Oxford University Press.

Brace, C. L. and D. P. Tracer, 1992 'Craniofacial Continuity and Change: A Comparison of Late Pleistocene and Recent Europe and Asia.' *The Evolution and Dispersal of Modern Humans in Asia*, ed. T. Akazawa, K. Aoki and T. Kimura. Tokyo: Hokusen-sha, 439–471.

Cavalli-Sforza, L. L., P. Menozzi and A. Piazza, 1994 *The History and Geography of Human Genes*. Princeton: Princeton University Press.

Conway, R. S., 1900 'The riddle of the nations.' *Current Review* 77: 74–81.

Francalacci, P., 1995 'DNA analysis of ancient desiccated corpses from Xinjiang.' *JIES* 23: 385–398.

———, 1998 'DNA analysis of ancient desiccated corpses from Xinjiang, China: Further results.' *The Bronze Age and Early Iron Age Peoples of Eastern Central Asia*, ed. V. Mair, 537–547. Washington and Philadelphia: *JIES* Monograph 26.

Han Kangxin, 1991 'Xinjiang gudai jumin de zhongzu renleixue he Weiwuer zu de tizhi tedian [Studies on the racial anthrop-ology of the ancient inhabitants of Xinjiang and the physical characteristics of the Uyghur people].' *Xiyu yanjiu* 2: 1–13.

———, 1993 *Sichou zhi lu gudai jumin zhongzu renleixue yanjiu [The Collected Papers about the Racial Anthropological Study of the Ancient Silk Road Inhabitants]*. Ürümchi: Xinjiang renmin chubanshe.

———, 1994 'The study of ancient human skeletons from Xinjiang, China.' *Sino Platonic Papers* 51.

———, 1998 'The physical anthropology of the ancient

populations of the Tarim Basin and surrounding areas.' *The Bronze Age and Early Iron Age Peoples of Eastern Central Asia*, ed. V. Mair, 558–570. Washington and Philadelphia: *JIES* Monograph 26.

Han Kangxin and Pan Qifeng, 1990 'Guanyu Wusun, Yuezhi de zhongshu [On the racial affinities of the Wusun and Yuezhi].' *Xiyu shi luncong* 3: 1–8.

Kohn, L. A. P., 1991 'The role of genetics in craniofacial morphology and growth.' *Annual Review of Anthropology* 20: 261–278.

de Lapouge, G. Vacher, 1899 *L'Aryen, son role sociale*. Paris.

Samolin, W., 1958–59 'Ethnographic aspects of the archaeology of the Tarim Basin.' *Central Asiatic Journal* 4: 45–67.

Shao Xingzhou and Wang Bo, 1991 'Tulufan pendi gumu renlu de zhonxi yanjiu – Yanghai gumu [Studies on the racial systematics of the human skulls from an ancient cemetery in the Turfan Basin – The ancient cemetery at Yanghe].' *Xinjiang wenwu* 3: 44–54.

Shao Xingzhou, Wang Jinglan, Cui Jing, Wang Bo, and Chang Xien, 1990 'Baozidong M41 gumu lugu de yanjiu [Studies of the skulls from the ancient tomb M41 at Bozdöng].' *Xinjiang wenwu* 1:23–31.

Sjøvold, T., 1984 'A report on the heritability of some cranial measurements and non-metric traits.' *Multivariate Statistical Methods in Physical Anthropology*, ed. G. N. van Vark and W. W. Howells, 223–246. Dordrecht and Boston: D. Reidel.

Taylor, G., 1921 'The evolution and distribution of race, culture, and language.' *Geographical Review* 11: 54–119.

Wang Bo, 1994 'Xinjiang Loulan Tieban He nü shi zhongzu renleixue yanjiu [Anthropological studies of the race of a female corpse from the Töwän River at Krorän in Xinjiang].' *Xinjiang daxue xuebao* 22.4: 68–71.

Zhao Tongmao, 1998 'The Uyghurs, a Mongoloid-Caucasoid mixed population: Genetic evidence and estimates of Caucasian admixture

in the peoples living in northwest China.' *The Bronze Age and Early Iron Age Peoples of Eastern Central Asia*, ed. V. Mair, 548–557. Washington and Philadelphia: *JIES* Monograph 26.

CHAPTER EIGHT
The Usual Suspects: The Indo-Iranians

Hiebert, F., 1994 *Origins of the Bronze Age Oasis Civilization in Central Asia*. Cambridge: American School of Prehistoric Research, Bulletin 42.

———, 1998 'Central Asians on the Iranian Plateau: A model for Indo-Iranian expansionism.' *The Bronze Age and Early Iron Age Peoples of Eastern Central Asia*, ed. V. Mair, 148–161. Washington and Philadelphia: *JIES* Monograph 26.

Kuzmina, E. E., 1994 *Otkuda prishli Indoarii?* Moscow: MGP 'Kalina'.

Mallory, J. P., 1994–95 'The Indo-European homeland: An Asian perspective.' *Bulletin of the Deccan College Post-graduate and Research Institute* 54–55: 237–254.

———, 1998 'A European perspective on Indo-Europeans in Asia.' *The Bronze Age and Early Iron Age Peoples of Eastern Central Asia*, ed. V. Mair, 175–201. Washington and Philadelphia: *JIES* Monograph 26.

Parpola, A., 1988 'The coming of the Aryans to Iran and India and the cultural and ethnic identity of the Dāsas.' *Studia Orientalia* 64: 195–302.

———, 1998 'Aryan languages, archaeological cultures, and Sinkiang: Where did Proto-Iranian come into being, and how did it spread? *The Bronze Age and Early Iron Age Peoples of Eastern Central Asia*, ed. V. Mair, 114–147. Washington and Philadelphia: *JIES* Monograph 26.

Sarianidi, Victor, 1998 *Margiana and Protozoroastrism*. Athens: Kapon.

Sims-Williams, N., 1996 'The Sogdian merchants in China and India.' *Cina e Iran: da Allesandro Magno alla Dinastia Tang*, eds. A. Cadonna and L. Lanciotti, 45–67. Florence: Leo S. Olschki.

CHAPTER NINE
Tocharian Trekkers

Adams, D. Q., 1984 'The position of Tocharian among the other Indo-European languages.' *Journal of the American Oriental Society* 104: 395–402.

———, 1999 *A Dictionary of Tocharian B*. Amsterdam and Atlanta: Rodopi.

Bailey, F. W., 1947 'Recent work in 'Tokharian'.' *Transactions of the Philological Society* 1947: 126–153.

Burrow, T., 1935 'Tokharian elements in the Kharoṣṭhī documents from Chinese Turkestan.' *Journal of the Royal Asiatic Society* 1935, 667–675.

———, 1937 *The Language of the Kharoṣṭhī Documents from Chinese Turkestan*. Cambridge: Cambridge University Press.

Chen Chien-wen, 1998 'Further Studies on the racial, cultural, and ethnic affinities of the Yuezhi.' *The Bronze Age and Early Iron Age Peoples of Eastern Central Asia*, ed. V. Mair, 767–784. Washington and Philadelphia: *JIES* Monograph 26.

Fukushima, Naoshirō, 1935 'On the designation-problem of the so-called Tokharian language.' *Fujioka hakushi kōseki kinen gengogaku ronbunshū*, 7–72. Tokyo: Iwanami.

Gamkrelidze, T. and V. I., 1991 'Les premiers Indo-Européens de la histoire: les ancêstres des Tokhariens en Asie Mineure ancienne.' *Revue des études géorgiennes et caucasiennes* 6: 265–296.

Hamp, E. P., 1998 'Whose were the Tocharians? Linguistic subgrouping and diagnostic idiosyncrasy.' *The Bronze Age and Early Iron Age Peoples of Eastern Central Asia*, ed. V. Mair, 307–346. Washington and Philadelphia: *JIES* Monograph 26.

Henning, W. B., 1965 'The first Indo-Europeans in history.' *Society and History: Essays in Honor of Karl August Wittfogel*, ed. G. L. Ulmen, 215–230. The Hague: Mouton.

Huang Shengzhang, 1985 'Shi lun suowei "Tuhuoluoyu" ji qi youguan de lishi dili he minzu wenti [A tentative discussion of the "Tocharian language" and related questions of history, geography and ethnicity].' *Xiyu shi luncong* 2: 228–268.

Krause, W. and W. Thomas, 1960–64 *Tocharisches Elementarbuch*. 2 vols. Heidelberg: Carl Winter Universitätsverlag.

Kuzmina, E. E., 1998 'Cultural connections of the Tarim Basin people and the pastoralists of the Asian steppes in the Bronze Age.' *The Bronze Age and Early Iron Age Peoples of Eastern Central Asia*, ed. V. Mair, 63–93. Washington and Philadelphia: *JIES* Monograph 26.

Laufer, B., 1917 *The Language of the Yüe-chi* [sic] *or Indo-Scythians*. Chicago: R. R. Donnelly and Sons.

Litvinsky, B. A., 1992 *Vostochny Turkestan v Drevnosti i Rannem Srednevekov'e*. Moscow: Nauka.

Mallory, J. P., 1998 'Speculations on the Xinjiang mummies.' *JIES* 23: 371–384.

Narain, A. K., 1987 'On the "first" Indo-Europeans: The Tokharian-Yuezhi and their Chinese homeland.' *Papers on Inner Asia* 2, ed. Y. Bregel, 1–29. Bloomington: Indiana University.

———, 1990 'Indo-Europeans in Inner Asia.' *The Cambridge History of Early Inner Asia*, ed. D. Sinor, 151–176. Cambridge: Cambridge University Press.

Pinault, G., 1989 'Introduction au tokharien.' *Actes des sessions de linguistique et de littérature* 7. Paris: Presses de l'École Normale Supérieure.

Ringe, D., 1990 'Evidence for the position of Tocharian in the Indo-European family?' *Die Sprache* 34: 59–123.

Ringe, D., T. Warnow, A. Taylor, A. Michailov and L. Levinson, 1998 'Computational cladistics and the position of Tocharian.' *The Bronze Age and Early Iron Age People of Eastern Central Asia*, ed. V. Mair, 391–414. Washington and Philadelphia: *JIES* Monograph 26.

Rong Xinjiang, 1995 'Longjia kao [On the tribe of Longjia].' *Zhongya xuekan* [*Journal of Central Asia*] 4: 144–160.

Sieg, E. and W. Siegling, 1921 *Tocharische Sprachreste*. Berlin and Leipzig: Walter de Gruyter.

Torday, L., 1997 *Mounted Archers: The Beginnings of Central Asian History*. Edinburgh: Durham Academic Press.

Van Windekens, A. J., 1976 *Le Tokharien confronté avec les autres langues indo-européennes*. 2 vols. Louvain: Centre international de dialectologie génerale.

Warnow, T., D. Ringe and A. Taylor, 1995 'Reconstructing the evolutionary history of natural languages.' *Institute for Research in Cognitive Science Report* 95–16.

Winter, W., 1984 *Studia Tocharica*. Poznan: Uniwersytet im. Adama Mickiewicza w Poznaniu.

CHAPTER TEN
Who Were the Mummies?

Adams, D. Q., 1998 'On the history and significance of some Tocharian B agricultural terms.' *The Bronze Age and Early Iron Age Peoples of Eastern Central Asia*, ed. V. Mair, 372–378. Washington and Philadelphia: *JIES* Monograph 26.

Charpentier, J., 1917 'Die ethnographische Stellung der Tocharer.' *Zeitschrift der Deutschen Morgenländischen Gesellschaft* 71: 347–388.

Jettmar, K., 1996 'Die Tocharer, ein Problem der ethnischen Anthropologie?' *Homo* 47:34–42.

Kuzmina, E. E., 1998 'Cultural connections of the Tarim Basin people and pastoralists of the Asian steppes in the Bronze Age.' *The Bronze Age and Early Iron Age Peoples of Eastern Central Asia*, ed. V. Mair, 63–93. Washington and Philadelphia: *JIES* Monograph 26.

Lin, Mei-cun, 1992 'Tocharian people: Silk road pioneers.' *Significance of Silk Roads in the History of Human Civilizations*, eds. Tadao Umesao and Toh Sugimura, 91–96. Osaka: National Museum of Ethnology.

Litvinsky, B. A., 1988 'The common ethnic and cultural background of East Turkestan and what is now Soviet Central Asia.' *Oriental Studies in the USSR: Annual 1987*, 183–199. Moscow: Nauka.

Mair, Victor H., 1998 'Die Sprachamöbe: An archeolinguistic parable.' *The Bronze Age and Early*

Iron Age Peoples of Eastern Central Asia, ed. V. H. Mair, 835–855. Washington and Philadelphia: *JIES* Monograph 26.

CHAPTER ELEVEN
Legacy

An Zhimin, 1993 'Shilun Zhongguo de Zaoqi Tongqi [A tentative discussion on China's early Copper/Bronze implements].' *Kaogu* 12: 1110–1119.

Bezold, C., 1919–20 'Sse-ma Ts'ien und die babylonische Astrologie.' *Ostasiatische Zeitschrift: Beiträge zur Kenntnis der Kultur und Kunst des Fernen Osten* 8: 42–49.

Bodde, D., 1961 'Myths of Ancient China.' *Mythologies of the Ancient World*, ed. Samuel Noah Kramer, 367–408. Garden City, New York: Anchor Books.

Chang, Tsung-tung, 1988 'Indo-European vocabulary in Old Chinese: A new thesis on the emergence of Chinese language and civilization in the Late Neolithic Age.' *Sino Platonic Papers* 7: 1–56.

Chernykh, E. N., 1992 *Ancient Metallurgy in the USSR.* Cambridge: Cambridge University Press.

Chiou-Peng, Tzehuey, 1998 'Western Yunnan and its steppe affinities.' *The Bronze Age and Early Iron Age Peoples of Eastern Central Asia*, ed. V. Mair, 280–304. Washington and Philadelphia: *JIES* Monograph 26.

Cook, R. S., 1995 'The etymology of Chinese Chén.' *Linguistics of the Tibeto-Burman Area*, 18.2: i–iii, 1–238.

Fitzgerald-Huber, L., 1995 'Qijia and Erlitou: the question of contacts

with distant cultures.' *Early China* 20:17–67.

Heine-Geldern, R., 1951 'Das Tocharerproblem und die Pontische Wanderung.' *Saeculum* 2.2: 225–255.

Lin Yün, 1986 'A reexamination of the relationship between bronzes of the Shang culture and of the Northern Zone.' *Studies of Shang Archaeology*, ed. K. C. Chang, 237–273. New Haven and London: Yale University Press.

Lu Liancheng, 1993 'Chariot and horse burials in ancient China.' *Antiquity* 67: 824–838.

Mair, V. H., 1990 'Old Sinitic $*m^y ag$, Old Persian *maguš*, and English "magician".' *Early China* 15: 27–47.

———, 1990 *Tao Te Ching: The Classic Book of Integrity and the Way.* New York: Bantam.

———, 1998 'Canine conundrums: Eurasian dog ancestor myths in historical and ethnic perspective'. *Sino-Platonic Papers* 87.

Miller, R. A., 1988 'Pleiades perceived: MUL.MUL to Subaru.' *Journal of the American Oriental Society* 108.1: 1–25.

Moran, H. A. and D. H. Kelley, 1969 *The Alphabet and the Ancient Calendar Signs.* Palo Alto: Daily Press.

Muhly, J., 1988 'The beginnings of metallurgy in the Old World.' *The Beginnings of the Use of Metals and Alloys*, ed. Robert Maddin, 2–20. Cambridge, Mass.: MIT Press.

Puett, M., 1998 'China in early Eurasian history: A brief review of recent scholarship on the issue.' *The Bronze Age and Early Iron Age Peoples of Eastern Central Asia*, ed. V. Mair, 699–715. Washington

and Philadelphia: *JIES* Monograph 26.

Pulleybank, E., 1966 'Chinese and Indo-Europeans.' *Journal of the Royal Asiatic Society*, 9–39.

Pulleybank, E., 1996 'Early contacts between Indo Europeans and Chinese with commentaries.' *International Review of Chinese Linguistics* 1: 1–50.

de Santilla, G. and H. von Dechend, 1983 *Hamlet's Mill: An Essay on Myth and the Frame of Time.* Boston: David R. Godine.

Shaughnessy, E., 1988 'Historical perspectives on the introduction of the chariot into China.' *Harvard Journal of Asiatic Studies* 48: 189–237.

———, 1989 'Western cultural innovations in China, 1200 BC' *Sino-Platonic Papers* 11.

Temple, R., 1986 *China: Land of Discovery.* Wellingborough: Patrick Stephens.

Watson, W., 1984 'An interpretation of opposites? Pre-Han bronze metallurgy in west China.' *Proceedings of the British Academy* 70: 327–358.

Yu Taishan, 1996 'Shuo Daxia de qianxi – jian kao Yun xing zhi Rong [On the migrations of the Daxia, together with an investigation of the Rong surnamed Yun]', Zhongguo Xian Qin shi xuehui and Luoyang shi dier wenwu gongzuodui, ed. *Xia wenhua yanjiu lunji*, 176–196. Beijing.

Zhang Zengqi, 1994 'Again on the influence and diffusion of the Scythian culture in the Yunnan Bronze Age.' *The Archaeology of the Steppe: Methods and Strategies*, ed. Bruno Genito, 666–699. Naples: Istituto Univerisario Orientale.

Sources of Illustrations

I: Photo Jeffery Newbury, *Discover Magazine* April 1994. II: Photo Jeffery Newbury, *Discover Magazine* April 1994. III: Photo Dolkun Kamberi. IV: Photo Jeffrey Newbury, *Discover Magazine* April 1994. V: Photo Jeffrey Newbury, *Discover Magazine* April 1994. VI: Photo Jeffrey Newbury, *Discover Magazine* April 1994. VII: Photo He Dexiu. VIII: Photo He Dexiu. IX: After Yu Zhiyong, *et. al.*, 1996, 'The most important findings at Niyä in the Täklimakan,' *China Culture Pictorial*, 1-2, 6. X: Photo Irene Good. XI: Photo Victor Mair. XII: Photo courtesy of Prof M. Yaldiz, Staatliche Museen zu Berlin, Museum für indische Kunst. XIII: After Le Coq, Albert von, 1913, *Chotscho*, Berlin, D. Reimer, 21. 1: Drawing by Maura Pringle. 2: From Bergman. (1939), pl. XIb. 3: Drawing by Maura Pringle, after Mair, Victor (1998), frontispiece. 4: Photo Victor Mair. 5: Photo Victor Mair. 6: Photo Victor Mair. 7: Photo Victor Mair. 8: Drawing by Victor Mair. 9: Drawing by Maura Pringle. 10: After Harley and Woodward (1987), fig. 8.5. 11: Mallory and Adams (1997), 79d. 12: Drawing by Maura Pringle. 13: After Khazanov, 1971, *Ocherki Voennogo Dela Sarmatov*. Moscow, Nauka, table 34. 14: After *Journal of the Hellenic Society* 48, 1928, pl. xi. 15: After Rudenko, S. , 1953, *Kul'tura Naseleniya Gornogo Altaya v Skifskoe Vremya*. Moscow, Nauka, fig. 163. 16: Drawing by Maura Pringle. 17: After Harley and Woodward (1987), fig. 10.9. 18: After Harley and Woodward (1987), fig. 11.3. 19: After de Silva, Anil, 1967, *The Art of Chinese Landscape Painting in the Caves of Tun-huang*, New York, Crown Publishing, 214-215. 20: After Harley and Woodward (1994), fig. 4.1. 21: After Needham, Joseph, 1959, *Science and Civilization in China*, Cambridge, Cambridge University

Press, vol. 3, 506, fig. 205a and b. 22: Drawing by Maura Pringle. 23: After Drège and Bührer (1989), 9. 24: Drawing by Maura Pringle. 25: Photo Victor Mair. 26: Drawing by Maura Pringle. 27: Drawing by Maura Pringle, after Mair (1998), frontispiece. 28: After *Xinjiangshiku bihua* (Wall Paintings of Xinjiang Caves), 1989. Zhongguo meishu quanji (Arts of China, Complete Collection), painting series 16, Beijing: Wenwu chubanshe, 24. 29: After Grünwedel, A., 1912, *Altbuddhistische Kultstätten in Chinesisch-Turkistan*, Berlin, Georg Reimer, 333, fig. 664. 30: After Stein, Aurel, 1921, *Serindia*, 4 vols, Oxford, Clarendon Press, plate LXII. 31: After von Gabain (1961), fig. 5. 32: After Wriggins, Sally, 1996 *Xuanzang: A Buddhist Pilgrim on the Silk Road*. Colorado and Oxford: Westview Press. 33: After Drège and Bührer (1989), 261. 34: After Erdélyi (1994), 561, fig. 2. 35: Drawing by Victor Mair. 36: After U.-Köhalmi, K., 1953, 'Über die Pfeifenden Pfeile der innenasiatischen Reiternomaden,' *Acta Orientalia Hungarica* 71.1, 14. 37: Drawing by Victor Mair. 38: Drawing by Maura Pringle. 39: Drawing by Maura Pringle. 40: After von Gabain (1961), 40, fig. 16. 41: After Daniels and Bright (1996), table 47.1, 48.2. 42: Junge, J., 1962, *Saka-Studien = Klio*, Beiheft 41, taf. II. 43: Drawing by Maura Pringle. 44: After von Gabain (1961), 67, fig. 39. 45: After Stein, Aurel, 1921, *Serindia*, Oxford, Clarendon Press, plate CXIII, N. xv. 152. 46: After Stein, Aurel, 1921, *Serindia*, Oxford, Clarendon Press, 349. 47: After Litvinsky (1992), 71, fig. 1. 48: After von Gabain (1961), 12, fig. 4. 49: After Daniels and Bright (1996), tables 30.1, 30.3, 30.5, 30.6. 50: After Mallory and Adams (1997), 300. 51: Drawing by Maura Pringle. **table p. 123:** After (with revisions) Frye

(1996), 248-249. 52: After Mallory and Adams (1997), 551. 53: After Mallory and Adams (1997), 127. 54: After Mallory and Adams (1997), 299. 55: After Mallory and Adams (1997), 297. 56: After Mallory and Adams (1997), 21. 57: Drawing by Maura Pringle. 58: Drawing by Maura Pringle, after Mair (1998), frontispiece. 59: After China Pictorial Publications, ed., 1989, *The Silk Road on Land and Sea*, Beijing, China Pictorial Publishing Company, 128, fig. 2. 60: After *Rōran ōkoku to yūkyū no bijo* (The Kingdom of Krorän and the Eternal Beauty) (1992), 73, fig. 178. 61: After Chen and Hiebert (1995), 258, fig. 7. 62: After Xinjiang Weiwuer Zizhiqu Wenhuating Wenwuchu and Xinjiang Daxue Lishi Xi Wenbo Ganbu Zhuanxiu Ban, 1989, 'Hami Yanbulake mudi,' *Kaogu xuebao* 3, fig. 27. 63: After Xinjiang Wenwu Kaogu Yanjiusuo, 1992, 'Hami Wupu mudi muzang,' *Xinjiang Wenwu* 3, 4, fig. 2. 64: After *Rōran ōkoku to yūkyū no bijo* (The Kingdom of Krorän and the Eternal Beauty) (1992), 105, fig. 280. 65: Tulufan Diqu Wenguansuo, 1984, 'Xinjiang Shanshan Subashi gu muzang,' *Kaogu* 1, 46, fig. 2. 66: Xinjiang Wenwu Kaogu Yanjiusuo, 1993, 'Shanshan Subeixi muqun yi hao mudi fajue jianbao', *Xinjiang Wenwu* 4, 2, fig. 2. 67: Drawing by Maura Pringle, after Mair (1998), frontispiece. 68: After Bergman (1939), 63, fig. 9. 69, 70: After Bergman (1939), pl. IVb. 71: After Bergman (1939), pl. Vd. 72: After Bergman (1939), 69, fig. 12. 73: Recomposited from Kamberi, (1994), 44, 9-12. 74: Recomposited from Bayinguoleng Menggu Zizhizhou Wenguansuo (1992), 4-6, figs. 5-7. 75: After Xinjiang Weiwuer Zizhiqu Bowuguan (1991), pl. 35. 76: Xinjiang Wenwu Kaogu Yanjiusuo and Hejing Xian Wenhuaguan, 1989, 'Hejing xian

Chawuhugou er hao mudi fajue jianbao,' *Xinjiang Wenwu* 4, 19, fig. 5. 77: Xinjiang Wenwu Kaogu Yanjiusuo and Hejing Xian Wenhuaguan, 1990, 'Hejing xian Chawuhuguo er hao mudi fajue jianbao,' *Xinjiang Wenwu* 1, 16, fig. 15. 78: After Debaine-Francfort (1989), 194, fig 14. 79: Xinjiang Shehui Kexueyuan Kaogu Yanjiusuo, 1981, 'Xinjiang Alagou shuxue muguo mu fajue jianbao,' *Wenwu* 1, fig. 5. 80: Photo Victor Mair. 81: After Debaine-Francfort, (1988), 201, fig. 21. 82: After An Zhimin, 1998, 'Cultural complexes of the Bronze Age in the Tarim Basin,' in *The Bronze Age and Early Iron Age Peoples of Eastern Central Asia*, ed. V. Mair, Washington and Philadelphia, vol. 1, 52, fig. 5-6. 83: Drawing by Maura Pringle, after Mair (1998), frontispiece. 84: After Stein, Aurel, 1921, *Serindia*, Oxford, Clarendon Press, pl. XXXV. 85: After Yu Zhiyong, *et. al.*, 1996, 'The most important findings at Niyä in the Täklimakan,' *China Culture Pictorial*, 1-2, 7. 86: After Stein, Aurel, 1921, *Serindia*, Oxford, Clarendon Press, plate LXXXIX, no. 27. 87: After Stein, Aurel, 1921, *Serindia*, Oxford, Clarendon Press, plate XXXIII. 88: Photo Victor Mair. 89: Photo Victor Mair. 90: Photo Victor Mair. 91: After von Le Coq (1928), *Buried Treasures of Chinese Turkestan*, London, George Allen and Unwin, 123. 92: After Grünwedel, A., 1912, *Altbuddhistische Kultstätten in Chinesisch-Turkistan*, Berlin, Georg Reimer, 58, fig. 116. 93: After Grünwedel, A., 1912, *Altbuddhistische Kultstätten in Chinesisch-Turkistan*, Berlin, Georg Reimer, 97, fig. 216. 94: After Grünwedel, A., 1912, *Altbuddhistische Kultstätten in Chinesisch-Turkistan*, Berlin, Georg Reimer, 148, fig. 336. 95: Drawing by Maura Pringle. 96: After *Rōran ōkoku to yūkyū no bijo* (The Kingdom of Kroän and the Eternal Beauty) (1992), 67. 97: Photo Reza, 1996, 'Xinjiang' *National Geographic*, March, 1996, 189.3, 50. 98: After Xinjiang Weiwuer Zizhiqu Shehui Kexue Yuan Kaogu Yanjiusuo, ed., 1985, *Xinjiang gudai minzu wenwu*, Beijing, Wenwu chubanshe, fig. 19. 99: After Stein (1928), fig. 173, by

permission of Oxford University Press. 100: After Bergman (1939), 136, fig. 32. 101: After Bergman (1939), 80, pl. VIc. 102: After Bergman (1939), 80, pl. VIb. 103: Photo Jeffrey Newbury, *Discover* Magazine April 1994. 104: Photo Dolkun Kamberi. 105: Photo Jeffery Newbury, *Discover* Magazine April 1994. 106: Photo Victor Mair. 107: Photo He Dexiu. 108: Photo Victor Mair. 109, 110: Photo Victor Mair. 111: Photo Victor Mair. 112: Photo Victor Mair. 113: Photo Victor Mair. 114: Photo Jeffrey Newbury, *Discover Magazine*, April 1994. 115, 116: Ma Chengyuan and Yue Feng eds., 1998 Archaeological Treasures of the Silk Road in Xinjiang Uygur Autonomous Region. Shanghai, Shanghai Translation Publishing House, pls. 132, 133. 117: After Rudenko, S., 1953, *Kul'tura Naseleniya Gornogo Altaya v Skifskoe Vremya*. Moscow, Nauka, 33 fig. 11. 118: After Rudenko, S., 1953, *Kul'tura Naseleniya Gornogo Altaya v Skifskoe Vremya*. Moscow, Nauka, fig. 80. 119: Kuzmin, N. Yu and O. B. Varlamov, 1988, Osobennosti pogrebal'nogo obryada plemen Minusinskoy Kotloviny na rubezhe nashey ery, *Metodicheskie Problemy Arkheologii Sibiri*, eds. R. S. Vasil'evsky and Yu. P. Kholyushkin, Novosibirsk, Nauka, 146-155. p. 151. 120: Arriaza, B., 1996, 'Preparation of the dead in coastal Andean preceramic populations.' In *Human Mummies: A global survey of their status and the techniques of conservation*, eds. K. Spindler, H. Wilfing, E. Rastbichler-Zissernig, D. zur Nedden, and H. Nothdurfter, Vienna and New York, 133, fig. 4. 121: Drawing by Eimear Nelis. 122: Drawing by Eimear Nelis. 123: After *Rōran ōkoku to yūkyū no bijo* (The Kingdom of Kroän and the Eternal Beauty) (1992), 72, fig. 177. 124: After Bergman (1939), pl. 26, 3. 125: After *Rōran ōkoku to yūkyū no bijo* (The Kingdom of Kroän and the Eternal Beauty) (1992), 82, fig. 203. 126: Drawing by Gillian Gilmore. 127: Drawing by Gillian Gilmore. 128: Photo Irene Good. 129: After Xinjiang Weiwuer Zizhiqu Shehui Kexue Yuan Kaogu Yanjiusuo, (1985), fig. 52. 130: Drawing by Gillian Gilmore after a photo by Victor Mair. 131: Photo Wang Luli. 132: Drawing by Gillian

Gilmore. 133: Bergman (1939), pl. vi. 134: Drawing by Victor Mair and Eimear Nelis. table p. 233: After Taylor (1921), 107, table vii. 135: Drawing by Gillian Gilmore. 136: Brace, C.L. and D.P. Tracer, 1992, 'Craniofacial continuity and change: a comparison of Late Pleistocene and recent Europe and Asia,' in *The Evolution and Dispersal of Modern Humans in Asia*, eds. T. Akazawa, K. Aoki and T. Kimura, Tokyo, Hokusen-sha, 26.2. 137: After Han Kangxin, 1998, 'The physical anthropology of the ancient populations of the Tarim Basin and surrounding areas,' in *The Bronze Age and Early Iron Age Peoples of Eastern Central Asia*, ed. V. Mair, Washington and Philadelphia, vol. 2, 566, fig. 2. 138: After Han Kangxin, 1998, 'The physical anthropology of the ancient populations of the Tarim Basin and surrounding areas.' In *The Bronze Age and Early Iron Age Peoples of Eastern Central Asia*, ed. V. Mair, Washington and Philadelphia, vol. 2, 559, fig. 1. 139: Han Kangxin, 1993, 'Luopu Shanpula gudai congzangmu rengu de zhongxi wenti,' in *Sichou zhi lu gudai jumin zhongzu renleixue yanjiu*, Ürümchi, Xinjiang renmin chubanshe, 322, fig. 2. 140: After Han Kangxin, 1998, 'The physical anthropology of the ancient populations of the Tarim Basin and surrounding areas,' in *The Bronze Age and Early Iron Age Peoples of Eastern Central Asia*, ed. V. Mair, Washington and Philadelphia, vol. 2, 569, fig. 4. 141: Photo Victor Mair. 142: After Mu Shunying, Qi Xiaoshen and Zhang Ping (1994), 82, fig. 201. 143: After von Gabain (1961), 29, fig. 7. 144: After von Gabain (1961), 34, fig. 11. 145: After Zhao Tongmao (1998), vol. 2 550. 146: Photo Victor Mair. 147: Drawing by Maura Pringle. 148: After Kuzmina (1994), 405, fig. 9. 149: After Gening, V. F., G. Zdanovich and V. V. Gening, 1992, *Sintashta*, Chelyabinsk, 154, fig. 72. 150: After Lamberg-Karlovsky, C., 1994, *Antiquity* 68, 399, fig. 1. 151: Drawing by Maura Pringle. 152: After Mandelshtam, A. M., 1968, *Pamyatniki Epokhi Bronzi v Yuzhnom Tadzhikstane*, Moscow, 21, 27, figs. 10, 16. table p. 271: After Thomas, Werner, 1969, 'Zur tocharischen Wiedergabe der Sanskrit-Verbe des

Udānavarga,' *Zeitschrift für vergleichende Sprachforschung* 83, 317–318. **table p. 273a:** After Thomas, Werner, 1954, 'Ein tocharischer Liebesbrief,' *Zeitschrift für vergleichende Sprachforschung* 71, 78-80. **table p. 273b:** After Pinault, G.-J., 1987, 'Epigraphie koutcheene,' in *Sites divers de la region de Koutcha*, eds. Huashan, Ch., S. Gaulier, M. Maillard and G. Pinault, Paris, LP1 and 2. **153:** Drawing by Maura Pringle. **154:** Drawing by Maura Pringle. **table p. 288:** After Adams, D. Q., 1984, 'The position of Tocharian among the other Indo-European languages,' *Journal of the American Oriental Society* 104: 395-402, and Van Windekens, A. J., 1976, *Le Tokharien confronté avec les autres langues indo-européennes*, 2 vols. Louvain, Centre international de dialectologie génerale. **155:** After Gamkrelidze, Thomas and Vyacheslav Ivanov, 1995, *Indo-European and the Indo-Europeans*, Berlin and New York, Mouton, vol. 2, 580-581. **156:**

After Devoto, G., 1962, *Origini Indeuropee*, Florence, Sansoni, 342, fig. 70. **157:** After Nichols, Johanna, 1997, 'The epicentre of the Indo-European linguistic spread,' in *Archaeology and Language*, eds. Roger Blench and Matthew Spriggs, London and New York, 135, fig. 8.7. **158:** Drawing by Maura Pringle. **159:** After Vadetskaya, E., 1986, *Arkheologicheskiye Pamyatniki v Stepyakh Srednego Yeniseya*, Leningrad, 20-21, table 2. **160:** Drawing by Maura Pringle. **161:** Drawing by Maura Pringle. **162:** After Rudenko, S., 1953, *Kul'tura Naseleniya Gornogo Altaya v Skifskoe Vremya*. Moscow, Nauka, pl. 24. **163ab:** After Debaine-Francfort (1989), 197, fig. 18.2. **163cd:** After Vadetskaya, E., 1986, *Arkheologicheskiye Pamyatniki v Stepyakh Srednego Yeniseya*, Leningrad, 20-21, table 2. **164:** Drawing by Maura Pringle. **165:** Drawing by Maura Pringle. **166:** After Temple (1986), 19, fig. 1. **167:** After

Temple, (1986), 66, fig. 90. **168:** After Temple (1986), 86, fig. 117. **169:** After Temple (1986), 72, fig. 46. **170:** After Lu Liancheng (1993), 827, fig. 4. **171:** After Gening, V. F., G. Zdanovich and V. V. Gening, 1992, *Sintashta*, Chelyabinsk, 215, fig. 116. **172:** After Mair (1990), 29, fig. 2. **173:** After Fitzgerald-Huber, (1995), 34, fig. 5b and 44, fig 7c; **174:** After Fitzgerald-Huber (1995), 34, fig. 5a and 45, fig. 8a. **175:** Drawing by Maura Pringle. **176:** After Zhang Zengqi (1994), 694, fig. 1. **177:** After Davis-Kimball, Jeannine, 1996, 'Tribal interaction between the Early Iron Age nomads of the southern Ural steppes, Semirechiye, and Xinjiang,' in *The Bronze Age and Early Iron Age Peoples of Eastern Central Asia*, ed. V. Mair, Washington and Philadelphia, vol. 1, 249, fig. 11.

Acknowledgments

In both the preparation and the editing of this book we have been fortunate to have enjoyed the assistance of numerous scholars whose help we acknowledge below with the usual proviso that any mistakes that have persisted are the fault of the authors. For the preparation of the maps: Maura Pringle; for the preparation of the line drawings: Gillian Gilmore, Eimear Nelis; for reading chapters: D. Q. Adams, E. J. W. Barber, Daniel Boucher, Larry Clark, Paolo Francalacci, Irene Good, James Russell Hamilton, Brian Hemphill, Louisa Fitzgerald Huber, David Keightley, Elfriede Regina Knauer, Adrienne Mayor, Takao Moriyasu, Donald Ringe, Charlotte Roberts, Richard Salomon, Nicholas Sims-Williams, Werner Sundermann, Oktor Skjærvø, David Utz, Werner Winter, David Curtis Wright, and Peter Zieme; for the use of photographs: Dolkun Kamberi, Håkan Wahlquist, Marianne Yaldiz; for the reference to the Shangma site: Lothar von Falkenhausen; for assistance in Xinjiang archaeology: Idris Abdursul, Sabit Ahmat, Du Gencheng, He Dexiu, Abdulkayum Hoja, Lü Enguo, Ahmet Rashid, Tian Lin, Wang Binghua, Wang Bo, Yu Zhiyong, Israfel Yusuf, Zhang Chuan, Zhang Yuzhong and Zhang Ping; for providing essential research materials: Eileen Murphy, Xu Wenkan; for generous aid: James Buchanan, and for moral support and encouragement: Eimear Mallory, Li-ching Chang and Thomas Krishna Mair.

Index